PAGES PACKED WITH ESSENTIAL INFORMATION

"Value-packed, unbeatable, accurate, and comprehensive."

—*The Los Angeles Times*

"The guides are aimed not only at young budget travelers but at the independent traveler; a sort of streetwise cookbook for traveling alone."

—*The New York Times*

"Unbeatable; good sight-seeing advice; up-to-date info on restaurants, hotels, and inns; a commitment to money-saving travel; and a wry style that brightens nearly every page."

—*The Washington Post*

THE BEST TRAVEL BARGAINS IN YOUR BUDGET

"All the dirt, dirt cheap."

—*People*

"Let's Go follows the creed that you don't have to toss your life's savings to the wind to travel—unless you want to."

—*The Salt Lake Tribune*

REAL ADVICE FOR REAL EXPERIENCES

"The writers seem to have experienced every rooster-packed bus and lunar-surfaced mattress about which they write."

—*The New York Times*

"[Let's Go's] devoted updaters really walk the walk (and thumb the ride, and trek the trail). Learn how to fish, haggle, find work—anywhere."

—*Food & Wine*

"A world-wise traveling companion—always ready with friendly advice and helpful hints, all sprinkled with a bit of wit."

—*The Philadelphia Inquirer*

A GUIDE WITH A SPIRIT AND A SOCIAL CONSCIENCE

"Lighthearted and sophisticated, informative and fun to read. [Let's Go] helps the novice traveler navigate like a knowledgeable old hand."

—*Atlanta Journal-Constitution*

"The serious mission at the book's core reveals itself in exhortations to respect the culture and the environment—and, if possible, to visit as a volunteer, a student, or a teacher rather than a tourist."

—*San Francisco Chronicle*

LET'S GO PUBLICATIONS

TRAVEL GUIDES

Australia
Austria & Switzerland
Brazil
Britain
California
Central America
Chile
China
Costa Rica
Costa Rica, Nicaragua & Panama
Eastern Europe
Ecuador
Egypt
Europe
France
Germany
Greece
Guatemala & Belize
Hawaii
India & Nepal
Ireland
Israel
Italy
Japan
Mexico
New Zealand
Peru
Puerto Rico
Southeast Asia
Spain & Portugal with Morocco
Thailand
USA
Vietnam
Western Europe
Yucatan Peninsula

ROADTRIP GUIDE

Roadtripping USA

ADVENTURE GUIDES

Alaska
Pacific Northwest
Southwest USA

CITY GUIDES

Amsterdam
Barcelona
Berlin, Prague & Budapest
Boston
Buenos Aires
Florence
London
London, Oxford, Cambridge & Edinburgh
New York City
Paris
Rome
San Francisco
Washington, DC

POCKET CITY GUIDES

Amsterdam
Berlin
Boston
Chicago
London
New York City
Paris
San Francisco
Venice
Washington, DC

LET'S GO
FLORENCE

RESEARCHERS

MARYKATE JASPER   **BERYL LIPTON**

IYA MEGRE MANAGING EDITOR
BEATRICE FRANKLIN RESEARCH MANAGER

EDITORS

COURTNEY A. FISKE   **SARA PLANA**
RUSSELL FORD RENNIE   **CHARLIE E. RIGGS**
OLGA I. ZHULINA

HOW TO USE THIS BOOK

ORGANIZATION. Coverage is divided into the following neighborhoods: the Duomo, P. della Signoria, Santa Maria Novella, San Lorenzo, San Marco, Santa Croce, the West Oltrarno, and the East Oltrarno. Neighborhood lines are fluid, but it should be apparent that each area has its own significant landmarks and unique character.

COVERING THE BASICS. The first chapter, **Discover** (p. 1), contains highlights of the city, complete with descriptions of Florence's neighborhoods and suggested itineraries to take you from one to ten days on the road. **Essentials** (p. 9) has all the info you'll need to navigate everything from Florentine transportation to bureaucracy. **Life and Times** (p. 41) should help you find your way around even more complex constructs: Florentine history, culture, and customs. Our **Beyond Tourism (p. 67)** chapter holds tons of options for travelers looking to volunteer, study, and work in Florence. **Practical Information (p. 79)** contains a list of local services, from libraries to fitness clubs, while the **Appendix** has a phrasebook and maps for each neighborhood.

WHEN TO USE IT

TWO MONTHS BEFORE YOU LEAVE. Our book is filled with practical information to help you before you go. **Essentials** (p. 9) has advice about passports, visas, plane tickets, insurance, and more. The **Accommodations** (p. 85) section can help you with booking a room from home.

ONE MONTH BEFORE YOU LEAVE. Take care of travel insurance and write down emergency numbers and hotlines to take with you. Make a list of packing essentials and shop for anything you need. Make any necessary reservations.

TWO WEEKS BEFORE YOU LEAVE. Start thinking about the things you don't want to miss during your stay. **Discover** (p. 1) is a good place to start, with suggested itineraries and Let's Go Picks. Page through the **Sights** (p. 113) and **Museums** (p. 135) chapters and see what catches your eye. Don't forget to consider some daytrips in **Tuscany** (p. 173); you may want to see more than just the one city.

ON THE ROAD. **Food** (p. 97) and **Nightlife** (p. 163) list plenty of options to feed your belly and your liver. If you want to indulge even more, try **Shopping** (p. 155); we list a section for souvenirs, but there's no shame in only buying things for yourself. The **Sights** (p. 113), **Museums** (p. 135), and **Life and Times** (p. 41) chapters are full of information and historical anecdotes about the art and architecture you'll see nearly every minute of every day. Speaking of which, we know that we're a pretty entertaining read, but don't forget to take your nose out of the book and look around every now and then.

CONTENTS

DISCOVER FLORENCE................1
Neighborhoods 2
ESSENTIALS........................9
Planning Your Trip 9
Safety and Health 17
Getting to Florence 22
Getting Around Florence 26
Keeping in Touch 30
Accommodations 33
Specific Concerns 36
LIFE AND TIMES....................41
History 41
Art and Architecture 47
Literature 56
Music 59
Religion 60
Culture 61
Holidays and Festivals 65
BEYOND TOURISM..................67
Volunteering 68
Studying 70
Working 73
PRACTICAL INFORMATION........79
Tourist and Financial Services 79
Local Services 79
Emergency and Communications 83
ACCOMMODATIONS................85
By Price 85
By Area 86
The Duomo 86
Piazza della Signoria 87
Santa Maria Novella 88
San Lorenzo 89
San Marco 92
Santa Croce 93
West Oltrarno 94
East Oltrarno 95
FOOD.............................97
By Price 98
By Area 99
The Duomo 99
Piazza della Signoria 100
Santa Maria Novella 102
San Lorenzo 103
San Marco 105
Santa Croce 107
West Oltrarno 109
East Oltrarno 111
SIGHTS..........................113
The Duomo 113
Piazza della Signoria 121

Santa Maria Novella 124
San Lorenzo 125
San Marco 127
Santa Croce 129
West Oltrarno 131
East Oltrarno 133
MUSEUMS........................135
Piazza della Signoria 135
Santa Maria Novella 144
San Lorenzo 145
San Marco 145
Santa Croce 148
The Oltrarno 149
SHOPPING AND ENTERTAINMENT....155
English Language Bookstores 155
Open-Air Markets 155
Clothing 157
Boutiques 157
Souvenirs 158
Cinema 160
Theater 160
Live Music 161
Spectator Sports 161
NIGHTLIFE.......................163
The Duomo 163
Piazza della Signoria 164
Santa Maria Novella 165
San Lorenzo 166
San Marco 167
Santa Croce 167
West Oltrarno 169
East Oltrarno 169
TUSCANY.........................173
Greve In Chianti 175
Siena 176
San Gimignano 187
Cortona 190
Arezzo 194
Pisa 197
Lucca 204
Monterosso 211
Vernazza 214
Corniglia 216
Manarola 216
Riomaggiore 218
APPENDIX........................220
Climate 220
Measurements 220
Language 221
INDEX...........................239

RESEARCHERS

Marykate Jasper   *Santa Maria Novella, Duomo, San Marco, Oltrarno (east), Siena, San Gimignagno, Cortona, Arezzo*

Already familiar with the inner workings of Let's Go after a summer spent as an Associate Editor, Marykate used her knowledge of format and flair to produce some truly stellar copy. Despite enduring the inconsistencies of the Florence tourist information office, the vagaries of Tuscan transportation, and the indignity of the Kimono of Shame, she fortified herself with all the red meat she could get her hands on and kept us in stitches with her irreverent and punny sense of humor. Her descriptions of various monastic orders alone deserve their own book.

Beryl Lipton   *San Lorenzo, Piazza della Signoria, Santa Croce, Oltrarno (west), Pisa, Viareggio, Lucca, Volterra*

The other half of the team that battled spotty internet connections and grumpy Italian workers, Beryl tackled the art-historic center of Florence, getting into fashion shows and onto restaurant rooftops along the way. Her steady consumption of gelato made us worry about her dietary health; her command of the Florentine nightlife scene, however, led us to think she was probably strengthened by all of that fresh dairy goodness—or maybe just on a sugar high. All in all, Beryl truly captured the essence of all that is quirky, beautiful, and pleasant in Florence.

STAFF WRITERS

Charlotte Alter   Daniel C. Barbero   Meagan Ann Michelson
Sanders Bernstein   Julia Cain   Sara Joe Wolansky
William Eck   Brianne Farrar   Anna Kathryn Kendrick
Elias Berger   Nick Charyk   Alexandra Perloff-Giles
C. Harker Rhodes   Ansley Rubinstein   Madeleine Schwartz
Anna Steim   Maria Vassileva

CONTRIBUTING WRITERS

Antonia Devine graduated from Princeton University in 2008 with a BA in Art and Archaeology and a certificate in Italian. She works in New York as a junior architect and plans to pursue a Masters in Architecture. Along the way, she'd like to return to Italy to "study" the food, art and culture.

Rosa Lowinger is an art conservator and writer based in Los Angeles. The 2009 Rome Prize fellow in conservation she is presently working on a book on art vandalism. She is the author of *Tropicana Nights: The Life and Times of the Legendary Cuban Nightclub.*

ACKNOWLEDGMENTS

BEATRICE THANKS: Marykate and Beryl, for putting up with everything that I asked you to do, and for making me laugh every time I read your marginalia. The RMs, for solidarity and everything else. Iya, for dorking it up with me and holding my hand through two books and a season of heart-wrenching SYTYCD obsession. The rest of LGHQ, for guidance, fun, impeccable music taste, and 🍂Discuss. My roommates, for making a couch a home. Team ML, for keeping up a virtual Vergnugenzelt throughout the summer. And my family, for letting me go yet again and teaching me about Italy in the first place. *Tanti grazie a tutti.*

EDITORS THANK: The Ed Team would first and foremost like to thank our lord (Jay-C) and savior (Starbucks, Terry's Chocolate Orange). We also owe gratitude to Barack Obama (peace be upon Him), the Oxford comma, the water cooler, bagel/payday Fridays, the HSA "SummerFun" team for being so inclusive, Rotio (wherefore art thou Rotio?), the real Robinson Crusoe, the Cambridge weather and defective umbrellas, BoltBus, Henry Louis Gates, Jr. (sorry 'bout the phone call), the office blog, gratuitous nudity, the 20-20-20 rule and bananas (no more eye twitches), the Portuguese flag, trips to the beach (ha!), sunbathing recently-married Mormon final club alums, non-existent free food in the square, dog-star puns, and last but not least, America. The local time in Tehran is 1:21am.

But seriously, to the MEs and RMs, our researchers (and all their wisdom on tablecloths and hipsters), LGHQ, HSA, our significant others (future, Canadian, and otherwise), and families (thanks Mom).

Publishing Director
Laura M. Gordon
Editorial Director
Dwight Livingstone Curtis
Publicity and Marketing Director
Vanessa J. Dube
Production and Design Director
Rebecca Lieberman
Cartography Director
Anthony Rotio
Website Director
Lukáš Tóth
Managing Editors
Ashley Laporte, Iya Megre,
Mary Potter, Nathaniel Rakich
Technology Project Manager
C. Alexander Tremblay
Director of IT
David Fulton-Howard
Financial Associates
Catherine Humphreville, Jun Li

Managing Editor
Iya Megre
Research Manager
Beatrice Franklin
Editors
Courtney A. Fiske, Sara Plana, Russell Ford Rennie, Charlie E. Riggs, Olga I. Zhulina
Typesetter
Rebecca Lieberman

President
Daniel Lee
General Manager
Jim McKellar

PRICE RANGES ❷❸❹
❶ FLORENCE ❺

Our researchers list establishments in order of value from best to worst, honoring our favorites with the Let's Go thumbs-up (🖑). Because the best *value* is not always the cheapest *price*, we have incorporated a system of price ranges based on a rough expectation of what you will spend. For **accommodations,** we base our range on the cheapest price for which a single traveler can stay for one night. For **restaurants,** we estimate the average amount one traveler will spend in one sitting. The table below tells you what you'll *typically* find in Florence at the corresponding price range, but keep in mind that no system can allow for the quirks of individual establishments.

ACCOMMODATIONS	RANGE	WHAT YOU'RE *LIKELY* TO FIND
❶	under €30	Campgrounds, HI hostels, basic dorm rooms, and the like. Expect bunk beds and a communal bath. Don't get too excited; there aren't many of these around Florence, especially in summer.
❷	€30-45	Upper-end hostels or lower-end *pensiones*. You may have a private bathroom, or there may be a sink in your room and a communal shower in the hall. Meals may be available cheaply to hostel guests.
❸	€46-60	A medium-sized room with a private bath, probably in a small but lovely hotel. Some amenities, like Wi-Fi, A/C, TV, or phone. Breakfast possibly included for your toast-hoarding convenience.
❹	€61-75	Similar to ❸, but should have more amenities or be in a more highly touristed or conveniently located area. Breakfast is often included in the price of your room.
❺	over €75	Large hotels, upscale chains, or smack up against the Duomo. If it's a ❺ and it doesn't have the perks or service you're looking for, you've probably paid too much.

FOOD	RANGE	WHAT YOU'RE *LIKELY* TO FIND
❶	under €7	Probably a slice of pizza or a sandwich from a bar; possibly buffet at *aperitivo* time—always a good call.
❷	€7-13	*Primo* and a drink, or even a full three-course lunch menu in a more residential neighborhoods.
❸	€14-20	Typically a sit-down meal. A three-course dinner menu or a *secondo* and dessert with a drink—plus that euro for tip.
❹	€21-27	Entrees are more expensive than ❸, but you're paying for quality service, ambience, and decor. Few restaurants in this range have a dress code, but you'll want to clean yourself up after a day of travel.
❺	over €27	Your meal might cost more than your hostel, but here's hoping it's something fabulous, famous, or involving a lot of good wine.

ABOUT LET'S GO

THE STUDENT TRAVEL GUIDE
Let's Go publishes the world's favorite student travel guides, written entirely by Harvard students. Armed with pens, notebooks, and a few changes of clothes stuffed into their backpacks, our student researchers go across continents, through time zones, and above expectations to seek out invaluable travel experiences for our readers. Because we are a completely student-run company, we have a unique perspective on how students travel, where they want to go, and what they're looking to do when they get there. If your dream is to grab a machete and forge through the jungles of Costa Rica, we can take you there. If you'd rather bask in the Riviera sun at a beachside cafe, we'll set you a table. In short, we write for readers who know that there's more to travel than tour buses. To keep up, visit our website, www.letsgo.com, where you can sign up to blog, post photos from your trips, and connect with the Let's Go community.

TRAVELING BEYOND TOURISM
We're on a mission to provide our readers with sharp, fresh coverage packed with socially responsible opportunities to go beyond tourism. Each guide's Beyond Tourism chapter shares ideas about responsible travel, study abroad, and how to give back to the places you visit while on the road. To help you gain a deeper connection with the places you travel, our fearless researchers scour the globe to give you the heads-up on both world-renowned and off-the-beaten-track opportunities. We've also opened our pages to respected writers and scholars to hear their takes on the countries and regions we cover, and asked travelers who have worked, studied, or volunteered abroad to contribute first-person accounts of their experiences.

FIFTY YEARS OF WISDOM
Let's Go has been on the road for 50 years and counting. We've grown a lot since publishing our first 20-page pamphlet to Europe in 1960, but five decades and 54 titles later our witty, candid guides are still researched and written entirely by students on shoestring budgets who know that train strikes, stolen luggage, food poisoning, and marriage proposals are all part of a day's work. This year, for our 50th anniversary, we're publishing 26 titles—including 6 brand new guides—brimming with editorial honesty, a commitment to students, and our irreverent style. Here's to the next 50!

THE LET'S GO COMMUNITY
More than just a travel guide company, Let's Go is a community that reaches from our headquarters in Cambridge, MA all across the globe. Our small staff of dedicated student editors, writers, and tech nerds comes together because of our shared passion for travel and our desire to help other travelers get the most out of their experience. We love it when our readers become part of the Let's Go community as well—when you travel, drop us a postcard (67 Mt. Auburn St., Cambridge, MA 02138, USA), send us an e-mail (feedback@letsgo.com), or sign up on our website (www.letsgo.com) to tell us about your adventures and discoveries.

For more information, updated travel coverage, and news from our researcher team, visit us online at www.letsgo.com.

DISCOVER FLORENCE

Thanks to the floods, wars, famine, and Black Death that haunted Europe during the early Renaissance period, sopping-wet, battle-weary, emaciated, and plagued Florence—or Firenze (Fee-REN-zeh; pop. 400,000)—was not a pleasant sight. In the late 14th century, however, Florence was able to etch itself into the history books. Florentines Boccaccio, Dante, and Giotto created trend-setting masterpieces and, in the 15th century, Florence had gained further artistic distinction as the Medici family amassed a priceless collection of works, supporting masters like Botticelli, Brunelleschi, Donatello, and Michelangelo, among other ninja turtles. Rivalries between families, political factions, neighboring towns, and artists led to increasingly impressive shows of power—now yours to enjoy in the resulting art and architecture. Think of it as capitalistic free-market competition, a bit of a rarity in Italy.

Today, you can't turn a corner in Florence without finding a famous church, museum, or building designed by Arnolfo di Cambio—and the attendant tour groups. The historical center must be one of the most crowded squares in Europe, but venture just a few blocks outside of Piazza della Signoria and you'll find homey *trattorie*, artisanal shops, and the block parties that comprise local Florentine nightlife. Cross the river to the hills of the Oltrarno or head to Fiesole to get breathtaking views of the city and the rolling Tuscan countryside. Nowhere else is there so much concentrated beauty, whether man-made or soil-born. There's definitely something in the water.

FACTS AND FIGURES

POPULATION: 367,569.

URBAN AREA: 39.5 sq. miles.

TUSCAN POPULATION: 3,701,000

AGE: Florentia was founded by Julius Caesar in 59 B.C., putting Florence at 2068 years old.

YEARS AS ITALY'S CAPITAL: 5, from 1865 to 1870.

NUMBER OF MEDICIS WHO HELD POSITIONS OF POLITICAL POWER: 17—including 3 Cardinals, 7 Grand Dukes, and our favorite, Piero the Gouty.

NUMBER OF UNESCO WORLD HERITAGE SITES: One... the entire city.

LITERS OF CHIANTI PRODUCED PER YEAR: 107,291,040.

WHEN TO GO

Few would dare call a Florentine **spring** anything less than heaven. The weather is pleasantly balmy (hovering around 50-70°F), although often rainy, but the tourists haven't caught on. By June, both the temperature and the tourist industry have picked up considerably. Florentine **summer** is sweltering (75-95°F) and congested, but you can catch major exhibitions, exciting festivals, and concerts under the stars. When the city gets too oppressive, head to the hills of

1

the surrounding Tuscan countryside. From late July to August, the locals leave town; you may not find as many *trattorie* or nightclubs open, but the crowds will subside. The trend continues into the **fall,** when the temperatures drop (45-60°F) and the prices do too. **Winter** brings cold (expect around 35-55°F), rain, and some of the lowest prices of the year; it also brings the holidays, which are a major to-do.

NEIGHBORHOODS

Florence is small and manageable, with plenty of large churches to serve as points of reference. In general, neighborhoods have been classified by the large churches and *piazze* that give them their names. Keep in mind that these boundaries are fluid and fairly arbitrary.

SANTA MARIA NOVELLA

Santa Maria Novella is dominated by the **train station,** the Dominican **basilica,** and the **piazza** that all bear its name. Stretching from the city center west along the Arno to the park Le Cascine, and northeast along the edge of the San Lorenzo area, the neighborhood is close enough to the center for convenience, but not quite as pricey as the real estate just around the Duomo. There are plenty of small churches and museums in the area, in addition to some restaurants with excellent fixed menus and, further west, some of the city's biggest nightclubs.

SAN LORENZO

San Lorenzo was once the stomping ground of the Medici, as attested by the beautiful **church** they funded here as their family parish. The neighborhood has few other notable sights, but is home to some cheap hostels, tasty restaurants, and a varied nightlife scene. For the purposes of this guide, this neighborhood encompasses the narrow triangle that stretches north from the Basilica di San Lorenzo, between the Santa Maria Novella area and San Marco.

THE DUOMO

This area needs no introduction. As the focal point of the city, the neighborhood around the Duomo is filled with art, architecture, and the people gawking at it all. Accommodations can be astronomically expensive, but there are a few of reasonable value that, though still pricey, have astounding views. Food tends toward the overpriced, but there are a few real gems tucked away—including some of the best gelaterias in the city.

PIAZZA DELLA SIGNORIA

Along with the Duomo area, this neighborhood composes the real center of Florence. Three of the most important **museums** in the world are located on this patch of land between P. del Duomo and the Arno. Predictably, establishments in the region are quite expensive, but there's a bit more price diversity than around the Duomo and a few good deals. At night, this neighborhood is a great place to find a chic bar for an *aperitivo*.

SAN MARCO

Renowned as the home of *David*, but this neighborhood (stretching northeast from the Duomo, in between San Lorenzo and Santa Croce) also plays host to a number of unique and interesting museums, including the **Museo Archeologico** and the **Opificio delle Pietre Dure.** More residential than the central neighborhoods, San Marco contains few hostels but many inexpensive hotels. The best meal deals in the area blink into existence at lunchtime, so keep an eye out for afternoon specials. Nightlife is minimal and mostly of the Irish pub variety.

SANTA CROCE

Santa Croce is capped by a truly outstanding **basilica** and stretches eastward along the Arno from the city center. Accommodations and other sights here are few and far between, which leaves room for the abundance of wonderful local restaurants and the welcoming nightlife (along **Via de' Benci** and in **Piazza Sant'Ambrogio** and **Piazza Ghiberti**) that characterize the area.

THE OLTRARNO

Across the river lies a land of promise. On the western side of the Oltrarno are the vast **Palazzo Pitti,** the verdant **Boboli Gardens,** and a host of **medieval churches,** while the hills on the east have pleasant walks and stunning city views. Then there are the cheap accommodations, the hearty local fare, and the *piazze* that overflow with nighttime fun. Who needs the Uffizi?

◪LET'S GO PICKS

BEST PROOF THAT SIZE REALLY DOESN'T MATTER: The beautiful, tiny **Tuscan hill towns** (p. 173). You thought we were going to say Michelangelo's **David** (p. 145), didn't you?

BEST REMINDER THAT NOT ALL GREAT ITALIAN ARTISTS WERE PAINTERS: The **Pozzo di Beatrice,** incongruously located in the **Museo Salvatore Ferragamo** (p. 144), juxtaposes the memory of the lyrical poet with the lyrical shoemaker.

BEST FREE SIGHT: We're torn between **Piazza Michelangelo** (p. 133), the **Ponte Vecchio** (p. 121), and the **Loggia della Signoria** (p. 121).

BEST DINNER THEATER: The **Teatro del Sale** (p. 107), in Santa Croce.

BEST FLORENTINE RIVALRY: Basilica di Santa Croce (p. 129) **v. Basilica di Santa Maria Novella** (p. 124). The Dominicans' and Franciscans' decidedly un-monastic desire to show each other up produced two beautiful churches and its own mini-feud, **Donatello v. Brunelleschi,** over who could make a better crucifix. Runners-up: the **Guelphs v. the Ghibellines,** the **Medicis v. everyone else.**

BEST GELATO IN FLORENCE: Sorry—you're going to have to figure that one out for yourself (although around the Duomo is a good place to start). Happy tasting!

4 • WWW.LETSGO.COM

DISCOVER

SUGGESTED ITINERARIES

ONE DAY

Trying to absorb Florence in a day will likely lead to shock or Stendhal syndrome. But if you have a note from your doctor and are willing to make some tough choices, it can be done. Spend the extra few euro and make reservations for everything you can; you'll save precious hours by not having to wait in line. The **Duomo** (p. 113)—plus its neighbors, the Battistero (p. 119) and the Campanile (p. 119)—and the **Uffizi** (p. 135) are obviously in; visit either the **Bargello** (p. 142) if you like sculpture or the **Palazzo Vecchio** (p. 143) if your tastes run to painting or history. Next up is the **Accademia** (p. 145), which actually doesn't take much time once you've had your fill of Michelangelo. Finally, hit a few of the best churches in town: **Santa Croce** (p. 129) is a must, and then either **Santa Maria Novella** (p. 124) or **San Lorenzo** (p. 125). Enjoy dinner in **Santa Croce** (p. 107) or the **Oltrarno** (p. 109) , and head to a local bar or one of the block-party-esque *piazze* to finish off the day.

THREE DAYS

Now we're beginning to get somewhere: you can definitely get to the most famous spots in Florence if you've got three days to do it. Plus, you'll have enough time to peek into the smaller, less mainstream sights—but not nearly enough time to see them all. Definitely read up about everything ahead of time and construct your plan of attack. Also consider whether you may want a break from the onslaught of medieval and Renaissance art by visiting something a bit different, like the **Museo Salvatore Ferragamo** (p. 144).

DAY ONE. Start off with a bang when you're still bright-eyed and bushy-tailed: take in the **Duomo** (p. 113) and its neighbors, the **Bargello** (p. 142), the **Uffizi** (p. 135), and the **Palazzo Vecchio** (p. 143). It's still worth it to make reservations for all the sights you can. Grab a quick and easy lunch from a *trattoria* in the center. Hang around in the **Piazza della Signoria** (p. 100) area for dinner and then a drink at a simple bar.

DAY TWO. Get to the **Accademia** (p. 145) when it opens and enjoy. After that, hit as many of Florence's major churches as you feel like: definitely **Santa Croce** (p. 129), and then take your pick from the rest of the best (**Santa Maria Novella** (p. 124), **San Lorenzo** (p. 125), **Orsanmichele** (p. 121), the **Badia** (p. 122), **Santa Trinità** (p. 125), **Santissima Annunziata** (p. 127), **Chiesa di Ognissanti** (p. 125). You can probably make it through at least three, and definitely don't rush—if you go too fast, all frescoes begin to look the same. Have dinner at a tasty *trattoria* in **Santa Croce** (p. 107), and then stick around for the neighborhood's nightlife scene (p. 167).

DAY THREE. In the morning, visit some of the smaller museums in Florence: pick three or so from among the **Casa di Dante** (p. 143), **Casa Buonarroti** (p. 149), **Palazzo Davanzati** (p. 141), **Museo di Storia della Scienza** (p. 143), **Opificio di Pietre Dure** (p. 147), **Macchine di Leonardo** (p. 145), **Casa di Rodolfo Siviero** (p. 152), **Museo Horne** (p. 148), and the **Museo Archeologico** (p. 146). Then, head across the river for an afternoon in the galleries of the **Palazzo Pitti (p. 149)** and the **Boboli Gardens** (p. 151), and wander up the hill to **San Miniato al Monte** (p. 133) and **Piazzale Michelangelo** (p. 133) for the stunning view. Eat in the **Oltrarno (p. 109)**, and if you still have the energy to stand check out one of the popular nightclubs in the **Santa Maria Novella** (p. 165) area. Alternatively, if you want a less high-octane evening, you can visit some of the spots along the southeastern side of the river (p. 169), where native Florentines go to grab a drink and enjoy the scenery.

 TIME CRUNCH. If you want to be even more efficient with your time, you can combine the attractions of Day Two and Day Three and then group them by neighborhood, rather than type. However, traipsing across the city is an artistic experience in itself.

FIVE DAYS

It is certainly possible to see most of Florence's landmarks in five days, although you will probably be overwhelmed and never want to hear the word "Renaissance" again. If you end up with some extra time on your hands, sit back at one of the city's elegant cafes with an espresso or a beer, or wander through some of the famous medieval streets, such as the **Borgo degli Albizi** (p. 120), which are lined with beautiful palaces but don't require entrance fees—or entrance, for that matter.

DAY ONE. Take your time and enjoy the **Duomo** (p. 113), **Battistero** (p. 119), **Campanile** (p. 119), and **Museo dell'Opera del Duomo** (p. 120). Spend what's left of the day at the **Uffizi** (p. 135) and the **Palazzo Vecchio** (p. 143).

DAY TWO. Enjoy a morning of sculpture in the **Bargello** (p. 142) and the **Accademia** (p. 145); move on to the other sights in San Marco—**Museo Archeologico** (p. 146), **Opificio delle Pietre Dure** (p. 147), **Chiesa della Santissima Annunziata** (p. 127), and the **Museo di San Marco** (p. 146)—in the afternoon.

DAY THREE. Begin the day at the **Basilica di Santa Croce** (p. 129). Then walk through the area around Piazza della Signoria, visiting the **Badia** (p. 122), **Orsanmichele** (p. 121), and **Palazzo Davanzati** (p. 141). Turn north to **San Lorenzo** and see its **church** (p. 125) as well as the nearby **Macchine di Leonardo** (p. 145) if the fancy strikes.

DAY FOUR. Spend some time in the **Santa Maria Novella** area. You can visit its **basilica** (p. 124) and the surrounding smaller sights: **Chiesa di Ognissanti** (p. 125), **Chiesa di Santa Trinità** (p. 125), **Cenacolo di Fuligno** (p. 125), **Museo Salvatore Ferragamo** (p. 144), and **Museo Fotografia Fratelli Alinari** (p. 144). There are often cool exhibits on in **Palazzo Strozzi** (p. 144). Finally, enjoy some greenery in the park of **Le Cascine**.

DAY FIVE. Time to cross the river and immerse yourself in the **Oltrarno**. You'll want to spend some time in the galleries of **Palazzo Pitti** (p. 149), and possibly pay a visit to the **Basilica di Santo Spirito** (p. 131), **Chiesa di San Felice** (p. 132), **Basilica di Santa Maria del Carmine** (p. 131), and **Casa Rodolfo Siviero** (p. 152). Enjoy the **Boboli Gardens** (p. 151), and then head up the hill to **San Miniato al Monte** (p. 133) and **Piazzale Michelangelo** (p. 133) to get a view of the territory you've just conquered.

GO GO GELATO!

Not that long ago, Italian news-papers published a study that claimed that you should only eat gelato in winter because summer consumption is bad for you—it freezes the small intestine. As the science then was dubious—it was probably just an attempt by some gluttonous scientists to scare away other gelato con-sumers—and has since been dis-proved, there's no reason not to indulge in the tasty Italian treat year around. Here's a list of the top 10 spots in Florence to keep you cool in the summer and, well, just to enjoy in the winter.

1. Badiani, V. dei Mille 20. Get the much imitated but never outdone Buontalenti, a mysterious gelato recipe found among 16th-century documents.

2. Vestri, Borgo Albizi 11/r. Master chocolate-makers making the best chocolate gelato in Florence.

3. Gelateria del Neri, V. dei Neri 26r. The best gelato in Florence? Mandarin and melon have been rumored to cause flavor explo-sions, while the chocolate and chili have been linked to an oral volcanic eruption...

SEVEN DAYS

If you've got a whole week ahead of you, go through our five-day itinerary and then get out of the city. You could spend a day in **Fiesole** (p. 173) doing more sightseeing and then a day of wine tasting in **Greve in Chianti** (p. 175). If you feel like heading farther afield, spend two days in **Siena** (p. 176) or two days in **Pisa** (p. 197).

TEN DAYS

Ten days in Tuscany will really give you a chance to see all of the things under the Tuscan sun. Take the five-day itinerary in Florence (or turn it into four—Day Two through Day Four can be compressed into just two days, if you leave a couple of things out and walk fast).

 A FINANCIAL NOTE. Traveling around Tus-cany is reasonably cheap, and lower costs of sights and food will help your wallet stay plump. Obviously, in most of these towns there is either no nightlife or a very inex-pensive scene. Hostels, however, are never easy to find; though hotels may be cheaper than in Florence, the fact that you can't find a €15 bed may be inconvenient.

DAYS SIX AND SEVEN. Take the train to **Siena** (p. 176) and spend two days exploring this Florentine rival. Make sure to see the **Campo** (p. 180)—well, you can't really miss it—the **Palazzo Pubblico** (p. 180), and the **duomo** (p. 181). Also don't forget to eat some Sienese delicacies, like *cinta senese* and *panforte*. The student population of the town pro-vides some amiable **nightlife** (p. 183).

DAY EIGHT. Hop on a bus and go deeper into wine country by visiting either **Radda in Chianti** (p. 184) or **Montepulciano** (p. 185). Whichever you choose, make sure to go wine tasting or even take a tour of a vineyard. There aren't many accommodations, so head back to **Siena** for the night; this will leave you conveniently located to continue on your Tuscan tour.

DAY NINE. The next stop is the lovely hillside town of **San Gimignano** (p. 186), known as the "City of the

Beautiful Towers." Here you can take in the town's medieval architecture and the views of the country below. San Gimignano is also famous for its wild boar *(cinghiale)* and its sweet white wine *(Vernaccia di San Gimignano)*. There are a few interesting sights—and one creepy one, the **Museo Pena di Morte and Museo della Tortura** (p. 190)—but the best way to spend the afternoon is simply wandering through the town itself. Don't forget to try a gelato from the **Pluripremiata Gelateria** (p. 188), which for our money may be the best ice cream in Tuscany.

DAY TEN. Finish off your trip with a visit to the even smaller and quainter **Cortona** (p. 190). If you are a big fan of beef, try to coordinate your sojourn so that you arrive for the **Sagra della Bistecca** in mid-August. Like San Gimignano, this town has some quite notable sights, but is most worth visiting simply for the ambiance. It is also conveniently host to an **HI hostel** (p. 191), which are few and far between outside of Florence.

4. Vivoli, V. Isola della Stinche, 7. By all accounts it is a sin to miss the *cioccolato al caffè* (chocolate with coffee) at this touristy but tasty shop.

5. Gelateria L'Alpina, V. Strozzi 12. Get the *croccante al rhum*.

6. Il Sorriso, V. Erbosa 70. While located on the outskirts of town, the walk is well worth the delicious fresh fruit gelati!

7. Carabe, V. Ricasoli 60. Serving gelato *à la siciliana*—there's more emphasis on the fruit and nut flavors here than at most *gelaterie*. The *limone* is to die for.

8. Il Re Gelato, V. Strozzi 8r. Gelato is normally very dense, with only about 25-30% air (compared to ice cream, which tends to approach 50%), but the gelato at this establishment is renowned for its airiness.

9. Grom, V. del Campanile. An expensive and extravagant chain.

10. Carapina, P. Oberdan 2r. The *frutti di bosco* is tremendous!

ESSENTIALS

PLANNING YOUR TRIP

 ENTRANCE REQUIREMENTS
Passport (see next page). Required for all non-EU citizens.
Visa (p. 11). Italy does not require visas for EU citizens and residents of Australia, Canada, Ireland, New Zealand, the US, and many more countries for up to 90 days. To find out if you need a visa, check with your respective Italian Embassy.
Study or Work Permit (p. 11). Required for all foreigners planning to study or work in Italy. See the **Beyond Tourism** chapter (p. 67) for more info.

EMBASSIES AND CONSULATES

ITALIAN CONSULAR SERVICES ABROAD

Australia: Embassy of Italy, 12 Grey St., Deakin, Canberra, ACT 2600 (☎+61 262 733 333; www.ambcanberra.esteri.it/Ambasciata_Canberra). **Consulate General of Italy,** 509 St. Kilda Rd., Melbourne VIC 3004 (☎+61 039 867 5744; www.consmelbourne. esteri.it). **Consulate General of Italy,** The Gateway, Level 45, 1 Macquarie Pl., Sydney, NSW 2000 (☎+61 029 392 7900; www.conssydney.esteri.it).

Canada: Embassy of Italy, 275 Slater St., 21st fl., Ottawa, ON K1P 5H9 (☎+1-613-232-2401; www.ambottawa.esteri.it). **Consulate General of Italy,** 3489 Drummond St., Montréal, QC H3G 1X6 (☎+1-514-849-8351; www.consmontreal.esteri.it).

Ireland: Embassy of Italy, 63/65 Northumberland Rd., Dublin (☎+353 16 60 17 44; www.ambdublino.esteri.it).

New Zealand: Embassy of Italy, 34-38 Grant Rd., P.O. Box 463, Thorndon, Wellington (☎+64 44 735 339; www.ambwellington.esteri.it). **Consulate General of Italy,** 102 Kitchener Rd., PO Box 31 121 Auckland (☎+649 489 9632).

UK: Embassy of Italy, 14 Three Kings Yard, London W1K 4EH (☎+44 207 312 2200; www.amblondra.esteri.it). **Consulate General of Italy,** 32 Melville Street, Edinburgh EH3 7HA (☎+44 131 226 3631; www.consedimburgo.esteri.it). **Consulate General of Italy,** Rodwell Tower, 111 Piccadilly, Manchester M1 2HY (☎+44 161 236 9024; www.consmanchester.esteri.it).

US: Embassy of Italy, 3000 Whitehaven St., N.W., Washington, DC 20008 (☎+1-202-612-4400; www.ambwashingtondc.esteri.it). **Consulate General of Italy,** 600 Atlantic Ave., Boston, MA 02110 (☎+1-617-722-9201; www.consboston.esteri.it). **Consulate General of Italy,** 500 N. Michigan Ave., Ste. 1850, Chicago, IL 60611 (☎+1-312-467-1550; www.conschicago.esteri.it). **Consulate General of Italy,** 690 Park Ave., New York, NY 10021 (☎+1-212-439-8600; www.consnewyork.esteri.it).

CONSULAR SERVICES IN ITALY

Australia: V. Antonio Bosio 5, Rome 00161 (☎06 85 27 21, emergency ☎800 87 77 90; www.italy.embassy.gov.au). Open M-F 9am-5pm.

Canada: V. Zara 30, Rome 00198 (☎06 85 44 41; www.dfait-maeci.gc.ca/canada-europa/italy/menu-en.asp). Open M-Th 8:30-11:30am.

Ireland: P. di Campitelli 3, Rome 00186 (☎06 69 79 121; www.ambasciata-irlanda.it). Open M-F 10am-12:30pm and 3-4:30pm.

New Zealand: V. Clitunno 44, Rome 00198 (☎06 85 37 501; www.nzembassy.com). Open M-F 8:30am-12:45pm and 1:45-5pm.

UK: V. XX Settembre 80a, Rome 00187 (☎06 42 20 00 01; www.britain.it). Open M-F Sept.-May 9am-5pm; June-Aug. 8am-2pm. Closed UK and Italian holidays.

US: V. Vittorio Veneto 119/A, Rome 00187 (☎06 46 741; www.usembassy.it). Consular services open M-F 8:30am-12:30pm. Closed US and Italian holidays.

TOURIST OFFICES

The **Italian Government Tourist Board (ENIT; l'Ente Nazionale Italiano per il Turismo)** provides information on Italy's culture, natural resources, history, and leisure activities. Visit their website, www.italiantourism.com, for info. Call ☎+1-212-245-4822 for a free copy of *General Information for Travelers to Italy*.

Australia: 46 Market St., Sydney, NSW 2000 (☎+61 02 926 216 66; http://www.enit.it/dovesiamo.asp?Lang=UK&sede=australia).

Canada: 175 E. Bloor St., Ste. 907 South Tower, Toronto, ON M4W 3R8 (☎+1-416-925-4882; http://www.enit.it/dovesiamo.asp?Lang=UK&sede=canada).

UK: 1 Princes St., London W1B 2AY (☎+44 20 7408 1254; www.italiantouristboard.co.uk).

US: 630 5th Ave., Ste. 1565, New York, NY 10111 (☎+1-212-245-5618; www.italiantourism.com).

DOCUMENTS AND FORMALITIES

PASSPORTS

REQUIREMENTS

Citizens of Australia, Canada, Ireland, New Zealand, the UK, and the US need valid passports to enter Italy and to re-enter their home countries. Italy does not allow entrance if the holder's passport expires in under three months beyond the stay; returning home with an expired passport is illegal and may result in a fine. Your passport will prove your most convenient method of identification and, if the photo was taken long ago, a source of humorous conversation.

NEW PASSPORTS

Citizens of Australia, Canada, Ireland, New Zealand, the UK, and the US can apply for a passport at any passport office or at selected post offices and courts of law. Citizens of these countries may also download passport applications from the official website of their country's government or passport office. Any new passport or renewal applications must be filed well in advance of the departure date, though most passport offices offer rush services for a steep fee. Note, however, that "rushed" passports still take up to two weeks to arrive.

ONE EUROPE. European unity has come a long way since 1957, when the **European Economic Community (EEC)** was created to promote European solidarity and cooperation. Since then, the EEC has become the **European Union (EU),** a mighty political, legal, and economic institution. On May 1, 2004, 10 South, Central, and Eastern European countries—Cyprus, the Czech Republic, Estonia, Hungary, Latvia, Lithuania, Malta, Poland, Slovakia, and Slovenia—were admitted into the EU, joining 15 other member states: Austria, Belgium, Denmark, Finland, France, Germany, Greece, Ireland, Italy, Luxembourg, the Netherlands, Portugal, Spain, Sweden, and the UK. On January 1, 2007, two others, Bulgaria and Romania, came into the fold, bringing the tally of member states to 27.

What does this have to do with the average non-EU tourist? The EU's policy of freedom of movement means that most border controls have been abolished and visa policies harmonized. Under this treaty, formally known as the **Schengen Agreement,** you're still required to carry a passport (or government-issued ID card for EU citizens) when crossing an internal border, but, once you've been admitted into one country, you're free to travel to other participating states. Most EU states are already members of Schengen (minus Cyprus) as are Iceland and Norway. EU newcomers Bulgaria and Romania are still in the process of implementing the free travel agreement. The UK and Ireland have opted out of the agreement, but have created their own Common Travel Area, whose regulations match those of Schengen.

For more important consequences of the EU for travelers, see **The Euro (p. 13)** and **Customs in the EU (p. 13).**

ESSENTIALS

PASSPORT MAINTENANCE

Photocopy the page of your passport with your photo as well as your visas, traveler's check serial numbers, and any other important documents. Carry one set of copies in a safe place, apart from the originals, and leave another set at home. Consulates also recommend that you carry an expired passport or an official copy of your birth certificate in a part of your baggage separate from other documents.

If you lose your passport, immediately notify the local police and your home country's nearest embassy or consulate. To expedite its replacement, you must show ID and proof of citizenship; it also helps to know all information previously recorded in the passport. In some cases, a replacement may take weeks to process, and it may be valid only for a limited time. Any visas stamped in your old passport will be lost forever. In an emergency, ask for immediate temporary traveling papers that will permit you to re-enter your home country.

VISAS, INVITATIONS, AND WORK PERMITS

VISAS

EU citizens do not need a visa. Citizens of Australia, Canada, New Zealand, and the US do not need a visa for stays of up to 90 days, but this three-month period begins upon entry into any of the countries that belong to the EU's **freedom of movement** zone. For more information, see **One Europe** (see this page). Those staying longer than 90 days may purchase a visa at an Italian consulate or embassy. A visa costs about €75 and allows the holder to spend between 90 and 365 days in Italy, depending on the type of visa. Double-check entrance requirements at the nearest Italian embassy or consulate (p. 9) for up-to-date info before departure. US citizens can also consult http://travel.state.gov.

Foreign nationals planning to spend over 90 days in Italy should apply within eight working days of arrival for a *permesso di soggiorno* (permit of stay).

Generally, non-EU tourists are required to get a permit at a police station or foreign office *(questura)* if staying longer than 20 days or taking up residence in a location other than a hotel or boarding house. If staying in a hotel or hostel, ask the staff to fill out the registration requirements for you and have the fee waived. There are steep fines for failing to comply.

Entering Italy to study requires a special visa. For more information, see the **Beyond Tourism** chapter (p. 67).

WORK PERMITS

Admittance to a country as a traveler does not include the right to work, which is authorized only by a work permit. For more information, see the **Beyond Tourism** chapter (p. 67).

IDENTIFICATION

When you travel, always carry at least two forms of identification on your person, including a photo ID. A passport and a driver's license will usually suffice. Never carry all of your IDs together; split them up in case of theft or loss and keep photocopies in your luggage and at home.

STUDENT AND YOUTH IDENTIFICATION

The **International Student Identity Card (ISIC),** the most widely accepted form of student ID, provides discounts on some sights, accommodations, food, and transportation, access to a 24hr. emergency help line, and insurance benefits for US cardholders. Applicants must be full-time secondary or post-secondary school students at least 12 years old. Because of the proliferation of fake ISICs, some services (particularly airlines) require additional proof of student identity. For travelers who are under 26 years old but are not students, the **International Youth Travel Card (IYTC)** also offers many of the same benefits as the ISIC.

Each of these identity cards costs US$22. ISICs and IYTCs are valid for one year from the date of issue. To learn more about ISICs and IYTCs, try www.myisic.com. Many student travel agencies (p. 23) issue the cards; for a list of issuing agencies or more information, see the **International Student Travel Confederation (ISTC)** website (www.istc.org).

The **International Student Exchange Card (ISE Card)** is a similar identification card available to students, faculty, and children aged 12 to 26. The card provides discounts, medical benefits, access to a 24hr. emergency help line, and the ability to purchase student airfares. An ISE Card costs US$25; call ☎+1-800-255-8000 (in North America) or ☎+1-480-951-1177 (from all other continents). For more info visit www.isecard.com.

CUSTOMS

Upon entering Italy, you must declare certain items from abroad and pay a duty on the value of those articles if they exceed the allowance established by Italy's customs service. Goods and gifts purchased at duty-free shops abroad are not exempt from duty or sales tax; "duty-free" means that you won't pay tax in the country of purchase. Duty-free allowances were abolished for travel between EU member states on June 30, 1999, but still exist for those arriving from outside the EU. Upon returning home, you must likewise declare all articles acquired abroad and pay a duty on the value of articles in excess of your home country's allowance. Jot down a list of any valuables brought from home and register them with customs before traveling abroad. It's a good idea to **keep receipts for all goods acquired abroad.**

CUSTOMS IN THE EU. As well as freedom of movement of people, travelers in the European Union can also take advantage of the freedom of movement of goods. This means that there are no customs controls at internal EU borders and travelers are free to transport whatever legal substances they like as long as it is for their own personal (non-commercial) use. Duty-free allowances were abolished on June 30, 1999, for travel between the original 15 EU member states; this now also applies to Cyprus and Malta. However, travelers between the EU and the rest of the world still get a duty-free allowance when passing through customs.

MONEY

CURRENCY AND EXCHANGE

The currency chart below is based on August 2009 exchange rates. Check the currency converter on websites like www.xe.com or www.bloomberg.com for the latest exchange rates.

EURO (€)		
	AUS$1 = €0.58	€1 = AUS$1.71
	CDN$1 = €0.65	€1 = CDN$1.54
	NZ$1 = €0.47	€1 = NZ$2.14
	UK£1 = €1.17	€1 = UK£0.85
	US$1 = €0.70	€1 = US$1.44

As a general rule, it's cheaper to convert money in Italy than at home. While currency exchange will probably be available in your arrival airport, it's wise to bring enough foreign currency to last for at least 24-72hr.

When changing money abroad, try to go only to banks or money changers *(cambio casas)* that have at most a 5% margin between their buy and sell prices. Since you lose money with every transaction, it makes sense to convert large sums at one time.

If you use traveler's checks or bills, carry some in small denominations (the equivalent of US$50 or less) for times when you are forced to exchange money at poor rates, but bring a range of denominations since charges may be applied per check cashed. Store your money in a variety of forms; ideally, at any given time you will be carrying some cash, some traveler's checks, and an ATM and/or credit card. All travelers should also consider carrying some US dollars (about US$50 worth), which are often preferred by local tellers.

 THE EURO. As of January 1, 2009, the official currency of 16 members of the European Union—Austria, Belgium, Cyprus, Finland, France, Germany, Greece, Ireland, Italy, Luxembourg, Malta, the Netherlands, Portugal, Slovakia, Slovenia, and Spain—has become the euro.

The currency has important—and positive—consequences for travelers hitting more than one Eurozone country. For one thing, money changers across the eurozone are obliged to exchange money at the official, fixed rate (below) and at no commission (though they may still charge a service fee). Second, euro-denominated traveler's checks allow you to pay for goods and services across the eurozone, again at the official rate and commission-free. At the time of printing, €1 = US$1.44 = CDN$1.54 = NZ$2.14 etc. For more info, check a currency converter (such as www.xe.com) or www.europa.eu.int.

TRAVELER'S CHECKS

Traveler's checks are one of the safest and most convenient means of carrying funds. However, they can also be one of the most frustrating means of spending money since fewer and fewer shops outside of tourist areas accept traveler's checks. American Express and Visa are the most-recognized brands. Many banks and agencies sell them for a small commission. Check issuers provide refunds if the checks are lost or stolen, and many provide additional services, such as toll-free refund hotlines abroad, emergency message services and assistance with lost and stolen credit cards or passports. Ask about toll-free refund hotlines and the location of refund centers when purchasing checks, and always carry emergency cash.

American Express: Checks available with commission at AmEx offices and select banks (www.americanexpress.com). AmEx cardholders can purchase checks by phone (☎+1-800-528-4800). Cheques for Two can be signed by either of 2 people traveling together. For purchase locations or more info, contact AmEx's service centers: in Australia ☎+61 2 9271 8666, in Canada and the US +1-800-528-4800, in New Zealand +64 9 583 8300, and in the UK +44 1273 571 600. In Italy, call ☎+39 067 2282.

Visa: Checks available at banks worldwide. For the location of the nearest office, call the Visa Travelers Cheque Global Refund and Assistance Center: in the UK ☎+44 800 895 078, in the US +1-800-227-6811; elsewhere, call the UK collect at +44 2079 378 091. Checks available in American, British, Canadian, European, and Japanese currencies, among others. Visa also offers TravelMoney, a prepaid debit card that can be reloaded online or by phone. For more information on Visa travel services, see http://usa.visa.com/personal/using_visa/travel_with_visa.html.

CREDIT, DEBIT, AND ATM CARDS

Where they are accepted, credit cards often offer superior exchange rates—up to 5% better than the retail rate used by banks and other currency-exchange establishments. Credit cards may also offer services such as insurance or emergency help and are sometimes required to reserve hotel rooms or rental cars. **MasterCard** (a.k.a. **EuroCard** in Italy) and **Visa** (e.g. **Carte Bleue** in Italy) are the most frequently accepted; **American Express** cards work at some ATMs and at AmEx offices and major airports.

The use of ATM cards is widespread in Italy. Depending on the system that your home bank uses, you can most likely access your personal bank account from abroad. ATMs get the same wholesale exchange rate as credit cards, but there is often a limit on the amount of money you can withdraw per day (usually around US$500). There is also typically a surcharge of US$1-5 per withdrawal, so it pays to be efficient.

Debit cards are as convenient as credit cards but withdraw money directly from the holder's checking account. A debit card can be used wherever its associated credit card company (usually MasterCard or Visa) is accepted.

The two major international money networks are **MasterCard/Maestro/Cirrus** (for ATM locations ☎+1-800-424-7787; www.mastercard.com) and **Visa/PLUS** (for ATM locations visit http://visa.via.infonow.net/locator/global/). Most ATMs charge a transaction fee that is paid to the bank that owns the ATM. It is a good idea to contact your bank or credit card company before going abroad; frequent charges in a foreign country can sometimes prompt a fraud alert, which will freeze your account.

> **PINS AND ATMS.** To use a cash or credit card to withdraw money from a cash machine (ATM) in Europe, you must have a four-digit Personal Identification Number (PIN). If your PIN is longer than four digits, ask your bank whether you can just use the first four or whether you'll need a new one. Credit cards don't usually come with PINs, so, if you intend to hit up ATMs in Europe with a credit card to get cash advances, call your credit card company before leaving to request one.
>
> Travelers with alphabetic, rather than numerical, PINs may also be thrown off by the lack of letters on European cash machines. The following are the corresponding numbers to use: 1 = QZ; 2 = ABC; 3 = DEF; 4 = GHI; 5 = JKL; 6 = MNO; 7 = PRS; 8 = TUV; 9 = WXY. Note that if you mistakenly punch the wrong code into the machine three times, it will swallow your card for good.

GETTING MONEY FROM HOME

If you run out of money while traveling, the easiest and cheapest solution is to have someone back home make a deposit to your bank account. Otherwise, consider one of the following options.

WIRING MONEY

It is possible to arrange a **bank money transfer,** which means asking a bank back home to wire money to a bank in Italy. This is the cheapest way to transfer cash, but it's also the slowest, usually taking several days or more. Note that some banks may only release your funds in local currency, potentially sticking you with a poor exchange rate; inquire about this in advance. Money transfer services like **Western Union** are faster and more convenient than bank transfers—but also much pricier. Western Union has many locations worldwide. To find one, visit www.westernunion.com or call in Australia ☎+61 1800 173 833, in Canada and the US+1 800-325-6000, in the UK+44 0800 735 1815, or in Italy at 800 788 935. To wire money using a credit card, call in Canada and the US ☎+1 800-CALL-CASH, in the UK+44 0800 833 833. Money transfers services, like remittances and access to emergency funds, are available to **American Express** cardholders in Italy; check www.amextravelresources.com before leaving. **Thomas Cook** also provides resources for international money transfers. See www.thomascook.com for more information.

US STATE DEPARTMENT (US CITIZENS ONLY)

In serious emergencies only, the US State Department will forward money within hours to the nearest consular office, which will then disburse it according to instructions for a US$30 fee. If you wish to use this service, you must contact the Overseas Citizens Services division of the US State Department (☎+1-202-501-4444, from US 888-407-4747).

COSTS

The cost of your trip will vary considerably, depending on where you visit, how you travel, and where you stay. The most significant expenses will probably be your round-trip (return) airfare to Italy (see **Getting to Florence By Plane,** (p. 22) and a railpass or bus pass.

STAYING ON A BUDGET

To give you a general idea, a bare-bones day in Florence (sleeping in hostels/guesthouses, buying food at supermarkets) would cost about US$50 (€32); a slightly more comfortable day (sleeping in hostels/guesthouses and the occasional budget hotel, eating one meal per day at a restaurant, going out at night) would cost about US$90 (€57); and, for a luxurious day, the sky's the limit. Don't forget to factor in emergency reserve funds (at least US$200) when planning how much money you'll need.

TIPPING AND BARGAINING

At many Italian restaurants, a service charge *(servizio)* or cover *(coperto)* is included in the bill. Locals sometimes do not give tips, but it is appropriate for foreign visitors to leave an additional 5-10% at restaurants for the waiter. A euro or two will suffice. Taxi drivers expect about a 5-10% tip, though Italians rarely tip them. Bargaining is common in Italy, but use discretion. Haggling is appropriate at markets, with vendors, and unmetered taxi fares (settle the price before getting in), but elsewhere, it is usually inappropriate. Hotel negotiation is more successful in uncrowded *pensioni* (Italian accommodations, which are sort of a middle ground between hotels and hostels). To get lower prices, show little interest. Don't offer what you can't pay; you're expected to buy once the merchant accepts your price.

TAXES

The **Value Added Tax** (**VAT;** *imposto sul valore aggiunta*, or IVA) is a sales tax levied in the EU. Foreigners making any purchase over €155 are entitled to an additional 20% VAT refund. Some stores take off 20% on-site. Others require that you fill out forms at the customs desk upon leaving the EU and send receipts from home within six months. Not all storefront "Tax-Free" stickers imply an immediate, on-site refund, so ask before making a purchase.

PACKING

Pack lightly: lay out only what you think you absolutely need, then pack half of the clothes and twice the money. The **Travelite FAQ** (www.travelite.org) is a good resource for tips on traveling light. The online **Universal Packing List** (http://upl.codeq.info) will generate a customized list of suggested items based on your trip length, the expected climate, your planned activities, and other factors.

Converters and Adapters: In Italy, electricity is 230 volts AC, enough to fry any 120V North American appliance. 220/240V electrical appliances won't work with a 120V current, either. Americans and Canadians should buy an **adapter** (which changes the shape of the plug; US$10-20) and a **converter** (which changes the voltage; US$10-20). Don't make the mistake of using only an adapter (unless appliance instructions explicitly state otherwise). Australians and New Zealanders (who use 230V at home) won't need a converter but will need a set of adapters to use anything electrical. For more on all things adaptable, check out http://kropla.com/electric.htm.

LIQUIDS IN THE AIR. Travelers should note new EU and US travel restrictions on liquids—including drinks, toiletries, and gels—on airplanes. At the time of printing , liquids could be transported only in containers of 100mL (3 fl. oz. in the US) or less. Each passenger could carry only as many containers as fit in a 1L (1 quart in the US) clear plastic bag. To avoid hassles, put as many of your liquids as possible in your checked luggage. Contact Florence's international airport for the latest policy.

Important documents: Don't forget your passport, traveler's checks, ATM and/or credit cards, adequate ID, and photocopies of all of the aforementioned in case these documents are lost or stolen (p. 11). Also check that you have any of the following that might apply to you: a hostelling membership card (p. 33); driver's license (p. 27); travel insurance forms (p. 19); ISIC (p. 12); and/or railpass or bus pass (p. 25).

SAFETY AND HEALTH

GENERAL ADVICE

In any type of crisis, the most important thing to do is **stay calm.** Your country's embassy abroad (p. 10) is usually your best resource in an emergency; registering with that embassy upon arrival in the country is a good idea. The government offices listed in the **Travel Advisories** box (see next page) can provide information on the services they offer their citizens in case of emergencies abroad.

LOCAL LAWS AND POLICE

In Italy, you will mainly encounter two types of police: the *polizia* (☎113) and the *carabinieri* (☎112). The *polizia* are a civil force under the command of the Ministry of the Interior, whereas the *carabinieri* fall under the jurisdiction of the Ministry of Defense and are considered a military force. Both, however, generally serve the same purpose—to maintain security and order in the country. In the case of attack or robbery, both will respond to inquiries for help.

DRUGS AND ALCOHOL

Needless to say, **illegal drugs** are best avoided altogether. In Italy, drugs including marijuana, cocaine, and heroin are illegal. An increase in cocaine and heroin addiction and trafficking have led Italian authorities to respond harshly to drug-related offenses. If you carry **prescription drugs,** bring copies of the prescriptions and a note from a doctor, and have them accessible at international borders. The drinking age in Italy is 16. Drinking and driving is prohibited and can result in a prison sentence. The legal blood alcohol content (BAC) for driving is under 0.05%.

SPECIFIC CONCERNS

DEMONSTRATIONS AND POLITICAL GATHERINGS

Americans should be mindful while traveling in Italy, as there is some anti-American sentiment. It is best to err on the side of caution and sidestep any political discussions. In general, use discretion and avoid being too vocal about your citizenship.

TERRORISM

Terrorism has not been as serious a problem in Italy as in other European countries, though the general threat of terrorism still exists. Exercise common sense and caution when in crowded, public areas like train or bus stations and open spaces like *piazze* in larger cities. The box below lists offices to contact and websites to visit to get the most updated list of your government's advisories about travel.

> **TRAVEL ADVISORIES.** The following government offices provide travel information and advisories by telephone, by fax, or via the web:
>
> **Australian Department of Foreign Affairs and Trade:** ☎+61 2 6261 1111; www.dfat.gov.au.
>
> **Canadian Department of Foreign Affairs and International Trade (DFAIT):** ☎+1-800-267-8376; www.dfait-maeci.gc.ca. Call or visit the website for the free booklet *Bon Voyage...But.*
>
> **New Zealand Ministry of Foreign Affairs:** ☎+64 4 439 8000; www.mfat.govt.nz.
>
> **United Kingdom Foreign and Commonwealth Office:** ☎+44 20 7008 1500; www.fco.gov.uk.
>
> **US Department of State:** ☎+1-888-407-4747, 202-501-4444 from abroad; http://travel.state.gov.

PERSONAL SAFETY

EXPLORING AND TRAVELING

To avoid unwanted attention, try to blend in as much as possible. Respecting local customs (in many cases, dressing more conservatively than you would at home) may ward off would-be hecklers. Familiarize yourself with your surroundings before setting out and carry yourself with confidence. Check maps in shops and restaurants rather than on the street. If you are traveling alone, be sure someone at home knows your itinerary and never tell anyone you meet that you're by yourself. When walking at night, stick to busy, well-lit streets and avoid dark alleyways. If you ever feel uncomfortable, leave the area as quickly and directly as you can. There is no sure-fire way to avoid all the threatening situations that you might encounter while traveling, but a good **self-defense course** will give you concrete ways to react to unwanted advances. **Impact, Prepare,** and **Model Mugging** (www.modelmugging.org) can refer you to local self-defense courses in Australia, Canada, Switzerland, and the US.

If you are using a **car,** learn local driving signals and wear a seat belt. Children under 40 lb. should ride only in specially designed car seats, available for a fee from most car-rental agencies. Study route maps before you hit the road and, if you plan on spending a lot of time driving, consider bringing spare parts. For long drives in desolate areas, invest in a cell phone and a roadside assistance program (p. 27). Park your vehicle in a garage or well-traveled area and use a steering-wheel locking device in larger cities. Sleeping in your car is the most dangerous way to get your rest, and it's illegal in many countries.

No one should hitchhike without careful consideration of the risks involved. Hitching means entrusting your life to a random person who happens to stop beside you on the road, and hitchers always risk theft, assault, sexual harassment, and unsafe driving.

POSSESSIONS AND VALUABLES

Never leave your belongings unattended; crime can occur in even the safestlooking hostel or hotel. Bring your own padlock for hostel lockers and don't ever store valuables in a locker. Be particularly careful on **buses** and **trains;** horror stories abound about determined thieves who wait for travelers to fall asleep. Carry your bag or purse in front of you where you can see it. When traveling with others, sleep in alternate shifts. When alone, be careful in selecting a train compartment: never stay in an empty one and always use a lock to secure your pack to the luggage rack. Use extra caution if traveling at night or on overnight trains. Try to sleep on top bunks with your luggage stored above you (if not in bed with you) and keep important documents and other valuables on you at all times.

There are a few steps you can take to minimize the financial risk associated with traveling. First, **bring as little with you as possible.** Second, buy a few combination **padlocks** to secure your belongings either in your pack or in a hostel or train-station locker. Third, **carry as little cash as possible.** Keep your traveler's checks and ATM/credit cards in a **money belt**—not a "fanny pack"—along with your passport and ID cards. Fourth, **keep a small cash reserve separate from your primary stash.** This should be about US$50 (US dollars or euro are best) sewn into or stored in the depths of your pack, along with your traveler's check numbers and photocopies of your important documents.

In Florence, **con artists** often work in groups and may involve children in their schemes. Beware of certain classics: sob stories that require money, rolls of bills "found" on the street, mustard spilled (or saliva spit) onto your shoulder to distract you while they snatch your bag. **Never let your passport or your bags out of your sight.** Hostel workers will sometimes stand at bus and train arrival points to recruit tired and disoriented travelers to their hostel; never believe strangers who tell you that theirs is the only hostel open. Beware of **pickpockets** in city crowds, especially on public transportation. Also, be alert in public telephone booths. If you must say your calling-card number, do so very quietly; if you punch it in, make sure no one can look over your shoulder.

PRE-DEPARTURE HEALTH

In your passport, write the names of any people you wish to be contacted in case of a **medical emergency** and list any **allergies** or **medical conditions.** Matching a prescription to a foreign equivalent is not always easy, safe, or possible, so, if you take **prescription drugs,** carry up-to-date prescriptions or a statement from your doctor stating the medications' trade names, manufacturers, chemical names, and dosages. While traveling, be sure to keep all medication with you in your carry-on luggage.

While it may be difficult to find brand name medications like Tylenol or Advil, these products can easily be identified by their common Italian drug names such as *acetaminofene* (acetaminophen), *paracetamolo* (paracetamol), and *ibuprofen* (ibuprofen).

IMMUNIZATIONS AND PRECAUTIONS

Travelers over two years old should make sure that the following vaccines are up to date: MMR (for measles, mumps, and rubella); DTaP or Td (for diphtheria, tetanus, and pertussis); IPV (for polio); Hib (for *Haemophilus influenzae* B); and HepB (for Hepatitis B). For recommendations on immunizations and prophylaxis, consult the Centers for Disease Control and Prevention (CDC; below) in the US or the equivalent in your home country and check with a doctor for guidance.

USEFUL ORGANIZATIONS AND PUBLICATIONS

The American **Center for Disease Control and Prevention (CDC; ☎ +1-800-CDC-INFO/232-4636;** www.cdc.gov/travel) maintains an international travelers' hotline and an informative website. Consult the appropriate government agency of your home country for consular information sheets on health, entry requirements, and other issues for various countries (see the listings in the box on **Travel Advisories,** p. 18). For quick information on health and other travel warnings, call the **Overseas Citizens Services** (☎ +1-202-647-5225) or contact a passport agency, embassy, or consulate abroad. For information on medical evacuation services and travel insurance firms, see the US government's website at http://travel.state.gov/travel/abroad_health.html or the **British Foreign and Commonwealth Office** (www.fco.gov.uk). For general health information, contact the **American Red Cross** (☎ +1-202-303-5000; www.redcross.org).

STAYING HEALTHY

Common sense is the simplest prescription for good health while you travel. Drink lots of fluids to prevent dehydration and constipation and wear sturdy, broken-in shoes and clean socks.

ONCE IN FLORENCE

ENVIRONMENTAL HAZARDS

Arid summer weather creates prime conditions for heat exhaustion and dehydration, so drink plenty of liquid.

Heat exhaustion and dehydration: Heat exhaustion leads to nausea, excessive thirst, headaches, and dizziness. Avoid it by drinking plenty of fluids, eating salty foods (e.g., crackers), abstaining from dehydrating beverages (e.g., alcohol and caffeinated beverages), and wearing sunscreen. Continuous heat stress can eventually lead to **heatstroke,** characterized by a rising temperature, severe headache, delirium, and cessation of sweating. Victims should be cooled off with wet towels and taken to a doctor.

INSECT-BORNE DISEASES

Many diseases are transmitted by insects—mainly mosquitoes, fleas, ticks, and lice. Be aware of insects in wet or forested areas. Use insect repellents such as DEET and soak or spray your gear with permethrin (licensed in the US only for use on clothing). **Mosquitoes**—responsible for malaria, dengue fever, and yellow fever—can be particularly abundant in wet, swampy, or wooded areas like those found in Tuscany. **Ticks**—which can carry Lyme and other diseases—can be particularly dangerous in rural and forested regions.

Lyme disease: A bacterial infection carried by ticks and marked by a circular bull's-eye rash of 2 in. or more. Later symptoms include fever, headache, fatigue, and aches and pains. Antibiotics are effective if administered early. Left untreated, Lyme can cause problems in joints, the heart, and the nervous system. If you find a tick attached to your skin, grasp the head with tweezers as close to your skin as possible and apply slow, steady traction. Removing a tick within 24hr. greatly reduces the risk of infection. Do not try to remove ticks with petroleum jelly, nail polish remover, or a hot match. Ticks usually inhabit moist, shaded environments and heavily wooded areas.

FOOD- AND WATERBORNE DISEASES

Prevention is the best cure: be sure that your food is properly cooked and that the water you drink is clean. Watch out for food from markets or street vendors that may have been cooked in unhygienic conditions. Other culprits are raw shellfish, unpasteurized milk, and sauces containing raw eggs. Buy bottled water or purify your own water by bringing it to a rolling boil or treating it with **iodine tablets;** note, however, that boiling is more reliable. While Italy's water is relatively clean, it is important to be wary in places like trains where water is not clean. The sign *"acqua non potabile"* means the water is not drinkable; *"acqua potabile"* means the water is sanitary. Even as a developed nation, Italy experienced an outbreak of stomach flu due to contaminated drinking water in Taranto in 2006.

> **Traveler's diarrhea:** Results from drinking fecally contaminated water or eating uncooked and contaminated foods. Symptoms include nausea, bloating, and urgency. Try quick-energy, non-sugary foods with protein and carbohydrates to keep your strength up. Over-the-counter anti-diarrheals (e.g., Imodium®) may counteract the problem. The most dangerous side effect is dehydration; drink 8 oz. of water with ½ tsp. of sugar or honey and a pinch of salt, try uncaffeinated soft drinks, or eat salted crackers. If you develop a fever or your symptoms don't go away after 4-5 days, consult a doctor. Consult a doctor immediately for treatment of diarrhea in children.

OTHER INFECTIOUS DISEASES

The following diseases exist all over the world. Travelers should know how to recognize them and what to do if they suspect they have been infected.

> **AIDS and HIV:** For detailed information on Acquired Immune Deficiency Syndrome (AIDS) in Italy, call the CDC's 24hr. National AIDS Hotline at ☎+1-800-232-4636. Note that Italy screens incoming travelers for AIDS, primarily those planning extended visits for work or study, and denies entrance to those who test HIV-positive. Contact the consulate of Italy for info.

> **Sexually transmitted infections (STIs):** Gonorrhea, chlamydia, genital warts, syphilis, herpes, HPV, and other STIs are easier to catch than HIV and can be just as serious. Though condoms may protect you from some STIs, oral or even tactile contact can lead to transmission. If you think you may have contracted an STI, see a doctor immediately.

OTHER HEALTH CONCERNS

MEDICAL CARE ON THE ROAD

Florence conforms overall to the standards of modern Western health care. Medical facilities tend to be better in private hospitals and clinics. Most Florentine doctors speak English; if they don't, they may be able to arrange for a translator. *Let's Go* lists info on how to access medical help in the **Practical Information** section (p. 79).

If you are concerned about obtaining medical assistance while traveling, you may wish to employ special support services. The **International Association for Medical Assistance to Travelers** (**IAMAT;** US ☎+1-716-754-4883, Canada +1-416-652-0137; www.iamat.org) has free membership, lists English-speaking doctors worldwide, and offers details on immunization requirements and sanitation. For those whose insurance doesn't apply abroad, you can purchase additional coverage.

ESSENTIALS

Those with medical conditions (such as diabetes, allergies to antibiotics, epilepsy, or heart conditions) may want to obtain a **MedicAlert** membership (US$40 per year), which includes, among other things, a stainless-steel ID tag and a 24hr. collect-call number. Contact the MedicAlert Foundation International (from US ☎888-633-4298, outside US +1-209-668-3333; www.medicalert.org).

WOMEN'S HEALTH

Women traveling in unsanitary conditions are vulnerable to **urinary tract (including bladder and kidney) infections.** Bring supplies from home if you are prone to infection, as they may be difficult to find on the road. **Tampons, pads,** and **contraceptive devices** are widely available, though your preferred brand may not be stocked—bring extras of anything you can't live without. Abortion (*aborto* or *interruzione volontaria di gravidanza*) is legal and may be performed in the first 90 days of pregnancy for free in a public hospital or for a fee in an authorized private facility. Except in urgent cases, a week-long reflection period is required. Women under 18 must obtain parental permission or a judge's consent. Availability may be limited in some areas, especially in the south, due to a "conscience clause" that allows physicians who oppose abortion to opt out of performing the procedure. The election of Pope Benedict XVI has sparked controversy over abortion, but no immediate policy changes are expected.

GETTING TO FLORENCE

BY PLANE

When it comes to airfare, a little effort can save you a bundle. For those with flexibility *and* patience, **standby flights** are one way to save; be prepared to spend all day at the airport for a week or more before finally boarding a plane. Call major airline companies for details (see **Commercial Airlines, p. 24**). Tickets sold by consolidators are also good deals, but last-minute specials, airfare wars, and charter flights often beat these fares. The key is to hunt around, be flexible, and ask about discounts. Students, seniors, and those under 26 should almost never pay full price for a ticket.

AIRFARES

Airfares to Florence peak between April and October, and holidays are also expensive. The cheapest times to travel are early spring and late fall. Midweek (M-Th morning) round-trip flights run cheaper than weekend flights, but they are generally more crowded and less likely to permit frequent-flier upgrades. Not fixing a return date ("open return") or arriving in and departing from different cities ("open-jaw") can be pricier than round-trip flights. Patching one-way flights together is the most expensive way to travel.

If Florence is only one stop on a more extensive globe-hop, consider a round-the-world (RTW) ticket. Tickets usually include at least five stops and are valid for about a year; prices range US$3000-8000. Try the airline consortiums **Oneworld** (www.oneworld.com), **Skyteam** (www.skyteam.com), and **Star Alliance** (www.staralliance.com). It is also cheaper to fly to Pisa (if departing from a European city) than going directly to Florence. The **Pisa**

International Airport (Aeroporto Internazionale Galileo Galilei) and Florence are conveniently connected by rail and bus.

Fares for round-trip flights to Florence from the US or Canadian east coast cost US$800-1500, US$550-700 in the low season (from mid-Oct. to mid-Dec. and Jan.-Mar.); from the US or Canadian west coast US$800-1600/600-1000; from the UK UK£175-300/100-200; from Australia AUS$1900-3000/1500-2000; from New Zealand NZ$2200-3500/1900-2400.

BUDGET AND STUDENT TRAVEL AGENCIES

While knowledgeable agents specializing in flights to Rome can make your life easy, they may not spend the time to find you the lowest possible fare—they get paid on commission. Travelers holding ISICs and IYTCs (p. 12) qualify for big discounts from student travel agencies. Most flights from budget agencies are on major airlines, but in high season some may sell seats on less reliable chartered aircraft.

The Adventure Travel Company, 124 MacDougal St., New York, NY 10021, USA (☎+1-212-674-2887; www.theadventuretravelcompany.com). Offices across Canada and the US including New York City, San Diego, San Francisco, and Seattle.

STA Travel, 2871 Broadway, New York, NY 10025, USA (24hr. reservations and info ☎+1-800-781-4040; www.statravel.com). A student and youth travel organization with offices worldwide, including US offices in Los Angeles, New York City, Seattle, Washington, DC and a number of other college towns. Ticket booking, travel insurance, railpasses, and more. Walk-in offices are located throughout Australia (☎+61 134 782), New Zealand (☎+0800 474 400), and the UK (☎+44 8712 230 0040).

COMMERCIAL AIRLINES

TRAVELING FROM NORTH AMERICA

Crossing the pond? Standard commercial carriers like **American** (☎+1-800-433-7300; www.aa.com), **United** (☎+1-800-538-2929; www.ual.com), and **Northwest** (☎+1-800-225-2525; www.nwa.com) will probably offer the most convenient flights, but they may not be the cheapest. Check **Air France** (☎+1-800-237-2747; www.airfrance.us), **Alitalia** (☎+1-800-223-5730; www.alitaliausa.com), **British Airways** (☎+1-800-247-9297; www.britishairways.com), and **Lufthansa** (☎+1-800-399-5838; www.lufthansa.com) for cheap tickets from destinations throughout the US to Florence. You might find an even better deal on one of the following airlines, if any of their limited departure points is convenient for you.

> **Finnair** (☎+1-800-950-5000; www.finnair.com). Cheap round-trips from New York City to Pisa; connections throughout Europe ($325).

> **KLM** (☎+44 8712 227 474; www.klmuk.com). Cheap tickets from London, Dublin, and elsewhere to Florence ($175).

TRAVELING FROM IRELAND AND THE UK

Cheapflights (www.cheapflights.co.uk) publishes bargains on airfare from the British Isles, but British and Irish globetrotters really looking to save should always fly on budget airlines. The following commercial carriers occasionally offer discounted fares or specials.

> **KLM** (☎+44 8712 227 474; www.klmuk.com). Cheap tickets from London, Dublin, and elsewhere to Florence (UK£70-200).

> **Alitalia** (☎+1-800-223-5730; www.alitaliausa.com). Affordable round-trips from London, Dublin, Edinburgh, and elsewhere to Florence (UK£180-280).

TRAVELING FROM AUSTRALIA AND NEW ZEALAND

When traveling from Australia and New Zealand to Florence chances are you might have to combine different airlines for the best deals. For more information, see **Flight Planning on the Internet** (p. 23). Below are airlines that list Florence as a destination. Make sure to check the schedule, as flights to Florence are often only available during seasonal peaks.

> **KLM** (☎+44 8712 227 474; www.klmuk.com). Flights from Auckland, Melbourne, Perth, and Sydney to Florence. (Operated jointly with Meridiana and Singapore airlines; AUS$2000-6000, NZD$4000-8000).

> **Qantas Air:** (in Australia ☎+61 13 13 13, in New Zealand +64 800 808 767; www.qantas.com.au). Flights to Florence (often partnered with other airlines; AUS$3000-6000).

BUDGET AIRLINES

For travelers who don't place a premium on convenience, we recommend **budget airlines** as the best way to jet around Europe. Travelers can often snag these tickets for illogically low prices (i.e., less than the price of a meal in the airport food court), but you get what you pay for: namely, minimalist service and no frills. In addition, many budget airlines fly out of smaller regional airports several kilometers out of town. You'll have to buy shuttle tickets to reach the airports of many of these airlines, so plan on adding an hour or so to your travel time. After round-trip shuttle tickets and fees for services that might come standard on other airlines, that €1 sale fare can suddenly jump to €20-100. Still, it's possible save money even if you live outside the continent by hopping a cheap flight to anywhere in Europe and using budget airlines to reach your final destination. Prices vary dramatically; shop around, book months ahead, pack light, and stay flexible to nab the best fares. For a more detailed list of these airlines by country, check out www.whichbudget.com.

easyJet (☎+44 871 244 2366, UK£0.10 per min.; www.easyjet.com). From London to Pisa (UK£25-90).

Ryanair (in Ireland ☎+353 0818 30 30 30, in the UK +44 0871 246 0000, elsewhere +35 3124 80856; www.ryanair.com). The cheapest flights (from £10 with taxes) from Dublin, Glasgow, Liverpool, and London to Pisa.

Sterling (in Denmark ☎+45 70 10 84 84, in the UK +44 0870 787 8038; www.sterling. dk). The 1st Scandinavian-based budget airline. Connects Denmark, Norway, and Sweden to 47 European destinations, including Florence (€80).

Transavia (in the UK ☎+44 020 7365 4997; www.transavia.com). From Copenhagen and Amsterdam to Pisa (€45).

BY TRAIN

Traveling to Florence by train from within Europe can be as expensive as flying, but allows travelers to watch the country unfold before them and grants the possibility of spontaneous stopovers before reaching the ultimate destination. Prices and number of trips per day vary according to destination, the day of the week, season, and other criteria. To find prices, schedules, and locations check **www.raileurope.com** or **www.voyages-sncf.com**.

Florence's main station is **Stazione Santa Maria Novella,** on the edge of the historic old town. Other small stations are **Firenze Campo Marte** (near Florence Stadium) and **Firenze Rifredi.** If you take an Intercity train to Florence, you may need to change at Rifredi for another train to Firenze S.M.N.

If traveling from Paris or most German towns, you can also take the overnight trains and sleep comfortably the entire way (€70-100). See p. 18 for info on train safety.

BY BUS

Though European trains are popular, in some cases buses prove a better option. Often cheaper than railpasses, international bus passes allow unlimited travel on a hop-on, hop-off basis between major European cities. Amsterdam, Athens, Istanbul, London, Munich, and Oslo are centers for lines offering long-distance rides across Europe. Bus travel within Italy has its own benefits and disadvantages; in remote parts of the country private companies offer cheap fares and are often the only option, though schedules may be unreliable.

Eurolines, 4 Vicarage Rd., Edgbaston, Birmingham B15 3ES, UK (☎+44 8705 80 80 80; www.eurolines.com). The largest operator of Europe-wide coach services. Unlimited 15-day (high season UK£195, under 26 and over 60 UK£165; low season UK£149/129); 30-day (high season UK£290/235; low season UK£209/169); or 60-day (high season UK£333/259; low season UK£265/211) travel passes that offer unlimited transit between 35 major European cities.

SITA, V. Santa Caterina da Siena 15, Florence, Italy (☎1 800 37 37 60; www.sita-on-line.it). Just to the west of **Stazione di Santa Maria Novella.** Offers a handful of long-distance services, most to southern Italy and Sicily.

BORDER CROSSINGS

The surrounding countries of France, Switzerland, and Austria can make great daytrips from Italy's border cities. Multiple-country rail passes are available through **RailEurope (www.raileurope.com)**. As a part of the EU, Italy only requires that travelers present a valid passport and ID to travel between EU nations. When traveling to France and Austria, no currency exchange is necessary. Switzerland, however, uses the Swiss franc (CHF).

GETTING AROUND FLORENCE

BY FOOT

Some of Italy's grandest scenery and Florence's historical sites can be seen only by **foot**. *Let's Go* features many daytrips, but native inhabitants and fellow travelers are the best source for tips. Professionally-run hiking and walking tours are often your best bet for navigating *la bell'Italia*. Hiking tours generally range from six to nine days long and cost US$2800-4000. Check out Ciclismo Classico (see above) for hiking options along the Amalfi Coast, and through Tuscany or Cinque Terre. The **Backpack Europe** website (www.backpackeurope.com) provides links to great hiking, walking, and kayaking options throughout Italy.

Everything in Florence is within walking distance. That said, if your feet fail you after treading through miles of marvels in the Uffizi or elsewhere, we're here to help.

BY BUS

Orange **ATAF buses** cover most of the city from 6am to 1am. Buy tickets at any newsstand, *tabaccheria*, or coin-operated ticket dispenser. Your trip will cost €1.20 for one ticket, €4.50 for 4 tickets, €5 for 1 day, or €12 for 3 days. Validate your ticket onboard using the orange machine or risk a €50 fine. Once validated, the ticket allows unlimited bus travel for the allotted time. From the train station, the ATAF information office (☎+39 055 80 04 24 500; www.ataf.net) is on the left and provides free maps. Open M-F 7:15am-1:15pm and 1:45-7:45pm, Sa 7:15am-1:15pm. Take bus #7 to Fiesole, #13 to Piazzale Michelangelo, and #17 if you're headed toward the area hostels.

Of the four so-called "night-bus routes," three operate only between 9pm and 1am. The only true night bus *(autobus notturno)* is bus 70.

 FERMATA FRENZY. Taking the bus in Italy is easy, affordable, and a great way to get around, but most bus stops that aren't in major *piazze* are only *fermata prenotata* stops, meaning the bus driver won't stop there unless he/she sees somebody waiting or someone onboard requests a stop. Drivers often miss travelers waiting quietly on the side of the road, so make your presence known. Wave your hands, step out on the curb, and make eye contact; you might feel silly but you'll feel worse if the bus drives right by.

BY TAXI

Taxis are available, but it may be best if you have your hotel or restaurant call ahead. Taxis can be called by phone and the nearest one available is sent to you through the company's radio system (☎+39 055 42 42, 055 47 98, 055 44 99, or

055 43 90). In Florence, it can be difficult to hail a cab from the curb. You either call for one or get one at the very few taxi stands. One popular taxi stand is at the central **Santa Maria Novella Train Station** and in a few major squares. Keep in mind that taxis in Florence are expensive. The meter starts at €2.54, on top of which you pay €0.82 per kilometer within the city limits (€1.47 per kilometer beyond). A cross-town ride will cost around €10, depending on traffic. Tipping is not expected, unless the driver helps you carry luggage.

BY CAR

In a nutshell, don't do it. Driving inside the historic center of Florence is virtually impossible. Only residents with permits are allowed to go there. Enforcement of the Limited Traffic Zone (ZTL) is by camera. Violators are tracked down and fined €90. Once you enter the forbidden zone, it is not humanly possible to pass only one camera, and each time you do, it is a separate fine.

As if that weren't enough, Florence has some of the teeniest streets in Europe, an amazingly fiendish one-way system that confuses even the locals, and some streets that come to an abrupt end with little or no warning.

Parking in the historic center is out of the question. It may only be done by residents with a permit, and all other cars are towed away instantly—if not sooner —to some unsavory suburb. It will cost you hundreds of euros to get yours returned. If you are still tempted to drive around Florence, keep in mind that gas *(benzina)* is exorbitantly priced at approximately €1.30 per liter.

If, for some unfathomable reason, you should choose to leave Florence and explore the rest of the country, you will find that Florence is connected by modern highways to the rest of Italy. With a vast network of narrow, winding roads, loosely enforced speed limits, and aggressive native drivers, touring Italy by car is a memorable experience. Despite the initial intimidation that may come from cruising bumper to bumper on a cliffside road along the Amalfi coast, with a little bit of courage and a decent helping of driving competence, car travel opens up corners of Italy that are not easily accessible.

The easiest way to get in and out of the city from the **A-1 Autostrada**—which connects Florence to Bologna, Milan and the North, and Rome and the South— is to use the **Firenze-Certosa** exit. This is the same route for those leaving for or arriving from Siena on the **FI-SI** highway. If you are arriving from or leaving for Pisa and the West on the A-11 Autostrada, it is best to go by way of Firenze-Certosa and use the A-1 to connect to and from the A-11.

Before setting off, know the laws of the countries in which you'll be driving. For an informal primer on European road signs and conventions, check out www.travlang.com/signs. The **Association for Safe International Road Travel** (**ASIRT**; ☎+1-301-983-5252; www.asirt.org) can provide more specific information about road conditions. ASIRT considers road travel (by car or bus) to be relatively safe in Italy.

DRIVING PERMITS AND CAR INSURANCE

INTERNATIONAL DRIVING PERMIT (IDP)

If you plan to drive a car while in Italy, you must be over 18 and have an **International Driving Permit (IDP),** though certain regions will allow travelers to drive with a valid American or Canadian license for a limited number of months.

Your IDP, valid for one year, must be issued in your own country before you depart. An application for an IDP usually requires one or two photos, a current local license, an additional form of identification, and a fee. To apply, contact your home country's automobile association. Be vigilant when purchasing an IDP online or anywhere other than your home automobile association. Many vendors sell permits of questionable legitimacy for higher prices.

CAR INSURANCE

Most credit cards cover standard insurance. If you rent, lease, or borrow a car, you will need a **green card,** or **International Insurance Certificate,** to certify that you have liability insurance and that it applies abroad. Green cards can be obtained at car rental agencies, car dealers (for those leasing cars), some travel agents, and some border crossings. Rental agencies may require you to purchase theft insurance in countries that they consider to have a high risk of auto theft.

RENTING A CAR

A single traveler won't save by renting a car (especially considering the high gas prices), but four usually will. It is always significantly less expensive to reserve a car from the US than from Europe. If you can't decide between train and car travel, you may benefit from a combination of the two; RailEurope and other railpass vendors offer **rail-and-drive** packages. **Fly-and-drive** packages are often available from travel agents or airline-rental agency partnerships.

You can rent a car from a US-based firm (Alamo, Avis, Budget, or Hertz) with European offices, from a European-based company with local representatives (Europcar), or from a tour operator (Auto Europe, Europe By Car, and Kemwel Holiday Autos) that will arrange a rental for you from a European company at its own rates.

Expect to pay €260 per week (€45-90 per day), though you might be able to find deals (without radio or A/C) as low as €150. By reserving in advance, non-residents of Italy are eligible for discounts of up to 60%. Insurance is required, augmenting the rates by as much as €55 a week. Paying by credit card may give you free insurance on rentals; check with your credit card company. All agencies require either a credit card or a cash deposit of at least €155, and most take only plastic.

Reserve ahead and pay in advance if at all possible. Always check if prices quoted include tax and collision insurance; some credit card companies provide insurance, allowing their customers to decline the collision damage waiver. Ask about discounts and check the terms of insurance, particularly the size of the deductible. To rent a car from most establishments in Italy, you need to be at least 18 years old. Some agencies require renters to be 25, and most charge those 18-24 an additional insurance fee of €12 per day. Be sure to ask about the insurance coverage and deductible, and always check the fine print. At most agencies, all that's needed to rent a car is a license from home, proof that you've had it for a year, and preferably an International Driver's Permit (see above). Car-rental agencies are concentrated in the **Borgo Ognissanti** area. Rental agencies in Italy include:

Alamo (in the US ☎+1-877-222-9075, in Italy +39 055 263 8733; www.alamo.com).

Auto Europe (in North America ☎+1-888-223-5555, in Italy +39 172 1011; www.autoeurope.com).

Avis (in Italy ☎+ 39 199-100-133; www.avis.com).

Budget (US ☎+1-800-527-0700, outside US ☎+1-800-472-3325; www.budgetrentacar.com).

Europcar International (in Italy ☎+39-055-318-609 ; www.europcar.com).

Europe by Car (☎+1-800-223-1516; www.europebycar.com).

Hertz (in the US ☎+1-800-654-3131, outside US ☎+1-800-654-3001; www.hertz.com).

Kemwel (☎+1-800-678-0678, reservations ☎+1-877-820-0668; www.kemwel.com).

ON THE ROAD

Italian roads range from the *autostrade*—superhighways with 130kph (80 mph) speed limit, increased to 150kph (93 mph) in some areas—to the narrow and sometimes unpaved *strade comunali* (local roads). Highways usually charge expensive tolls, often best paid with a credit card. In cities the speed limit is usually 50kph (31 mph). Headlights must be on when driving on the *autostrada*. For more driving rules and regulations, check *Moto Europa* (www.ideamerge.com/motoeuropa) or *In Italy Online* (www.initaly.com/travel/info/driving.htm).

DANGERS

Mountain roads can have steep cliffs and narrow curves; exercise caution if you must drive in the Dolomites or the Apennines. Be careful on minor roads in the countryside, as many are not well maintained and best taken at a slow and steady pace.

CAR ASSISTANCE

The **Automobile Club d'Italia (ACI)** is at the service of all drivers in Italy, with offices located throughout the country (www.aci.it). In case of breakdown, call ☎116 for assistance from the nearest ACI. On superhighways use the emergency telephones placed every 2km. For long drives in desolate areas, invest in a roadside assistance program and a cell phone, but be aware that use of phones en route is only permitted with a hands-free device.

BY TWO-WHEELER

While there are hills north and south of the center of town, almost all of the historic center of Florence is easy for two-wheeler travelers, because it is as flat as a crepe. But there is a catch: traffic is terrible, and buses, trucks, cars, motorcycles, motorbikes, bicycles, and pedestrians are all competing for almost no space at all, so you'd better pay attention.

BICYCLE

Cycling is a convenient and fun way to explore central Florence. It's not obligatory to wear a helmet, and many locals don't bother, but most outlets will provide one. The city runs a public bike-hire service, known as **Mille e Una Bici (A Thousand and One Bikes,** which is something of an overstatement) with bikes available at eight points around the city, including the main one just in front of the Santa Maria Novella train station. Bikes cost up to €8 a day for non-residents. Hours vary from one spot to the next, but many points are not open on weekends.

Renting a bike is easy in Italy; look for *noleggio* (hire) signs. If you want to bring your own, some airlines will count a bike as your second piece of luggage; many now charge extra (one-way US$80-160). Rules vary by airline, but usually bikes must be packed in a cardboard box with the pedals and front wheel detached; many airlines sell bike boxes at the airport (at least US$15). Most ferries let you take your bike for free or for a nominal fee, and you can always ship your bike on trains. Renting a bike beats bringing your own if you plan to stay in one or two regions, and some hostels rent bicycles for low prices. In

ESSENTIALS

addition to **panniers** (US$40-150) to hold your luggage, you'll need a good **helmet** (US$10-40) and a sturdy **lock** (from US$30). *Let's Go* lists bike rental stores in the **Transportation** section of towns and cities whenever possible. **Ciclismo Classico,** 30 Marathon St., Arlington, MA 02474, USA (☎+1-800-866-7314; www.ciclismoclassico.com), offers beginner to advanced level trips across Italy, including Sardinia, the Amalfi Coast, Southern Italy, Sicily, Piedmont, and the Veneto. Listed below are some of the most popular outlets in Florence:

Alinari, V. Guelfa 85/r (☎+39 055 28 05 00; www.alinarirental.com; road bikes €2.50 per hour; mountain bikes €3 per hour).

Florence by Bike, V. San Zanobi 91/r and Via San Zanobi 120-122/r (☎+39 055 48 89 92; www.florencebybike.it). Standard bicycles €13 per day, mountain bikes €19 per day, scooters from €31 per day.

MOPEDS

Often a *motorino* (scooter) is the most convenient method of transportation to reach sights in places with unreliable bus or train connections. *Motorini* are everywhere in Florence. Everyone seems to own one, and just as many seem to have been injured on one. If you want to sacrifice safety for speed and style, you can rent one; no special license is required, though a helmet most definitely is. Gas and insurance may or may not be included in the rental price. If you have never driven a scooter before, Florence's minuscule streets and heavy traffic is not the place to test your maneuverability.

KEEPING IN TOUCH

BY EMAIL AND INTERNET

While Internet is a relatively common amenity throughout Italy, Wi-Fi is not, and as a general rule, the prevalence of both decreases the further you travel from urban areas. In Rome, it may be possible to find Internet but not Wi-Fi. In smaller towns, even a basic Internet connection may be hard to come by. Rates range from €2-6 per hour. While it's possible in some places to forge a remote link with your home server, in most cases this is a much slower (and more expensive) option than using free **web-based email accounts** (e.g., www.gmail.com). **Internet cafes** and the occasional free Internet terminal at a public library or university are listed in the **Practical Information.** For additional cybercafes in Italy, check out http://cafe.ecs.net., and www.cybercaptive.com.

Laptop users can occasionally find internet cafes that will allow them to connect their laptops to the internet. Travelers with wireless-enabled computers may be able to take advantage of an increasing number of internet "hot spots," where they can get online for free or for a small fee. Newer computers can detect these hot spots automatically; otherwise, websites like www.jiwire.com, www.wififreespot.com, and www.wi-fihotspotlist.com can help you find them.

WARY WI-FI. Wireless hot spots make Internet access possible in public and remote places. Unfortunately, they also pose **security risks.** Hot spots are public, open networks that use unencrypted, unsecured connections. They are susceptible to hacks and "packet sniffing"—ways of stealing passwords and other private information. To prevent problems, disable ad hoc mode, turn off file sharing and network discovery, encrypt your email, turn on your firewall, beware of phony networks, and watch for over-the-shoulder creeps.

BY TELEPHONE

CALLING HOME FROM ITALY

Prepaid phone cards are a common and relatively inexpensive means of calling abroad. Each comes with a Personal Identification Number (PIN) and a toll-free access number. You call the access number and then follow the directions to enter your PIN. To buy prepaid phone cards, check online for the best rates; www.callingcards.com is a good place to start. Online providers generally send your access number and PIN via email, with no actual "card" involved. You can also call home with prepaid phone cards purchased in Italy (see **Calling Within Italy, p. 31**).

Another option is to purchase a **calling card,** linked to a major national telecommunications service in your home country. Calls are billed collect or to your account. To call home with a calling card, contact the operator for your service provider in Italy by dialing the appropriate toll-free access number (listed below in the third column).

Placing a collect call through an international operator can be expensive, but may be necessary in case of an emergency. You can frequently call collect without even possessing a company's calling card just by calling its access number and following the instructions.

> **PLACING INTERNATIONAL CALLS.** To call Italy from home or to call home from Italy, dial:
> 1. The **international dialing prefix.** To call from **Australia,** dial 0011; **Canada** or the **US,** 011; **Ireland, New Zealand,** or the **UK,** 00; **Italy,** 00.
> 2. The **country code** of the country you want to call. To call **Australia,** dial 61; **Canada** or the **US,** 1; **Ireland,** 353; **New Zealand,** 64; the **UK,** 44; **Italy,** 39.
> 3. The **city/area code.** *Let's Go* lists the city/area codes for cities and towns in Italy opposite the city or town name, next to a ☎, as well as in every phone number. If the first digit is a zero (e.g., 020 for London), omit the zero when calling from abroad (e.g., dial 20 from **Canada** to reach **London**).
> 4. The **local number.**

CALLING WITHIN ITALY

The simplest way to call within the country is to use a coin-operated phone. Prepaid phone cards (available at newspaper kiosks and tobacco stores, or *tabaccherie*), usually save time and money in the long run.

CELLULAR PHONES

Cellular phones *(telefonini)* are a convenient and inexpensive option for those planning longer visits to Italy. Pay phones are increasingly hard to come by, making cell phones a good alternative for tourists. You won't necessarily have to deal with cell phone plans and bills; prepaid minutes are widely available and phones can be purchased cheaply or even rented, avoiding the hassle of pay phones and phone cards.

The international standard for cell phones is **Global System for Mobile Communication (GSM).** To make and receive calls in Italy you will need a GSM-compatible phone and a **SIM (Subscriber Identity Module) card,** a country-specific, thumbnail-sized chip that gives you a local phone number and plugs you into the local network. Many SIM cards are prepaid, and incoming calls are often free. You can buy additional cards or vouchers (usually available at convenience stores) to "top up" your phone. For more info on GSM phones, check out www. telestial.com, www.orange.co.uk, www.roadpost.com, or www.plane-tomni.com. Companies like **Cellular Abroad** (www.cellularabroad.com) rent cell phones that work in a variety of destinations around the world.

For those with unlocked cell phones (call your cell phone service provider to check if your phone is locked or to ask them to unlock it), Italian SIM cards can be purchased for €10 at **Vodafone** stores throughout the city (and phone credit can be purchased after that). €0.16 per minute with a €0.16 connection fee. Open M-F 11am-7pm. **Webpuccino**, P. Madonna, V de' Conti 22r (☎055 277 6469; www. webpuccino.it). Phone rental €30 and comes with €5 of local credit and €3 of international credit. You get free incoming calls while in Italy, free calls from Florence to all landlines in Italy, free calls between students with the same carrier inside Florence (home zone). **3 Store** (☎055 21 55 26, www.tre.it), near the duomo at V. Martelli 20r. Check website for alternate locations and rates. €39 to purchase a phone, and then buy credit.

GSM PHONES. Just having a GSM phone doesn't mean you're necessarily good to go when you travel abroad. The majority of GSM phones sold in the United States operate on a different frequency (1900) than international phones (900/1800) and will not work abroad. Tri-band phones work on all three frequencies (900/1800/1900) and will operate through most of the world. Additionally, some GSM phones are SIM-locked and will only accept SIM cards from a single carrier. You'll need a SIM-unlocked phone to use a SIM card from a local carrier when you travel.

TIME DIFFERENCES

Italy is 1hr. ahead of Greenwich Mean Time (GMT) and observes Daylight Saving Time.

BY MAIL

SENDING MAIL HOME FROM ITALY

Airmail is the best way to send mail home from Italy. **Aerogrammes,** printed sheets that fold into envelopes and travel via airmail, are available at post offices. Write "airmail" or *"per posta aerea"* on the front. Most post offices charge exorbitant fees or simply refuse to send aerogrammes with enclosures. Surface mail is by far the cheapest and slowest way to send mail. It takes one to two months to cross the Atlantic and one to three to cross the Pacific—good for heavy items you won't need for a while, such as souvenirs. Delivery times and package shipping costs vary; inquire at the post office *(ufficio postale)*.

SENDING MAIL TO ITALY

To ensure timely delivery, mark envelopes "airmail," *"par avion,"* or *"per posta aerea."* In addition to the standard postage system whose rates are listed below, **Federal Express** (in Australia ☎+61 13 26 10, in Canada and in the US +1-800-463-3339, in Ireland +353 800 535 800, in New Zealand +64 800 733 339, the UK +44 8456 0708 09; www.fedex.com) handles express mail services to Italy. Sending a postcard within Italy costs €0.20 while sending letters (up to 20 kg) domestically requires €7.

There are several ways to arrange pick up of letters sent to you while you are abroad. Mail can be sent via **Fermo Posta** (General Delivery) to almost any city or town in Italy with a post office, and it is generally reliable, if occasionally untimely. Address **Fermo Posta** letters like so:

Dante ALIGHIERI
c/o Ufficio Postale Centrale
FERMO POSTA
48100 Florence
Italy

The mail will go to a special desk in the central post office, unless you specify a post office by street address or postal code. Note that the postal service may ignore this specification. It is usually safer and quicker, though more expensive, to send mail express or registered. Bring your passport (or other photo ID) for pickup; there may be a small fee. If the clerks insist that there is nothing for you, ask them to check under your first name as well. *Let's Go* lists post offices in the **Practical Information** section.

American Express's travel offices throughout the world offer a free **Client Letter Service** (mail held up to 30 days and forwarded upon request) for cardholders who contact them in advance. Some offices provide these services to non-cardholders (especially AmEx Travelers Cheque holders), but call ahead to make sure. *Let's Go* lists AmEx locations in **Practical Information;** for a complete list, call ☎+1-800-528-4800 or visit www.americanexpress.com/travel.

ACCOMMODATIONS

HOSTELS

Many hostels are laid out dorm-style, often with large single-sex rooms and bunk beds, although private rooms that sleep from two to four are becoming more common. They sometimes have kitchens and utensils for your use, breakfast and other meals, storage areas, laundry facilities, internet, transportation to airports, and bike or moped rentals. However, there can be drawbacks: some hostels impose a maximum stay, close during certain daytime "lockout" hours, have a curfew, don't accept reservations, or, less frequently, require that you do chores. In Italy, a dorm bed in a hostel will average around €15-25 and a private room around €25-30 per day.

 A HOSTELER'S BILL OF RIGHTS. There are certain standard features that we do not include in our hostel listings. Unless we state otherwise, you can expect that every hostel has no lockout, no curfew, free hot showers, some system of secure luggage storage, and no key deposit.

HOSTELLING INTERNATIONAL

Joining the youth hostel association in your own country (listed below) automatically grants you membership privileges in **Hostelling International (HI)**, a federation of national hostelling associations. Non-HI members may be allowed to stay in some hostels, but they will have to pay extra to do so. HI hostels are scattered throughout Italy and are typically less expensive than private hostels. HI's umbrella organization's website (www.hihostels.com), which lists the web addresses and phone numbers of all national associations, can be a great place to begin researching hostelling in a specific region. Other hostelling websites include www.hostels.com and www.hostelplanet.com.

Most HI hostels also honor **guest memberships**—you'll get a blank card with space for six validation stamps. Each night you'll pay a nonmember supplement and earn one guest stamp; six stamps make you a member. This system works well most of the time, but in some cases you may need to remind the hostel reception. A new membership benefit is the **FreeNites program,** which allows hostelers to gain points toward free rooms. Most student travel agencies (p. 23) sell HI cards, as do all of the national hostelling organizations listed below. All prices listed below are valid for a one-year membership.

Australian Youth Hostels Association (AYHA), 422 Kent St., Sydney, NSW 2000 (☎+61 2 9261 1111; www.yha.com.au). AUS$42, under 26 AUS$32.

Hostelling International-Canada (HI-C), 205 Catherine St., Ste. 400, Ottawa, ON K2P 1C3 (☎+1-613-237-7884; www.hihostels.ca). CDN$35, under 18 free.

Hostelling International Northern Ireland (HINI), 22-32 Donegall Rd., Belfast BT12 5JN (☎+44 28 9032 4733; www.hini.org.uk). UK£15, under 25 UK£10.

Youth Hostels Association (England and Wales), Trevelyan House, Dimple Rd., Matlock, Derbyshire DE4 3YH (☎+44 1629 592 600; www.yha.org.uk). UK£16, under 26 UK£10.

Youth Hostels Association of New Zealand Inc. (YHANZ), Level 1, 166 Moorhouse Ave., P.O. Box 436, Christchurch (☎+64 3 379 9970, in NZ 0800 278 299; www.yha.org.nz). NZ$40, under 18 free.

Hostelling International-USA, 8401 Colesville Rd., Ste. 600, Silver Spring, MD 20910 (☎+1-301-495-1240; www.hiayh.org). US$28, under 18 free.

OTHER TYPES OF ACCOMMODATIONS

HOTELS, GUESTHOUSES, AND PENSIONS

Hotel singles in Italy cost about US$40-80 (€25-50) per night, doubles US$ 60-140 (€40-90). In many lower budget establishments, you'll typically share a hall bathroom; a private bathroom will cost extra. Some hotels offer "full pension" (all meals) and "half pension" (no lunch). Smaller guesthouses and pensions are often cheaper than hotels. If you make **reservations** in writing, indicate your night of arrival and the number of nights you plan to stay. The hotel will send you a confirmation and may request payment for the first night.

BED AND BREAKFASTS (B&BS)

For a cozy alternative to impersonal hotel rooms, B&Bs (private homes with rooms available to travelers) range from acceptable to sublime. Rooms in B&Bs generally cost US$40-80 (€20-50) for a single and US$60-140 (€70-90) for a double in Italy. Many websites provide listings for B&Bs; check out **Bed & Breakfast Inns Online** (www.bbonline.com), **BedandBreakfast.com** (www.bedandbreakfast.com), or **BNBFinder.com** (www.bnbfinder.com).

AGRITURISMO

Frequently omitted by mainstream travel guides and ignored by local tourist offices, *agriturismo* is a pleasurable, leisurely, and inexpensive way to visit the Italian countryside. Local families open their homes to guests and provide reasonably-priced meals. The host family and guests gather around the table each night, sharing bottles of homemade wine, fresh vegetables from the garden, and stories that last far into the night. These houses, however, are usually only accessible by car—a tranquil remoteness that simply adds to their charm, provided that you can reach them. If you're looking to truly experience the laid-back Italian lifestyle, hearty cuisine, local wines, and sweeping countryside vistas, *agriturismo* is the best way to spend your time and money. To find *agriturismo* options in your region, consult local tourist offices or check out the **Associazione Nazionale per l'Agriturismo, l'Ambiente e il Territorio** (**National Association of Agrotourism, Environment and Territory;** www.agriturist.it).

ESSENTIALS

UNIVERSITY DORMS

Many **colleges** and **universities** open their residence halls to travelers when school is not in session; some do so even during term time. Getting a room may take a couple of phone calls and advanced planning, but rates tend to be low, and many offer free local calls and Internet access. For a list of student housing opportunities in Italian cities, write to The **Italian Ministry of Education,** Vle. Trastevere 76/A, 00153 Rome (☎+39 06 58 491; www.pubblica.istruzione.it), and ask for a *Guide for Foreign Students*.

HOME EXCHANGES AND HOSPITALITY CLUBS

Home exchange offers the traveler various types of homes (houses, apartments, condominiums, villas, even castles in some cases), plus the opportunity to live like a native and cut down on accommodation fees. For more information, contact **HomeExchange.com Inc.** (☎+1-310-798-3864 or toll-free 800-877-8723; www.homeexchange.com) or **Intervac International Home Exchange** (☎05 19 17 841; www.intervac.com).

Hospitality clubs link their members with individuals or families abroad who are willing to host travelers for free or for a small fee to promote cultural exchange and general good karma. In exchange, members usually must be willing to host travelers in their own homes. **The Hospitality Club** (www.hospitalityclub.org) is a good place to start. **Servas** (www.servas.org) is an established, more formal, peace-based organization, and requires a fee and an interview to join. An Internet search will find many similar organizations, some of which cater to special interests (e.g., women, GLBT travelers, or members of certain professions). As always, use common sense when planning to stay with or host someone you do not know.

LONG-TERM ACCOMMODATIONS

Travelers planning to stay in Italy for extended time periods may find it most cost-effective to locate an **apartment** for rent *(affittasi)*. A basic one-bedroom or studio apartment in Florence will range €500-2000 per month. Besides the rent itself, prospective tenants are frequently required to front a security deposit (usually one month's rent and the last month's rent).

A good place to check for apartments is Florence's **craigslist** (http://florence.it.craigslist.it/), a forum for renters and rentees where you can see others' listings or post your own housing needs. For regional listings, try http://affittistudenti.studenti.it and www.secondamano.it.

SPECIFIC CONCERNS

SUSTAINABLE TRAVEL

Italy's government focuses on cultural restoration while natural resources are overlooked and underappreciated. As the number of travelers on the road rises, the detrimental effect they can have on natural environments is an increasing concern. *Let's Go* promotes the philosophy of sustainable travel. Through a sensitivity to issues of ecology and sustainability, today's travelers can be a powerful force in preserving and restoring the places they visit.

Ecotourism, a rising trend in sustainable travel, focuses on the conservation of natural habitats—mainly, on how to use them to build up the economy without exploitation or overdevelopment. Travelers can make a difference by doing advance research, by supporting organizations and establishments that pay attention to their carbon "footprint," and by patronizing establishments that strive to be environmentally friendly. Recently, ecotourism has been getting more creative, interesting and diverse. Opportunities in Italy can be found at **www.ecoturismo-italia.it,** an Italian nonprofit that works in conjunction with other international organizations. For information on environmental conservation, see the resources below or the **Beyond Tourism** (p. 67) section of this book.

ECOTOURISM RESOURCES. For more information on environmentally responsible tourism, contact one of the organizations below:

Conservation International, 2011 Crystal Dr., Ste. 500, Arlington, VA 22202, USA (☎+1-800-429-5660 or 703-341-2400; www.conservation.org).

Green Globe 21, Green Globe vof, Verbenalaan 1, 2111 ZL Aerdenhout, the Netherlands (☎+31 23 544 0306; www.greenglobe.com).

International Ecotourism Society, 1301 Clifton St. NW, Ste. 200, Washington, DC 20009, USA (☎+1-202-506-5033; www.ecotourism.org).

United Nations Environment Program (UNEP; www.unep.org).

WOMEN TRAVELERS

Women exploring on their own inevitably face some additional safety concerns. Single women can consider staying in hostels that offer single rooms that lock from the inside or in religious organizations with single-sex rooms. It's a good idea to stick to centrally located accommodations and to avoid solitary late-night treks or metro rides. Always carry extra cash for a phone call, bus, or taxi. **Hitchhiking is never safe** for lone women or even for two women traveling together. Look as if you know where you're going and approach older women or couples for directions if you're lost or feeling uncomfortable in your surroundings. Generally, the less you look like a tourist, the better off you'll be. Dress conservatively, especially when visiting Florentine churches and religious sites. Wearing a conspicuous **wedding band** sometimes helps to prevent unwanted advances.

Your best answer to verbal harassment is no answer at all; feigning deafness, sitting motionless, and staring straight ahead at nothing in particular will usually do the trick. The extremely persistent can sometimes be dissuaded by a firm, loud, and very public *"Vai via"* or *"Vattene"* ("Go Away!"). Don't hesitate to seek out a *poliziotto* (police officer) or a passerby if you are being harassed. Memorize the emergency numbers in places you visit, and consider carrying a whistle on your keychain. A self-defense course will both prepare you for a potential attack and raise your level of awareness of your surroundings (see **Personal Safety**, p. 18). Also, it might be a good idea to talk with your doctor about the health concerns that women face when traveling (p. 22).

GLBT TRAVELERS

It is difficult to characterize the Italian attitude toward gay, lesbian, bisexual, and transgender (GLBT) travelers. Homophobia is still in issue in some regions, but Florence has easily accessible gay scenes. Away from the larger cities, however, gay social life may be difficult to find. The online newspaper **365gay.com** has a travel section. **Babilonia** and **Guida Gay Italia** can be found at newsstands, and **Pride** and **GayClubbing** (both free) can be found at most gay venues. Florence also offers a variety of gay *discoteche* (nightclubs) and bars. Listed below are contact organizations, mail-order catalogs, and publishers that offer materials addressing some specific concerns. **Out and About** (www.planetout.com) offers a website and a newsletter addressing gay travel concerns.

Arcigay, V. Don Minzoni 18, 40121 Bologna (☎051 64 93 055; www.arcigay.it). Provides resources for homosexuals and helps combat homophobia throughout the peninsula. Holds dances and other special events. Website contains addresses and phone numbers of city centers.

Gay.It, V. Ravizza 22/E, 56121 Pisa (www.gay.it). Provides info on gay life in Italy. Associated website in English (www.gayfriendlyitaly.com) gives regional info on nightlife, homophobia, gay events, and more.

Giovanni's Room, 345 S. 12th St., Philadelphia, PA 19107, USA (☎+1-215-923-2960; www.giovannisroom.com). An international lesbian and gay bookstore with mail-order service (carries many of the publications listed below).

International Lesbian and Gay Association (ILGA), 17 Rue de la Charité, 1210 Brussels, Belgium (☎+32 2 502 2471; www.ilga.org). Provides political information, such as homosexuality laws of individual countries.

TRAVELERS WITH DISABILITIES

Travelers with disabilities should inform airlines and hotels of their disabilities when making reservations, as some time may be needed to prepare special accommodations. Call ahead to restaurants, museums, and other facilities to find out if they're wheelchair accessible. Guide-dog owners should inquire as to the quarantine policies of each destination country.

Rail is probably the most convenient form of transport for disabled travelers in Europe: many stations have ramps, and some trains have wheelchair lifts, special seating areas, and specially equipped toilets. All Eurostar, some InterCity (IC), and some EuroCity (EC) trains are **wheelchair-accessible,** and CityNightLine trains and Conrail trains feature special compartments. For those who wish to rent cars, some major **car-rental** agencies (e.g., Hertz) offer hand-controlled vehicles. Look for pamphlets on accessibility from local tourist offices; a list of publications can be found at **www.coinsociale.it.**

ESSENTIALS

Accessible Italy, Via C. Manetti 34, 47891 Dogana, Repubblica di San Marino (☎+39 378 05 49 94 11 11; www.accessibleitaly.com). Provides tours to Italy for travelers with disabilities. Proceeds go toward improving handicap-access to attractions in Italy. Also organizes handicap-accessible weddings in Italy.

Accessible Journeys, 35 W. Sellers Ave., Ridley Park, PA 19078, USA (☎+1-800-846-4537; www.disabilitytravel.com). Designs tours for wheelchair users and slow walkers. The site has tips and forums for all travelers.

TMobility International USA (MIUSA), 132 E. Broadway, Ste. 343, Eugene, OR 97401, USA (☎+1-541-343-1284; www.miusa.org). Provides a variety of books and other publications containing information for travelers with disabilities.

Society for Accessible Travel and Hospitality (SATH), 347 5th Ave., Ste. 605, New York, NY 10016, USA (☎+1-212-447-7284; www.sath.org). An advocacy group that publishes free online travel info. Annual membership US$49, students and seniors US$29.

MINORITY TRAVELERS

Like much of Western Europe, Italy has experienced a wave of immigration from Africa, Eastern Europe, and South America in recent years that has spurred some racial tension, especially over competition in the local economy. Particularly in southern Italy, travelers belonging to racial minorities or members of non-Christian religions may feel unwelcome or experience some hostility. Tension has always existed in Italy regarding gypsies from Romania and other parts of Eastern Europe. In terms of safety, there is no easy answer. Men and women should always travel in groups and avoid unsafe parts of town. The best answer to verbal harassment is often not to acknowledge it. A number of advocacy groups for immigrant rights have sprouted up throughout Italy, including **Associazione Almaterra** (☎+39 01 12 46 70 02; www.arpnet.it) and **NOSOTRAS** (☎+39 05 52 77 63 26; www.nosotras.it). The following organizations work to combat discrimination in Italy and can give advice and help in the event of an encounter with racism.

Associazione Arci, V. dei Monti di Pietralata 16, 00157 Rome (☎06 41 50 95 00; www.attivarci.it). Extensive organization that promotes citizen rights, democracy, and inclusivity. Fights to end discrimination and racism on the peninsula.

Casa dei Diritti Sociali FOCUS, V. dei Mille 6, 00185 Rome (☎06 44 64 61 13; www.dirittisociali.org). Volunteer organization promoting solidarity with and among immigrant populations and multiculturalism through youth outreach and political advocacy.

Ucodep, V. Madonna del Prato 42, 52100 Arezzo (☎05 75 40 17 80; www.ucodep.org) Works to advance human rights, social justice, nonviolence, and intercultural exchange.

DIETARY CONCERNS

With all of Italy's delicious carnivorous offerings, vegetarians may feel left out. While there are not many strictly vegetarian restaurants in Italy, it is not difficult to find vegetarian meals. To avoid confusion in restaurants, make sure you tell your waiter *"Non mangio carne"* ("I don't eat meat") or say that you would like your pizza or pasta sauce *"senza carne, per favore"* ("without meat, please"). Before you head to Italy, check out the **Italian Vegetarian Association (AVI),** V. XXV Aprile 41, 20026 Novate Milanese, Milano (www.vegetariani.it), which also offers *Good Vegetarian Food* (Italian Vegetarian Association, 2004; €12), a guide to vegetarian tourism in Italy.

The travel section of **The Vegetarian Resource Group's** website, at www.vrg. org/travel, has a comprehensive list of organizations and websites that are geared toward helping vegetarians and vegans traveling abroad. Vegetarians will also find numerous resources on the web; try www.vegdining.com, www.happycow.net, and www.vegetariansabroad.com.

Lactose intolerance also does not have to be an obstacle to eating well in Italy. Though it may seem like everybody but you is devouring pizza and gelato, there are ways for even the lactose intolerant to indulge in local cuisine. In restaurants ask for items without *latte* (milk), *formaggio* (cheese), *burro* (butter), or *crema* (cream); or order the cheeseless delicacy, *pizza marinara*.

Travelers who keep **kosher** should contact synagogues in larger cities for info on kosher restaurants. Your own synagogue or college Hillel should have access to lists of Jewish institutions across the nation. Check out **www.shamash.org/kosher/** for an extensive database of kosher establishments in Italy. A good resource is the *Jewish Travel Guide*, edited by Michael Zaidner (Vallentine Mitchell; US$18). Travelers looking for halal restaurants may find www.zabihah.com a useful resource.

LET'S GO ONLINE. Plan your next trip on our newly redesigned website, **www.letsgo.com.** It features the latest travel info on your favorite destinations as well as tons of interactive features: make your own itinerary, read blogs from our trusty Researchers, browse our photo library, watch exclusive videos, check out our newsletter, find travel deals, and buy new guides. We're always updating and adding new features, so check back often!

ESSENTIALS

LIFE AND TIMES

As one of the world's most impressive artistic capitals, Florence offers a lifestyle and culture infused with the Renaissance heritage of some of the most notable writers, sculptors, and painters across the globe. In 1252, it was the first city to mint its own gold coin called the florin, and in 1430, to erect a nude statue in a public place. It is the birthplace of the 15th century Renaissance and boasts three decades of cultural and intellectual flourishing during the reign of Medici dynasty, a family of generous patrons who emptied their piggy banks to fund the arts. Fortunately, much of the art and historic architecture has been preserved to this day and can be viewed in original form. (The most notable exception is Michelangelo's *David* in P. della Signoria, which is actually a fake.) With a unique blend of history and modernity, Florence's medieval streets showcase glitzy glamour of Gucci as well as family-run businesses and artisan shops with homemade jewelry and one-of-a-kind foodstuffs. Ultimately, students of art history and visitors with artistic leanings will feel right at home wandering the halls of the Uffizi or taking a break in the shadow of the Duomo. The less artistically-inclined will be just as entertained—but it might be a good idea to brush up on your Ninja Turtle knowledge before you go.

HISTORY

HUMBLE BEGINNINGS

Florence, the consummately civilized city, owes its beginnings to the **Etruscans,** who established a settlement at **Fiesole.** The spot was very near the modern city, known as Faesulae to their Roman successors. Fiesole, a town famed for its priests and school of augury—i.e., interpreting the gods' will based on birds' flight patterns; and you thought your job as weird—was part of a larger Etruscan civilization that by the sixth century BC spanned much of central Italy, including a little town called Rome. As that city came into its own right, the area of Fiesole fell to them, and by 265 BC all of Etruria was ruled from the Seven Hills. It was several centuries until the town would amount to much. Hey, Rome wasn't built in a day either.

AVE CAESAR

In the year of his consulship, **Julius Caesar** established new cities for veterans of his campaigns, doling out farmsteads across the Republic's territory. One of these new colonies was **Florentia,** "the flourishing one," whose construction began in 30 BC near old Fiesole and occupied the strategic crossing of the Arno River with many other streams. Many of Florence's great avenues trace back to the original plan, including **Via del Corso, Via degli Strozzi, Via Roma,** and **Via Calimala.** The forum of the Roman Republic now commemorates the Italian Republic as **Piazza della Repubblica.** The old walls followed **Via del Proconsolo, Via de'**

Cerretani, and Via de' Tornabuoni and, to the south, a rough line from Piazza Santa Trinità to the Palazzo Vecchio. The next era of construction was in the AD second century under Hadrian, who put his name to the baths and amphitheater.

TUSCAN TURNABOUT

When Rome relapsed, Florence fluctuated. Impoverished by the general economic and social collapse, the city played different roles under different conquerors. Under Diocletian in the late fourth and early fifth centuries, Florence became a regional capital, and Christianity took firm hold in Florence. The barbarian invasions placed the city under Lombard control in the fifth century, with brief interludes of Byzantine intervention. Florence assumed a place of prominence in the new order, entering the Duchy of Tuscia, including Tuscany, Umbria, and Corsica, created in 800 by the Holy Roman Emperor, Charlemagne. Over the next centuries, the city became a seat of power, from which the warlike and proud Countess Matilda Canossa challenged the Emperor, Henry IV, himself. You go, girl.

IMPERIAL IMPASSE

For repeatedly showing up the Emperor in most unladylike fashion, the duchy was dismantled after Matilda's death. For the following decades, northern Italy and Tuscany were a motley collection of warring city-states. Florence was ruled by its own city council, or *commune*, composed of aristocrats and powerful merchants who shared out the *signoria*, top government posts. The guilds, or *arti*, also exercised power. The flourishing city conquered nearby Fiesole in 1123 and began to grow thick with churches and towers built by the families of the new order. New city walls were built 50 years later. But Florence could not wall itself off from the quagmire of imperial politics; the ruling families began to organize into pro-imperial Ghibellines, mostly noble families tied to the feudal order, and pro-papal Guelphs, merchants interested in local independence. The political became violent with the murder of Buondelmonte dei Buondelmonti, a Guelph, on the Ponte Vecchio in 1216. This struggle dominated Florence for centuries, including famous Florentines such as Dante Alighieri (see Literature, p. 56), best-known for his *Divina Commedia* but also author of *De Monarchia*, a tract defending the universal authority of the Empire.

NATURAL DISASTERS

Florence's problems went from manmade to natural when a devastating flood washed through the city in 1333, killing many and washing away the Ponte Vecchio. The upside of the deluge was a construction craze that completed the Palazzo Vecchio (see Sights, p. 113) and other monuments. There was no silver lining, however, to the Black Death, which arrived at the early date of 1348 due to Florence's heavy maritime trade and contact with sailors returning from the East. The disease halved Florence's population, and war resumed at about the same time. Over the next decades, the city overcame its problems to conquer San Gimignano, Volterra, Pistoia, Prato, and Pisa. One of the city's more unusual leaders was the Englishman Sir John Hawkwood, a mercenary leader who arrived in the area in 1375. Giovanni Acuto, as he became known, first extorted the city, which paid him not to attack. They faced their own problems, including a proletarian revolt of the *ciompi* (wool carders) in 1378. Later, however, he became commander-in-chief of the city's armies, saving Florence from Milanese conquest in the 1390s.

CLUB MEDICI

By the 15th century, the city's government had largely fallen into the hands of a single family, the **Albizi**—but the increasing wealth of the banker **Giovanni di Bicci de' Medici** made him a man to be reckoned with. Florence was the seat of his international financial empire, and his son, **Cosimo**, was so feared by the Albizi that they exiled him in 1433. In response, Cosimo, who had managed the finances of the Papacy and become the wealthiest man of the age, single-handedly caused the first capital flight in history, pulling out nearly all the banking interests and forcing the Albizi to surrender. During his long reign, he allied with the Sforzas of Milan, paying them handsomely for use of their mercenary soldiers. The Medicis' power was so great that **Pope Pius II** called Cosimo "master of all Italy," and until his death in 1464 Florence enjoyed a rare peace, blossoming into a city of 70,000 people. A patron of the arts and champion of the Renaissance, he bankrolled the **Duomo** (p. 113) and such artists as **Brunelleschi, Donatello,** and **Fra Angelico.** He also drew the church council that attempted to reunite the Catholic and Orthodox churches in Florence, and heavily supported the University of Florence, which became a new center of humanist thought. His library, later called the **Laurentian Library** (see **Sights,** p. 127), included manuscripts ferreted out from the West and East, was opened to the public, and employed many of the best-regarded scholars of Italy. The "Father of the Fatherland," as he was posthumously titled, died at peace—but the future of Florence would be troubled.

ALL IN THE FAMILY

Cosimo's son Piero occupied himself mostly with political machinations. His successor in 1469, his 20-year-old son **Lorenzo,** also kept up Florence's pretenses of republican government, but made very clear where the power was. Soon enough he would face challengers to that power—the **Pazzi** family, Pope-backed rivals of the Medici. In 1478, they mounted a coup, slaying Lorenzo's brother Giuliano during Mass but missing Lorenzo, who rallied his troops and destroyed the Pazzi. Enraged, **Pope Sixtus IV** excommunicated Lorenzo and organized an alliance of Naples and the Papal States against Florence. Lorenzo managed to defuse the

LOCAL LEGEND

MEDICI DRUG LORDS

Ever wonder about the polka-dotted Medici crest plastered on nearly every building in Florence? Although scholars offer various explanations for the six buttons adorning the city's most famous dynastic emblem, some speculate that the dots are actually pills, alluding to some pharmaceutical family lore. Like most stories about pill-pushing, this one puts the illustrious Medici family in a sketchy breach of medical ethics.

Back in the day before the MCATs or modern skepticism, an enterprising Medici ancestor was in the business of selling pills he promised could cure any ailment. A farmer who lost his donkey came to this crafty "doctor" and asked him for help. The doctor sold him six pills and told the farmer to take them while wandering around looking in places a donkey might be tempted to go. After three days of popping pills and roaming the back roads of Tuscany screaming his donkey's name, this intelligent fellow finally stumbled upon his pet eating some delicious thistle. The farmer widely proclaimed this discovery a miracle, and the story of the six "magical" pills catapulted the doctor to great fame and fortune. The doctor capitalized on his placebo success and founded the Medici family, whose name means "doctors" in Italian.

At the time of printing, none of the famous Medicis have a medical degree, nor has anyone been convicted of prescription fraud.

situation, however, and reformed the government to concentrate power for himself. Lorenzo's court included luminaries such as **Leonardo da Vinci** and **Botticelli.** Under this behind-the-scenes ruler, the Renaissance—the explosion in learning and cultural achievement that would shift the whole of European culture—began in Florence. To his credit, Lorenzo set a precedent of refusing royal or noble title, though his ego did force him to take the title "the Magnificent." Whether credit is assigned to the Medicis' patronage, the culture of the Italian city-state, or the great men of that flourishing, the city of Florence would make a permanent place for itself. Unfortunately, the Medici began to face competitors, and their banking branches in London, Bruges, and Lyon collapsed as Lorenzo entertained a costly and lavish court. The next family head, **Piero the Unfortunate,** lived up to his title rather than the illustrious achievements of his predecessors. Unable to manage the delicate balance of Italian politics, Piero lost out as Charles VIII of France gained the upper hand against Florence, marching into the city at the head of an army and sacking the Medici palace.

BAPTISM BY FIRE

With the Medicis dispersed, the Republic was reactivated. The leadership gap was instead filled by **Girolamo Savonarola,** a populist priest with a radical, messianic agenda. The Ferrara-born preacher had arrived in the city in 1481, hectoring sinners at the **Chiesa di San Marco** (see p. 146). The Florentine masses, seeking respite from the turmoil and tumult of the past years, found solace in his promise of a pure paradise on earth. In 1494, Savonarola took over the city government, establishing a theocratic Republic that banned drinking, prostitution, gambling, ostentatious clothes, and any other fun pastimes. Great **bonfires of the vanities** were set up to destroy books and possessions of the old era, and child police marched around the city ratting on adults who were not hip to the times. Many priceless artifacts were destroyed by this proto-Puritan and his followers; rumor has it that Botticelli, swept up in the fervor, burned several of his own paintings. As Savonarola's anger crossed over into bans on commerce and trade—and when his predictions for the end of the world didn't pan out—unrest began to grow. The Pope demanded that Savonarola come to Rome, and the Franciscans, rivals of the dictator's Dominican order, began to foster street violence. The council of the city finally stood up to Savonarola, and after a 1498 trial, he was burned at the stake as a heretic in the **Piazza della Signoria** (p. 121).

RETURN OF THE MEDICI

After that experiment, Florence was receptive to the return of secular rule under **Giovanni de' Medici,** who returned in 1512, backed by a Spanish army. The Medici family returned to their exalted position in the city's political and social life, and their status only improved when the same Giovanni was elected **Pope Leo X** one year later; his apartments in the **Palazzo Vecchio** (p. 143) remain to this day. Over the past years, however, Florence had lost its position as economic center. Although the Medici's position was reinforced by Giovanni's elevation to the papacy, the sack of Rome by the mutinous Imperial army in 1527 prompted a rebellion in Florence in the last attempt to reinstate the old republic. After an eleven-month siege in 1530, nevertheless, the combined armies of the Emperor and the Pope forced the Medicis back onto the throne, creating the blatant hereditary title of Duke. The Medicis were now firm agents of Imperial interests in Italy, but family strife continued to wreak violence. After a number of family feuds, the long-lived **Cosimo il Giovane** managed to rule

Florence until 1574, becoming Grand Duke of Tuscany. In this period the city and its provinces flourished, the city government returned to solvency after decades of disarray, and the Medici resumed their traditional role as patrons of the arts and sciences, building the **Uffizi** (p. 135).

A HUNDRED YEARS OF QUIETUDE

Over the next century, other regional powers eclipsed the grand city as an economic and political center, and other capitals of Europe took over its role as a cradle of art, science, and culture. The successors of Cosimo il Giovane, Francesco and Ferdinando, were capable rulers, and **Cosimo II** invited **Galileo Galilei,** a native of the Duchy of Tuscany, to Florence after his troubles with the Church began. Aside from that, the following reigns spanned an era known as Florence's "forgotten centuries." Few discoveries or creations of note came from Florence, and a three-year **plague** beginning in 1630 put a vicious halt to the life of the city. Terrible plague was followed by harsh rule in the form of **Cosimo III,** who persecuted the Jews and was virtually an arm of the Inquisition. His successor was the alcoholic, **Gian Gastone,** who effectively gave up Florence's independence, only managing to preserve the city as a state separate from the rule of the Emperors. As he lay sick, the European powers assigned the duchy to **Francis,** duke of Lorraine and husband of the Empress, **Maria Theresa** of Austria. The great Medici collection of art and artifacts passed to Gian Gastone's sister, Anna Maria, who in her death in 1743 mandated that the objects never leave Florence.

AUSTRIAN FLORENCE

The **Habsburg** monarchs ruled the city from afar, with a succession of regents sitting in the Grand Duchy. Under their rule, the Inquisition was curbed and the duchy's government moved out of the medieval past and into the beginnings of the **Enlightenment,** with a reliable administration and taxation. Nevertheless, Florence was definitely a colony of **Vienna,** and the city was not at ease until the succession of a resident Grand Duke, **Pietro Leopoldo.** Brother to the Austrian Emperor, Josef II, Pietro abolished the cruel punishments and Inquisition, introduced names for the winding streets of the city, and built schools that admitted the Tuscan peasantry for the first time. However, he was never popular with the residents, who resented the cold, foreign meddler as much as the absentee regents of old. Upon the death of his brother, Pietro ascended to the throne of the Habsburgs, leaving his son, **Ferdinando,** in charge of Tuscany just in time for Napoleon's ruthless invasion.

BUONGIORNO, BONAPARTE

After scattering the Habsburg forces, French forces simply occupied Tuscany for five years, while **Napoleon Bonaparte** reorganized the entire region into the new **Kingdom of Etruria,** with its capital in Florence. The new crown was gifted to **Louis** of the House of Bourbon as recompense for the Bourbon's loss of the Duchy of Parma. King Louis took over in 1801, but died a mere two years later. His successor, **Louis II,** was four years old and thus not particularly remarkable as a leader. Napoleon changed his mind about the whole enterprise in 1807, abolishing the kingdom and splitting Tuscany into three departments of France.

RESTORATION

Like so many places in Europe, the end of Napoleonic rule meant an uneasy return of the previous tenant, meaning Ferdinando was back. Unlike many monarchs, however, his rule was not tumultuous, and for the 10 years before his death in 1824, reforms on the city and duchy allowed for peace between the sovereign and subjects. His son ruled similarly, avoiding the temptation to turn the clock back and accepting the tide of Italian nationalism which was beginning to surge. **Leopoldo II** allowed a great measure of freedom in speech and debate, and intellectuals from across Italy, including the writers **Ugo Foscolo**, **Alessandro Manzoni** and **Giacomo Leopardi,** descended on the city. Uprisings against the Austrian rulers in Milan were joined by support sent by the Grand Duke of Tuscany, who decided that revolution was more dangerous than the wrath of his relatives. In 1848, Florence, like all the great cities of Europe, saw discontent on a level not seen since the French Revolution; a **republic** was proclaimed by radical liberals, and Leopold II fled the city. As soon as Austria began to menace the city, however, the legislature begged Leopold II to return. Nevertheless, nation was proving stronger than city, and in 1859 the Grand Duke was forced out, the last to rule over the city.

UNIFICATION

A year later, the provisional government declared the union of the Grand Duchy to the Kingdom of Piedmont, which by 1861 had gobbled up nearly all of Italy, proclaiming itself the new, unified **Kingdom of Italy.** The new monarch, **Vittorio Emanuele,** and his government began casting around for a national capital; the natural choice of Rome was still a stubborn papal holdout, so in 1865 they chose Florence. This city of 115,000 people was bolstered overnight by an army of 30,000 bureaucrats and officials, transforming the city. In the five short years that Florence served as the Italian capital, it took its present form. The broad *viali* that ring the city were paved, large new *piazze* were built, and the entire north and northwestern sections of the city were planned and built. This wave of construction did not stop when the capital moved, and in 1888 **electricity** came to the city. (The microwave, however, would heed another century.) For several decades, many ancient facades, medieval walls, and palaces were torn in the modernizing frenzy, with most of the city's architectural losses dating to this era.

FLORENCE AT WAR

At the beginning of **World War I,** Florence was little affected. By 1917, however, rationing and the loss of 11,000 men from the Florentine region had ravaged the city. After the war, reconstruction efforts centered on the new factories including the Pignone smelters in the Rifredi area, northwest of the city's center. With the rise of industry in Florence came an increased working class, which lay the foundations for Florence as a center of radical politics, initially dominated by the **communists.** In 1920, the **fascists** had come to Florence, and like the ex-socialist **Benito Mussolini,** the city's discontented classes moved to fascism en masse. On the 28th of October, 1922, as Mussolini stormed Rome, fascist forces in Florence seized the city's telecommunications, railway station, and municipal buildings. Florentine fascism was so energetic that Mussolini had to rein in the local **Blackshirts,** but in gratitude for their loyalty he built the city the new **stadium** (p. 161) at **Campo di Marte** and the new train station at **Santa Maria Novella** (p. 124). These baubles were not worth the conflict to come, which brought intense Allied bombing. Much of Florence's priceless art was transported out of the city, and most of it was saved one way or another. But the following surrender of Italy in 1943 did not bring relief, as the Germans quickly occupied the north, including Florence. The Allies would not make it to the city until 1944.

MODERNITÁ

Work on the ruined parts of Florence began quickly, with the **Ponte alla Vittoria**, **Ponte Santa Trinità**, and others reconstructed. The city would take on new leadership under the flamboyant, deeply religious mayor **Giorgio La Pira**, who used the power of the city government to house the poor and distribute largesse, positioning him as the hero of the city's working classes. The city followed most of northern Italy in the postwar economic boom, but disaster struck in 1966, with a massive flood that saw the **Arno** turn into a raging monster wiping out millions of books and works of art. Restorative work is still going on to this day. Today, Florence has become a center of international tourism, one of the pre-eminent cities of Italy, and notorious for the survival of Communist politics in "Red Tuscany." Remarkably free from Italy's old friends, the Mafia and its siblings, the largest project of modern times has been the decades-old plan to build a new city center in the Castello district. For the moment, however, Florence's economy and society are dominated by the tourists and students that drive the city centre, with most of the city's other industries clustered along the Prato.

LIFE AND TIMES

ART AND ARCHITECTURE

Once you've huffed and puffed up the 463 steps to the top of Florence's **Santa Maria del Fiore** (p. 113) and you peer out into a terra-cotta *paradiso*, you realize this city is one, big artistic masterpiece—or rather, *capolavoro*. From Giotto's **belltower** (p. 119) to Michelangelo's strapping **David** (p. 145), Florence is bursting with an exceptional artistic heritage. It was, after all, the birthplace of all birthplaces, the starting point of the Renaissance in the 13th century.

LET'S GET IT STARTED

ETRUSCANS. Before the Romans ruled the roost, the **Etruscans** were the most powerful civilization in Italy. Although their prehistoric origins are mysterious, the Etruscans left behind a fascinating artistic heritage. Etruscan art—essentially the first art in Italy—exhibits a unique blend of Greek, Egyptian, oriental, and native elements. Archaeological finds indicate that the Etruscans were skilled in architecture, sculpture, painting, pottery, jewelry-making, and metal-working. Tombs and temples comprise the majority of Etruscan finds to date—not surprising, as the civilization believed strongly in an afterlife. Fortunately, present-day Florence holds one of the world's most impressive collections of Etruscan art at the

700-400 BC Etruscan civilization scatters its tombs and temples throughout Italy.

19 BC Roman poet Virgil finishes his *Aeneid*.

AD 380 Christianity becomes the official religion of the Roman Empire.

Museo Archeologico Nazionale di Firenze (p. 146), located in the Palazzo della Crocetta. Among the Etruscan treasures housed in the museum are the bronze Chimera of Arezzo, the Sarcophagus of Laerthia Seianti, and the Sarcophagus of the Amazons, as well as many other pieces dating from as far back as the fifth century BC.

BYZANTINE BIBLE STUDY

1059-1128 AD St. Miniato puts his own head on his shoulders. Ew.

Reputed as the last great Byzantine artist, Cimabue (before 1251-1302) is usually affiliated with the schism between old and new artistic traditions in western Europe. With Cimabue, the "new" tradition was ushered in. Among Cimabue's major works are the Santa Trinità Madonna, now on display at Florence's the Uffizi (p. 135) and the Church of Santa Croce (p. 129). Among his pupils was the Sienese painter Duccio. Their relationship was a complicated one, and the extent to which Duccio imitated Cimabue's work is still a hot topic of debate. Byzantine art was primarily concerned with translating Biblical text into visual media according to strict conventions of artistic and architectural form. Eventually, the Byzantine tradition would fuse with Roman, Carolingian, Ottonian, and other influences—and thus, the Romanesque style was born.

THE MIDDLE AGES

1250-1300 The dolce stil nuovo has its literary heyday.

HOPELESS ROMANESQUE

1266-73 Thomas Aquinas writes the Summa Theologica.

1278-1442 Santa Maria Novella and Santa Croce are constructed... but, would endure architectural Botox over the years.

1314 Dante's Inferno is published. Burn, baby, burn.

Reputedly the first Romanesque structure in all of Tuscany, the Basilica di San Miniato al Monte was completed between 1059 and 1128. From the geometric marble facade to the astounding mosaic of Christ between the Virgin and St. Minias on the interior, this building is quite an artistic feat. Legend has it that Saint Miniato was an Armenian prince who trekked to Florence to evangelize; he was ultimately decapitated by the tyrannical emperor Decius. The situation truly came to a head when, after being executed, Miniato allegedly picked up his—uh, noggin—placed it back on his body, and traipsed across the Arno to the cave at Monte alla Croce where he had lived as a hermit, now the location of the Romanesque church that bears his name.

GOTHIC GLAMOUR

1327 Petrarch meets Laura, and his heart goes "pidder padder."

1334 Giotto finishes his freestanding campanile at Santa Maria del Fiore.

In the late 13th century, the French introduced the Italians to a new trend—going Goth. The Gothic architectural style celebrated the vast, lit spaces created by the new technology of vaulted ceilings and enormous, vibrant rose windows. Florence contains some remarkable examples of Gothic architecture, both sacred and secular. The Ponte Vecchio (p. 121)—or "Old Bridge"—crosses the Arno at its narrowest point. During World War II, all of the other bridges in Florence were demolished but, fortunately, Hitler spared this landmark.

Today, this piece of Gothic architecture is lined with the most extravagant jewelry shops you could ever imagine. The Dominican **Santa Maria Novella** (p. 124) and Franciscan **Santa Croce** (p. 129) are probably the most prominent examples of sacred Gothic architecture in Florence. Interestingly, both of the structures have undergone facelifts over the years. Although the majority of Santa Maria Novella was executed in the Gothic style between about 1278 and 1350, the facade of the building is in the Renaissance style, added by **Leon Battista Alberti** in 1470. Santa Croce was built between 1294 and 1442, but its Gothic revival facade and *campanile* were not added until the 19th century.

The new Florentine Gothicism inevitably introduced some major players to the Italian art scene. **Gentile da Fabriano** (c. 1370-1427) was perhaps the foremost Italian painter of the International Gothic movement. In 1423, he completed the masterful *Adoration of the Magi* to adorn the Church of **Santa Trinità** (p. 125). Today, the painting is housed in the Uffizi (p. 135). **Giotto di Bondon,** or simply Giotto (c. 1267-1337), straddled artistic epochs, painting at the tail end of the Gothic movement and helping to usher in the Renaissance. Although very little of Giotto's life is known, he was reputedly Cimabue's pupil. One work of art that sure can be ascribed to Giotto is the free-standing belltower, or *campanile*, of **Santa Maria del Fiore** (p. 119), a prime piece of Florentine Gothic architecture. Despite these and a few others, Gothic architecture never quite reached its heyday in Italy the way it did in other European countries. But not to worry—Italy would more than compensate with its next few generations of artistic *virtuosi* during the Renaissance.

WE REPRESENT THE FLORENTINE GUILDS

Throughout the Middle Ages, much of the Florentine art scene was dominated by the guild system—the core of economic activity in medieval Florence. Guilds or *arti* were organized into a hierarchical scheme, with seven major guilds *(arti maggiori)*, five middle guilds *(arti mediane)*, and seven minor guilds *(arti minori)*. Sculptors were included in one of the minor guilds, **Maestri di Pietra e Legname** (the Masters of Stone and Wood). Painters, on the other hand, were included in one of the major guilds, **l'Arte dei Medici e Speziali** (the Guild of Doctors and Druggists). Classifying painters with doctors and pharmacists may initially seem odd—but remember that painters actually had to purchase their pigments from apothecaries. In 1349, a group of Florentine painters established **Compagnia di San Lucca** (Confraternity of Saint Luke), an organization separate from the guild system and local politics. The church **Orsanmichele** (p. 121) still stands as a testament to the significance of guilds in medieval times. Strangely enough, the building was originally a grain store, but it was fully converted into a church by 1404. In the late 14th century, all of the major Florentine guilds were asked to provide

c. 1430-40 Donatello creates the *David,* a free-standing, hat-wearing nudie.

1420-36 Brunelleschi uses his math skills to create Florence's Duomo.

c. 1420-55 Fra Angelico endorses humanism. What a rebel.

1431-38 Lucca della Robbia creates the *cantorie.*

statues of their patron saints to adorn the front of the church. Today, some of the original statues are located in the museum within the church. In the15th century, the Medici family rose to power, and transformed Florence into a center of humanist learning and artistic flourishing.

LIFE AND TIMES

1345 The Ponte Vecchio is completed. Today you can leave a lock with your lover.

1350-53 Boccaccio writes the *Decameron*, which would influence Chaucer's *Canterbury Tales*.

1401 Ghiberti's bronze doors are victorious.

1404 Orsanmichele ditches the silo for the sacristy.

ONCE MORE, WITH FEELING

EARLY RENAISSANCE

Housed at the **Bargello** (p. 142), **Donatello's** (c. 1386-1466) bronze **David** sports only a hat, boots, and sword. In fact, this free-standing nude truly pushed artistic boundaries and revolutionized the medium of sculpture. Donatello continued to break from the earlier, restrained artistic tradition with his wooden **Mary Magdalene**, representing a pathetic, emaciated and repentant figure. Today, the sculpture can be seen in the **Museo dell'Opera del Duomo** (p. 120), which also contains the famous *cantorie* (singing galleries) crafted by **Luca della Robbia** (c. 1400-82). He also produced countless works in terra cotta with a glazy finish, including the circular depictions of Apostles in the **Pazzi Chapel**. His works are also featured in the Chapel of the Crucifix in the **Basilica of San Miniato al Monte** (p. 133).

Towering above many other Renaissance architects was **Filippo Brunelleschi** (1377-1446). Math nerds, take heed—the aesthetic wonders of Florence are not merely for the humanities-minded. In fact, Renaissance architecture was founded upon Brunelleschi's mathematical studies of Roman building techniques. His most famous work is the dome over **Santa Maria del Fiore** (p. 113), boasting a diameter of over 40m. The cloister attached to Santa Croce, the **Pazzi Chapel**, is another geometric masterpiece by Brunelleschi. His contemporary, **Lorenzo Ghiberti** (c. 1381-1455), created the impressive bronze doors of the cathedral, described by Michelangelo as "the Gates of Paradise." In the 1401 contest to determine whose doors were most worthy of the baptistery, Ghiberti's design even defeated that of Brunelleschi. Ooh, burn. Another prominent architect of the period was **Leon Battista Alberti** (1404-72), who created the facade of **Santa Maria Novella** (p. 124), which illustrates his mastery of visual perspective.

An unlikely artist, **Fra Angelico** (c. 1400-55) personified the tension between medieval and Renaissance Italy. Though a member of a militant branch of Dominican friars which opposed humanism on principle, he created works that exhibit the techniques of space and perspective endorsed by humanistic artists, now on display at the **Museo della Chiesa di San Marco** (p. 146). **Masaccio** (1401-28) filled chapels with angels and gold-leaf and is credited with the first use of mathematical laws of perspective. His figures in the **Brancacci Chapel** (p. 131) served as models for Michelangelo and Leonardo. **Fra Filippo Lippi** (1406-69) was influenced by both Fra Angelico and Masaccio, but he also introduced innovative methods to the medium of painting. He experimented with new techniques in color and perspective, some of his works possessing an almost sculptural dimensionality. Among his most famous works is *The Coronation of the Virgin*, immortalized in a description at the end of Robert Browning's poem "Fra Lippo Lippi," written in the voice of the 15th-century painter. A pupil of Fra Angelico, **Benozzo Gozzoli** (c. 1421-1497) fused his mastery of nature scenes and portraits to create the *Procession of the Magi* for the **Palazzo Medici-Riccardi** (p. 127). Perhaps the most well-known Florentine painter of the period is **Sandro Botticelli** (1444-1510), whose *Birth of Venus* and *Primavera (Spring)* epitomize the Renaissance, and are both on display at the Uffizi (p. 135). The former depicts the goddess of love, standing upon a seashell as she emerges from the sea—a full-grown newborn. In the midst of the zephyr, she methodically wraps herself in her own golden locks. Venus appears yet again in *Primavera*—this time, fully clothed and surrounded by Cupid and the three Graces.

HIGH RENAISSANCE

From 1450 to 1521, the torch of artistic distinction passed between Leonardo and Michelangelo. Branching out from the disciplines of sculpture and painting, **Leonardo da Vinci** (1452-1519) excelled in subjects ranging from geology, engineering, and musical composition to human dissection and armaments design. Leonardo was—obviously—born in Vinci, a small Tuscan town just outside of Florence. Although some of his most famous works (like *The Last Supper*) are located in Milan, you can still get a taste of Leonardo in Florence. The **Museum of Leonardo da Vinci** (p. 145) contains wooden models of the innovative machines he designed in his sketchbook, including everything from hydraulic and aviatic devices.

Michelangelo Buonarroti (1475-1564) was an artistic jack of all trades. Although his major painted masterpieces are housed in Rome, Florence is home to many of his sculptural and architectural *capolavori* (masterpieces). In fact, you can genuflect at his tomb, located in the **Church of Santa Croce** (p. 129). He completed the designs for the **Laurentian Library** (p. 127), located close to the Duomo. His unfinished work, *Slaves*, is located in Florence's **Accademia** (p. 145), along with what is perhaps his most famous sculpture, **David**. The sculpture is different from its predecessors in that it depicts David before his Biblical skirmish with Goliath. Positioned in a contrapposto stance in all his nude glory, David's a whole lot of man.

Other prominent Renaissance artists include **Raffaello** (1483-1520), a draftsman who created technically perfect figures. Although his frescoes in the Vatican Museum are probably his most famous pieces, several of his portraits are on display in the Uffizi Gallery (p. 135) and Palazzo Pitti (p. 149) in Florence. In Venice, **Giovanni Bellini's** (c. 1430-1516) prolific protégé, **Titian** (1488-1576) created masterful paintings, notable for their realistic facial expressions and rich

1482 Botticelli's *Venus* arises from the sea.

1498 Leonardo da Vinci puts the last touches on *The Last Supper*.

1501-4 Michelangelo sculpts his *David*. Thank you, Michelangelo.

1513 Machiavelli writes *The Prince*.

1535 Parmigiano paints his Mannerist *Madonna with the Long Neck*.

1538 Titian creates the *Venus of Urbino*, now at Florence's Uffizi.

1482 Botticelli's *Venus* arises from the sea.

1498 Leonardo da Vinci puts the last touches on *The Last Supper.*

1501-4 Michelangelo sculpts his *David.* Thank you, Michelangelo.

1513 Machiavelli writes *The Prince.*

1535 Parmigiano paints his Mannerist *Madonna with the Long Neck.*

1538 Titian creates the *Venus of Urbino,* now at Florence's Uffizi.

1550 Niccolò di Raffaello begins work on the Boboli Gardens, but dies in the same year; Vasari gives us the aesthetic scoop in his *Lives of the Artists.*

colors. Titian's voluptuous *Venus of Urbino* is located at the Uffizi, and many of his other paintings are scattered throughout Florence's museums.

MIND YOUR MANNERISM

Emerging as a reaction to classicism, the Mannerist style dominated the High Renaissance from the 1520s until the birth of the Baroque style around 1590. Originating in Rome and Florence, Mannerist works are characterized by a self-conscious sense of aestheticism. Artists of the movement experimented with unusual colors and proportionalities. **Andrea del Sarto** (1486-1530) was one of the definitive painters of the Florentine Mannerist movement, and like Fra Lippo Lippi, one of the "narrators" of a Robert Browning poem. Sarto's famous works include his frescoes at the **Basilica della Santissima Annunziata di Firenze** (p. 127), as well as those on the life of St. John the Baptist adorning the Cloister of the Barefoot, or **Chiostro dello Scalzo** (p. 128). Also in the Mannerist style, the *Deposition* by **Jacopo da Pontermo** (1494-1557) can be seen at the Church of Santa Felicità. **Parmigiano** (1503-40) created the *Madonna of the Long Neck,* a piece emblematic of the movement's intentional distortions, and located in the Uffizi Gallery. One of the most adept portraitists of the period, **Bronzino** (1503-1572) helped transform Florentine Mannerism, with such paintings as *Portrait of a Young Girl with a Prayer Book.* Another painter, **Jacopo Tintoretto** (1518-94), a Venetian Mannerist, was the first to paint multiple light sources within a single composition. Among his works housed at the Uffizi (p. 135) are *Leda and the Swan* and *Saint Augustine Heals the Cripples.*

The Mannerist period is also known for its architecture, exemplified by artisans such as **Niccolò di Raffaello** (1500-50), who began the **Boboli Gardens** (p. 151) at the rear of the Palazzo Pitti in the same year he died. **Bernardo Buontalenti** (c. 1536-1608), one of the architects who continued the construction of the gardens, built a grotto that bears his name; the Grotto di Buontalenti boasts Mannerist frescoes produced by Bernardino Poccetti, called Barbatelli (1548-1612). Also on display in the Boboli Gardens are several Mannerist sculptures created by **Giambologna** (1529-1608). Another prominent Mannerist sculptor in Renaissance Florence was Baccio Bandinelli, whose *Hercules and Cacus* still stands in the **Piazza della Signoria** (p. 121).

IF IT AIN'T BAROQUE, DON'T FIX IT

A 17th-century stylistic hybrid born of the Counter-Reformation and monarchy, Baroque composition combined Mannerism's intense emotion with the Renaissance's grandeur to achieve a new expressive theatricality. Heavy on drama, emotion, and richness, Baroque art attempted to inspire faith in the Catholic Church and respect for earthly power. Painters of this era favored naturalism, a commitment to portraying nature in its raw state. One of the early Baroque painters in Italy was Giovanni da San Giovanni, also called **Giovanni Mannozzi** (1592-1636), whose frescoes ornament the interior of the Palazzo Pitti (p. 149). **Caravaggio** (1573-1610), the epitome of Baroque painters, relied heavily on chiaroscuro and naturalism to create dramatically unsettling images. It is even rumored that he used the corpse of a prostitute recovered from Rome's Tiber River as a model for the Virgin Mary's body in *Death of the Virgin*. This provocative painting is located in the Louvre in Paris, although a handful of Caravaggio's works are on display at Florence's Uffizi Gallery (p. 135).

Another Baroque painter, **Orazio Gentileschi** (1562-1639), was heavily influenced by the works of Caravaggio. Orazio's daughter **Artemesia** joined the family business, becoming one of the most important female painters in Italian history. Although born in Rome, she spent a period in Florence, during which time she produced such Baroque pieces as *Judith and her Maidservant* and *The Conversion of the Magdalene*. **Gianlorenzo Bernini** (1598-1680), a prolific High Baroque sculptor and architect, is best known for his overwhelming colonnade of St. Peter's Piazza and the awesome baldacchino inside the cathedral. Today, a few of his lesser known works are located in Florence. Another Baroque architect whose works are surely visible in Florence is **Buontalenti**. In addition to having a hand in the Boboli Gardens, he was one of the pioneers of ornate Baroque stage design and theatre architecture. Late Baroque sculptor **Giovanni Battista Foggini** (1652-1725) applied artistic methods he learned in Rome to such Florentine buildings as **Santa Maria del Carmine** (p. 131). Toward the end of the Baroque period, however, this grand style began to give way to the delicacy and elaborate ornamentation of **Rococo**, a light and graceful method originating in 18th-century France. Rococo motifs include seashells, clouds, flowers, and vines carved into woodwork and stone edifices. While artists in Florence remained enamored with the Baroque style, **Giovanni Battista Tiepolo** (1696-1770) in Venice mastered the Rococo style.

NINETEENTH-CENTURY ART

NEOCLASSICISM

French-influenced Neoclassicism abandoned the overly detailed Rococo and dramatic Baroque methods in favor of a purer, more ancient construction. At first, the shift was almost too subtle to notice, primarily because the Neoclassical artists had no new inspiration on which they could base their Neotraditional works. With the early 17th-century discovery and excavation of Herculaneum and Pompeii,

1602 Shakespeare writes *Troilus and Cressida,* inspired by Chaucer, who was inspired by Boccaccio.

1606 A prostitute's corpse may or may not have served as Caravaggio's model for *Death of the Virgin.*

1633 Galileo is tried before the Inquisition. Who could have expected it?

1803 Neoclassical artist Pietro Benvenuti becomes director of Florence's Accademia.

LIFE AND TIMES

however, Neoclassical artists quickly found their ancient muses in the form of recovered artifacts. After the Medici reign diminished, the **Lorraine** family came to power, bringing with them a taste for the Neoclassical style that had originated in France. A friend of the sculptor **Antonio Canova** (1757-1822), Tuscan artist **Pietro Benvenuti** (1769-1844) promoted the formal aspects of Neoclassicism, and became the director of Florence's Accademia in 1803. In the next generation of Italian Neoclassicists was **Luigi Sabatelli** (1772-1850), a painter inspired by the French artist Antoine-Jean Gros. Among his works that can be seen in Florence today are his frescoes in the Hall of the Iliad in the Palazzo Pitti (p. 149). Among the many other Florentine sites that offer a taste of Neoclassicism is the **Villa del Poggio Imperiale**. In the 19th century, the structure underwent Neoclassical renovations, headed by **Gaspare Maria Paoletti** (1727-1813), **Pasquale Poccianti** (1774-1858), and **Giuseppe Cacialli** (1770-1828). Limited parts of the building can still be visited today.

SEE, SPOT, PAINT

c. 1850 The Macchiaioli group forms in Florence. Those guys really knew how to manipulate a paintbrush.

During the mid-19th century, a group of politically- and aesthetically-rebellious artists convened at the Caffè Michelangiolo in Florence to shoot the intellectual breeze. This congregation—the **Macchiaioli group**—anticipated French Impressionism and was spearheaded by **Telemaco Signorini** (1835-1901), **Giovanni Fattori** (1825-1908), and **Silvestro Lega** (1826-1895). The group opposed the strict Neoclassical style and believed that a painting's meaning lay in its *macchie* (spots) of color rather than in its narrative. A technique called "blotting," which abruptly juxtaposed patches of color through manipulations with a dry paint brush, was used to depict politicized scenes of battle and outspoken responses to everyday life. Many of the works of these revolutionary, proto-Impressionist artists are on display at the Modern Art Gallery in the Palazzo Pitti (p. 149), including Signori's *Leith*, Fattori's *La Rotonda dei Bagni Palmieri*, and Lega's *Bersaglieri Leading Prisoners*.

1855 Robert Browning composes the dramatic monologues "Fra Lippo Lippi" and "Andrea del Sarto."

1870s Giovanni Verga gets nitty gritty, ushering in the *verismo* movement.

1883 *Pinocchio* has no strings, but Collodi has lots of success.

TWENTIETH-CENTURY ART

BACK TO THE FUTURISM. The Italian Futurist painters, sculptors, and architects of the early 20th century brought Italy to the cutting edge of art. Inspired by Filippo Tommaso Marinetti's (1876-1944) **Futurist Manifesto** of 1909, these Italian artists loved to glorify danger, war, and the 20th-century machine age. At the 1912 Futurist exhibition in Paris, painters and sculptors went beyond Cubism to celebrate the dynamism and energy of modern life by depicting several aspects of moving forms. Rival Futurist school sprung up in Milan and Florence, with **Marinetti, Umberto Boccioni** (1882-1916), and **Gino Severini** (1883-1966) dominating the former group, and **Carlo Carrà** and **Ardegno Soffici** (1879-1964) heading the lat-

1906 Amedeo Modigliani enrolls in a school to study nudes—purely for art's sake.

ter group. Although you're not likely to come across any of his major works in Florence, **Giorgio de Chirico** (1888-1978) was another figure who changed the face of Italian art. Educated in both Athens and Greece, de Chirico depicted eerie scenes dominated by mannequin figures, empty spaces, and steep perspective. During a stint in Florence in 1909, he created such works as *The Enigma of the Oracle*. Although his mysterious and disturbing style, called **Pittura Metafisica**, was never successfully imitated, he inspired early Surrealist painters.

PERFECTLY RATIONAL. Other 20th-century Italian artists include **Amadeo Modigliani** (1884-1920), a sculptor and painter who was highly influenced by African art and Cubism. Quite the wise student, he enrolled in Florence's Free School of Nude Studies (Scuola Libero di Nudo) in 1906. Another influential 20th-century figure was **Marcello Piacentini** (1881-1960), who created fascist architecture that imposed sterility upon classical motifs. **Architectural Rationalism**—a style sanctioned by Mussolini—was a movement predicated upon the idea that the structure of a building should strictly conform to its purpose. In Florence, the **Santa Maria Novella Train Station** is a prime example of Rationalism. Completed in 1935, the station was designed by **Giovanni Michelucci** (1891-1990), a pioneer of modern architecture who also had hand in the 1950s renovation of the Uffizi. In 1938, Piacentini designed the looming EUR in Rome (Esposizione Universale Roma) as an impressive reminder of the link between Mussolinian fascism and Roman imperialism. Piacentini also designed the **Odeon Theater** in Florence's **Piazza Strozzi**.

THIS MODERN ART. In the Postwar Era, Italian art lacked unity but still produced noteworthy artists. Although their major works are not on display in the city of Florence, their aesthetic visions forever changed the face of Italian art. **Argentinean Lucio Fontana** (1899-1968), who split his time between his native country and Italy, pioneered **Spatialism,** a movement to bring art beyond the canvas toward a synthesis of color, sound, movement, time, and space. His *taglio* (slash) canvases of the mid-1950s created a new dimension for the 2D surface with a simple linear cut. Conceptual artist **Piero Manzoni** (1933-63) created a scandal in 1961 when he put his feces (allegedly) in 90 small cans labeled *Artist's Shit*, setting the price of the excrements at their weight in gold. In May 2007 Sotheby's sold a can for €124,000. In the late 1960s **Arte Povera** bridged the gap between art and life by integrating cheap everyday materials into pieces of art. **Michelangelo Pistoletto** (1933-) caused a clamor with his *Venus in Rags* (1967), a plaster cast of the classical Venus facing a pile of old rags, on display in Turin. In 1984, he brought his controversial art to Florence's **Forte Belvedere** for a solo exhibition. While eclipsed by its Renaissance past, contemporary art in Italy thrives in select museums and at the bi-annual **Florence Biennale,** held at the **Fortezza da Basso**, and showcasing the recent work of artists from Italy and around the world.

1909 Filippo Tommaso Marinetti writes the *Futurist Manifesto*; Giorgio de Chirico paints *The Enigma of the Oracle*.

1921 Pirandello composes *Six Characters in Search of An Author.*

1932-34 Florence's Santa Maria Novella Train Station is constructed in the Rationalist style.

1950s Piero Manzoni decides to slash canvases.

1967 Michelangelo Pistoletto creates a stir with his *Venus in Rags.*

1997 Dario Fo miffs the Catholic Church, but scores a Nobel Prize in literature.

2003 Matthew Pearl's *The Dante Club* is published. Dante may or may not approve.

LIFE AND TIMES

LITERATURE

Early Italian literature was dominated by such figures as **Cicero** (106-43 BC), **Julius Caesar** (100-44 BC), and **Ovid** (43 BC-AD 17), before sliding into the Dark Ages and the trend of authorial anonymity among secular writers. Although the tumult of medieval life discouraged most literary creativity in the late 13th century, the Tuscan muses were about to awake, introducing some of the most prominent writers in history.

DOLCE STIL NUOVO

The "sweet new style" was the prevailing poetic style in Florence from about 1250 to 1300. The lyric poets who popularized this movement—called the *stilnovisti*—composed tender sonnets, *ballate*, and *canzoni*, influenced by the French troubadours' theme of ▓courtly love. The mellifluous verses of the *stilnovisti* are characterized by introspection and often present sophisticated, idealized images of female beauty. Bolognese **Guido Guinizelli** (c. 1240-1276) was one of the early forerunners of the movement, along with **Florentines Lapo Gianni** (c. 1270-1332) and **Guido Cavalcanti** (c. 1255-1300), whose works include *Canzone D'Amore* (Song of Love). Another *stilnovisto*, **Cino da Pistoia** (1270-c. 1336) wrote countless poems about mutual love, in addition to serving as ambassador to Florence in the early 14th century. The poet from this group who indisputably attained rockstar status was **Dante Alighieri** (1265-1321). It was actually Dante who coined the term *dolce stil nuovo* in Canto 24 of his *Purgatorio*—but we already knew he was clever.

THE TUSCAN TRIFECTA

Dante, Petrarch, and Boccaccio are principally responsible for resuscitating Italian literature in the late 13th century. This elite Tuscan trio was regally called the **Tre Corone (Three Crowns).** The *capolavori* (masterpieces) of these three literary giants helped solidify the Tuscan dialect as the official Italian language.

ABANDON ALL HOPE, YE WHO ENTER HERE. Although scholars do not agree on the precise dates of the literary Renaissance, many argue that the work of **Dante Alighieri** marked its inception. Dante is considered the father of modern Italian literature, which explains why Florence—in fact, all of Italy—abounds with memorial statues of his grimacing visage. He was one of the first poets in all of Europe to write using the *volgare* (common vernacular; Florentine, in Dante's case) instead of Latin. In his epic poem *La Divina Commedia*, he roams the three realms of the afterlife *(Inferno, Purgatorio, Paradiso)* with Virgil as his guide, meeting famous historical and mythological figures and his true love, ▓Beatrice. In the work, Dante calls for social reform and indicts all those who contributed to Florence's moral downfall, including Popes and political figures—especially those who ordered his own political exile. A testament to his literary prowess, Dante has inspired countless authors over the years, from Geoffrey Chaucer in the 14th century, to Matthew Pearl, author of *The Dante Club* in 2003. Today, a small museum (p. 143) is located in what was supposedly Dante's home near the P. della Signoria in Florence.

YOU WHO HEAR THE SOUND, IN SCATTERED RHYMES. Petrarch (1304-74), a lyric poet and the second titan of the 13th century, more clearly belongs to the literary Renaissance. A scholar of Latin, Petrarch dismissed Scholasticism, instead favoring a return to the classics, and is often described as "the father of Humanism." His most famous works are the sonnets he wrote to a married woman named Laura, collected in Il Canzoniere, also called the *Rime sparse*, or "scattered rhymes." Eventually, Petrarch's beloved Laura fell victim to the bubonic plague—but, of course, he was compelled to continue dedicating verses to her. In the later years of his life, after much city-hopping, Petrarch ultimately met the same end as his beloved Laura. His literary legacy is, however, eternal. The Petrarchan sonnet—the counterpart to the English or Shakespearean sonnet—is divided into eight lines (the octave) and six lines (the sestet). You know a writer's the real deal when he lends his name to a poetic form.

DO AS WE SAY, AND NOT AS WE DO. The third member of this literary triumvirate was **Giovanni Boccaccio** (1313-75), who, like his contemporary Petrarch, was a renowned humanist. Boccaccio's earlier works include *Il Filocolo* and *Il Filostato;* the former laid the foundations for Italian prose, while the latter is a poem that inspired both Chaucer's *Troilus* and Shakespeare's *Troilus and Cressida*. Undoubtedly, Boccaccio's most famous work is the *Decameron,* a collection of 100 stories that range in tone from suggestive to vulgar—in one, a gardener has his way with an entire convent. Admiring Boccaccio's entertaining literary genius, Chaucer based several of his Canterbury Tales on episodes that appear in the Decameron. Late in his life, Boccaccio returned to writing in Latin and, after a stint of lecturing on his predecessor Dante in Florence, he died at his family home in Certaldo, Italy.

RENAISSANCE MEN

IMPROV ASYLUM. The 14th century saw the rise of *la Commedia dell'Arte*, a form of improvised theater with a standard plot structure and characters. Each character had its own mask and costume and a few fixed personality traits. The most famous character, Arlecchino **(Harlequin),** was easily identified by his diamond-patterned costume, similar to the motley worn by Shakespeare's fools.

THE FRESH PRINCE AND FRIENDS. By the 15th and 16th centuries, Italian authors were reviving classical sources in new ways. **Alberti** (1404-72) put his visual expertise into writing, articulating his aesthetic views in his treatises *On Sculpture*, *On Architecture*, and *On Painting*. At the pinnacle of the Renaissance, Florentine **Niccolò Machiavelli** (1469-1527) wrote *Il Principe* (The Prince), a grim assessment of what it takes to gain political power. In the spirit of the Renaissance, specialists in other fields tried their hands at writing. The designer of the Palazzo degli Uffizi, **Giorgio Vasari** (1511-74) stopped redecorating Florence's churches to produce the ultimate primer on art history and criticism, *The Lives of the Artists*. Mannerist sculptor and native Florentine, **Benvenuto Cellini** (1500-71) wrote about his art in **The Autobiography.** Finally, **Michelangelo** (1475-1564) proved to be a prolific composer of sonnets in this period, believe it or not.

STARRY, STARRY WRITER. Pisa-born **Galileo Galilei** (1564-1642) is known for his revolutionary contributions to astronomy and mathematics, as well as his development of the scientific method. Luckily, this genius's pen was not inert, and it is because of his literary works that we are able to understand his scientific accomplishments. Among the works he wrote early in his career is *De Motu (On Motion)*. Although never published, the book reveals Galileo's conceptions of cause-effect relationships and free falling objects. In *Siderius Nuncius (The Sidereal Messenger)*, he recorded the observations he made with his new and improved version of the telescope. His most controversial work, *Dialogo sopra i due massimi sistemi del mondo, tolemaico e copernicano (Dialogue Concerning the Two Chief Systems, Ptolemaic and Copernican)* was finished in 1630. The book is a conversation between a layman (Sagredo), a ridiculed Aristotelian (Simplicio), and a figure serving to express Galileo's own heliocentric opinions (Salviati). The papacy was upset by the fact that the book so clearly endorsed the Copernican theory of the universe, and so Galileo was tried in the Inquisition, and ultimately ordered to remain under house arrest indefinitely. Rumor has is that, after being forced to recant his heliocentric views, Galileo murmured, "Eppur, si muove" ("And yet, it moves").

MODERN TIMES

"ALL TOGETHER NOW." The 19th century brought Italian unification and the need for one language. Nationalistic "Italian" literature, an entirely new concept, grew slowly. *Racconti* (short stories) and poetry became popular in the 1800s. Sicilian **Giovanni Verga** (1840-1922) created a brutally honest depiction of destitute Italians, which ushered in a new tradition of portraying the common man in art and literature, a movement known as *verismo* (contemporary, all-too-tragic realism). In 1825, **Alessandro Manzoni's** (1785-1873) historical novel, *I Promessi sposi*, established the Modernist novel as a major avenue of Italian literary expression.

LOOK MA, NO STRINGS. Carlo Collodi (1826-1890) contributed to Italian unification as a journalist and solider before ultimately turning to children's literature. In 1883 he composed the whimsical **Storia di un burratino** *(Story of a Marionette)*, also called *Le avventure di Pinocchio (The Adventures of Pinocchio)*. In the opening lines, Maestro Ciliegia (Master Cherry) finds a peculiar piece of lumber, and the rest is history. Pinocchio continues to enchant children, now in his innocuous Disney format, with the precocious and sometimes diabolic antics of a puppet.

THE POST-MEN COMETH. In the 20th century, cutting-edge postmodernism ran rampant throughout Italy. Most of the prominent authors from this time, however, were not from Florence, a city which arguably had her literary heyday in the 13th century. Postmodern Italian writers sought to undermine the concept of objective truth that was so dear to the *verismo* movement. Nobel Prize winner **Luigi Pirandello** (1867-1936) deconstructed theatrical convention and explored metatheater in works like his 1921 *Sei personaggi in cerca d'autore (Six Characters in Search of an Author)*. During the terror of Mussolini, anti-fascist fiction exploded as writers related their horrific personal and political experiences under the dictator. The most prolific of these writers, **Alberto Moravia** (1907-90), wrote the ground-breaking *Gli indifferenti (The Time of Indifference)*, which was promptly censored for its subtle attacks on the fascist regime. In 1947 **Primo Levi** (1919-87) wrote *Se questo è un uomo (If This is a Man)* about his experience as a prisoner in Auschwitz. Several female writers also gained popularity, including **Grazia Deledda** (1875-1936), **Elsa Morante** (1912-85), and **Natalia Ginzburg** (1916-91). Writers like **Cesare Pavese** (1908-50) and **Beppe Fenoglio** (1922-63) brought the cinematic trend of *neorealismo* to the novel. **Italo Calvino** (´1923-85) exemplified the postmodern era with the magic realism of his 1957 *Il barone rampante (The Baron in the Trees)* and by questioning the act of reading and writing in *Se una notte d'inverno un viaggatore (If On a Winter's Night a Traveler)*. In 1997, playwright **Dario Fo's** (b. 1926) satires brought him both denunciation by the Catholic Church and the Nobel Prize for literature.

ITALY SEEN THROUGH FOREIGN EYES

DUNANT, SARAH. *The Birth of Venus.* Set in the 15th century; Alessandra falls in love with an artist, while Savonarola reigns over Florence.

ELIOT, GEORGE. *Romola.* Deceit, politics, and martyrdom in Savonarola's Florence. Noticing a pattern here?

FORSTER, E.M. *A Room With a View.* Victorian love and coming-of-age in Florence.

HOWELLS, WILLIAM DEAN. *Indian Summer.* Three's company; a romantic comedy set in Florence, starring one man and two women.

HUXLEY, ALDOUS. *Time Must Have a Stop.* Sebastian Barnack is educated in Florence for the summer.

JAMES, HENRY. *Portrait of a Lady.* A large legacy and multiple suitors, but life is still tough for Isabel Archer.

MAYES, FRANCIS. *Under the Tuscan Sun.* A woman's soul-searching in the heart of Italy, which inspired the 2003 movie of the same name.

RUSHDIE, SALMAN. *The Enchantress of Florence.* A smokin' hot princess bridges the gap between Renaissance Florence and Mughal India.

RUSKIN, JOHN. *Mornings in Florence.* A guide to Florentine art for the English traveler.

LIFE AND TIMES

MUSIC

Thank goodness for Florence—without it, Italian music might never have gotten beyond Gregorian chants. As Italy started to emerge from the late Middle Ages, Florence took the cultural initiative and pushed music in the right direction. (Similar things were happening in France, of course, but you'll have to learn about that on another trip.) The Florentine influence on the Italian musical scene became prominent in the middle of the 14th century, a period known as the **Trecento** ("Three Hundred"—it took place in the 1300's, but they dropped the thousands' place). Leaving behind the old monastic monophony, with every voice singing the same melody, Florentine composers like **Francesco Landini** and **Lorenzo da Firenze** gave rise to a new polyphonic music—different voice parts singing different lines to produce changing harmonies.

A few hundred years later, Florence gave Italy its greatest gift to the musical world (and the greatest headache to the non-musical world)—the invention of opera. In the 1590s, a group of Florentine musicians and intellectuals called the **Florentine Camerata** decided that polyphony was getting out of hand. In an effort to bring back the music of the Greek world—going Greek was cool in the Renaissance—they began writing songs to imitate the old Greek tragedies, which they thought had been entirely sung on stage. In 1597, the first complete opera was written: *Dafne*, music by **Jacopo Peri**, lyrics by **Ottavio Rinuccini.** That work was lost, though the second opera ever written, *Euridice* (by the same team, aided by **Giulio Caccini**) survives to the present day.

Today, Florence continues its proud operatic tradition with the **Maggio Musicale Fiorentino**, a celebration of opera founded in 1933 as one of the first music festivals in Italy. Running each year from late April to early June, the festival generally involves performances of four operas. In addition, the festival has spawned a full season of concert, ballet, and theater performances to enliven Florence's musical life from October to April. There is also a thriving modern music scene, with live jazz and hip DJs at many new bars and clubs.

FEATURING FLORENCE. The Italian film industry dates back to 1905 when the first movie studio started rolling its cameras in the city of Turin. In the following decade, however, the industry took a liking to Rome's predictable weather and unpredictable scenery and re-established itself in the capital city. Today, as the Italian film industry expands, Florence's medieval charm and stunning architecture make the city an unparalleled backdrop for movies, and there have been a number of notable films shot primarily in the city. Some include *A Room With a View* (1985), *Hannibal* (2001), and *Tea With Mussolini* (1999), the latter of which was by Franco Zeffirelli, the famous Florentine director who also dabbled in radio, theatre, and opera. Every November to December, the city of Florence also holds the **Festa dei Popoli,** a renowned national and international film festival. Movies and documentaries from around the world are screened in their original languages with Italian subtitles if necessary. Popcorn, anyone?

RELIGION

As you probably won't be surprised to learn, the vast majority of Florence's population is (at least nominally) Catholic. After all, somebody has to attend services in all of the incredibly beautiful churches—and there are well over 200 places of worship inside the city limits, though a few have been deconsecrated and put to secular use. (For details, see most of the sights listed in this guide, p. 113.) According to legend, the city of Florence became a Roman Catholic diocese in the first century, around the same time that Rome did. In fact, the system of dioceses assigning a bishop formal authority over a certain territory didn't really take hold until the fourth century or so—when the Roman Emperors stopped throwing Christians to the lions—but Florence definitely got its own right away. A thousand years or so later, the city (and the church hierarchy) had grown enough that **Pope Martin V** decided Florence deserved a promotion, and so made it an Archdiocese on May 10, 1419. Since then, two archbishops of Florence have gone on to become Popes—**Pope Clement VII** in 1523, and **Pope Leo XI** in 1605. Unsurprisingly, both were Medicis. Neither one had a particularly glorious career. Pope Clement VII watched Rome get sacked by the army of the Holy Roman Emperor, and had to pay a ransom of 400,000 ducats to keep his own life; he also excommunicated King Henry VIII, thereby losing all of England to the Protestant Reformation. **Leo XI,** on the other hand, didn't manage to do anything that disastrous; in fact, he didn't manage to do anything at all. Catching an illness at his coronation, he died just 26 days later. The Italians gave him the posthumous nickname Papa Lampo ("Lightning Pope") in memory of the brevity of his reign.

Today, around 90% of the people living within the boundaries of the Archdiocese of Florence declare themselves Roman Catholics. If that number seems high, realize that it actually represents a protracted decline of Catholicism in Florence; back in 1950, an astonishing 99.4% of the population were members of the Roman Church. Over 700 priests officiate in the city, under the leadership of Archbishop **Giuseppe Betori,** who took office in September of 2008.

Beside the overwhelming Catholic presence, there are smaller populations in Florence practicing other religious traditions. The history of the Jewish community in the city dates back to the late 1300s, including the construction of its beautiful **synagogue** (p. 130). Much more recently, the Muslim community established its first Florentine **mosque** in 1991. Meanwhile, the interdenominational **Community of Protestant Churches in Europe (CPCE)** has selected to hold its next General Assembly in Florence, in the autumn of 2012. Florence is also famous for its religious—or at least religiously-inspired—festivals, including the **Easter Sunday Scoppio del Carro ("Explosion of the Cart")** fireworks display. The city celebrates its patron saint, John the Baptist, in the **Festival of Saint John** every June 24.

Though religious sensitivities are on the wane, it's important for tourists to remain conscientious about respecting churches, cathedrals, and other places of religious significance. Dress modestly—long pants for men, covered shoulders for women—when visiting these sites, avoid disrupting services, and be aware that some churches may not allow photography. (Flashes can damage fragile paintings and mosaics.) In general, remember that these buildings are places of worship first, and tourist attractions second.

CULTURE

THE ART OF DINING

LA CUCINA ITALIANA

GREAT EXPECTATIONS. In Italy, food is as much a part of the cultural heritage as Verdi and Michelangelo. True Italian cuisine is far more than spaghetti and meatballs or eggplant parmesan, and those accustomed to your typical Italian restaurant elsewhere may be surprised by the variety or regional cuisines in Italy. Each region of Italy has its own distinct culinary style often based on foods grown or raised in the local area. Southern Italy is home to citrus orchards, olive groves, and fields of durum wheat for pasta. The world's first *pizzeria*, still in business, started on the streets of Naples in Campania, which is also famous for its cheeses like Mozzarella di Bufala, Ricotta, and Mascarpone. Southern Italian chefs exploit their proximity to the sea in a variety of local seafood specialties. Northern Italian cuisine is known for its use of rice, polenta, cheeses, and butter or lard (with the notable exception of Liguria, home to olive oil-based basil pesto). Main courses often involve some sort of game or wild fowl like rabbit, quail, or grouse.

UNDER THE TUSCAN SUN. Most of what we think of as Italian food, including bruschetta, bolognese sauce, and cured meats comes from central Italy, where Tuscany is located. In fact, while Florentine food is often associated with humble peasant dishes, some argue that it was at the court of the Medici in Florence that Italian cuisine was born. Food in Florence is largely based around meat dishes—like the famous *bistecca alla fiorentina*—but the region also boasts excellent olive oils, sheep milk cheeses, and white beans called *fagioli*. Above all, Florentine cuisine is characterized by its use locally grown produce and seasonal flavors.

A TAVOLA! (TO THE TABLE!)

SLOW AND SAVORY. Whatever the region, all Italians take time to savor each course and enjoy the company of those sharing the meal. A traditional Italian dinner will include an *antipasto* (appetizer), a *primo piatto* (starch-based first course like pasta or risotto), a *secondo piatto* (meat or fish), a *contorno* (vegetable side dish), and finally the *dolce* (dessert), followed by *caffè* (espresso) and sometimes an after-dinner liqueur like *limoncello*. Given the length of a true Italian meal, it should come as no surprise that it was the Italians who championed the Slow Food movement to combat Americanized fast food.

WATER EVERYWHERE. Tap water is safe to drink throughout Italy, but most Italians prefer to drink bottled water. Bottled water is available either sparkling *(aqua gassata* or *frizzante)* or still *(aqua naturale* or *non-gassata)*. If you want tap water, you can ask for *acqua del rubinetto*, but waiters may be reluctant to serve it to you.

FAST FOOD, ITALIAN STYLE

THE FAST AND THE FLAVORY. Not every meal in Italy is an elaborate feast. Breakfast, or *la colazione*, in Italy is usually very simple, consisting of a quick coffee and a *cornetto* (croissant) at a neighborhood bar. Standing at the counter is often cheaper than sitting at a table. While weekends may mean long drawn-out lunches that last most of the afternoon, during the work week, Italians often grab a *panino* (sandwich) or a salad for *il pranzo* (lunch). *La cena* (dinner) usually begins at 8pm, and tends to be the lengthiest meal of the day. Nevertheless, there are quicker and cheaper alternatives. *Trattorie* and *osterie* are more budget-friendly than *ristoranti*. *Pizzerie* in Italy specialize in individual, made-to-order thin-crust pizzas, usually cooked in a wood oven. Other options for Italians on the go include the *tavola calda* (cafeteria-style prepared food vendor), *rosticceria* (grill), and *gastronomia* (food shop that prepares hot dishes for takeout). If you're cooking at home or planning a picnic, a *salumeria* (deli selling a variety of cured meats) or an *alimentari* (grocery shop) may be your best bet. Open-air markets are great places to find fresh locally-grown produce. And while many Italians do go to different specialty stores to do their shopping, supermarkets like STANDA or Coop exist in cities, like Florence.

CHECK, PLEASE!

TIPPING POINTS. Most restaurants have a *coperto* (cover charge), which includes table settings, bread and water. When it comes to tipping, Italians don't tip as much as Americans. Most restaurants include a modest *servizio* (service charge) in *il conto* (the bill). If the service warrants it, leave your waiter a little extra on the table.

CLEAN PLATES. If you're in a *pizzeria*, you can ask to take the rest of your pizza home with you, but otherwise Italians shy away from doggy bags. Portions are smaller in Italy, though, and the food is so delicious you're unlikely to have leftovers anyway!

IN VINO VERITAS

"GOOD WINE NEEDS NO BUSH." Despite its reputation for living in the shadow of wine-loving French neighbors, Italy is home to some of the oldest wine-producing regions in the world. Greek and Etruscan settlers grew grapes to make wine long before the Romans started established their own viticultural practices in Italy in the second century BC. Modern Italy continues to be one of the foremost exporters of vintage spirits, responsible for nearly one-fifth of global wine production. Today, over one million vineyards and 2000 varieties of grapes are grown in Italy's warm climes and rocky hills before *la vendemmia* (the grape harvest) in September or October.

WINO FOREVER. To determine the quality of a wine, look for the classification on the bottle. Independently tested wine will bear the label **DOCG** (*Denominazione di Origine Controllata e Garantita*), the sign of a high quality wine. Wines that follow regional regulations are labeled **DOC** (*Denominazione di Origine Controllata*), while wines produced in a specific area bear the label IGT (*Indicazione Geografica*). **Vino da Tavola** is a catch-all term for otherwise unclassifiable table wines.

THE DAYS OF WINE AND ROSES. Tuscany is best known for its Sangiovese grapes, crushed to make the region's popular **Chianti,** as well as the "noble" red vino **Nobile di Montepulciano** and white **Trebbiano.** Beginning in the 80s, Tuscany began to blend native grape varietals with some foreign ones like Cabernet Sauvignon and Merlot to create "Super Tuscans," which includes **Chianti Classico.**

 CORK YOUR WALLET! Wine snobs may spend €50 on a bottle of aged *riserva*, but wines in the €6-12 range can often be sublime. The most respected wine stewards in the nation regularly rank inexpensive wines above their costly cousins. Expense can equal quality, but it's wiser to go for the high end of a lower-grade wine than the low end of a higher-grade wine.

CUSTOMS AND ETIQUETTE

PROJECT RUNWAY. Italian designers dominate the fashion world and it's no secret the Italians care about looking good. Walk around any *piazza* and you'll see stylish Italian women striding across the cobblestones in high heels, their hair flying in the breeze, radiating an air of confidence and effortless chic. You may not be able to master the Italian attitude in a short visit, but you can blend in by avoiding telltale tourist attire like shorts, sneakers, athletic T-shirts, and baseball caps. Conservative clothing (covered shoulders and knee-length skirts or dresses for women) is mandatory when visiting places of worship.

ESPRESSO YOURSELF. When you ask for a *caffè* in Italy, expect a demitasse of espresso, not a big mug of filtered coffee. If you want American-style coffee, ask for a *caffè Americano.* On a hot day, a *caffè freddo* (iced coffee) may do the trick. A *caffè latte* is hot milk mixed with coffee, while a *cappuccino* is an espresso infused with steamed milk and a *caffè macchiato* is espresso "stained" with a drop of steamed milk. Coffee consumed after breakfast should not have milk in it. Ordering a cappuccino after a meal is a sure sign you're not Italian and will be laughed at by waiters.

SOME RESERVATIONS. Reservations are only necessary at the fanciest Italian restaurants. If you would like to make a reservation in advance, you would say, *"Vorrei fare una prenotazione."*

AROUND THE CLOCK. In Italy, as in most of Europe, time is based on the 24hr. day rather than the 12hr. clock. So, for example, 4pm would be expressed as 16:00.

YOU'RE TOAST. Italians often say *"Buon appetito!"* ("Enjoy your meal!") when the first course is served. If you are toasting with a drink, you say *"Salute!"* ("To your health!").

SIGN LANGUAGE? Italians express themselves not only through their rapid-fire speech but also through hand gestures. Animated gesticulation may be used to punctuate speech or to shade a word or phrase with a meaning it may lack. Note, however, that like dialects, certain hand signals can have different meanings depending on the region.

YOURS, MINE, AND HOURS. Shops in Italy generally open from about 9am to 1pm, when they close for lunch, before reopening in the afternoon. Most shops are open for at least a half day on Saturday, but few are open on Sundays. Large supermarkets and department stores, however, are usually open all day Monday through Saturday, and part of the day on Sunday. Most restaurants in Italy open for two separate shifts every day. Restaurants generally begin lunch service around midday and continue until 3pm. Most restaurants open for dinner at about 7pm and stay open until at least 11pm. Banks throughout Italy are open Monday to Friday 8:30am-1:30pm, and 3:30-4:30pm. Pharmacies are generally open 9am-12:30pm and 3:30-7:30pm, though there is always a 24hr. pharmacy nearby. Post offices in Italy are open daily Monday through Saturday from 8:30am until 6:30pm.

SHOPPING SPREE. Each year, in January and July, the *saldi* (sales) is the talk of the town. Stores generally begin selling their merchandise at 30% off in the second week of January and July, and the discount generally increases to at least 50% as the weeks go on. If you get there by late February or August, though, be prepared for most of the inventory to be gone.

SIZE ME UP. Italy uses the continental European sizing system, which differs from both American and British sizes.

WOMEN'S CLOTHING										
US	2	4	6	8	10	12	14	16	18	20	22
ITALY	36	38	40	42	44	46	48	50	52	54	56

WOMEN'S SHOES										
US	5½	6½	7	7½	8	8½	9	10	10½	20	22
ITALY	35	36	37	38	38½	39	40	41	42	54	56

MEN'S CLOTHING										
US	34	36	38	40	42	44	46	48	18	20	22
ITALY	44	46	48	50	52	54	57	58	52	54	56

MEN'S SHIRTS										
US	14	14½	15	15½	16	16½	17	17½	18	20	22
ITALY	36	37	38	39	40	41	42	43	52	54	56

MEN'S SHOES										
US	6	6½	7	7½	8	8½	9	9½	10	10½	11-11½
ITALY	39	40	40½	41	41½	42	42½	43	43½	44-44½	45

HOLIDAYS AND FESTIVALS

Like their countrymen in other major Italian cities, the Florentines always find a reason to celebrate. (It's a fact: Italy has one of the highest rates of alcohol consumption in all of Europe.) In particular, the weather of spring presents ideal conditions to hold numerous festivals unique to the city, luring tourists and locals to fill the streets. Every Easter Sunday in April, the spectacular **Scoppio del Carro** is held in the square beneath the Duomo cathedral in keeping with medieval tradition. As part of the slightly bizarre festivities, a mechanical dove is used to explode an enormous cart of fireworks in front of the cathedral. Late summer (August) and winter are not quite as holiday-happy as the spring, yet there are still many notable events, many of which are related to both the visual and performing arts including painting, sculpture, music, dance, drama, and film. Here are some festivals found only in Florence:

DATE	FESTIVAL	INFO
Easter Sunday	Scoppio del Carro	See **Religion**, p. 60.
Last week of April	Mostra Mercato Internazionale dell'Artigianato	An exhibition of European arts and crafts.
April-June	Maggio Musicale (May of Music)	The city's largest arts festival with music, dance, and drama. See **Music**, p. 59.
May 23	Celebrazioni per la Morte di Savonarola	
Sunday after Ascension Day (40 days after Easter)	Festa del Grillo (Festival of the Cricket)	
Late June	Pitti Immagine Uomo	The second round of a nationwide men's fashion show.
June 24	Festa di San Giovanni Battista (Feast of Saint John)	The feast day of Florence's patron saint, with impressive fireworks and traditional events. See **Religion, p. 60**.
Around June 24	Gioco del Calcio Storico (Old-fashioned Soccer Match)	
July-August	Florence Dance Festival	
Summer	Rime Rampanti	The Europa dei Sensi program hosts series of nightly cultural shows featuring music, poetry, and food from a chosen European country.
Summer	Opera Festival	Opera performances throughout Tuscany often featuring such classics as Aida and Il Flauto Mágico.
Oct-April	Amici della Musica (Friends of Music)	Concert season.
September 7-8	Festa della Rificolona (Paper Lantern Festival)	
November-December	Festa dei Popoli	Nationals and international film festival.

LIFE AND TIMES

BEYOND TOURISM

A PHILOSOPHY FOR TRAVELERS

HIGHLIGHTS OF BEYOND TOURISM IN FLORENCE

TEACH ENGLISH to Italian schoolchildren in **rural summer camps** (p. 75).

LEARN the secrets of Tuscan cuisine at a decadent **cooking course** (p. 73).

PAINT an almost-Renaissance masterpiece while studying at **art school** (p. 72).

As a tourist, you are always a foreigner. Sure, hostel-hopping and sightseeing can be great fun, but connecting with a foreign country through studying, volunteering, or working can extend your travels beyond tourist traps. We don't like to brag, but this is what's different about a *Let's Go* traveler. Instead of feeling like a stranger in a strange land, you can understand Florence like a local. Instead of being that tourist asking for directions, you can be the one who gives them (and correctly!). All the while, you get the satisfaction of leaving Italy in better shape than you found it. It's not wishful thinking—it's Beyond Tourism.

As a **volunteer** in Florence, you can roll up your sleeves, cinch down your Captain Planet belt, and get your hands dirty doing anything from farming grapes to restoring frescoes. This chapter is chock-full of ideas to get involved, whether you're looking to pitch in for a day or run away from home for a whole new life in Italian activism.

Ahh, to **study** abroad! It's a student's dream, and when you find yourself reading Dante while sipping a glass of Chianti, it actually makes you feel sorry for those poor tourists who don't get to do any homework while they're here. Florence is a study abroad mecca, and you can find classes on virtually anything art- or Italy-related. Learn how to paint like Botticelli, read Machiavelli in the original Italian, or recreate that delicious *ribollita* you had last night for dinner—all while enjoying the vibrant community of Italian and foreign students that call Florence their (perhaps temporary) home.

Working abroad is one of the best ways to immerse yourself in a new culture, meet locals, and learn to appreciate a non-US currency. Yes, we know you're on vacation, but we're not talking about normal desk jobs—we're talking about teaching conversational English or interning at a fashion house in the name of funding another month of globe-trotting. Finding jobs in Italy is notoriously difficult, even for Italians, and for non-EU citizens can be horribly frustrating. However, the prevalence of tourism in Florence means that those who speak fluent English or another foreign language can be in high demand—just keep in mind the bureaucratic and legal issues that may be involved.

SHARE YOUR EXPERIENCE. Have you had a particularly enjoyable volunteer, study, or work experience that you'd like to share with other travelers? Post it to our website, www.letsgo.com!

VOLUNTEERING

Feel like saving the world this week? Volunteering can be a powerful and fulfilling experience, especially when combined with the thrill of traveling in a new place. Italy lacks the history of a philanthropic tradition that other countries, such as the United States, have enjoyed; volunteer opportunities can be difficult to find. Most Italian volunteer programs focus on the more impoverished regions to the south of the peninsula or those devastated by the recent Abruzzo earthquake. However, a current focus on issues like immigration and healthcare have resulted in a new push for public service outlets, especially for young people. And, of course, the prevalence of Catholicism provides some opportunities for social work.

Most people who volunteer in Florence do so on a short-term basis at organizations that make use of drop-in or once-a-week volunteers. The best way to find opportunities that match your interests and schedule may be to check with a hub of the English-speaking expat community, such as the **British Institute** (P. degli Strozzi 2, ☎055 26 77 81; www.britishinstitute.it) or a Florentine organization well-known for its social work. As always, read up before heading out.

Those looking for longer, more intensive volunteer opportunities usually choose to go through a parent organization that takes care of logistical details and often provides a group environment and support system—for a fee. There are two main types of organizations—religious and secular—although there are rarely restrictions on participation for either. Websites like **www.volunteerabroad.com, www.servenet.org,** and **www.idealist.org** allow you to search for volunteer openings both in your country and abroad.

> **I HAVE TO PAY TO VOLUNTEER?** Many volunteers are surprised to learn that some organizations require large fees or "donations," but don't go calling them scams just yet. While such fees may seem ridiculous at first, they often keep the organization afloat, covering airfare, room, board, and administrative expenses for the volunteers. (Other organizations must rely on private donations and government subsidies.) If you're concerned about how a program spends its fees, request an annual report or finance account. A reputable organization won't refuse to inform you of how volunteer money is spent. Pay-to-volunteer programs might be a good idea for young travelers who are looking for more support and structure (such as pre-arranged transportation and housing) or anyone who would rather not deal with the uncertainty of creating a volunteer experience from scratch.

ECOTOURISM

The rolling hills of Tuscany, with their vineyards and olive groves, are incredibly popular destinations for expensive package ecotours. However, a savvy traveler willing to sweat a bit can find a virtually free way to enjoy the land that lies under the Tuscan sun.

Workaway.Info, (www.workaway.info). Provides listings for work and volunteer opportunities, many on farms throughout Tuscany. Volunteers are expected to work at least 5hr. a day in exchange for room and board. €18 registration fee for 2 years.

World-Wide Opportunities on Organic Farms (WWOOF Italia), V. Casavecchia 109, Castagneto Carducci 57022, Livorno (www.wwoof.it). Provides a list of organic farms that introduce volunteers to tasks like harvesting olives, grapes, and even bamboo. Knowledge of farming not necessary, although volunteers should be physically capable and willing to work hard. Many opportunities at farms and vineyards around Tuscany. Membership fee €25.

ART, CULTURE, AND RESTORATION

Florence's rich cultural heritage, which dates back to ancient Rome, is increasingly in danger of crumbling or being overrun by modern life. Art restoration volunteering played an especially prominent part in Florentine history in the aftermath of the flood of 1966 (see **Life and Times**, p. 47). Volunteers looking for a labor-intensive way to engage with Italy's historical past should research groups that specialize in landmark preservation.

Earthwatch (☎+44 18 6531 8831; www.earthwatch.org). Organizes trips for volunteers and ecotourists, including one that focuses on helping at an archeological site of a Roman villa in Pisa. UK1395 for 2 weeks, including room and board.

ResponsibleTravel.com, 3rd Floor, Pavilion House, 6 Old Steine, Brighton BN1 1EJ, UK (☎+44-127-360-0030; www.responsibletravel.com). Various volunteer opportunities including cultural and environmental preservation projects of variable length. Program fee €460-975, depending on project.

Lorenzo de'Medici, 3600 Bee Caves Rd., Austin, TX 78746, USA (☎+1-877-765-4536; www.lorenzodemedici.org), or Via Faenza 43, Florence 50123 (☎055 28 73 60). Summer programs in Florence and Tuscany with work in archaeology or art restoration. Also offers semester study abroad courses. Programs from US$1700.

YOUTH AND THE COMMUNITY

Community-based projects are among the most rewarding volunteer experiences. The programs listed below promote interactive humanitarian work through English-language programs and projects aimed at assisting the disadvantaged. Knowledge of Italian may be necessary.

Association for Intercultural Exchanges and Activities (AFSAI), Vle. dei Colli Portuensi 345 B2, Rome 00151 (☎06 53 70 332; www.afsai.it). Founded independently in 1958, AFSAI collaborates with the **European Voluntary Service (EVS) and Youth for Europe** (a work exchange program) to arrange cultural exchange and volunteer programs with homestays for Italians and non-Italians aged 16-30. Small fee for some programs.

iBO Italia, V. Montebello 46A, Ferrara 44101 (☎0532 24 32 79; www.iboitalia.org). Italian organization that places volunteers in 2-4 week work camps throughout Italy. Volunteers aid families, communities, and youth associations. Provides simple accommodations and board. 18+.

International Internship and Volunteer Network, P.O. Box 574, Largo, FL 33779, USA (☎+1-727-252-8480; www.iivnetwork.com). Volunteer and internship placements in social work, among other areas. 18+. US$1550 fee.

International Partnership for Service-Learning and Leadership, 1515 SW Fifth Ave., Suite 606, Portland, OR 97201, USA (☎+1-503-954-1812; www.ipsl.org). Study abroad program in Siena with 15-20hr. per week of volunteer work in education, healthcare, or immigrant and refugee assistance. 1 month in summer US$5750; semester $15,525.

Ireos, V. dei Serragli 3/5, Florence (☎055 21 69 07; www.ireos.org). A GLBT organization that works with public health and counseling.

VIDES, 5630 W. Commerce st., San Antonio, TX 78237, USA (☎+1-210-435-1919; www.vides.us). Catholic organization, but accepts non-Catholics open to living with a religious family. Placements in educational, developmental, and outreach services in Italian communities. Some religiously-oriented; youth ministry, for example. Free.

STUDYING

VISA INFORMATION. Italian bureaucracy often gives international visitors the run-around, but there are ways to minimize paperwork confusion. Just remember that all **non-EU citizens** are required to obtain a visa for any stay longer than three months. For info and applications, contact the Italian embassy or consulate in your country (see **Essentials, p. 9**). Before applying for a student visa, however, be sure to obtain the following documentation: valid passport, visa application form (available from most embassy websites), four passport-size photographs, proof of residency, and complete documentation on the course or program in which you are participating. If you are under the age of 18, you will also need an affidavit of financial support from parents, and your parents' most recent bank statement. All **non-EU citizens** are also required to register with the *Ufficio degli Stranieri* (Foreigners' Bureau) at the *questura* (local police headquarters) to receive a *permesso di soggiorno* (permit to stay) within eight days of arrival. The kit required to complete the *permesso di soggiorno* can be obtained and submitted at most major post offices. The same documentation is necessary for the *permesso di soggiorno* as for the visa; additionally, applicants must have the required *permesso di soggiorno* form and a *Marco da Bollo,* which costs €15 and is available at most Italian *tabaccherie*. **EU citizens** must apply for a *permesso di soggiorno* within three months, but they do not need a visa to study in Italy. Once you find a place to live, bring your *permesso di soggiorno* (it must have at least one year's validity) to a records office. This certificate will both confirm your registered address and expedite travel into and out of Italy. Make sure to check with your local Italian embassy or consulate in case visa requirements have changed recently.

It's completely natural to want to play hookey on the first day of school when it's raining and first period Trigonometry is meeting in the old cafeteria, but when your campus is Florence and your meal plan revolves around *bistecca* and *pappa al pomodoro,* what could be better than the student life?

A growing number of students report that studying abroad is the highlight of their learning careers. If you've never studied abroad, you don't know what you're missing—and, if you have studied abroad, you do know what you're missing. Study-abroad programs range from basic language and culture courses to university-level classes, often for college credit (sweet, right?). In order to choose a program that best fits your needs, research as much as you can before making your decision—determine costs and duration as well as what kinds of students participate in the program and what sorts of accommodations are provided. The diversity of classes offered in Florence is infinite—everything from an ordinary college curriculum taught in a Tuscan classroom to specialized courses in art, Italian literature, or Renaissance history.

In programs that have large groups of students who speak English, there is a trade-off. You may feel more comfortable in the community, but you will not have the same opportunity to practice a foreign language or to befriend other international students. For accommodations, dorm life provides a better opportunity to mingle with fellow students, but there is less of a chance to experience the local scene. If you live with a family, you could potentially build lifelong friendships with natives and experience day-to-day life in more depth, but you might also get stuck sharing a room with their pet iguana. Conditions can vary greatly from family to family.

UNIVERSITIES

Most university-level study-abroad programs at Florentine universities are conducted in Italian, although many programs offer classes in English as well as lower-level language courses. Savvy linguists may find it cheaper to enroll directly in a university abroad, although getting college credit may be more difficult. You can search **www.studyabroad.com** for various semester-abroad programs that meet your criteria, including your desired location and focus of study. If you're a college student, your friendly neighborhood study-abroad office is often the best place to start. Given the prevalence of available programs in Florence, make sure you shop around a bit to find one that really strikes your fancy.

AMERICAN PROGRAMS

Virtually every American university will offer some sort of study abroad program in Florence. The programs below do not limit enrollment to students of a parent organization.

American Institute for Foreign Study (AIFS), College Division, River Plaza, 9 W. Broad St., Stamford, CT 06902, USA (☎+1-800-727-2437; www.aifsabroad.com). Organizes programs and internships for high-school and college study in universities in Florence.

CET Academic Programs: Italian Studies Program in Siena, Florence, and Sicily, 1920 North St. NW, Ste. 200, Washington, D.C. 20036, USA (☎+1-800-225-4262; www.cetacademicprograms.com). Only open to the public for the summer term, this Vanderbilt University program offers art history courses and traveling seminars. Summer program US$8490-8990; includes medical insurance and housing.

Council on International Educational Exchange (CIEE), 300 Fore St., Portland, ME 04101, USA (☎+1-207-553-4000 or +1-800-407-8839; www.ciee.org). A comprehensive resource for work, academic, and internship programs in Italy. Places high school students in Italian schools for study abroad semesters.

School for International Training (SIT) Study Abroad, 1 Kipling Rd., P.O. Box 676, Brattleboro, VT 05302, USA (☎+1-888-272-7881 or 802-258-3212; www.sit.edu/studyabroad) runs **The Experiment in International Living** (☎+1-800-345-2929; www.experimentinternational.org). 3- to 5-week summer programs offer high-school students cross-cultural homestays, community service, cooking classes, ecological adventure, and language training in Italy. Many programs include portions of travel in Tuscany. US$6800, including airfare.

ITALIAN PROGRAMS

Students have been studying in Florence for centuries—after all, the *Accademia* was once an art school. If you really want to be immersed in Florentine culture, why not study it in depth by enrolling in a program that opens your eyes, ears, or stomach? A further benefit of such courses is that they will often be filled with a diverse array of Europeans—if not Italians— meaning that you'll get a bit more of a foreign experience that taking a class with a kid who grew up two towns away from you in the States.

LANGUAGE SCHOOLS

Old lady making snarky comments to you in the plaza? Impudent cashier at the *trattoria?* Cute moped girl that is totally into you? To communicate is to be human, and without the local language in your toolbelt, you're up a creek without a *pala*. Fear not! Language school here to help.

While language school courses rarely count for college credit, they do offer a unique way to get acquainted with the culture and language of Tuscany. Schools can be independently run or university affiliated, local or international, youth-oriented or full of old people—the opportunities are endless, and the city is crammed with them. Their programs are also good for high -school students who might not feel comfortable with older students in a university program. Some worthwhile organizations include:

Centro Culturale Giaccomo Puccini, V. Amerigo Vespucci 173, 55049 Viareggio (☎05 84 43 02 53; www.centropuccini.it). 2- to 24- week language courses at all levels in a Tuscan beach town. Professional Italian and cultural courses available. 16+. Additional accommodations fee for apartment or homestay. Program costs €260-2520. €70 registration fee.

Centro Fiorenza, V. Santo Spirito 14, Florence 50125 (☎055 23 98 274; www.centro-fiorenza.com). Students live in Florence and are immersed in Italian. Internship program available for advanced speakers. Program also offers courses on the island of Elba, although hotel accommodations there are expensive. 1- to 5-week course (20 lessons per week) from €200.

Eurocentres, 56 Eccleston Sq., London SW1V 1PH, UK (☎+44 20 7963 8450; www.eurocentres.com). Language programs for beginning to advanced students with homestays in Florence.

Koinè, V. de' Pandolfini 27, Florence 50122 (☎055 21 38 81; www.koinecenter.com). Language lessons (group and individual), cultural lessons, wine tastings, and cooking lessons. Courses offered in Florence, Lucca, Bologna, Cortona, and Elba. 1-4 week courses €190-4780. Accommodations not included. Deposit €150.

FINE ARTS

All those hours spent looking at Florentine art will undoubtedly stir your creativity. What better way to channel it than taking a class in drawing or sculpture? Check out the following programs for info:

Aegean Center for the Fine Arts, Paros 84400, Cyclades, Greece (☎+30 22 84 02 32 87; www.aegeancenter.org). Italian branch located in Pistoia. Instruction in arts, literature, creative writing, voice, and art history. Classes taught in English. Fees cover housing in a 16th-century villa, meals, and excursions to Rome, Venice, and Greece. University credit on individual arrangement. 14-week program in the fall €8800.

Art School in Florence, Studio Art Centers International, Palazzo dei Cartelloni, Via Sant'Antonio 11, Florence 50123 (☎+1-212-248-7225; www.saci-florence.org). Affiliated with Bowling Green State University. Studio arts, art history, Italian studies. Apartment housing. 6 credits summer US$5550; 15 credits semester US$14,900.

CULINARY SCHOOLS

Fearing Italian food withdrawal? These classes will make your returning home a little less unbearable and teach you all about the diversity of Tuscan cuisine and agriculture.

Apicius, The Culinary Institute of Florence, V. Guelfa 85, Florence 50129 (☎055 26 58 135; www.apicius.it). Professional and non-professional food and wine studies in historic Florence. Cooking courses in English; Italian-language classes available. Prices for weekly non-professional programs €1265-5750; includes room and board. Masters in Italian cuisine €10,550. Enrollment fee €120.

Cook Italy (☎34 90 07 82 98; www.cookitaly.com). Region- or dish-specific cooking classes. Venues include Bologna, Cortona, Florence, Lucca, Rome, and Sicily. Courses 3- to 6- nights from €1250; housing, meals, and recipes included.

Organic Tuscany, Localita Pino, Certaldo (FI) 50052, Italy (☎03 47 32 89 333 in Italy, +1-347-417-5907 in the US; www.organictuscany.com). Cooking classes in the Tuscan countryside, plus excursions to surrounding towns and tastings of local produce. Some courses are vegetarian. 1-week course €1400.

The International Kitchen, 330. N. Wabash #2613, Chicago, IL 60611, USA (☎+1-800-945-8606; www.theinternationalkitchen.com). A leading provider of cooking school vacations to Italy. Traditional cooking instruction in beautiful settings for individuals and groups. Program locations include the Amalfi Coast, Liguria, Tuscany, and Venice. Courses 2-10 nights; 1-day classes also available. Programs start at US$220.

WORKING

We haven't yet found money growing on trees, but we do have a team of dedicated Researchers looking high and low. In the meantime, Florence is filled with great opportunities to earn a living and travel at the same time. As with volunteering, work opportunities tend to fall into two categories. Some travelers want long-term jobs that allow them to integrate into a community, while others seek out short-term jobs to finance the next leg of their travels. In Italy, short-term work in agriculture, the service sector, and tourism is the easiest to come by. Though job hunters must navigate the inevitable challenge of Italy's soaring unemployment rates and the premium that Italian employers place on both practical experience and advanced degrees, take heart: with a little research in advance, long-term opportunities are not out of the realm of possibility. **Transitions Abroad** (www.transitionsabroad.com) and **Jobs Abroad** (www.jobsabroad.com) offer far more updated online listings for work over any time span than we could possibly list here.

Check out weekly job listings in *Corriere della Sera*'s **Corriere Lavoro** (online at trovolavoro.it) or *Il Sole 24 Ore*'s **Cercolavoro Giovani,** which specializes in listings for recent university graduates. **GoAbroad.com** (www.internabroad.com/Italy.cfm) has a user-friendly online database of internship listings in Italy. Youth Info Centers' **Informagiovani** (www.informagiovani-italia.com) in each region target both Italians and visitors and offer free information on work regulations, employment trends, volunteer programs, and study opportunities.

MORE VISA INFORMATION. Working legally in Italy as a foreigner is a bureaucratic challenge regardless of your nationality. **EU passport holders** do not require a special visa to live or work in Italy. They do require a permit to stay *(permesso di soggiorno per lavoro)*, which grants permission to remain in Italy for the duration of employment. To obtain a *permesso di soggiorno*, EU citizens must register at the local police headquarters *(questura)* within eight days of arrival for a permit to search for work *(ricevuta di segnalazione di soggiorno)*. **Non-EU citizens** seeking work in Italy must possess an Italian work permit *(autorizzazione al lavoro in Italia)* before entering the country. Only a prospective employer can begin the process, guaranteeing that the individual has been offered a position. Permits are authorized by the Provincial Employment Office and approved by the police headquarters before being forwarded to the employer and prospective employee. The prospective employee must then present the document, along with a valid passport, in order to obtain a work visa. **Non-EU citizens** must also obtain both the *permesso di soggiorno* and a workers' registration card *(libretto di lavoro)* which will function as an employment record for up to ten years. Visit the **Italian Ministry of Foreign Affairs** website (www.esteri.it) or the **US Embassy** site (http://italy.usembassy.gov) for more information.

LONG-TERM WORK

If you're planning on spending a substantial amount of time (more than 3 months) working in Florence, search for a job well in advance. International placement agencies are often the easiest way to find employment abroad, especially for those interested in teaching. Although they are often only available to college students, **internships** are a good way to ease into working abroad. Many students say the interning experience is well worth it, despite low pay (if you're lucky enough to get paid at all). Be wary of advertisements for companies offering to get you a job abroad for a fee—often times, these same listings are available online or in newspapers. Many of the reputable organizations below also offer study abroad (p. 70) programs.

Center for Cultural Interchange, 746 N. LaSalle Dr., Chicago, IL 60610, USA (☎+1-312-944-2544; www.cci-exchange.com/abroad/intern.shtml). 1-3 month volunteer internships in Florence. Opportunities in business, accounting and finance, tourism, and social service. 20+. At least 2 years of college-level Italian required. US$7090-10,590. Tuition includes Italian language course, health insurance, and homestay with half-board.

English Yellow Pages, V. Belisario 4/B, 00187 Rome (☎06 47 40 861 or 97 61 75 28; www.englishyellowpages.it). Resources for English-speaking expats in Italy run by an American who relocated to Italy in 1982 to teach English. Includes job listings, classifieds, photos, blogs, and more.

Global Experiences, 168 West St., Annapolis, MD 21401, USA (☎+1-877-432-27623; www.globalexperiences.com). Arranges internships with companies in Florence. Fields include law, international business, tourism, graphic design, and fashion. 10-week programs start at €4950 and include intensive language training, accommodation, emergency medical travel insurance, and full-time on-site support.

Institute for the International Education of Students, 33 N. LaSalle St., 15th fl., Chicago, IL 60602, USA (☎+1-800-995-2300; www.iesabroad.org). Internships for academic credit in Siena based on availability, background, skills, and language ability. Past assignments in fashion, photography, journalism, business consulting, museum studies, and psychological research. Semester-long programs from around US$17,000. Includes tuition for up to 19 credits, orientation, housing, and medical insurance.

World Endeavors, 3015 E. Franklin Ave., Minneapolis, MN 55406, USA (☎+1-866-802-9678; www.worldendeavors.com/Italy). 3- to 6-month internships in Florence in a wide variety of fields from craft apprenticeships to sports management with professional football teams. 3-month internships from US$4650 include intensive Italian training and various English-speaking support services.

TEACHING ENGLISH

While some elite private American schools offer competitive salaries, let's just say that teaching jobs abroad pay more in personal satisfaction and emotional fulfillment than in actual cash. Perhaps this is why volunteering as a teacher instead of getting paid is a popular option. Even then, teachers often receive some sort of a daily stipend to help with living expenses. In almost all cases, you must have at least a bachelor's degree to be a full-fledged teacher, although college undergraduates can often get summer positions teaching or tutoring. Though the demand for English teachers in Italy is high, the competition is stiff. Finding a teaching job as a non-EU citizen can be especially tough. Beyond the usual difficulty of obtaining permits, many language schools require EU citizenship and most prefer British citizens to other English speakers.

Many schools require teachers to have a **Teaching English as a Foreign Language (TEFL)** certificate. You may still be able to find a teaching job without one, but certified teachers often find higher-paying jobs. Some schools within Italy that grant TEFLs will even offer both classroom instruction and practical experience or a leg up in job placement when you earn your certificate. The Italian-impaired don't have to give up their dream of teaching, either. Private schools usually hire native English speakers for English-immersion classrooms where no Italian is spoken. (Teachers in public schools will more likely work in both English and Italian.) Placement agencies or university fellowship programs are the best resources for finding teaching jobs. The alternative is to contact schools directly or to try your luck once you arrive in Italy. In the latter case, the best time to look is several weeks before the start of the school year, or as early as February or March for summer positions. The following organizations are extremely helpful in placing teachers in Italy.

Associazione Culturale Linguistica Educational (ACLE), V. Roma 54, San Remo 18038, Imperio (☎01 84 50 60 70; www.acle.org). Non-profit association working to bring theater, arts, and English language instruction to Italian schools. Employees create theater programs in schools, teach English at summer camps, and help convert a medieval home into a student art center. Knowledge of Italian useful. On-site accommodations and cooking facilities included. Ages 20-30. Camp counselor salary of €220-260 per week.

International Schools Services (ISS), 15 Roszel Rd., P.O. Box 5910, Princeton, NJ 08543, USA (☎+1-609-452-0990; www.iss.edu). Hires teachers for more than 200 overseas schools, including occasionally in Italy. Candidates should have teaching experience and a bachelor's degree. 2-year commitment is the norm.

Office of Overseas Schools, US Department of State, 2201 C St. NW, Washington, D.C. 20520, USA (☎+1-202-647-4000; www.state.gov/m/a/os). Provides an extensive list of general info about teaching overseas. See also the **Office of English Language Programs** (http://exchanges.state.gov/education/engteaching).

BEYOND TOURISM

AU PAIR WORK

Au pairs are typically women (although sometimes men) aged 18-27 who work as live-in nannies, caring for children and doing light housework in foreign countries in exchange for room, board, and a small spending allowance or stipend. One perk of the job is that it allows you to get to know Italy without the high expenses of traveling. Drawbacks, however, can include mediocre pay and long hours. Unfortunately, with the recent adoption of laws that severely limit the availability of work visas for non-EU citizens in Italy, au pairing has become less common, especially for stays longer than 3 months (the maximum visa-free visiting period). The Italian government will not grant au pair-specific visas so it is imperative that au pairs take necessary steps with prospective employers to obtain work permits and visas (see **More Visa Information, p. 74**). In Italy, average weekly pay for au pair work is about €65. Much of the au pair experience depends on the family with which you are placed. The agencies below are a good starting point for looking for employment.

Childcare International, Trafalgar House, Grenville Pl., London NW7 3SA, UK (☎+44 20 8906 3116; www.childint.co.uk).

InterExchange, 161 6th Ave., New York City, NY 10013, USA (☎+1-212-924-0446 or 800-AU-PAIRS/287-2477; www.interexchange.org).

Roma Au Pair, V. Pietro Mascagni 138, Rome 00199 (☎33 97 79 41 26; www.romaaupair.it). Provides information on and listings for au pair placement throughout Italy, though generally in Rome.

SHORT-TERM WORK

Believe it or not, traveling for long periods of time can be hard on the wallet. Many travelers try their hand at odd jobs for a few weeks at a time to help pay for another month or two of touring around. Romantic images of cultivating the land in a sun-soaked vineyard may dance in your head, but in reality, casual agricultural jobs are hard to find in Italy due to the prevalence of foreign migrant workers who are often willing to work for minimal pay. Those looking for agricultural jobs will have the best luck looking in the northwest during the annual fall harvest or volunteer with **WWOOF** (p. 68). Another popular option is to work several hours a day at a hostel in exchange for free or discounted room and/or board. Most often, these short-term jobs are found by word of mouth or by expressing interest to the owner of a hostel or restaurant. Due to high turnover in the tourism industry, many places are eager for help, even if it is only temporary.

Italian with a French Accent

Spring semester of my junior year, I studied in the Middlebury program in Florence. I felt out of place from the start. College-bound students in Italy don't apply to scores of universities across the peninsula; instead, they attend their local universities and continue to live with their parents. At lunchtime, they either return home or find a cafe where they smoke and eat with childhood friends. As an American and a non-smoker, I did not fit in. It didn't help that my still-unsteady speech pattern made me reluctant even to try weaving myself into these long-established traditions and friend groups. As for academics, since I was an art history major I decided that a class on Gentile da Fabriano, an Italian Renaissance painter, would be a safe and enjoyable bet for my mandatory Italian-only class. I was only partially wrong.

Although my professor was Italian, I could barely understand him. I had spent the past two months learning the nuances of Tuscan accents—the soft ci and the 'h' in lieu of 'c'—in anticipation of dialectic-heavy instruction. Unfortunately for me, my professor was from Brescia, in Northern Italy. His 'r's rolled in unfamiliar places and he spoke from the back of this throat instead of the front of his mouth. Was he speaking with a French accent? Or, as I believed during particularly incomprehensible monologues, was it actually French in an Italian accent?

Ironically, he was the professor who enabled me to participate in Italian student life. Given the aforementioned insular nature of Italian universities, the students were expecting a Tuscan. They weren't used to hearing his accent either. I saw them pause over words or look over to their neighbors' notes just as often as I was lunging for my pocket dictionary. They also, as I learned from watching a never-ending rotation of students, rarely attended class, since our grades depended entirely on a single final. Emboldened by our shared plight, I offered my dutifully-acquired notes to some of the girls I had become friendly with. In return for my messy, sometimes-indecipherable compendium, they volunteered to prepare me for the final: a terrifying individual oral exam conducted in Italian. During the test, I would stand in front of the professor and answer whatever questions he posed on themes, dates or names. I would get my grade on the spot and, if I was unhappy with it, I could sign up to take it again. This is standard in Italy.

Although this ability is almost unheard of in America, it was another aspect that I found daunting and unfair. Any student can sit in on the exam, watching his compatriot flourish or founder. The interloper can gain insight about materials covered and questions asked, while also acting as intimidating audience for the student at the front.

" ...they volunteered to prepare me for the final: a terrifying individual oral exam"

Despite my initial fears, the course ended spectacularly. After the exam, my professor complimented my speaking ability. Although I'm proud of my hard-earned academic and linguistic accomplishments, I am prouder of how I navigated the Italian university system, making friends along the way. I am also delighted that I was not the most foreign person in the room; apparently, over the course of a semester, I had become more Florentine than I realized. It was the Northern professor with the rolling 'r's who was out of place in the class, not me. I don't think he minded, either.

Antonia Devine graduated from Princeton University in 2008 with a BA in Art and Archaeology and a certificate in Italian. She works in New York as a junior architect and plans to pursue a Masters in Architecture. Along the way, she'd like to return to Italy to "study" the food, art and culture.

PRACTICAL INFORMATION

TOURIST AND FINANCIAL SERVICES

TOURIST OFFICES

Informazione Turistica provides information in major foreign languages on tourist attractions, events, directions, available tours, and general emergency information. Offices are run through the **City of Florence, the Comune di Firenze,** and the **Agenzia per il Turismo di Firenze.** At P. Della Stazione 4 (☎055 21 22 45; turisimo3@comune.fi.it), across the *piazza* from the station's main exit. Open M-Sa 8:30-7pm, Su and holidays 8:30am-2pm. At Borgo Santa Croce 29r (☎055 23 40 444; turismo2@comune.fi.it). Open Mar.-Oct. M-Sa 9am-7pm, Su and holidays 9am-2pm; Nov.-Feb. M-Sa 9am-5pm, Su and holidays 9am-2pm. At V. Cavour 1r (☎055 29 08 32; infoturismo@provincia.fi.it). At Amerigo Vespucci Airport (☎055 31 58 74). Open daily 8:30am-8:30pm. At V. Manzoni 16 (☎055 23 320; info@firenzeturismo.it). Open M-F 9am-1pm.

AUDIO GUIDES

Walking Tour Shop, V. dei Cimatori (☎055 215 358), on the corner of P. De' Cerchi. Open daily 9am-6pm. €12 for 1½hr.

BUDGET TRAVEL

Centro Turistico Student and Youth, V. Borgo La Croce 42r (☎055 28 95 70; www.cts.it). Transalpino tickets and ISICs available. Open M-F 9:30am-1pm and 2:30-6pm, Sa 9:30am-12:30pm. MC/V. Branch at V. Maragliano 86 (☎055 33 41 64). Open M-F 9-1pm and 3-7pm, Sa 10am-1pm.

CONSULATES

UK, Lungarno Corsini 2 (☎055 28 41 33; www.ukinitaly.fco.gov.uk). Open M-F 9:30am-12:30pm and 2:30-4:30pm. **US,** Lungarno Amerigo Vespucci 38 (☎055 26 69 51; www.florence.usconsulate.gov). For more info, see **Essentials,** p. 10.

LOCAL SERVICES

LUGGAGE STORAGE AND LOST PROPERTY

Luggage Storage (☎055 23 52 190). At the far end of the train station, beside platform 16, toward the bus depot. €4 for 1st 5hr., €0.60 per hr. 6-12hr., €0.20 per hr. thereafter; max. 5 days. Must present identification. Open daily 6am-midnight. Cash only.

Ufficio Oggetti Rinvenuti(☎055 23 56 120), next to the baggage deposit in train station. **City Council Lost Property Office,** V. Circondaria 19 (☎055 32 83 942 or 32 83 943), holds all property handed in at Police Headquarters, Carabinieri, and Railway Police Offices. Inqui-

TYPES OF PASTA

No food screams "Italy!" louder than pasta. Italians, on average, consume over 60 pounds of pasta every year. Embrace the carbs and indulge in these noodles:

1. Acomo pepe: Italian for "pepper corn," this tiny bread-shaped pasta is well worth your hard-earned dough.

2. Fettucine: Many versions contain eggs, but true Italian fettucine is egg free.

3. Farfalle: Ordinarily, butterflies in your stomach provide an undesirable sensation, but in this case you might want to make an exception. Meaning "butterflies" in Italian, this medium-sized pasta is crimped to resemble a bow-tie.

4. Gnocchi: These small dumplings are either made from a mix of potato and flour or semolina.

5. Capelli d'Angelo: Derived from the Latin word for hair, this heavenly pasta is known as Angel Hair in the United States.

6. Capellini: Like Angel's Hair, but cut from an angel on Rogaine.

7. Gemelli: Meaning "twins" in Italian, some find this twisted pasta twice as nice as its competitors.

8. Vermicelli: Derived from the Latin *verme*, meaning worms. Give this thin, round pasta a try before the *vermes* get a shot at you!

9. Penne Rigate: From the Latin word for feathers, a worthwhile feather in your cap (or stomach).

10. Spaghetti: Last but not least, this most famous of pastas comes for the Italian word for strings.

ries about property left in taxis should first be made at the urban police offices and then at the City Council Offices.

ENGLISH-LANGUAGE BOOKSTORES

Feltrinelli International Bookstore, V. Cavour 12 (☎055 29 21 96). Open M-Sa 9am-7:30pm. Via de'Cerretani 30/32r (☎055 23 82 652). Open M-F 9:30am-8pm, Sa 10am-8pm, Su 10:30am-1:30pm and 3-6:30pm. A large chain with an equally large selection. MC/V.

Mel Bookstore, V. de'Cerretani 16r (☎055 28 73 39). The English language selection and the long hours make this location one of your best bets for finding something other than our travel guide to read on the train. Open M-F 9am–midnight and Su 10am-midnight.

Paperback Exchange, V. delle Oche 4r (☎055 28 73 39; www.papex.it). Probably the best selection of children's books in English. In addition to both fiction and nonfiction bestsellers, the store also has an eclectic, ever-changing selection of used books fun to hunt through. Trade-ins welcome. Open M-F 9am-7:30pm and Sa 10:30am-7:30pm.

Edison, P. della Repubblica 27r (☎055 21 31 10; www.libreriaedison.it). The usual selection of travel guides and fiction. Open M-Sa 9am-midnight, Su 10am-midnight.

BM, Borgo Ognissanti 4r (☎055 29 45 75). A host of more unique guidebooks, tailored to special interests like shopping or cuisine, and a wide fiction selection that includes mysteries, sci-fi, and bestsellers. 20% discount on all books by American or English publishers. Open M-Sa 9:30am-7:30pm. AmEx/MC/V.

LAUNDROMATS

Wash and Dry (☎055 58 04 480; www.washedry.it). Self-service locations throughout the city. Wash and dry €3.50 each. Detergent €1. **Branches:** V. dei Servi 105r, V. della Scala 52/54r, V. del Sole 29r, Borgo San Frediano 39r, Via dei Serragli 87r, V. Nazionale 129r, V. Ghibellina 143r, V. Dell'Agnolo 21r.

PUBLIC TOILETS

Available throughout the city for a fee (€0.60). **Santa Maria Novella Station,** open daily 8am-8pm. V. della Stufa 25; open daily Nov.-Mar. 10am-8pm, Apr.-Oct. 9am-10pm. **Borgo Santa Croce 29r,** open daily Nov.-Mar. 10am-8pm, Apr. 1-Oct. 31 9am-10pm. **Central Market,** V. dell' Ariento 14, open daily 2-7:30pm. **Ple. Michelangelo,** Vle. Galiliei, open daily 10am-10pm. **V. dello Sprone,** open daily Nov.-Mar. 10am-8pm, Apr.-Oct. 9am-10pm. **V. San Augustine 8,** open M-F 10-1pm and 3-7pm, Sa-Su 9am-2pm. **Piazza Ghiberti,** inside Mercato Sant'Ambrogio, open 7am-2pm.

GYMS

Palestra Ricciardi, Borgo Pinti 75 (☎055 24 78 444; www.palestraricciardi.it). Cardio and fitness rooms, plus classes like yoga, spinning, and pilates. Check website for class schedules. Open M-F 8am-10pm, Sa 9:30am-6pm, Su 10am-2:30pm.

Fit Village Studio, V. il Prato 40r (☎055 23 82 138; www.fitvillagestudio.com) and **Fit Village Tribu',** V. Caccini 13A (☎055 43 60 479). Both offer a huge variety of classes, 1 nearly every hr. 10am-9pm, in styles as varied as yoga, salsa, pilates, and hip-hop. Fit Village Tribu' has a wider selection, but is very far from the center. Check the website for schedules for both locations.

THE ITALIAN KEYBOARD. You'll find yourself using an Italian keyboard at some point during your journey, and you'll notice that the keyboard has some oddities. Here's a brief guide to the important absentees:

@: Located at the lower right-hand corner of the ç key. Press that key and the right-hand ALT key at the same time to get @.

': Ever important in English contractions, the apostrophe is located on the question mark key on Italian keyboards, in the uppermost row.

#: In case you're quantifying on your computer, this symbol is located on directly to the right of the ç/@ key. You'll notice that it's also located in the right-hand corner of that key. Therefore, do the same thing that you did with @–hold down the key and right-hand ALT at the same time.

Tropos, V. Orcagna 20A (☎055 67 83 81; www.troposfirenze.it). An extremely sleek and luxurious fitness center with gym, classes, pool, and spa. Open M-F 8am-10pm, Sa 8am-8pm, Su 9am-1pm.

BIKE RENTALS

Alinari Rental, V. San Zenobi 38r (☎055 28 05 00; www.alinarirental.com). Motorcycles €21-31 per hr., €45-55 per 5hr., €65-75 per day. Scooters €10-15/25-35/30-55 and €75-125 per weekend. Bicycles €3/7-13/12-18/24-36 and €45-80 per week.

Florence by Bike, V. San Zenobi 120r (☎055 48 89 92; www.florencebybike.it). Bicycles, scooters, and motorcycles by the day (from €14.50, €68, and €99, respectively). Also offers a bike tour of the city center. Open Apr.-Oct. daily 9am-7:30pm, Nov.-Mar. M-Sa 9am-1pm and 3:30-7:30pm.

I Bike Florence, V. de' Lamberti 1 (☎055 01 23 994; www.ibikeflorence.com). Hosts daily bike tours of Florence (€29) and the surrounding Chianti region (€70 on a bike, €120 on a scooter).

CAR RENTALS

In addition to numerous options at the airport, there are some locations nearer to the city center.

Avis, V. Borgognissanti 128r (☎055 21 36 29; www.avis.com). Open M-Sa 8am-7pm, Su 8am-1pm.

Hertz, V. Masso Finiguerra 33 (☎055 23 98 205; www.hertz.com). Open from mid-Mar. to Nov. M-Sa 8am-7pm, Su 8am-1pm; from Dec. to mid-Mar. M-F 8am-7pm, Sa 8am-2pm, Su 8am-1pm.

Thrifty, V. Borgognissanti 134r (☎055 28 71 61; www.thrifty.it). Open M-Sa 8:30am-7pm.

LIBRARIES

Biblioteca Berenson, V. dei Vincigliata 26 (☎055 60 32 51; www.itatti.it), at the Harvard University Center for Italian Renaissance Studies, in the Villa I Tatti. This glorious library houses a collection of materials on late Middle Ages to Renaissance Italy. Unfortunately, it is only open to current and former I Tatti appointees, or those holding at least a

A DAMPER ON THE INTERWEBS

Even more terrifying than leaving your comfort zone when traveling abroad can be leaving your wireless zone. In 2005, officials in Italy made that leap of faith a bit more difficult when they began requiring legal identification of all public internet users. As part of an anti-terror law, public internet access providers at bars, cafes, and other internet points are required to keep photo copies of IDs and have tracking software, which logs the sites visited. Though Italians seem relatively unfazed by the rule, for web-starved tourists this means more passport-touting and a nearly impossible search to find free wireless hotspots.

Further legislation in the country requires all blogs to register with the state, and a series of laws has attempted to keep the freedom of the ·net under lock. One case by the Italian state against torrent site The Pirate Bay requested that all internet service providers block the site, and funnel traffic through a site run by the major record labels. Another case involved pressing criminal charges against Google after a questionable video on Youtube.

While the US has birthed internet staples, Italy has certainly illustrated its tough side regarding the perils of the interweb. Thus, despite the recent partnership between America and Italy in the car industry, a race on the information superhighway would be no contest.

Master's degree or equivalent. Written requests can be made for exceptions. Open Sept.-July M-F 9am-6pm.

Biblioteca Nazionale Centrale di Firenze, P. dei Cavalleggeri 1 (☎055 24 91 91; www.bncf.firenze.sbn. it). The main public library in Florence since the 18th century. A vast collection of scholarly works, rare manuscripts, and periodicals, plus a variety of consultation services. You can apply for a tessera *utente* or a *tessera visitazione* (the latter gives you consultation access only). "Tourist" visits are not allowed, but reservations for guided group tours are. Open M-F 8:15am-7pm, Sa 8:15am-1:30pm. Collections and rooms have differing hours, call or check website for details.

Children's Lending Library, in the American church on V. B. Rucellai 9 (☎032 83 28 27 57). If you really need to get your hands on a comforting copy of *Harry Potter,* this is the place to go. Collection of books for children 16 and under. Open M 11am-noon, W 11am-1:30pm and 4-6pm, Su 10am-1pm.

Harold Acton Library, at the British Institute of Florence, Lungarno Guicciardini 9 (☎055 26 77 82 70; www.britishinstitute.it). Stunning collection of books in both English and Italian, specializing in history, art, music, and literature. Also contains an extensive selection of periodicals, mostly British or Italian. Memberships €20 for 1 month; €40 for 3 months, students €35; €65/50 for 1 year. Open Sept.-July M-F 10am-6:30pm.

GLBT RESOURCES

Arcigay (☎05 16 49 30 55; www.arcigay.it). Head office in Bologna. Available in English. One of the oldest and largest GLBT organizations in Italy. Extensive information on resources, events, and GLBT-friendly establishments. The regional office for Tuscany is found at www.arcigay.it/toscana (in Italian).

Azione Gay e Lesbica Firenze, V. Pisana 32 (☎055 22 02 50; www.azionegayelesbica.it). Exclusively Florence-focused. Provides information on the GLBT scene in the city. Hosts parties, festivals, exhibitions, and film screenings. Open M, Tu, Th 6-8pm.

Ireos, V. dei Serragli 3 (☎055 21 69 07; www.ireos.org). Involved in the health, culture, and well-being of the Florentine GLBT community. Library/resource center. Helps to host events throughout the city. Phone counseling. Psychiatric counseling Tu and F by appointment, and free, anonymous HIV tests once a month with counseling (6-7:30pm; call for appointment). Open M-Th 6-8pm, W 11am-1pm.

WOMEN'S RESOURCES

Artemisia, V. del Mezzetta 1/interiore (adult women ☎055 60 23 11, minors ☎055 60 13 75; www.

artemisiacentroantiviolenza.it). Social, psychological, and legal counseling as well as group therapy for victims of physical and psychological abuse.

Libreria delle Donne, V. Fiesolana 26 (☎055 24 03 84). Feminist bookstore specializing in works on lesbianism, gender theory, history of women, and books by female authors. Also hosts events and has info on women's groups throughout the city. Open M 4-8pm, Tu-F 9:30am-1pm and 4-8pm.

EMERGENCY AND COMMUNICATIONS

EMERGENCY NUMBERS

Emergency: ☎113 or ☎055 31 80 00

Police: Tourist Police, Ufficio Stranieri, V. Zara 2 (☎055 49 771). For visa or work-permit problems. Open M-F 9:30am-1pm. To report lost or stolen items, go around the corner to **Ufficio Denunce,** V. Duca d'Aosta 3 (☎055 49 771). Open M-Sa 8am-8pm.

Municipal Police: ☎055 32 831, in emergency ☎055 32 85.

Fire Station: ☎115 or 055 24 18 41.

PHARMACIES

Farmacia Comunale (☎055 28 94 35), by track 16 at the train station.

Molteni, V. dei Calzaiuoli 7r (☎055 28 94 90).

All'Insegna del Moro, P. San Giovanni 20r. All open 24hr. AmEx/MC/V.

MEDICAL SERVICES

Tourist Medical Services, V. Lorenzo il Magnifico 59 (☎055 47 54 11). English-, German-, and French-speaking doctors with 70 specialists. In P. Duomo (☎055 21 22 21). Open M-F 8am-8pm, doctors on-call 24hr.

Ospedale Santa Maria Nuova, P. Santa Maria Nuova 1 (☎055 27 581), near the Duomo.

INTERNET ACCESS

Internet Train, V. Guelfa 54/56 (☎055 26 45 146), V. dell'Oriolo 40r (☎055 26 38 968), Borgo San Jacopo 30r (☎055 265 7935), V. Giacomini 9 (☎055 50 31 647), V. de'Benci 36r (☎055 26 38 555), V. Alamanni 5a (☎055 28 69 92), V. Porta Rossa 38r (☎055 27 41 037), Lungarno B. Cellini 43r (☎055 38 30 921). Over 26 €4.30 per hr., under 26 €3.20 per hr. Wi-Fi €2.50 per hr. Open daily 10am-10:30pm.

POST OFFICE

V. Pellicceria 3 (☎055 27 36 480), off P. della Repubblica. Open M-F 8:15am-7pm, Sa 8:15am-12:30pm. **Postal Code:** 50100.

PRACTICAL INFORMATION

ACCOMMODATIONS

ACCOMMODATIONS BY PRICE

UNDER €30 (❶)

Alekin Hostel (p. 88)	PDS
Campeggio Michelangelo (p. 95)	EO
▓Holiday Rooms (p. 90)	SL
Hostel AF19 (p. 87)	Duomo
Hostel Veronique (p. 88)	PDS
Hotel Benvenuti (p. 93)	SM
▓Ostello Archi Rossi (p. 90)	SL
Ostello Santa Monaca (p. 94)	WO
Pensione La Scala (p. 89)	SMN
Soggiorno Prestipino (p. 87)	PDS

€30-45 (❷)

Albergo Sampaoli (p. 93)	SM
Florence Room Bed & Breakfast (p. 89)	SMN
Hotel Anna's (p. 91)	SL
Hotel Armonia (p. 91)	SL
Hotel Crocini (p. 88)	SMN
Hotel Dali (p. 87)	Duomo
Hotel Duca d'Aosta (p. 88)	SMN
Hotel Garden (p. 89)	SMN
Hotel Joli (p. 89)	SMN
Hotel San Marco (p. 92)	SM
Hotel Tina (p. 92)	SM
Hotel Varsavia (p. 88)	SMN
Leonardo House (p. 88)	PDS
Locanda Gallo (p. 93)	SM
Locanda Giovanna (p. 91)	SL
Pensione Ferretti (p. 87)	PDS
▓Soggiorno Luna Rossa (p. 90)	SL
Soggiorno Magliani (p. 92)	SM

€46-60 (❸)

Albergo Margaret (p. 88)	SMN
Albergo Universo (p. 89)	SMN
C.S.D.—Gould Institute (p. 94)	WO
▓Hotel Abaco (p. 88)	SMN
Hotel Aldini (p. 87)	Duomo
Hotel Ariston (p. 94)	SC
Hotel Bigallo (p. 86)	Duomo
Hotel Bijou (p. 89)	SMN

€46-60 CON'T

Hotel Cimabue (p. 93)	SM
▓Hotel Consigli (p. 88)	SMN
Hotel Deco (p. 92)	SL
Hotel Desirée (p. 88)	SMN
Hotel Giappone (p. 89)	SMN
Hotel Leonardo da Vinci (p. 89)	SMN
Hotel Lombardia (p. 92)	SL
▓Hotel Medici (p. 86)	Duomo
Hotel Monica (p. 91)	SL
Hotel Montreal (p. 89)	SMN
Hotel Panorama (p. 93)	SM
Hotel Patrizia (p. 89)	SMN
Hotel Serena (p. 89)	SMN
Hotel Toscana (p. 88)	PDS
Locanda degli Artisti (p. 91)	SL
▓Locanda Orchidea (p. 86)	Duomo
Ninna Nanna Bed & Breakfast (p. 91)	SL
Pensione Maria Luisa de'Medici (p. 87) Duomo	
Sognando Firenze Bed & Breakfast (p. 95)	EO
Tourist House (p. 89)	SMN
Vasari Palace Hotel (p. 92)	SL

€61-75 (❹)

Hotel Arizona (p. 94)	SC
Hotel Boboli (p. 94)	WO
Il Porcellino Tourist House (p. 87)	PDS
Tourist House Battistero (p. 91)	SL
Tourist House Duomo (p. 92)	SL

OVER €75 (❺)

Albergo Merlini (p. 91)	SL
Casa Guidi (p. 94)	WO
▓Hotel Bretagna (p. 87)	PDS
Hotel Gioia (p. 93)	SM
Hotel Il Perseo (p. 87)	Duomo
Hotel La Scaletta (p. 94)	WO
Hotel Mario's (p. 90)	SL
Hotel Porta Faenza (p. 92)	SL
Hotel Villa Liberty (p. 95)	EO
▓Relais Cavalcanti (p. 87)	PDS

EO = East Oltrarno	SM = San Marco
PDS = Piazza della Signoria	SMN = Santa Maria Novella
SC = Santa Croce	WO = West Oltrarno
SL = San Lorenzo	

Because of the constant stream of tourists, it is best to reserve a room at least 10 days ahead, especially for visits in the summer or during Easter. Not only will this save you from a night stranded at the train station, but it will also save you from unnecessary expenses; many establishments up their prices as the number of available rooms decreases. Most *pensioni*(boarding houses) prefer reservations in writing with at least one night's deposit; others simply ask for a phone confirmation.

To avoid unlisted service fees, don't book reservations over the internet. The best prices are almost always obtained directly from hotel owners, and haggling works at smaller establishments. Florence has so many budget accommodations that it's usually possible to find a room without a reservation, but last-minute options are often of a lower quality. Hotel owners are typically willing to suggest alternatives if their establishments are full, so don't hesitate to ask. Complaints should be lodged with the **Tourist Rights Protection Desk,** V. Cavour 1r (☎055 29 08 32/33; open M-Sa 8:30am-6:30pm, Su 8:30am-1:30pm.) or the **Servizio Turismo,** V. Alessandro Manzoni 16 (☎055 23 320; uff.turismo@provincia.fi.it. Open M-F 9am-1pm).

The city strictly regulates hotel prices via a one-to-five star system, so look for the green "*albergo*" sign outside of an accommodation to see its ranking. Proprietors must charge within the approved range for their category and must also post these rates in a place visible to guests. Most places will pin these rates behind the reception desk, but some establishments choose to post them on their website, and so be aware that the "maximum price" listed on some establishment's websites may refer to the legal limit on price, and not to any amount ever actually charged for a room. For **long-term housing** in Florence, check bulletin boards; classified ads in *La Pulce*, published three times weekly (€2); or *Grillo Fiorentino*, a free monthly paper. Reasonable prices range €500-2000 per month.

ACCOMMODATIONS BY AREA

THE DUOMO

"Budget" is a relative term in the area near the Duomo, where surprisingly scarce accommodations are usually squeezed between upscale stores and tourist-trap restaurants. Anything in the student price range that isn't a hostel will probably be low on amenities, but the location and the views in this neighborhood are unbeatable.

- ▨ **Locanda Orchidea,** Borgo degli Albizi 11 (☎055 24 80 346; www.hotelorchideaflorence.it). Turn left off V. Proconsolo from the Duomo. Dante's wife was born in this 12th-century *palazzo*. Rooms have marble floors and famous Renaissance prints. Clean shared baths. Singles €55; doubles €75; triples with shower €90-100; quads €120. Cash only. ❸

- ▨ **Hotel Medici,** V. dei Medici 6 (☎055 28 48 18). A 6-story student favorite. Top-floor terrace looks out over unbelievable views of the Duomo and Campanile. Breakfast included; we recommend dining on the aforementioned terrace. No A/C. Singles €50; doubles €75; quads €100. MC/V. ❸

- **Hotel Bigallo,** Vicolo degli Adimari 2 (☎055 21 60 86; www.hotelbigallo.it). Sumptuous furnishings and an unbeatable location beside the Baptistery make this the Hotel Savoy of the budget-savvy. Each room equipped with satellite TV, mini-bar, and A/C. Some rooms have views of the Duomo. Breakfast included. Internet €5 per hr. Doubles €60. Cash only. ❸

Hostel AF19, V. Ricasoli 9 (☎055 23 98 665; www.academyhostels.com). A bright and spacious hostel with multi-floor suites and a location literally steps from the Duomo. A/C. Safety lockers. Laundry €5. Free Wi-Fi in the lobby. Lockout 11am-2pm. 2- to 6-bed dorms €28-36. Cash preferred. AmEx/MC/V. ❶

Hotel Il Perseo, V. de'Cerretani 1 (☎055 21 25 04; www.hotelperseo.it). Exit the train station and take V. de' Panzani, which becomes V. de'Cerretani. Aussie-Italian couple and English-speaking staff welcome travelers to a recently renovated 3-star hotel with 20 sophisticated rooms and large, gleaming baths. All have A/C and satellite TVs; some have views of the Duomo. Intimate bar and TV lounge decorated with proprietor's art. Breakfast included. Free Wi-Fi. Singles €115; doubles €155, economy double €145; triples €180; quads €215; suite €250. 5% discount if you pay cash on arrival. AmEx/MC/V; AmEx not accepted for online reservations. ❺

Hotel Dali, V. dell'Oriuolo 17 (☎055 23 40 706; www.hoteldali.com). A welcoming and well-loved place with hand-painted touches and a friendly staff. Shared bathrooms. Singles €40; doubles €65; triples €90. AmEx/MC/V. ❷

Hotel Aldini, V. Calzaiuoli 13 (☎055 21 47 52). A place so mom-and-pop they don't even have business cards. Cheery rooms with hardwood floors. A/C. Breakfast included. Singles €50; doubles €70. AmEx/MC/V. ❸

Pensione Maria Luisa de' Medici, V. del Corso 1 (☎055 28 00 48). A basic hotel with eclectic pieces of art pasted to every spare inch of wall space. Curfew midnight. Double for 1 €50-60, for 2 €70-80; quads €120-130. Cash only. ❸

PIAZZA DELLA SIGNORIA

Most P. della Signora accommodations target the wealthy clientele that shop at the neighborhood's high-end stores. Though they are high quality, your best bet is to save money and stay somewhere else. Florence is easily walkable, and you'll probably find that getting a cheaper room slightly farther from the main attractions is worth it.

🖾 **Hotel Bretagna,** Lungarno Corsini 6 (☎055 28 96 18; www.hotelbretagna.net). Gilded common rooms with 200-year-old porcelain plates, spacious breakfast hall, elegant bar, and a small balcony with an incredible view of the river. Doubles €110, with river view and jacuzzi €140-150. Prices 35% lower Nov.-Mar. AmEx/MC/V. ❺

🖾 **Relais Cavalcanti,** V. Pellicceria 2 (☎055 21 09 62). From P. della Repubblica walk down V. Pellicceria toward the Arno past the Central Poste. Wake up to the scent of roses in a room with antique furniture and gold-trimmed headboards. All rooms with satellite TVs, A/C, and Wi-Fi. Complimentary coffee, tea, and sweets in a shared kitchen. Singles €70-80; doubles €90-120; triples 130-150. MC/V. ❻

Soggiorno Prestipino, V. del Moro 22 (☎055 21 00 90). Clean and functional rooms near Santa Maria Novella. Wi-Fi. Dorms €19-28; singles €35-45; doubles €40-65; triples €75-90. ❶

Pensione Ferretti, V. delle Belle Donne 17 (☎055 23 81 328; www.hotelferretti.com). Dainty and affordable rooms on the edge of Santa Maria Novella. The helpful manager stores luggage for guests after check-out. Breakfast included. Free Wi-Fi. Singles with shared bath €40; doubles €50; triples €90; quads €110. Cash only. ❷

Il Porcellino Tourist House, P. del Mercato Nuovo 4 (☎055 28 26 86; www.hotelporcellino.com). Named after a bronze boar that also gives its name to the market outside the door, these sunny rooms come with breakfast and use of a common kitchen. High-season singles €70; doubles €100. Low-season singles €50; doubles €80. AmEx/MC/V. ❹

Hotel Toscana, V. del Sole 8 (☎055 21 31 56). Spotless and well-equipped rooms. Continental breakfast included 7:30-10am. Internet access. Reception 24hr. Check-in 2pm. Check-out 11am. High-season singles €60; doubles €79; triples €90, quads €110. Low-season singles €38; doubles €49; triples €65; quads €80. AmEx/MC/V. ❸

Leonardo House, V. Trebbio 4 (☎055 26 08 998). All the modern comforts in this conveniently located hotel. Kitchen access. Free lounge computer. Free Wi-Fi. Dorms (available Oct.-Mar.) €15; doubles €40-50, with private bath €50-60. ❷

Alekin Hostel, V. Porta Rossa 6, 4th fl. (☎055 26 08 332). A wall of thank you notes pays tribute to the owner's hospitality, for good reason. Bare-bones but clean rooms come with shared baths and Wi-Fi. Quiet hours after 11pm. Doubles €25-35 per person; quads €17-25 per person. Cash only. ❶

Hostel Veronique, V. Porta Rossa 6, 2nd fl. (☎333 15 03 014). Owned by the same woman as Alekin and run by her son, these rooms are similarly plain but provide larger windows and more light during the day. Doubles €25-35 per person; quads €17-25 per person. Cash only. ❶

SANTA MARIA NOVELLA

Budget accommodations in this area provide easy access to the Duomo, train station, and *centro storico*, but the convenience will cost you.

Hotel Abaco, V. dei Banchi 1 (☎055 23 81 919; www.abaco-hotel.it). Convenient location, helpful staff, and extravagant rooms. Each room is a masterpiece named after a Renaissance great. Each with phone and TV. Breakfast included. Wi-Fi. Singles €60; doubles €70-95; triples €110. MC/V. ❸

Hotel Consigli, Lungarno Amerigo Vespucci 50 (☎055 21 41 72; www.hotelconsigli. com). Once the playground of a Renaissance prince, this riverside palace is a sunlit sanctum of vaulted ceilings, sweeping frescoes, and marble stairs. The rooms are enormous, cool, and quiet, and the balcony and breakfast room look out over postcard-perfect views of the Arno. A/C. Breakfast included. Wi-Fi €3 per hr., €5 per 2hr., €7 per 3hr. Parking €15 per day. Singles €60-90; doubles €60-150. AmEx/MC/V. ❸

Albergo Margaret, V. della Scala 25 (☎055 21 01 38; www.dormireintoscana.it/margaret). Enthusiastic English-speaking staff and large rooms with terraces, TV, A/C, and ivory decor. Breakfast included. Wi-Fi. Curfew midnight. Singles €50-60; doubles €70, with full bath €90. Cash only. ❸

Hotel Duca D'Aosta, V. Fiume 17 (☎055 21 15 95; www.hotelducadaosta.eu), 5min. from Santa Maria Novella station. Homey touches and sunny windows in rooms with A/C and TVs. Breakfast included. Reception 24hr. Singles €40-55; doubles €60-80; triples €85. MC/V. ❷

Hotel Crocini, Corso Italia 28 (☎055 21 29 05; www.hotelcrocini.com), next door to the Teatro Comunale, 15min. from Santa Maria Novella station. Family-run establishment outfits its classic rooms with satellite TV and spacious showers. No A/C. Free Wi-Fi. Reception 24hr. Singles €39; doubles €49. AmEx/MC/V. ❷

Hotel Varsavia, V. Panzani 5 (☎055 21 56 15; www.hotelvarsavia.com). A palatial marble reception area leads to clean, modern rooms. Rooms come with hair dryers, A/C, and satellite TV. Breakfast included. Singles €40; doubles €70. MC/V. ❷

Hotel Desirée, V. Fiume 20 (☎055 23 82 382; www.desireehotel.com). Delicately detailed decor and the occasional room with a view—snag one if you can. A/C. Breakfast included. Singles €50-70; doubles €75-85; triples €100-120. MC/V. ❸

Hotel Garden, P. Vittorio Veneto 8 (☎055 21 26 69; www.hotelgarden.firenze.it), 10-15min. from Santa Maria Novella station. This basic hotel woos travelers with its high ceilings and lovely garden. Wi-Fi in lobby. Singles €35, with bath €45; doubles €48/68; 6-person suite €120. AmEx/MC/V. ❷

Hotel Jolì, V. Fiume 8, 3rd fl. (☎055 29 20 79; www.hoteljolifirenze). Simple, spacious rooms in a convenient location. A/C. Breakfast included. Free Wi-Fi. Singles €45, with bath €50; doubles €65/75. AmEx/MC/V. ❷

Albergo Universo, P. Santa Maria Novella 20 (☎055 29 38 90; www.hoteluniversoflorence.com). A hip, modern hotel with funky patterned wallpaper and a convenient location across from the Chiesa Santa Maria Novella. All rooms come with A/C, hair dryers, TVs, and baths. Breakfast included. Wi-Fi €3 per 30min., €5 per day. Singles €60; doubles €60-86; triples €110. AmEx/D/MC/V. ❸

Tourist House, V. della Scala 1 (☎055 26 86 75; www.touristhouse.com). With only 10 rooms in the building, you'll really get the chance to know the owners of this inviting, personal guesthouse. TV and A/C in each room. Breakfast included. Free Wi-Fi. Singles €50-78; doubles €70-95. MC/V. ❸

Hotel Montreal, V. della Scala 43 (☎055 23 82 331; www.hotelmontreal.com). A classic hotel with red-and-gold decor and a commitment to customer service. Singles €55; doubles €70. MC/V. ❸

Florence Room Bed & Breakfast, V. Fiume 1 (☎055 21 26 17; www.florenceroom.it). A quiet hotel outfitted in ivory and dusky pink with prints of Renaissance masterpieces in every room. A/C and TV in each room. Breakfast included and delivered to your room. Wi-Fi available—ask at reception. Singles €39-50; doubles €70-85. ❷

Hotel Giappone, V. dei Banchi 1, 3rd fl. (☎055 21 00 90; www.hotelgiappone.com). Classic hotel with sizeable rooms equipped with TVs and A/C. Small shared baths. Free Wi-Fi. Singles €55; doubles €70-75. MC/V. ❸

Hotel Leonardo da Vinci, V. Guido Monaco 12 (☎055 35 77 51; www.leonardodavincihotel.net), 10min. from Santa Maria Novella Station. A meticulously designed minimalist hotel that looks far more expensive than it is. A/C and TV in each room. Wi-Fi in internet room. Singles €60; doubles €80; triples €120. AmEx/MC/V. ❸

Hotel Serena, V. Fiume 20 (☎055 28 04 47; www.albergoserena.it). A clean-cut establishment with checkered quilts and wide windows. All rooms come with safe deposit boxes, hair dryers, A/C, and TVs. Singles €55; doubles €80. AmEx/MC/V. ❸

Pensione La Scala, V. della Scala 21, 2nd fl. Quirky boarding house-style accommodation with an eclectic ensemble of old-fashioned rooms. Singles €25-30, with bath €40; doubles €40-60/65. Prices subject to change with season. Cash only. ❶

Hotel Patrizia, V. Montebello 7 (☎055 28 23 14; www.hotelpatriziaflorence.com). A simple hotel with a vintage feel. Luggage storage available at reception. Singles €50-65; doubles €65-95; triples €90-110; quads €110-125. ❸

Hotel Bijou, V. Fiume 5 (☎055 21 41 56; www.hotel-bijou.it). A classic hotel housed in a grandiose old Florentine home. A/C. Singles €50, with breakfast €55; doubles €65/75. Ask about the €66 bargain triple upstairs. AmEx/MC/V. ❸

SAN LORENZO

From P. della Stazione, V. Nazionale leads to budget hotels and comfortable hostels that are just minutes away from both the Duomo and the train station. The accommodations on V. Nazionale, V. Faenza, V. Fiume, and V. Guelfa are inexpensive, but rooms facing the street may be noisy due to the daily throngs of pedestrians. Occasionally, a lucky guest might get a room with

MOVIN' ON UP

Christmas aside, most religious holidays in my life have been pretty quiet. Most times I didn't even realize that they were going on. But when Florence celebrated the feast day of its patron, **San Giovanni Battista** (St. John the Baptist), I may not have known what was going on, but I knew it was something. The city simply shut down. *Trattorie, pizzerie,* pharmacies, and even a full half of the tourist traps in P. del Duomo were closed for the entire day. When night fell, the usually-raucous Florentines were unusually quiet. There was no one in the streets—like the Black Death all over again, minus the contagion.

They were all on the rooftops. Having navigated the ladder to the roof of Ruth's Kosher Restaurant (p. 107), I found out where everyone had been hiding. Come dark on San Giovanni, the city heads skyward for the famous fireworks display in the Oltrarno. Shouts, hoots, and opinionated banter bounced between the roofs of Florence, where viewers clung to lighting rods, ladders, and even the tiles of their steep roofs in order to watch the hour-long extravaganza. Our neighbors on Ruth's (mercifully) flat roof had ice cream; the party down the block was drinking wine. Apparently, the party hadn't stopped for the holidays. The Florentines had just moved it up in the world, if only for a day.

—Marykate Jasper

a spectacular view of the Florentine skyline. The vibrant marketplace surrounding the Basilica di San Lorenzo and a few delicious eateries offer a lively yet peaceful escape from the nearby chaos of the area between the Duomo and the Uffizi Gallery. San Lorenzo's proximity to the center makes it relatively safe at night, but as always, use caution when alone.

Ostello Archi Rossi, V. Faenza 94r (☎055 29 08 04; www.hostelarchirossi.com). You'll feel the Florentine creative vibe as soon as you see the frescoes painted in the reception by local art students. Each of the 30 spotless rooms comes with a PC, locker, and shared bathroom. Archi Rossi boasts a romantic garden, free Wi-Fi, computer use, and a free walking tour every morning with an English-speaking guide. Breakfast included; features bacon and eggs. Complimentary pasta dinners also occasionally served. Luggage storage available. Reception 24hr. Dorms €18-25; singles €25-35. MC/V. ❶

Holiday Rooms, V. Nazionale 22 (☎055 28 50 84; www.marcosplaces.com). Owner Marco has been known to meet guests at the train station to help them with their baggage—a small taste of the conveniences and perks to come. Hardwood beds and satin curtains adorn 8 quiet rooms equipped with satellite flatscreen TVs, computers, Wi-Fi, and laundry access. Kitchen available. Rooms €25-40 per person. Discounts at some local restaurants. ❶

Soggiorno Luna Rossa, V. Nazionale 7, 3rd fl. (☎328 62 51 017; www.marcosplaces.com). From the Piazza Stazione near Santa Maria Novella Station, walk to V. Nazionale until you reach Marco's other place. Wake up in a brightly decorated room to the morning sun streaming through the spectacular stained-glass windows of this centrally located hostel. 18 private rooms available, 3 with shared bathrooms. Each with Wi-Fi, computer, satellite flatscreen TV, and free international calls. Kitchen available. Rooms €25-40 per person. ❷

Hotel Etrusca, V. Nazionale 35 (☎055 23 96 885). Guarded by a gated glass door and a receptionist who only permits entrance to guests of the hotel. 6 rooms no more than 2 blocks from Santa Maria Novella and the Basilica di San Lorenzo. Although the small common area in the lobby is spare, TV and Wi-Fi are available. Credit cards may be used to reserve the room; otherwise cash only.

Hotel Mario's, V. Faenza 89 (☎055 21 68 01; www.hotelmarios.com). From Santa Maria Novella Station, go down V. Cennini and turn left on V. Faenza. Marrying the old world charm of a 17th-century Florentine building with modern comforts, the hotel owner Leonardo and his brothers like to help each and every guest make their stay memorable. The clean rooms, hardwood ceilings and floors, stained-glass windows, and attentive staff make the splurge worth it. The welcoming common room features a coffee and spirits bar, black leather couches, and chess boards. Doubles €90-130. MC/V. ⑤

Albergo Merlini, V. Faenza 56 (☎055 21 28 48; www.hotelmerlini.it). From Santa Maria Novella station, go down V. Cennini and turn right onto V. Faenza. Hidden inside the 18th-century Barbera Palace, this charming hotel features elegant rooms with hardwood floors and stained-glass windows. The spacious breakfast room with breathtaking views and high ceilings is perfect for admiring the Duomo. Free internet. Doubles €75; triples €90. AmEx/MC/V. ⑤

Ninna Nanna Bed & Breakfast, V. San Zanobi 37 (☎055 49 32 757). This 3-room lodging offers the atmosphere of a cozy home away from home. The petite Italian lady who runs the B&B doesn't speak much English, but she more than overcompensates with her warm hospitality. Each room has a small balcony, TV, and internet. Breakfast included. Doubles €50, with bath €60. Cash only. ❸

Locanda degli Artisti, V. Faenza 56 (☎055 21 38 06; www.hotelazzi.it). From Santa Maria Novella station, go down V. Cennini and turn right onto V. Faenza. Antique record players and authentic paintings adorn this bohemian-style inn. The sunny breakfast room serves as a better lounge than the terrace—which only offers a view of a caved-in roof—and is closer to the small bar counter (open 24hr.). Turkish bath and library open to guests. Breakfast included. Free Wi-Fi. Doubles €50-100; triples €75-125. Prices vary seasonally. Dorms occasionally offered during the low season. AmEx/MC/V. ❸

Hotel Anna's, V. Faenza 56 (☎055 23 02 714; www.hotelannas.com). From Santa Maria Novella station, go down V. Cennini and turn right onto V. Faenza. Tucked away in the heart of Palazzo Barbera, Hotel Anna occupies a space once belonging to an important editorial firm. The recently renovated and spotless rooms have internet and TVs. Breakfast included and delivered to the room. Singles €40; doubles €50. Prices drop by about €10-15 during the low season. AmEx/MC/V. ❷

Locanda Giovanna, V. Faenza 69 (☎055 23 81 353). 7 well-kept rooms, some with delightful garden views, provide a relaxing and quiet atmosphere. Singles have shared bath. The friendly Italian owner, Giovanna, doesn't speak much English, but her daughter can usually help out. Singles €30; doubles €60, with a cot €75; triples €80. Cash only. ❷

Hotel Monica, V. Faenza 66 (☎055 28 38 04; www.hotelmonicaflorence.com). From Santa Maria Novella Station, take V. Cennini and turn left onto V. Faenza. Located in an old Florentine building and furnished with terra-cotta floors, the functional rooms come with wrought-iron beds, TVs, and free Wi-Fi. Breakfast included; take it on the sunny terrace, nestled among flower-laden balconies. Book at least a month in advance for a discount or check the website for special promotions. Singles €60; doubles €70. MC/V. ❸

Tourist House Battistero, V. de' Cerretani 1 (☎333 83 79 256; www.touristhousebattistero.it). Within 2min. of the Duomo, Battistero is located on the 1st floor of a renovated 15th-century palace. The rooms come in different sizes, but each has its own A/C, bath with shower, and TV. The doubles boast large windows and magnificent views, while the larger rooms feature a kitchen. The studio can be rented by the week. Triples €70. Low season discounts. AmEx/MC/V. ❹

Hotel Armonia, V. Faenza 56 (☎055 21 22 46). The small hall, decorated with American film posters and black and white photos, gives this family-owned pension a retro charm. The 7 rooms are clean, well-maintained, and offer a striking panorama from their balconies. Free Wi-Fi. Singles €35-50; doubles €50-70. MC/V. ❷

Tourist House Duomo, V. de' Cerretani 1 (☎055 28 33 08; www.touristhouseduomo.com). From the Duomo, walk 3min. down V. de' Cerretani. The quiet rooms, furnished in antiquated style and equipped with all the modern comforts, come with private baths, A/C, TVs, and telephones. Doubles €65-85. Prices vary seasonally. AmEx/MC/V. ❹

Hotel Deco, V. Panzani 7 (☎055 28 44 69; www.hoteldeco.it). This hotel sports light aqua walls and large dried flowers in the interior of a neoclassical palace. A multilingual selection of TV stations and Wi-Fi keep you connected to the rest of the world, while the hotel's quiet atmosphere keeps you shielded from the noise of Santa Maria Novella outside. A/C and private bath in each room. Breakfast included. Singles €50-60; doubles €60-70; triples €90-100. AmEx/MC/V. ❸

Hotel Lombardia, V. Panzani 19 (☎055 21 52 76; www.hotellombardia.it). Just minutes from Santa Maria Novella, Lombardia's best kept secret is its friendly and helpful staff. Clean, functional rooms with TVs. Continental breakfast included. Open bar 7:30-11:30pm. Doubles €50-70. AmEx/MC/V. ❸

Hotel Porta Faenza, V. Faenza 77 (☎055 21 79 75; www.hotelportafaenza.it). From Santa Maria Novella Station, go down V. Nazionale and take a second left onto V. Faenza. This 18th-century house, once owned by a Florentine merchant family, boasts fancy brickwork, marble stairs, and hardwood, while offering an array of modern comforts. All the rooms come with large windows, satellite TV, and free Wi-Fi. Breakfast included. High season rooms €130-140; low season rooms €80-90. AmEx/MC/V. ❺

Vasari Palace Hotel, V. B. Cennini 9 (☎055 21 27 53; www.hotelvasari.com). From Santa Maria Novella Station, cross through P. Adua onto V. Cennini. This former monastery enchants its guests with marble staircases and majestic common areas that feature high ceilings, white couches, fireplaces, and a piano. The rooms, by contrast, are sparse and lit with fluorescent lights, but functional and clean. Continental breakfast served in the spacious breakfast room. Singles €50; doubles €60. AmEx/MC/V. ❸

SAN MARCO

Unlike almost every other neighborhood in the city, San Marco is sparse when it comes to lodgings. Crammed with former convents and academic buildings, the area feels residential even though it is a few blocks away from the main *piazze*. Many travelers find that the amenities and peaceful atmosphere (what you're paying for here) in this neighborhood are worth the extra walk.

Hotel Tina, V. San Gallo 31 (☎055 48 35 19; www.hoteltina.it). Family-run pension with pleasant blue decor welcomes guests into large carpeted rooms with comfortable plush furniture. Breakfast included. Free Wi-Fi. Singles €30-40; doubles with shower €45-75, with bath €70-80; triples €65-90; quads €80-120. MC/V. ❷

Soggiorno Magliani, V. Santa Reparata 1 (☎055 28 73 78). An inexpensive, no-frills establishment with very few amenities but a sweet, attentive family as staff. Bright rooms with desks and minimal decoration branch off a winding hallway with shared bathrooms. If you're just looking for a room, or maybe just looking to experience life under the care of an old Italian grandmother, this is the place for you. No A/C. Singles €38; doubles €48; triples €65-75; quads €80. Cash only. ❷

Hotel San Marco, V. Cavour 50 (☎055 28 18 51; www.hotelsanmarcofirenze.it), just a few feet away from P. San Marco. Sunlit white walls and bright bedspreads. Quiet rooms away from the street available on request. Breakfast included; enjoy it while watching *calcio* on the communal TV. A/C and Wi-Fi. Singles €35-50; doubles €65; quads €108. Cash only. ❷

Hotel Gioia, V. Cavour 25 (☎055 28 28 04; www.hotelgioia.it). A professional establishment with classy rooms. Frequented by both businessmen and tourists. Each room has satellite TV, mini-bar, A/C, and safe. Breakfast included; room service available. Wi-Fi. Singles €80; doubles €89; quads €130. MC/V. ❺

Hotel Benvenuti, V. Cavour 112 (☎055 57 39 09; www.benvenutihotel.it). Friendly staff and a quiet, relaxing atmosphere make up for the minimal decor and slightly inconvenient location. A/C available. Breakfast included. Free Wi-Fi. Singles €20-30, with private bath €33-35; doubles €55; quads €72. AmEx/MC/V. ❶

Hotel Cimabue, V. Bonifacio Lupi 7 (☎055 47 19 89; www.hotelcimabue.com). A delicately decorated hotel with glossy, quilted comforters and a quaint breakfast room. Despite its popularity with families, it still feels quiet and relaxed. A/C and TV in each room. Breakfast included. Wi-Fi. Singles €55; doubles €75; quads €115. AmEx/MC/V. ❸

Albergo Sampaoli, V. San Gallo 14 (☎055 28 48 34; www.hotelsampaoli.it). Well-lit rooms, each with Wi-Fi, DVD player, and fan. Large common room. Fridge available on each floor. Reception 24hr. Singles €30-60, with bath €35-74; doubles €44-55/45-84; triples €75-120; quads €90-140. Extra bed €25. 5% discount with reservation. ❷

Hotel Panorama, V. Cavour 60 (☎055 23 82 043; www.hotelpanorama.fi.it). Unusually heavy on the amenities for its price range, this hotel compensates for its essentially unadorned rooms with a host of extras. Be sure to take advantage of the vistas from the rooftop veranda. Each room has A/C, TV, hairdryer, and free Wi-fi. Some have views of the distant Duomo. Singles €55; doubles €75-85; quads €100-105. AmEx/MC/V. ❸

Locanda Gallo, V. San Gallo 73r (☎055 46 20 095; www.florencebeds.com). Although the stairway leading to this 3rd fl. *locanda* (inn) could use a bit of TLC, the 7 rooms themselves are large, sunlit, and well-maintained by the kind host. There aren't any real common spaces, so this place might be best if you're looking for a more private hotel experience. A/C. Free Wi-Fi. Singles €40-50; doubles €60-70; triples €120; quads €90-100. Cash only. ❷

SANTA CROCE

The distance from the city center and the residential atmosphere of the neighborhood has left Santa Croce without many options for the wayward tourist. Still, a couple of gems can be found.

THE TOWN BICYCLES

I knew that Italians are known for their love of the *moto*, but I had no idea that the enthusiasm extended to its less-mechanical predecessor.

Eighteen clowns piling into a Beetle while juggling have nothing on the bicyclists cruising the streets of Florence. Young and old use their two-wheelers as an integral part of their daily lives. Dr. Seuss would've gone nuts with the material he'd have here.

I've heard of a bicycle built for two, but for four? For a mom and three kids? For a man, a bucket, and a six-foot ladder?

Florence is a super biker-happy city; over 28,000 cyclists peddle their way around town, by the city council's last estimate.

And by 2010, it'll put down over 100km in new bike paths, promoting their program like everything else is promoted today—sex. "*+Bici +Baci*" ("More bicycles, More kisses") is the newest slogan, and though it's hard to explain, it still makes sense—nothing's sexier than being environmentally friendly.

—Beryl Lipton

Hotel Arizona, V. Luigi Carlo Farini 2 (☎055 24 53 21; www.arizonahotel.it). There's nothing here of the barren desert that gives this hotel its name except the glint of the rooms' gold wallpaper and the warmth of the hotel staff. A/C. Continental breakfast included. Wi-Fi available for a fee. Singles €60-85; doubles €89-139. 10% discount for stays over 4 nights. AmEx/MC/V. ❹

Hotel Ariston, V. Fiesolana 40 (☎055 24 76 980; www.hotelaristonfirenze.it). The replica of Michelangelo's *David* in the lobby pays homage to the artistic spirit of the city. Large rooms, each with a TV, offer a quiet escape from the chaos of the city center. Bar downstairs. Singles €55; doubles €90; quads €130. AmEx/MC/V. ❸

WEST OLTRARNO

Though this part of town is a bit farther from the center, the walk along the River Arno is peaceful and picturesque, and the cost may be a fraction less than that of comparable accommodations in the center.

C.S.D.—Gould Institute, V. dei Serragli 49 (☎055 21 25 76; www.istitutogould.it). From P. Santo Spirito, turn right onto V. Sant'Agostino and take a left at the end onto V. dei Serragli; the hostel is through the courtyard, so buzz yourself in. Run by a Protestant church, this establishment donates its profits to the special-circumstances children who also reside or receive services in another portion of the complex. Once part of the church, the common areas are high-ceilinged and pleasant, and the rooms rival those of many area hotels. Private and shared bathrooms. Free Wi-Fi. Reception M-F 8:45am-1pm and 3-7:30pm, Sa 9am-1:30pm and 2:30-6pm. No check-in Su and holidays. Prices depend on garden view and terrace. Singles €50-55; doubles €56-66; triples €75; quads €92. MC/V. ❸

Ostello Santa Monaca, V. Santa Monaca 6 (☎055 26 83 38; www.ostello.it). Basic rooms on the cheap. Enjoy a discounted meal at a local restaurant or wash-and-dry laundry service for €6.50 per load. Fans of late-night showers, hope you like them cold: hot water shuts off midnight-6am every night. Common room open 7am-1am. Microwave and stove-top available. Free internet. Check-in 6am-2am. Lockout 10am-2pm. Curfew 2am. 16- to 22-bed dorms €17; 10-bed dorms €18; 8-bed dorms €18.50; 6-bed dorms €19; 4-bed dorms €20. AmEx/MC/V. ❶

Hotel La Scaletta, V. Guicciardini 13 (☎055 28 30 28; www.hotellascaletta.it). Cross the Ponte Vecchio and continue on V. Guicciardini. Gorgeous rooms with antique furnishings, elegant sitting areas, a pleasant breakfast room, and a rooftop terrace with a spectacular view of Boboli Gardens. Wi-Fi in common room and some bedrooms. Low-season singles €50; doubles €60; triples €80; quads €100. High season singles €100; doubles €125; triples €140; quads €160. AmEx/MC/V. ❺

Hotel Boboli, V. Romana 63 (☎055 22 98 645; www.hotelboboli.com). The curved designs of the wire frame headboards and blue floral wallpaper create delicately antique-styled rooms that mirror the elegance of the nearby Boboli Gardens. Specials available online. Doubles from €65; triples from €85; quads from €99. AmEx/MC/V. ❹

APARTMENT

Casa Guidi, P. San Felice 8 (☎04 15 22 24 81). Once the home of poets Elizabeth and Robert Browning, this 3-bedroom apartment is now in the care of The Landmark Trust, an organization that rents historic buildings and residences in order to raise funds for restoration and preservation. The apartment sleeps up to 6 people and includes use of beautiful high-ceilinged rooms restored to their 19th century splendor. €230-370 per night. Prices vary seasonally. MC/V. ❺

EAST OLTRARNO

Accommodations in this scenic area of the city are generally both pricey and removed from the action: not a great combination for travelers relying on public transportation and a tight budget. Things get a lot greener in the Oltrarno, though, and if you just want to stay somewhere away from the scorching summer sun, the shaded gardens and air-conditioned rooms in the Oltrarno may be your best option.

Campeggio Michelangelo, V. Michelangelo 80 (☎055 68 11 977; www.ecvacanze.it), beyond Ple. Michelangelo. Take bus #13 from the station to the Camping 1 stop (15min., last bus 11:25pm). Chain campsite is family-geared and very crowded, but offers good (if distant) views of the city and a shaded olive grove. Market and bar available. Towels €1.50. Laundry €7. Internet €3 per hr. Reception daily 7am-11pm. €9.30-11 per person. April-Nov. 2-person tent €36. MC/V over €100. ❶

Sognando Firenze Bed and Breakfast, V. Giampaolo Orsini 115 (☎055 68 32 78; www.sognandofirenze.it). Boasts a bright breakfast room overlooking the street, neat yellow rooms with A/C, and private bathrooms. Breakfast included. Free Wi-Fi. Singles €60; doubles €70; triples €85; quads €105. MC/V. ❸

Hotel Villa Liberty, Vle. Michelangelo 40 (☎055 68 10 581; www.hotelvillaliberty.com). Antique villa meets Art Deco. Surrounded by peaceful private gardens and tucked into the green slopes of Ple. Michelangelo. Although a bit out of the way—a 15min. walk from Ponte Vecchio—it offers amenities like a hot tub, bar, bike rental, and A/C. Breakfast included. Free Wi-Fi. Doubles €85; triples €120; quads €140. ❺

FOOD

Florentine cuisine developed from the peasant fare of the surrounding countryside. Characterized by saltless bread and rustic dishes prepared with fresh ingredients and simple recipes, Tuscan food ranks among Italy's best. White beans and olive oil are two staple ingredients, often served together as a *contorno*, or side dish. One famous specialty is bruschetta, toasted bread doused with olive oil and garlic, usually topped with tomatoes and basil. For *primi*, Florentines favor the Tuscan classics *minestra di fagioli* (a white bean and garlic soup) and *ribollita* (hearty bean, bread, and black cabbage stew). Florence's classic *secondo* is *bistecca alla Fiorentina* (thick sirloin steak on the T-bone); locals order it *al sangue* (very rare; literally "bloody"), though it's also available *al punto* (medium) or *ben cotto* (well-done). The best local cheese is *pecorino*, made from sheep's milk. Other popular ingredients include shrimp (usually with the eyes and head still intact) and *cinghiale* (wild boar). A liter of house wine usually costs €3.50-6 in a *trattoria*, but stores sell cheap bottles (€2.50). The most famous local wine is *chianti classico*, a red wine typically produced in Florence's rural surroundings and distinguished by a black rooster on the bottle. The local dessert is *cantuccini di prato* (hard almond cookies with egg yolk) dipped in *vinsanto* (a rich dessert wine made from raisins).

Buy fresh produce at the **Mercato Centrale,** between V. Nazionale and San Lorenzo. (Open June-Sept. M-Sa 7:30am-2pm; Oct.-May M-Sa 7am-2pm and 4-8pm.) For basics, head to the **STANDA,** V. Pietrapiana 1r. Turn right on V. del Proconsolo and the first left on Borgo degli Albizi. Continue through P. Gaetano Salvemini; the supermarket is on the left. (Open M-Sa 8am-9pm, Su 9am-9pm. MC/V.) **Il Centro** supermarket chains are located throughout the city. Central locations include V. Ricasoli 109r (☎055 28 77 18; open M-Sa 8am-8pm, Su 10am-7pm), V. Il Prato 72r (☎055 21 03 04; open M-Sa 8am-8pm, Su 9am-7pm), and V. de' Ginori 41r (☎055 21 03 54; open M-Sa 8am-9pm, Su 9am-7pm). Beware of overpriced *alimentari* along V. Faenza. Several health food markets cater to vegetarians, two of which draw inspiration from the American book **Sugar Blues.** One is at V. XXVII Aprile 46r-48r, 5min. from the Duomo. (☎055 48 36 66. Open M-Sa 9am-1:30pm and 5-7:30pm, Su 9am-1:30pm. Closed one week in Aug. V.) The other, renamed **Ha-Tha Maya,** is next to the Istituto Gould, in the Oltrarno at V. dei Serragli 57r. (☎055 26 83 78. Open Sept.-July daily 8am-1:30pm and 4-7:30pm; Aug. M-F and Su 8am-1:30pm and 4-7:30pm, Sa 8am-1:30pm. MC/V.)

COVER YOUR... Many of the restaurants in Florence have a cover charge of €1-3, but not all of them advertise it clearly. Some even avoid mentioning it all until you've received your bill. To avoid the sort of nasty surprise that can amount to more than half of a budget meal (€5 pasta dish + €3 cover = a lot more expensive than you planned), look at the bottom of the menu. Even if you don't see one listed, be sure to ask the waiter upfront if there is any cover charge—before you sit down. It's neither a rude nor a stupid question, so you can avoid offending both the waitstaff and your wallet.

FOOD BY PRICE

UNDER €7 (❶)

50 Rosso (p. 102)	SMN
A Casamia (p. 107)	SC
Amon Specialità Egiziani (p. 102)	SMN
Antica Gelateria Fiorentina (p. 103)	SL
Antico Noe (p. 99)	Duomo
Bar Bano (p. 105)	SL
Bar Cabras (p. 104)	SL
Bar Sant'Agostino (p. 110)	WO
Caffè Astra (p. 104)	SL
Caffè Michelangiolo (p. 104)	SL
Caffè Rosanó (p. 106)	SM
Caffè Vecchio Mercato (p. 108)	SC
Caffelatte (p. 107)	SM
Caffetteria Raffaella (p. 104)	SL
Cantinetta dei Verazzano (p. 100)	Duomo
Danny Rock (p. 101)	PDS
🏴Gelateria del Neri (p. 100)	PDS
Gelateria La Carraia (p. 109)	WO
Gelateria Pitti (p. 110)	WO
Gelatissimo (p. 108)	SC
Gran Caffe San Marco p. 105)	SM
🏴Grom (p. 99)	Duomo
La Loggia degli Albizi (p. 100)	Duomo
La Mescita (p. 105)	SM
La Pagnotta (p. 108)	SC
L'Angolo della Pizza (p. 108)	SC
Mr. Kebab House (p. 108)	SC
Perchè No! (p. 101)	PDS
Ristorante "Leonardo" (p. 99)	Duomo
Salumeria Verdi (p. 108)	SC
Snack Bar Lele (p. 106)	SM
VinOlio (p. 105)	SM
Vivoli (p. 101)	PDS

€7-13 (❷)

Bar Capitol (p. 101)	PDS
Bar Galli (p. 105)	SL
Boccadama (p. 108)	SC
Buongustai (p. 100)	PDS
Caffe Landucci (p. 105)	SL
Cardillac Cafe (p. 106)	SM
Hemingway (p. 110)	WO
Il Principe (p. 108)	SC
Il Ristoro dei Perditempo (p. 110)	WO
I'pizzachiere (p. 111)	EO
La Casalinga (p. 110)	WO
Le Volpi e l'Uva (p. 111)	EO
Nabucco Wine Bar (p. 106)	SM
Ok Bar (p. 99)	Duomo
Osteria Pizzeria Zio Gigi (p. 99)	Duomo
Pizzeria Ostaria Centopoveri (p. 102)	SMN
Pizzeria Baccus (p. 103)	SMN
Ristorante Dioniso (p. 105)	SM

€7-13 CON'T (❷)

Ristorante Il Vegetariano (p. 106)	SM
Rosticceria Alfio Beppe (p. 106)	SM
Rosticceria Il Pirata (p. 102)	SMN
🏴Ruth's Kosher Vegetarian (p. 107)	SC
The William (p. 108)	SC
Trattoria al Trebbio (p. 103)	SMN
Trattoria Anita (p. 101)	PDS
Trattoria Belle Donne (p. 102)	SMN
Trattoria Contadino (p. 102)	SMN
Trattoria dell'Orto p. 109)	WO
🏴Trattoria Le Mossacce (p. 99)	Duomo
Trattoria Mario (p. 103)	SL
Trattoria Nerone (p. 104)	SL

€14-20 (❸)

4 Leoni (p. 109)	WO
Acquacotta (p. 107)	SC
Angels (p. 99)	Duomo
Gattabuia (p. 111)	EO
l'Brincello (p. 104)	SL
l'brindellone (p. 110)	WO
La Beppe Fioriai Trattoria (p. 111)	EO
La Grotta di Leo (p. 103)	SMN
Le Campane (p. 108)	SC
Le Colonnine (p. 108)	SC
Mamma Toscana (p. 104)	SL
Osteria de' Benci (p. 101)	PDS
Ristorante Da Mimmo (p. 106)	SM
Ristorante dei Fagioli (p. 107)	SC
Ristorante La Spada (p. 102)	SMN
Ristorante Le Fonticine (p. 104)	SL
Seme d'Uva (p. 109)	WO
Semolina (p. 108)	SC
Trattoria Baldini (p. 103)	SMN
Trattoria da Giorgio (p. 102)	SMN
Trattoria dei Matti (p. 105)	SL
Tre Merli (p. 103)	SMN
Valle dei Cedri (p. 108)	SC

€21-27 (❹)

Cammillo (p. 109)	WO
Caruso Jazz Cafe (p. 101)	PDS
Dante (p. 109)	WO
Filipepe (p. 111)	EO
Il Giova (p. 107)	SC
Il Latini (p. 100)	PDS
MaMMaMia (p. 102)	PDS
Osteria Santo Spirito (p. 110)	WO
Ristorante Acqua al 2 (p. 99)	Duomo
🏴Teatro del Sale (p. 107)	SC
Trattoria Zàzà (p. 103)	SL

OVER €27 (❺)

Osteria dell'Olio (p. 100)	Duomo
Ristorante Il Paiolo (p. 107)	SM

FOOD

EO = East Oltrarno PDS = Piazza della Signoria SC = Santa Croce SL = San Lorenzo	SM = San Marco SMN = Santa Maria Novella WO = West Oltrarno

FOOD BY AREA

THE DUOMO

The Old City is for the eyes, not the tastebuds. Most of these places will fill up at lunchtime just because they're within walking distance of the Duomo.

▣ **Grom,** V. del Campanile (☎055 21 61 58), off P. del Duomo to the left of the Campanile. The kind of gelato you'll be talking about in 50 years. As fresh as it gets; sublimely balanced texture. Large store is standing-room only and flooded with tourists and locals. Cups €2-5, cones €2-4. Open daily Apr.-Sept. 10:30am-midnight, Oct.-Mar. 10:30am-11pm. ❶

▣ **Trattoria Le Mossacce,** V. del Proconsolo 55r (☎055 29 43 61; www.trattorialemossacce.it). The sort of place that you just don't expect near the Duomo, Mossacce seats strangers shoulder-to-shoulder and whips out Tuscan specialties. *Primi* €5-8.50. *Secondi* €5.50-10. Cover €1. Open daily noon-2:30pm and 7-9:30pm. ❷

Ok Bar, V. de Servi 97r (☎055 21 71 49). A one-stop shop for any dish that your stomach could demand, this all-purpose bar serves up everything from American breakfast (toast and omelette €6) to four-cheese and shrimp risotto (€8.50). The to-go display is filled with pizza (€3), *panini* (€2.50-5), and pastries (€4-8). *Primi* €6-9.50. *Secondi* €6-14. Open daily 7am-midnight. MC/V. ❷

Antico Noe, Volta di San Piero 6r (☎055 23 40 838). When you're sick of reheated *rosticceria panini*, head to Antico Noe for freshly crafted sandwiches. Flavorful combinations like stuffed chicken, peppers, and mozzarella (€4) and roast pork, pecorino, and eggplant (€4). Popular vegetarian plates €3.80. Open Ma-Sa noon-midnight. Cash only. ❶

Ristorante Self-Service "Leonardo," V. Pecori 11, 1st floor. For a throwback to your middle school days, hop into the cafeteria-style lunch line at Leonardo and enjoy the budget-friendly *menù del giorno*. *Primi* from €3.80. *Secondi* from €4.80. Open M-F and Su 11:45am-2:45pm and 6:45pm-12:45am. Cash only. ❶

Ristorante Acqua al 2, V. della Vigna Vecchia 40r (☎055 28 41 70; www.acquaal2.it), behind the Bargello. Both the location and reputation for unique dishes beckon travelers and locals to this closet-sized restaurant. Salads from €7.50. *Primi* €8-12. *Secondi* €8-22. Cover €1. Open daily 7:30pm-1am. Reservations strongly recommended. AmEx/MC/V. ❹

Osteria il Gatto e la Volpe, V. Ghibellina 15r (☎055 28 92 64). American students crowd this restaurant to satisfy their late-night carb cravings. The pasta is filling and the atmosphere's fun, but the divine complimentary bread may just be the best part of the meal. Open daily noon-2pm and 7pm-midnight. MC/V.

Angels, V. del Proconsolo 29r (www.ristoranteangels.it). This trendy restaurant combines medieval and modern conceptions of elegance, filling its stone, stained-glass room with sleek, shining furniture. Metal candelabras meet gauzy curtains in one of the area's dinner hotspots, where fashionable Italians and tourists come to wine and dine. *Primi* €12. *Secondi* €12-20. Open daily noon-11:30pm. AmEx/MC/V. ❸

Osteria Pizzeria Zio Gigi, V. Folco Portinari 7r (☎055 21 55 84). Generous portions and a playful staff make this uncrowded *osteria*'s lunch special (*primo, secondo, and contorno* €8) a must. Open daily noon-2:30pm and 7-10:30pm. MC/V. ❷

FOOD

PICNIC SPOTS

Sick of being cooped up in museums and churches? Here are some of the best spots to kick back with a *panino* and enjoy Florence *al fresco*.

1. Piazza Santa Croce. Popular with everyone from gypsies to hash dealers, P. Santa Croce is the perfect spot from which to people-watch. Plus, it contains some wide benches convenient for spreading out snacks.

2. Piazzale Michelangelo. The view of the city from this hilltop *piazza* is worth the cramp in your leg from the hike up. Although the immediate *piazza* is popular with photo-snappers, wander just a few more steps down the road to find yourself in perfect Tuscan solitude.

3. Boboli Gardens. In true Italian form, the most desirable picnic spot in the city also has the crotchetiest regulations. Large meals are technically not allowed, but you can easily sneak smaller snacks into this elegant horticultural mecca. If James Bond picnicked, he would do it here.

4. Piazza Santo Spirito. On the other side of the Arno from the Duomo and Uffizi, this intimate piazza features fountains, trees, and benches largely unclogged by visitors.

5. Cascine Park. Located on the banks of the Arno, this leafy park is the perfect spot to watch kayakers glide down the river. Popular

Osteria dell'Olio, P. dell'Olio 10r (☎055 21 14 66; www.osteriadellolio.com). 300 years ago, P. dell'Olio was home to an open air market for olive oil vendors. Today, this upscale *osteria* bottles house oil and uses only quality local products in its original dishes. *Primi* €10-26. *Secondi* €24-36. 30% student discount. Open daily noon-3:30pm and 7pm-midnight. MC/V. ❺

Cantinetta dei Verrazzano, V. dei Tavolini 18-20r (☎055 26 85 90). Many come for the huge wine selection, but Verrazzano's decadent cakes and pies (from €4 a slice) are the real reason to make the trip. AmEx/MC/V. ❶

La Loggia degli Albizi, Borgo degli Albizi 39r (☎055 24 79 574). A hidden treasure, this quiet bakery offers an escape from tourist throngs. Pastries from €0.80. Coffee from €0.80, served at table €1.50. Open M-Sa 7am-8pm. ❶

PIAZZA DELLA SIGNORIA

Near the *piazza*, options tend to be limited to overpriced tourist-fare; if you're looking for a meal, **Buongustai** is your best bet within the immediately surrounding block. However, P. della Signora is just as overrun by quality gelato as it is by tourists. Hold off on getting your ice cream from just any old bar and walk a bit out of the square to Gelateria dei Neri, Perche No, or Vivoli; it's worth the extra couple of blocks—and it'll help burn off those extra calories.

🍽 **Gelateria dei Neri,** V. dei Neri 20-22r (☎055 21 00 34). Follow the street between Uffizi and Palazzo Vecchio. Just big enough for a counter and the waiting line, this gelateria is the locals' favorite. Serves generous scoops of creative flavors like *crema giotto* (a blend of coconut, almond, and hazelnut) and equally delicious classics like pistachio. Cones and cups from €1.50. Open daily 11am-midnight. Cash only. ❶

Buongustai, V. dei Cerchi 15 (☎055 29 13 04). Walk north from Palazzo Vecchio. After a day at the nearby Duomo, Bargello, and P. della Signoria, relax at this quirky and casual spot. Make sure to try the house special *Piatto del Buongustai* (Tuscan salami, cheese, and pickled vegetables; €10). *Primi* €4.50-6.50. *Secondi* €6.50-10. Open M-Th 9:30am-3:30pm, F-Sa 8:30-11pm. Cash only. ❷

Il Latini, V. dei Palchetti 6r (☎055 21 09 16; www.illatini.com). Waiting in line has never been so pleasant. Il Latini's host offers complimentary glasses of white wine and cheese to those waiting outside. *Primi* €5-10. *Secondi* €14-23. Open Tu-Su noon-2:30pm and 7:30-10:30pm. AmEx/MC/V. ❹

Vivoli, V. Dell' Isola Del Stinche 7r (☎055 29 23 34, www.vivoli.it). From Palazzo Vecchio, take Borgo dei Greci and turn left on V. Bentaccordia. Delicious treats. Coneheads take heed: the spoonfuls of sugar only come in cups here. Cups from €1.70. Open Tu-F 7:30am-midnight, Su 9:30am-midnight. Cash only. ❶

Caruso Jazz Café, V. Lambertesca 14/16r (☎055 26 70 207; www.carusojazzcafe.com). Enjoy a dinner of fresh pasta in this coral-colored, marble establishment, set to the soundtrack of Billie Holiday and other jazz greats. Th-F 9pm-midnight live jazz. *Primi* €6-8. *Secondi* €9-18. Cover €2. AmEx/MC/V. ❹

Perché No!, V. dei Tavolini 19r (☎055 23 98 969). From the Duomo, take V. de Calzaioli toward the Arno and turn left onto V. Tavolini before the P. della Signoria. The neon "gelateria" light may seem out of place in this high-end area, but patrons have been drawn by the shop's name ("Why not!") and homemade flavors, like cheesecake and macadamia nuts, for decades. Cones and cups from €2. Open in spring and summer M, W-F, and Su 11am-11:30pm, Th 11am-8pm, Sa 11am-noon; in fall and winter daily noon-8pm. Cash only. ❶

Osteria de' Benci, V. de' Benci 13r (☎055 23 44 923), on the corner with V. dei Neri. Savory portions of Tuscan classics like carpaccio (€13). Outdoor seating available. *Primi* €10. *Secondi* €10-17. Cafe open daily 8am-midnight. Restaurant open daily 1-2:45pm and 7:30-10:45pm. AmEx/MC/V. ❸

Trattoria Anita, V. del Parlascio 2r (☎055 21 86 98), behind Palazzo Vecchio. A casual Tuscan restaurant that provides authentic cuisine at reasonable prices near P. della Signoria. The changing daily lunch *menù* includes *primo*, *secondo*, and a vegetable side dish (€8). Grilled beefsteak or veal with a salad €12. Open M-Sa noon-2:30pm and 7-10pm. AmEx/MC/V. ❷

Bar Capitol, V. de' Neri, behind the Uffizi. If you find yourself too famished after a long day at the Uffizi to go any further than across the street, this restaurant provides outdoor seating and friendly service to get you going again. If you're looking for a different kind of pick-me-up, it is also a *tabacchi* and serves alcohol. *Primi* €6. *Secondi* €8-10. Open daily 7am-8pm. Cash only. ❷

Danny Rock, V. de' Pandolfini 13r (☎055 23 40 307; www.dannyrock.it), 3 blocks northwest of the Bargello. Casual *pizzeria* with outdoor patio and large dining room. Favored by local students. Check out the *menù* of the day and the list of burgers, but you'll find better pizza elsewhere. Take-out available. Pizza from €5. Cover €2. Open July-Aug. M-F noon-3:30pm and 7pm-1am, Sa 7pm-2am, Su 7pm-1am; Sept.-June M-F noon-3:30pm and 7pm-1am, Sa 7pm-2am, Su noon-3:30pm and 7pm-1am. MC/V. ❷

with Florentines attempting to escape the tourist hubbub.

6. Piazza Della Repubblica. In the heart of the city, this *piazza* has the architectural pull of the adjacent P. del Duomo without the heavy traffic.

7. Steps of San Miniato. In the same vertical direction as Ple. Michelangelo, the steps of San Miniato have an unforgettable view of the Tuscan hills outside the heart of the city.

8. Piazza della Signoria. The tourists, peddlers, and occasional jugglers and mimes make this *piazza* a little crowded, but nothing beats a date with David.

9. Piazza de Santissima Annunziata. A straight shot down V. de Servi away from the Duomo, this intimate *piazza* is usually nearly deserted except for the pigeon-friendly equestrian statue of Duke Ferdinand I. It also has a killer view of the Duomo in the distance.

10. Casa di Dante. For those with an active imagination, the small courtyard outside Dante's house is the perfect place to wallow in historical angst. Picture Dante sitting in the same place, eating a similar panino, waiting for ◪**Beatrice** to pass by. Nothing adds flavor like unrequited love.

MaMMaMia, V. Val di Lamona 1 (☎055 28 05 94), inside P. di Mercato Nuovo. Though the service is less cheery than the bright entrance and sunflowers inside would suggest, this restaurant offers outdoor seating, a convenient location, and menu specials for shopping tourists and locals in the area. *Primi* €8-14. *Secondi* €11-19. Open daily 11am-11pm. MC/V. ❹

SANTA MARIA NOVELLA

Any area this close to a train station is bound to feed its share of travelers. Tourist traps and chains crowd the avenues close to the station. That said, some of the cheapest food in the city can be found here. The *menù turistico*, as ominous as it sounds, can often end up being a good value if it includes a *secondo*. Santa Maria Novella has the best selection of ready-made and self-service eateries in the city.

Trattoria Contadino, V. Palazzuolo 69-71r (☎055 23 82 673). Casual, homestyle meals in a dining room with black and white decor and a relaxed atmosphere. You're sure to leave feeling stuffed—the only option is a multi-course *menù* that includes *primo, secondo*, a vegetable dish, bread, and house wine. Lunch €10. Dinner €11.50. ❷

Ristorante La Spada, V. della Spada 62r (☎055 21 87 57; www.laspadaitalia.com). This classic *cucina* serves Tuscan dishes ranging from the familiar (ravioli €9) to the uniquely Florentine (rabbit on a spit €10.50). Take a peek into the attached *rosticceria* (deli-kitchen) to watch the chef grilling your dishes in the open-air flame oven. The lunch *menù* (€11) includes *primo, secondo*, fruit salad, and drink. Check for nightly dinner deals. Cover €2.50. ❸

Trattoria da Giorgio, V. Palazzuolo 54. Probably the only place in Florence where you'll see a bead curtain and a Botticelli in the same room, da Giorgio keeps the decor unconventional and the menu unpretentious. *Menù* includes *primo, secondo*, vegetable, and ¼L of wine. Lunch *menù* €11. Dinner *menù* €12. Cover €1. Open M-Sa noon-2:30pm and 6-11pm. AmEx/MC/V. ❸

Rosticceria Gastronomia Il, Il Pirata, V. dei Ginori 56. Heaping helpings of hit-the-spot comfort food. As you chow down on your cheesy, meaty medley, check out the multilingual array of messages that guests have left on the wall and consider adding your own. The all-you-can-eat dinner buffet (with beer €8, with wine €9.50) is unbeatable. Buffet 6-9:30pm. Open M-Sa 11am-10pm. Cash only. ❷

Pizzeria and Ostaria Centopoveri, V. Palazzuolo 31r (☎055 21 88 46; www.icentopoveri.it). Deliciously gooey pizza you'll need a knife and fork to tackle. The lunch special (€8) includes a pizza, bread, and *caffè*. Or check out the Ostaria for the special *menù* (€10) that includes *primo, secondo*, water, and *caffé*. Both open daily noon-3pm and 7pm-midnight. ❷

Amon Specialità e Panini Egiziani, V. Palazzuolo 26-28r (☎055 29 31 46). This Egyptian alleyway take-out whips up kebabs (€3.50-3.90), falafel (€3), hummus (€2.80), and kofta for hungry Florentines on the go. Kebab sandwiches are stuffed with generous heaps of juicy shaved meat. Open daily noon-3pm and 6-11pm. Cash only. ❶

50 Rosso, V. Panzani 50r (☎055 28 35 85). The tasty grub at this snack bar—king of the ubiquitous takeout joints—will redefine the way you look at reheated *panini*. Choose from a variety of sandwiches to go (€2.50) or treat yourself to an espresso (€0.90) or cappuccino (€1.20). There's no table charge, so sit down and have a chat with the friendly staff. Open daily 6:30am-12:30am. ❶

Trattoria Belle Donne, V. delle Belle Donne (☎055 23 82 609). Flowers spill from every corner of this local favorite, where the customers sit on wooden stools and embrace the peasant roots of Tuscany's now world-famous cuisine. Brush up on your Italian, because there's no English menu. *Risotto al carciofi* €10. *Misto trippato toscano* €8.50. Open M-F noon-2:30pm and 7-10:30pm. MC/V. ❷

Trattoria Garga, V. del Moro 48r (☎055 23 98 898). Candle-lit dinner done a little differently: Garga's guests enjoy gourmet food while surrounded by motley murals and eclectic paintings. The husband-and-wife team behind this eatery also runs some local cooking classes. Signore Garga's arias from the kitchen don't cost extra. Open daily 9:30-11pm. AmEx/MC/V.

Trattoria Baldini, V. Il Prato 96r (☎055 28 76 63; www.trattoriabaldini.com). A family-friendly restaurant with a relaxed atmosphere and affordable menu. Most dishes, like the veal steak with parmesan (€13.50) and lamb cutlet (€12), run under €14. over €2. Open M-F noon-3pm and 7:30-10:30pm, Su 10am-3pm. ❸

Tre Merli, V. del Moro 11r (☎055 28 70 62). 2nd entrance at V. dei Fossi 12r. Head here for a sumptuous dinner served in an eclectic dining room close to the river. *Menù* (€15) includes *primo, secondo,* and wine. Cover €2. Open daily 11am-10:30pm. AmEx/MC/V. ❸

La Grotta di Leo, V. della Scala 41-43r (☎055 21 92 65). Always packed for dinner, this eatery makes for a loud, fun meal surrounded by heaps of tourists and a smattering of locals. Come for the tourist *menù* (€12) which includes *primo, secondo,* a vegetable dish, and drink. AmEx/MC/V. ❸

Trattoria al Trebbio, V. del Trebbio 47-49r (☎055 28 70 89). The seating for al Trebbio spills out into the street, lining the sidewalks and clustering the intersection with V. del Moro. Hop into one of their colorful chairs for a savory meal, like risotto with smoked buffalo mozzarella (€8), or just enjoy a streetside treat from their €4 dessert menu. Open daily noon-2:30pm and 7-11pm. ❷

Pizzeria Baccus, V. Borgo Ognissanti 45r (☎055 28 37 14; www.baccus.it). It may be named for the god of wine, but it's the pizza that's divine. Pizza and a drink €8. ❷

SAN LORENZO

The convenience afforded by San Lorenzo's proximity to major attractions is not without its drawbacks—touristy eateries and overpriced *gelaterias* that carry ice cream made from powders rather than fresh fruit. Still, there are a few gems—appreciated by locals and visitors alike—that carry delicious, fresh food for affordable prices.

Trattoria Mario, V. Rosina 2r, near P. del Mercato Centrale. Despite the 45min. wait, this family-run restaurant has proven its worth. Be prepared to share tables with other patrons. ½ portions are available on select dishes, and all courses are created with entirely fresh ingredients; there isn't a freezer in the whole place. Try the *ribollita* (soup with beans, bread, vegetables; €4.50), the *pollo fritto* (fried chicken) on M, or come for fish F. Be sure to arrive early in the afternoon before ingredients run out and some dishes are no longer available. Open M-Sa 12-3:30pm. Cover €0.50. Cash only. ❷

Trattoria Zàzà, P. del Mercato Centrale 16r (☎055 21 54 11). 3 outdoor areas and 4 themed indoor rooms set the scene for a delicious meal of fresh pasta at this 30-year-old favorite—but they still don't provide enough seating for all the hungry visitors—so be prepared to wait in line. Specializes in traditional Tuscan grilled meats. *Primi* €8-10. *Secondi* €11-22. Open daily 11am-11pm. AmEx/MC/V. ❹

Antica Gelateria Florentina, V. Faenza 2A. Every day, some of the best gelato in the Duomo area is prepared with fresh milk and fruit at this *gelateria.* The painted walls and the knowledgeable staff impart some of the treat's rich history. Enjoy nearly 30 flavors like *nocciola* (hazelnut) and *napole,* a fruit native to Italy. Cones and cups €1.60-4. Open daily noon-1am. Cash only. ❶

FOOD

THE HIDDEN DEAL

MERCATO CENTRALE

The Mercato Centrale is the perfect way to eat as the Italians do, without paying through the nose. Stocked with everything from massive buffalo mozzarella to wild boar meat, the Mercato Centrale is the city's oldest food market, selling the freshest Tuscan ingredients to the most discerning Italian cooks since the days before refrigerators.

Some tourists come to see or smell, but few think to stock up on ingredients for a delicious and portable lunch. The endless variety of fresh bread and cheese make an excellent and cheap combination, and don't forget to throw in a world-famous tomato from the produce section upstairs.

If you're willing to haggle a bit, you can get an excellent meal for two for under €10. Most vendors will even let you taste a piece of their product for free, which can add infinite variety to your menu, but make sure not to take advantage of their generosity.

V. del' Ariento, in the center of the popular San Lorenzo market, though you might have trouble finding the entrance through the sea of street vendors outside. Follow V. Faenza from P. del Duomo, make a right on V. Nazionale, then a quick right on V. del'Ariento. Open M-Sa 7am-2pm.

Bar Cabras, V. Dei Panzani 12r (☎055 21 20 32). For coffee and pastries near Santa Maria Novella, there's no better place. The older couple that has owned the small cafe for nearly half a century serves you sweets to the melody of classic rock. Enjoy custard-filled *torta della nonna* (€0.90), cannoli (€2.5), waffles (€3), and sandwiches (€3.5). ❶

Trattoria Nerone, V. Faenza 95r (☎055 29 12 17). With the dim lighting of a wine cellar, Trattoria Nerone features warm decor, elegantly painted walls, and precious figurines on the tables. Enjoy the creamy cheese topping of the thin crust pizza (€8) in the cozy atmosphere or choose the quiet outdoor seating on a sunny day. Open daily 11:30am-11pm. AmEx/MC/V. ❷

l'Brincello, V. Nazionale 110r (☎055 28 26 45). Painted scenes from Florence's past and Chianti wine bottles hanging from the ceiling give l'Brincello a warm ambience and historical character. Take a seat in one of the colorful chairs as the amiable chef prepares you one of the delicious daily specials like *rotolo ricotta e spinaci* (€7) or *bistecca alla fiorentina* (€20). Cover €1. Open Sept.-July noon-3pm and 7-11pm. MC/V. ❹

Ristorante Le Fonticine, V. Nazionale 79r (☎055 28 21 06; www.lefonticine.com). Owner Gian-Piero insists that his restaurant is a public place, thus the 3 generations worth of art that occupy the walls. Explore the kitchen on your way to the main dining area. Fresh pasta made daily. *Primi* €8-14. *Secondi* €9-20. Open Tu-Sa noon-2:30pm and 7-10pm. AmEx/MC/V. ❸

Mamma Toscana, V. San Antonino 34r (☎055 28 22 496). Salad and biscotti come with a meal that is delivered quickly by the young owners in a welcoming space, decorated with Christmas lights and flags of football clubs. *Primi* €5-8. *Secondi* €6-15. Open Tu-Su 10am-3pm and 6-11pm. AmEx/MC/V. ❸

Caffetteria Raffaella, V. Santa Caterina de' Alessandria 26. A bright and spacious cafe offering pastries like the *pasta sfoglia con mela* (€0.90) and *panini* (€2.50-3). Comfortable lights, tasteful decor, and original art from local artists create the perfect place for a quick snack or coffee break. Open M-F. Cash only. ❶

Caffè Astra, V. de' Cerretani 58r (☎055 23 02 710; www.sinisgalli.com). Stylish and conveniently located near the Duomo, Caffè Astra offers a full coffee and alcohol bar, upstairs lounge, and roof garden. Stop in for the melt-in-your-mouth buttermilk cookies (€0.30) or the *aperitvo con buffet* special everyday 5-9pm, which features a free buffet of pizza and *panini* with a €5 drink purchase. ❶

Caffè Michelangiolo, V. Cavour 21 (☎055 29 52 64; www.caffemichelangiolo.com), inside the Galleria Michelangelo. From 1850 to 1862, this spot was the meeting ground for the Macchiolia, a group of rebellious young painters who skipped class at the Accademia to discuss new directions in art. Today, you can treat yourself to an espresso (€0.80) or hot chocolate (€1.10) in the reopened coffee shop. Beer €3.50. Mixed drinks €4. Open daily 11am-6pm. Cash only. ❶

Bar Bano, V. Nazionale 163. Though steps away from a busy tourist area, the cafe has a pleasant, neighborly ambience with outdoor seating close to P. Della Indipendenza. Locally-made gelato €1.5-4. Sandwiches €2.5-3. Open daily 7am-1pm. Cash only. ❶

Bar Galli, V. de Banchi 14r (☎055 21 37 76). An Italian cafe by day and a Japanese restaurant by night, Bar Galli satisfies the craving for authentic Tuscan pasta and culturally diverse dishes. Grab the fish special of the day during the week or the ramen (€7-10) in the evenings. *Primi* €5-7. *Secondi* €7. Sa Japanese food. Open T-Su 12:30-2:30pm and 7-10pm. ❷

Trattoria dei Matti, V. Borgo San Lorenzo 31r (☎055 21 49 92). The outdoor seating and brick-lined interior with garlic cloves and wagon wheels gives this centrally located *pizzeria* a quirky charm—what else from the *trattoria* of fools? Pasta ranges from macaroni with salmon (€6) to spaghetti with clams, shrimps, and mussels (€13). Dishes also include tripe (€7) and pepper steak (€22). Daily specials. Open daily 11am-11pm. MC/V. ❸

Caffe Landucci, V. Borgo San Lorenzo 7r (☎055 21 26 80). A bit more expensive than other cafes in the area, Landucci lures diners into its sophisticated establishment with an enticing selection of fruit tarts and pastries. Outdoor seating available. Overpriced homemade gelato €3-6. Sandwiches €3-5. *Primi* €7.50. *Secondi* €8.50. Open daily 7am-8:30pm. AmEx/MC/V. ❷

SAN MARCO

Considering the number of sights in San Marco, the lunchtime food scene is surprisingly low on tourist traps. Because it's more residential than the city's other popular *piazze*, you'll find locals on lunch break at many of the area eateries, even those within a few blocks of the Accademia. Cafes and snack bars abound, so a cheap, quality meal is easy to come by. Dinner, however, is a bit more difficult; unlike the city center, San Marco isn't littered with *trattorie* vying for your business, so there's a greater temptation just to stop and eat as soon as you find a place that's open. You'll know you've found a good spot when you hear some Italian spoken (or shouted) at the other tables.

La Mescita, V. degli Alfani 70r, near the intersection with V. dei Servi. Look for the "Vino" sign above the door. La Mescita is a wonderful hole-in-the-wall that posts its prices on construction paper and writes the daily menu in marker. They'll quickly heat up your choice of the day's offerings and bring it to your table, but if you're aiming to save money, take it to go, because there's a €1 table service charge. *Panini* €1.60-3.50. *Primi* €4-5. *Secondi* €3-6. Open M-Sa 8am-9pm. ❶

VinOlio, V. San Zanobi 126r (☎055 48 99 57). On the corner with V. delle Ruote. Locals on lunch break dive into the chairs for hearty *primi* (€5.50-7) like pasta in ragu (€5.50) and roast beef with potatoes (€6). While the black-and-white photos and profusion of wine bottles may suggest a lazy, epicurean style, the incredibly speedy service at this restaurant caters to a crowd that has to be back at work soon. Open M-Sa 7:30am-1am. AmEx/MC/V. ❶

Ristorante Dioniso, V. San Gallo 16r (☎055 21 78 82). This blue-and-white Greek gem has won the local lunch crowd with its outgoing, energetic waiters and welcoming atmosphere. Lunch specials (€9) include fish, meat, and vegetarian options, all of which come with an extensive accompaniment of side dishes. Cover €1.50. Open M-Sa noon-3pm and 7:30pm-midnight, Su 7:30pm-midnight. AmEx/MC/V. ❷

Gran Caffè San Marco, P. San Marco 11r (☎055 21 58 33; www.grancaffesanmarco.it). This aptly-named colossus incorporates a *pasticceria*, a self-service restaurant, and a

FOOD

PIAZZALE MICHELANGELO

If your head and wallet are aching from the prices of downtown Florence, then step off the beaten tourist path. Only a few hundred yards off the main drags, you'll hardly feel as though you're in the city at all.

For one such route—which, incidentally, leads you directly to one of the most breathtaking vantage points over Florence, the Ple. Michelangelo—cross the Ponte Vecchio to its southern bank. Before reaching the Palazzo Pitti, take a left and cut through onto the Costa San Giorgio, which will take you up a long hill and into a sun-dappled residential area. Farther on, you will reach the impressive walls and expansive grounds of Fort Belvedere. Follow V. di Belvedere down the hill until you reach V. del Monte alle Croci on your right. This street will lead you up to a set of stone steps on your left, which ends at the Ple. Michelangelo.

The route is a full afternoon of walking, but if you bring your camera along and time it right, you will finish with some priceless, postcard-quality photos of Florence. Just think: the Duomo at sunset. Spectacular, and worth every step.

pizzeria in one sprawling complex. Skip the pizza, but come early in the lunch period to get their self-service food when it's hot. Lasagna day is not to be missed: their gooey-soupy-cheesy version is absolutely delicious. *Panini* €2.30-3.50. *Primi* €4.50-4.80. *Secondi* €4.50-6.50. Open daily 8am-10pm. MC/V. ❶

Cardillac Café, V. degli Alfani 57r. With a manic miscellany of local art on the walls and a foosball table in the back room, Cardillac oozes university vibe. There's a great stash of free nightlife info by the door, and the lunch *menù* is the definition of student food: a "big size" pizza with beer or a glass of wine is just €7 noon-3pm. Open M-Sa 8am-1am. Kitchen open 8am-3pm. Cash only. ❷

Nabucco Wine Bar, V. XXVII Aprile 28 (☎055 47 50 87). From 6:30-10:30pm, Nabucco runs a relaxed *aperitivo con buffet* (€6.50-7) that offers a quiet, less-crowded alternative to the kitsch nearby. With a wide selection of bruschetta, vegetables, finger sandwiches, and cold pasta dishes, this buffet has enough on offer to constitute a legitimate meal—even by non-Italian standards. International breakfast €8.50-13. Open M-Sa 6:30am-11:30pm. MC/V. ❷

Caffe Rosanó, V. San Gallo 29-31r. Look for the "Campus Bar" sign above the door. Local workers crowd this small cafe for a cold lunch and a hot drink, so if you're looking to rub elbows (literally) with some genuine Florentine, head here for a salad or cold pasta dish (€3.50-4.50) followed by coffee or espresso. Open M-Sa 7am-7:30pm. Cash only. ❶

Ristorante Da Mimmo, V. San Gallo 57-59r (☎055 48 10 30). A Tuscan farmhouse dropped into a Medici *palazzo*. Corn husks hang from the frescoed arches and loud conversations bounce off the marble walls. You won't need a reservation to sit down, but because of its popularity with the locals, you'll need one to sit inside. *Primi* €8-10. *Secondi* €11-16. Cover €3. AmEx/MC/V. ❸

Snack Bar Lele, V. Gino Capponi 12-14r (☎055 39 88 764). Head here early in the lunch hours to grab your pick of the *panini* (€2)from the enormous heap of sandwiches to the left of the door. Or enjoy a combo meal (€6.50) of a pizza or focaccia, a side dish, and water. Open M-F 7am-7pm. MC/V. ❶

Rosticceria Alfio Beppe, V. Cavour 118/120r. You can see the chickens rotating on their spits in the open-air oven at this charge-by-the-kilo *rosticceria*. The assertive, amiable staff is quick with suggestions, service, and a smile, so even if you just stop in to browse, you may find yourself leaving with a helping or two of whatever just came out of the oven. *Primi* €3.50. *Secondi* €2-8. Open M-F and Su 8am-9pm. MC/V. ❶

Ristorante Il Vegetariano, V. delle Ruote 30r (☎055 47 50 30), off V. San Gallo. True to its name, this self-service restaurant is a vegetarian's dream. Enjoy filling dishes in the peaceful bamboo garden (no pandas). Salads €4-5.50. *Primi* from €5.50. *Secondi* from €7. Open Sept.-July Tu-F 12:30-3pm and 7:30pm-midnight, Sa-Su 7pm-midnight. Cash only. ❷

Caffelatte, V. degli Alfani 39r (☎055 24 78 878). Originally opened as a butcher shop, this *latteria* now specializes in organically-grown and vegetarian foods. Also serves as the local milk shop, so anything dairy that they're serving is bound to be fresh and scrumptious. Scones with fresh cream €3.50. Espresso €2. Cover €1. Open M 8am-9pm, Tu-Su 8am-midnight. Cash only. ❶

Ristorante Il Paiolo, V. del Corso 42r (☎055 21 50 19; www.ristoranteilpaiolo.it). The cheerful owners of this restaurant are equally friendly to customers and the environment, serving an eco-conscious menu (€29), numerous vegetarian dishes, and fresh fish from the market every day. The delicious meals are pretty pricey (€20-30), but worth the splurge. Cover €3. Open daily noon-3pm and 7-11pm. AmEx/MC/V. ❺

SANTA CROCE

The restaurants cater to a local crowd, making for an abundance of great *trattorie* and *pizzerie*.

▨ **Teatro del Sale,** V. dei Macci 111r (☎055 20 01 492). It's "members only" at this private club, but the slight fee and mission statement ensure that the pretensions end here. In a high-arched, hardwood theatre, Fabio Picchi picks the freshest ingredients and announces each delicious course from his open kitchen. Once the last piece of mouthwatering dessert has been snatched off the plate, the entertainment begins, ranging from music lessons to theatrical performances—but many shows are in Italian, so plan ahead. Breakfast €7; lunch €20. Membership fee €5. Open Tu-Sa 9-11am, noon-2:15pm, and from 7:30pm until the end of the show. Reservations required. AmEx/MC/V. ❹

▨ **Ruth's Kosher Vegetarian Restaurant,** V. Luigi Carlo Farini 2A (☎055 24 80 888). Carnivorous Christians, be not afraid! There are plenty options for you, as well. Photos of Woody Allen and Kafka look on as wise owner Simcha makes everyone feel part of the community, serving hummus (€6), pasta (€7), and couscous (€13-15). Students enjoy special dinners W nights for €10. Free Wi-Fi. Open M-Th and Su noon-2:30pm and 7:30-10:30pm, F noon-2:30pm. AmEx/MC/V. ❷

A Casamia, P. de Ghiberti 5r (☎055 26 38 223). Crisp, clean decor means that eating so cheap never looked so good. Each weekday, choose from 3 different *primo, secondo,* and *contorno* offerings, have some bottled water, and enjoy a *caffè* for just €6, including cover. *Primo* and beverage €3.30. Open Tu-Su 11:30am-3pm and 6:30pm-2am. ❶

Acquacotta, V. dei Pilastri 51r (☎055 24 29 07). Sweet and simple, with flowered ceramic ware on the shelves and cream-colored walls, this Tuscan *trattoria* serves fresh pasta and seasonal dishes. Stop in for lunch when you can choose a *primo*, like ravioli stuffed with pheasant and truffle cream sauce, and a *secondo*, like beef filet with *Chianti Classico* sauce, for €12.50. Reservations recommended for weekend dinner. *Primi* €7-11. *Secondi* €12-20. Open Tu-Su noon-2:30pm and 7-11pm. AmEx/MC/V. ❹

Il Giova, Borgo la Croce 73r. Colorful tables and amphibian designs on the counter tiles create a tropical vibe in this gourmet restaurant. The highlights are duck breast with red onion and figs (€15) and sliced steak with truffle (€16). *Primi* €7-8.50. *Secondi* €11-18. Open M-Sa 12:30-3pm and 7:30-11pm. AmEx/MC/V. ❹

Ristorante del Fagiioli, Corso Tintori 47r., just a few steps from the touristy V. de' Benci and Chiesa di Santa Croce. Don't be intimidated by the Italian menu; the English-speaking owner will gladly translate. *Primi* €8-9. *Bistecca alla Fiorentina* €33 per kg. ❸

FOOD

L'Angolo Della Pizza, V. dei Macci 78r (☎055 24 51 49). At €1 a slice, *l'angolo* (the angle) of these pizzas is clearly "right." Splurge and get a calzone for €2. Seating is limited. Open M-F 8am-3:30pm. Cash only. ❶

Il Principe, V. dell'Agnolo 93r (☎055 24 03 50). Forget Burger King and really have it your way at "The Prince," where you have a say in the type of meat (or non-meat), cheese, and vegetables that go inside your choice of bread. *Normale* pizza €3.50-8. *Grande* pizza €7-16. Open daily 10:30am-midnight. Cash only. ❷

Semolina, P. Lorenzo Ghiberti 87r (☎055 23 47 584). A golden dragon and a pharaoh painted on the walls greet you in this whimsical restaurant. *Spaghetti alla carrettiera* (€6) is the spicy specialty. Pizza €5-8. *Primi* €6-15. *Secondi* €12-18. Open daily 12:30-3pm and 7:30-11:30pm. AmEx/MC/V. ❸

Valle dei Cedri, Borgo Santa Croce 11r (☎055 23 46 340; www.valledeicedri.com). Take a break from Tuscany in this Lebanese restaurant with a shawarma meal (€14) and shish kebab (€12), or mix things up with *Lahm bi Agin* (Lebanese pizza; €5). Open M-Sa 7pm-midnight. AmEx/MC/V. ❸

Le Campane, Borgo la Croce 87r. Family-run restaurant with an impressive brick oven. Have anything from *bistecca alla fiorentina* (€37 per kg) to pizza (*normale* €4-9; *grande* €9-20). *Primi* €6-9. *Secondi* €10-15. Cover €1.60. Open daily 1-3pm and 7-11:30pm. MC/V. ❸

The William, V. Magliabechi 7-11r (☎055 26 38 357). Conveniently close to P. Santa Croce, this English pub still pays homage to Florentine culture with a beautiful frescoed ceiling. For lunch, choose from pasta (€6), pizza (€7), hamburger or roast beef with a potato side (€8), or a meat dish with pasta (€12). Happy hour M-W 6-11pm; 2 lagers €7, 3 vodka shots €5. Th-F evenings live music. Open daily 12:30-3:30pm and 7:30-10:30pm. AmEx/MC/V. ❷

La Pagnotta, P. Sant'Ambrogio. Royal blue walls and gold Florentine fleur-de-lis in this corner bakery make the delicious pizza and pastries look good. *Torta di semolina* (traditional Tuscan cake) €1.50. Open M-Sa 7am-7pm. Cash only. ❶

Le Colonnine, V. de' Benci 6r (☎055 23 46 417). This restaurant's location on the corner of a fork-in-the-road conceals a surprisingly large, classy indoor seating area. Simple but satisfying lunch menu. Come for dinner for a more extensive selection. *Primi* €7-9. *Secondi* €10-13. Open daily noon-3:30pm and 6:30-11:30pm. MC/V. ❸

Gelatissimo, V. di San Giuseppe 4r. You'll find sugar and spice in this gelateria's eponymous specialty, which includes saffron, rose water, and pistachio. Balance out all that herbal taste with one of the more traditional flavors. Cups and cones from €1.50. Cash only. ❶

Boccadama, P. Santa Croce 25/26r (☎055 24 36 40). Yellow walls, olive curtains, and writing desks make this a cute place to stop for a lunch if you can't make it out of the square, but don't let your curiosity convince you to open the table drawers; you may not want to know what past diners have left for you there. *Primi* €7-9. *Secondi* €10. AmEx/MC/V. ❷

Salumeria Verdi, V. Giuseppe Verdi 36r (☎055 24 45 17). For a quick and yummy bite near Santa Croce, try the daily pasta offerings at this little food counter. *Primi* €3. *Secondi* €4.50. Open M-Sa 8:30am-8pm. MC/V. ❶

Mr. Kebab House, V. dei Pilastri 26. You'll be drawn by the tantalizing smell before you even see the place. Students get a €0.50 discount off the €3.50 falafels and kebabs. Cash only. ❶

Caffè Vecchio Mercato, Borgo la Croce 71r. Since the mid-19th century, a bar similar to this has stood on the same spot, providing tobacco products, coffee, wine, and pastries to quickly satisfy every fix. Coffee €0.90; cocktails €5. MC/V over €10. ❶

WEST OLTRARNO

Without the steady stream of tourists that other parts of Florence enjoy, restaurants in this area keep prices low and quality high to attract the locals who frequent these stops. There are fewer of the cookie-cutter *trattorie* than you'll find elsewhere, meaning that many of the restaurants have their own unique, often pleasant, personality.

Dante, P. Nazario Sauro 12r (☎055 21 92 19; www.ristorantedante.net). Let the doorman welcome you in and enjoy a comfortable meal surrounded by the restaurant's own brand of wine, bottled by a local winery. Students can enjoy it for free with a special deal that includes a free drink and no cover charge. *Primi* €6-18. *Secondi* €10-22. Cover €2. Open daily 12pm-1am. AmEx/MC/V. ❹

Cammillo, Borgo San Jacopo 57r (☎055 21 24 27). Bow-tied and mustachioed, the experienced waiters will make you feel at home in this *trattoria*. The Impressionist artwork gives it the air of a true Italian restaurant from the date scene in a black-and-white movie. *Primi* €10-15. *Secondi* €16-25. MC/V. ❹

Seme d'uva, V. dell'Orto 25r (☎055 22 86 471). The friendly staff provides a relaxed and intimate dining experience focused around a seasonally changing menu. The large, colorful paintings on the walls were made by local, amateur artists. Try the meat ravioli with cream sauce (€7.50) and *crespelle alla fiorentina* (pasta envelopes filled with asparagus and cheese, €8). *Primi* €7-9. *Secondi* €12-16. Open M-Sa 7-10:30pm. Cash only. ❸

4 Leoni, V. dei Vellutini 1r (☎055 21 85 62; www.4leoni.com). The culinary roar of these 4 lions has captured the attention of Dustin Hoffman and Isabella Rossellini. The old brick of years gone by shows in parts against the mustard yellow walls. The *fiocchetti di pera* (pear and parmesan in pasta pouches; €10) are a sweet and cheesy delight. *Primi* €8-18. *Secondi* €9-25. Cover €1.50. Open M-Tu and Th-Su noon-2:30pm and 7-10:30pm, W 7-10:30pm. AmEx/MC/V. ❸

Gelateria La Carraia, P. Nazario Sauro 25r (☎055 28 06 95). Hanging on the walls of this shop, *Mona Lisa* is clearly smiling at the wonderfully creamy and inexpensive selection of gelato. Candy-striped green walls and a bouquet of multi-colored cones add whimsy to this already sweet spot. Cones from €1. Cups from €1.30. Cash only. ❶

Trattoria dell'Orto, V. dell'Orto 35a (☎055 22 41 48). Get carried away by the sweet smell of fresh focaccia. Enjoy your meal either in the warmly lit inside or the enclosed outside seating area in the back. *Primi*

GET YOUR €500'S WORTH

There's no shortage of fine dining in Florence, but travelers with some spare change (or a little more) should stop by **Enoteca Pinchiorri,** one of the most legendary restaurants in Europe. Rated the 32nd best restaurant in the world by *Restaurant* magazine, Enoteca Pinchiorri's offerings include vegetable stew with ginger and black truffle and spinach and ricotta dumplings topped with creamy lobster *fricassee*. Giorgio Pinchiorri and his wife Annie Féolde own the place, with Féolde holding the reins as head chef.

Of course, a meal at Enoteca Pinchiorri will cost you. Most diners recommend the tasting menu; although there are several options, the eleven-course menu will cost you €300. The restaurant also houses one of the best wine cellars in the region, holding around 145,000 bottles of wine, which will drive the price up even further. Wine flights, offering diners a selection of five wines to sample throughout the night, start at around €175. If you happen to have around €500 to spare—and who doesn't?—why not try a meal at Enoteca Pinchiorri?

V. Ghibellina 87 (☎055 24 27 77), Santa Croce. Jacket recommended. Open Tu-W 7:30-10pm, Th-Sa 12:30-2pm and 7:30-10pm. Closed 3 weeks in August.

YOU ARE WHAT YOU (RUMIN)ATE

Don't let the fact that it is made from *abomaso*, the cow's fourth stomach, deter you from ordering a *lampredotto* sandwich. Dating back nearly a thousand years, this traditional "poor-man's dish" is a distinctively Florentine specialty you don't want to miss.

A more tender version of *trippa* (tripe, the cow's first stomach), another food stall mainstay, lampredotto is first boiled in a broth of herbs and vegetables, then sliced and served on a roll with green (parsley-based) or hot sauces.

Bread in Florence is generally baked without salt, which can render it a little bland, but in this case, the saltiness of the meat offsets the blandness of the roll.

Make sure to get all the fixings—ask for it *bagnato* (covered in the broth) and with salsa verde and piccante. Finally, round out the experience with a glass of red wine.

If you're brave enough to try it, the best place to get a tender, succulent *panino con lampredotto* is on the street, from one of the local vendors found throughout Florence.

€6.50-8. *Secondi* €8-10. Open W-Su 12:30-2:30pm and 5:30-11:30pm. AmEx/MC/V. ❷

La Casalinga, V. dei Michelozzi 9r (☎055 21 86 24; www.trattorialacasalinga.it). *"Qui si viene a mangiare, a ridere, a chiaccherare"* ("One comes here to eat, to laugh, and to chat") is the motto of this local *trattoria* serving rustic Italian fare in an amicable environment. Open daily 12-2:30pm and 7-10pm. ❷

Hemingway, P. Piattellina 9r (☎055 28 47 81). Mint blue walls and shelves of books set the tone in this chocolate-centered cafe named for the American author. Each table has its own elegant personality, but there exists a delicate bookishness throughout, from the narrative menu descriptions to the crowd of hip students and spectacled older couples. Milkshakes often include sweet liquor, like the *Quando ti alzi* (white chocolate ice cream, Bailey's Irish Cream, milk, and dry sparkling white wine; €9), and coffee (€4-7.50) is served with a chocolate spoon. Open M-Th 4:30pm-1am, F-Sa 4:30pm-2am, Su 3:30pm-1am. MC/V. ❷

Osteria Santo Spirito, P. Santo Spirito 16r (☎055 23 82 383). Aged doors, bright red walls, and dangling whirligigs. Conveniently located in the lively *piazza*, its bamboo-shaded outdoor seating area helps ensure an enjoyable meal in a creatively comfortable environment both inside and out. *Primi* €7-15. *Secondi* €14-28. Cover €2. Open daily 12-11:30pm. ❹

Gelateria Pitti, P. Pitti 2r (☎329 84 79 426). Homemade flavors in a small shop with friendly service. Cones and cups €1.50. Open daily 10am-11pm. Cash only. ❶

l'brindellone, P. Piattellina 10r (☎055 21 78 79). Respectfully sporty, this restaurant is named for the elaborate container that carries the Eucharist on Easter Sunday, but the many sports photos decorating its walls betray a less holy and more casual vibe. *Primi* €5-9. *Secondi* €8-12. ❸

Il Ristoro dei Perditempo, Borgo San Jacopo 48r (☎055 26 45 569). A classier version of the typical *pasticierria*, this food counter offers daily specials and a dining area lit by lace-covered lights at antique writing desk tables. A giant picture window offers a wonderful view of Ponte Vecchio and the Arno River below. *Primi* €5-7. *Secondi* €6-9. Open M noon-4pm, Tu-Su noon-10pm. ❷

Bar Sant'Agostino, V. Sant'Agostino 38r. A small, comfortable bar with a TV-equipped seating area and no cover. Grab one of the daily specials from the food counter for a real deal. *Primi* €3-5. Open daily 6am-9pm. Cash only. ❶

EAST OLTRARNO

The eateries in this area attract a lot of locals. While that means you're getting quality, you also won't find a lot of cheap eats here.

Gattabuia, Lungarno Cellini 13-15r (☎055 68 14 449; www.gattabuia.com). Even with 2 stories of space, this locally lauded restaurant still struggles to fit everyone into a table. Famous for its freshly crafted creative pizzas, Gattabuia is guaranteed to make you wait for your meal, but when your wait is awash in wine and conversation, who's complaining? Pizza €5-12. *Primi* €9-12. Cover €2. Open M and W-Su. Reservations recommended on weekends. MC/V. ❸

i'pizzachiere, V. San Miniato 2/1 (☎055 24 66 332). A pint-sized *pizzeria* with Latin music on the speakers and steaming-hot servings. Local workers frequently hop in to order a quick bite to go. Limited seating. Pizza €6-8, family size €15. Calzones €8. Open M and W-Su 11am-11pm. MC/V. ❷

La Beppa Fioraia Trattoria Pizzeria, V. dell'Erta Canina 6r (☎055 23 47 681; www.beppafioraia.it). Brush up on your Italian before hitting this secluded *trattoria*—the menu's entirely in Italian and no one's around to translate. Nestled at the base of a Tuscan hillside, this colorful, low-ceilinged eatery affords a charming view of the old city wall. *Primi* €8-10. *Secondi* €14-18. Open daily 12:30pm-2:30pm and 7:30pm-11:30pm. AmEx/MC/V. ❸

Filipepe, V. San Niccolo 39r (☎055 20 01 397; www.filipepe.com). A romantic escape lit only by covered lamps and candles, Filipepe would be the perfect date spot if seafood were a little sexier. The scrumptious dishes are often prepared with fresh ingredients (bring mints). Be sure to ask about the plate of the day. *Primi* €6-14. *Secondi* €14-20. Open daily 7:30pm-midnight. AmEx/MC/V. ❹

Le Volpi e l'uva, P. dei Rossi 1 (☎055 23 98 132; www.levolpieluva.com). Wall-to-wall wine bottles on the left, floor-to-ceiling wine glasses on the right, and a giant bunch of grapes dead center. If the decor doesn't make it obvious, the tipsy, teeming crowd at the tables certainly will: Le Volpi is all about the *vino*. Red wine €3.50-8 per glass, white €3.50-4.50. Cheese and salami platters €7-8. Open M-Sa 11am-9pm. AmEx/MC/V. ❷

FOOD

SIGHTS

Considering the Duomo's views, the perfection of Santo Spirito's nave, and the overwhelming array of art in the Uffizi Gallery, it's hard to take a wrong turn in Florence. Medieval churches, Renaissance basilicas, Baroque fountains, and 19th-century museums all cluster together in a city bursting with masterpieces from every era of Western civilization. Enjoy.

No matter which sights you choose to see, though, there are a few general pieces of advice that pertain to many of them. First and foremost, most important sights are best visited in the morning—the earlier the better. Not only do you avoid the crowds, but in the summer you miss the crushing heat that descends upon the city. During the afternoons, you can visit some of the countless smaller museums and galleries, or do as the Italians do and take a siesta. Remember that most churches are only open from 8:30am to 12:30pm and from 4 to 7pm, so plan accordingly. Many of them also close on certain days (see our handy chart, p. 114). If you are planning to visit one of the city's countless churches, remember to dress appropriately or you will be asked to leave, or worse, don't what our researchers came to know as the "kimono of shame." A final note about sightseeing in Florence: hours of operation are always subject to change—nation-wide strikes, a proprietor's whim, and everything in between can and will thwart your plans, so be ready to throw your hands up, let out a yell of frustration, and go buy some gelato. To avoid interminable waits for Florence's most renowned attractions, make phone reservations by calling Firenze Musei. (☎055 29 48 83; www.firenzemusei.it. Open M-F 8:30am-6:30pm, Sa 8:30am-12:30pm.)

THE DUOMO

▨DUOMO (CATTEDRALE DI SANTA MARIA DEL FIORE)

Open M,W, and F 10am-5pm; Th 10am-4:30pm; Sa 10am-4:45pm; Su 1:30-4:45pm. Shortest wait just before opening. Mass daily 7:30, 8:30, 9:30am, and 6pm. Su Mass 7:30, 9, 10:30am, and 12:30pm. English Mass Sa 5pm. Free. Ask inside the entrance to the left about free guided tours in English.

In 1296, the city fathers commissioned Arnolfo di Cambio to erect a cathedral so magnificent that it would be "impossible to make it either better or more beautiful with the industry and power of man"—or, more specifically, with the industry and power of Pisa and Siena, who by the late 13th century had already built towering cathedrals that made Florence's current church, St. Reparata, look like a peasant's hovel. Arnolfo intended to outshine his hometown's rivals; Santa Maria del Fiore would express both the glory of God *and* the glory of Florence—it's no coincidence that "Fiore" and "Fiorentina" (Florentine) come from the same word. Arnolfo designed a nave so massive in size that the technology necessary to erect a dome over it did not even exist yet. Wowed by his work here and in Santa Croce, in 1300 the city declared him exempt from paying taxes for life. Unfortunately, Arnolfo didn't live to enjoy his tax-free life for very long. He died in 1302, after completing only the lower half of the front facade. His successors only enlarged the scheme of the project, adding extra bays and upping the ante on the nave's height and width.

SIGHTS & MUSEUMS CLOSINGS	DAILY	M MORNING	M AFTERNOON	TU MORN.	TU AFTERNOON	W MORN.	W AFTERNOON
ACCADEMIA		Closed.	Closed.				
BARGELLO		Closed 2nd and 4th of the month.	Closed 2nd and 4th of the month.				
BASILICA DI SAN LORENZO							
BATTISTERO							
BIBLIOTECA NAZIONALE CENTRALE							
BRUNELLESCHI'S DOME							
CASA BUONARROTI							
CASA DI RODOLFO SIVIERO			Closed.	Closed.	Closed.	Closed.	Closed.
CASA GUIDI		Closed.	Closed Nov.-Mar.	Closed.	Closed.	Closed.	Closed.
CENACOLO DI FULIGNO		Closed.	Closed.		Closed.	Closed.	Closed.
CENACOLO DI SANT'APOLLONIA		Closed 2nd and 4th of the month.	Closed.		Closed.		Closed.
CENACOLO DI SANTO SPIRITO		Closed.	Closed.	Closed.	Closed.	Closed.	Closed.
CHIESA DI OGNISSANTI	Closed 12:30-4pm.						
CHIOSTRO DELLO SCALZO		Closed.		Closed.	Closed.	Closed.	Closed.
CIMITERO DEI PROTESTANTI	Closed noon-3pm.						
CRYPT OF ST. REPARATA							
DUOMO							
MUSEO ARCHEOLOGICO		Closed.				Closed.	Closed.
MUSEO DEGLI ARGENTI & MUSEO DELLA PORCELLANA		Closed 1st and last of the month.	Closed 1st and last of the month.				
MUSEO DEGLI INNOCENTI							
MUSEO DELL'OPERA DEL DUOMO							
MUSEO DI SAN MARCO		Closed 2nd and 4th of the month.	Closed.		Closed.		Closed.
MUSEO DI STORIA DELLA SCIENZA					Closed.		
MUSEO HORNE			Closed.		Closed.		Closed.
MUSEO MARINO MARINI				Closed.	Closed.		

SIGHTS & MUSEUMS CLOSINGS	TH MORN.	TH AFTERNOON	F MORN.	F AFTERNOON	SA MORN.	SA AFTERNOON	SU MORN.	SU AFTERNOON
ACCADEMIA								
BARGELLO								
BASILICA DI SAN LORENZO							Closed.	Closed Mar.-Oct.
BATTISTERO						Closed 1st of the month.		Closed.
BIBLIOTECA NAZIONALE CENTRALE						Closed.	Closed.	Closed.
BRUNELLESCHI'S DOME							Closed.	Closed.
CASA BUONARROTI			Closed.	Closed.	Closed.	Closed.		
CASA DI RODOLFO SIVIERO	Closed.	Closed.	Closed.	Closed.			Closed Sept.-June.	Closed.
CASA GUIDI	Closed.	Closed.	Closed.	Closed Nov.-Mar.	Closed.	Closed.	Closed.	Closed.
CENACOLO DI FULIGNO		Closed.	Closed.	Closed.		Closed.	Closed Sept.-June.	Closed.
CENACOLO DI SANT' APOLONIA		Closed.		Closed.		Closed.	Closed 1st, 3rd, and 5th of the month.	Closed.
CENACOLO DI SANTO SPIRITO	Closed.	Closed.	Closed.	Closed.		Closed Nov.-Mar.	Closed.	Closed.
CHIESA DI OGNISSANTI							Closed.	
CHIOSTRO DELLO SCALZO	Closed.		Closed.	Closed.	Closed.		Closed.	Closed.
CIMITERO DEI PROTESTANTI								
CRYPT OF ST. REPARATA							Closed.	Closed.
DUOMO							Closed.	
MUSEO ARCHEOLOGICO				Closed.		Closed.		Closed.
MUSEO DEGLI ARGENTI & MUSEO DELLA PORCELLANA								
MUSEO DEGLI INNOCENTI								
MUSEO DELL'OPERA DEL DUOMO								
MUSEO DI SAN MARCO								
MUSEO DI STORIA DELLA SCIENZA								
MUSEO HORNE								
MUSEO MARINO MARINI								

SIGHTS

SIGHTS & MUSEUMS CLOSINGS	DAILY	M MORN.	M AFTERNOON	TU MORN.	TU AFTERNOON	W MORN.	W AFTERNOON
MUSEO NAZIONALE ALINARI DELLA FOTOGRAFIA	Closed 1:30-4pm.					Closed.	Closed.
MUSEO SALVATORE FERRAGAMO				Closed.	Closed.		
MUSEO ZOOLOGICO		Closed 1st and last of the month.	Closed 1st and last of the month.				
OPIFICIO DELL PIETRE DURE			Closed.		Closed		Closed.
ORSANMICHELE		Closed.	Closed.				
ORTO BOTANICO				Closed Oct- Mar.	Closed Oct-Mar	Closed.	Closed.
PALAZZO DAVANZATI		Closed 1st, 3rd, and 5th of the month.	Closed.		Closed.		Closed.
PALAZZO MEDICI						Closed.	
PALAZZO PITTI		Closed.	Closed.				
PALAZZO VECCHIO							
SANTA CROCE							
SANTA MARIA DEL CARMINE				Closed.	Closed.		
SANTA TRINITA	Closed noon-4pm.						
SANTISSIMA ANNUNZIATA	Closed 12:30-4pm.						
SANTO SPIRITO	Closed 12:30-4pm.					Closed.	Closed.
SYNAGOGUE							
UFFIZI		Closed.	Closed.				

A 16th-century Medici rebuilding campaign removed the Duomo's incomplete Gothic-Renaissance facade. The walls remained naked until 1871, when Florentine architect Emilio de Fabris won the commission to create a facade in the Neo-Gothic style. The patterned green-white-and-red marble walls are impressively grand, especially when viewed from the southern side.

Today, the Duomo claims one of the world's longest naves. It rises 100m into the air, making it as high as the surrounding Tuscan hills and visible from nearly every corner of the city. Its 44 stained glass windows, dating from 1388-1445, also represent the largest collection of ancient stained glass in any Italian church. Though ornately decorated on the outside, the church's interior is rather chilly and stark; unadorned dark stone was believed to encourage humble devotion. One notable exception to this sober style is the extravagant group of frescoes on the dome's ceiling, where visions of the apocalypse glare down at visitors in a stunning display of color and light. Notice Paolo Uccello's celebrated monument to the mercenary captain Sir John Hawkwood on the cathedral's left wall and his *trompe l'oeil* clock on the back wall. This 24hr. timepiece runs backward, starting its cycle at sunset, when the *Ave Maria* is traditionally sung.

SIGHTS

SIGHTS & MUSEUMS CLOSINGS	TH MORN.	TH AFTERNOON	F MORN.	F AFTERNOON	SA MORN.	SA AFTERNOON	SU MORN.	SU AFTERNOON
MUSEO NAZIONALE ALINARI DELLA FOTOGRAFIA								
MUSEO SALVATORE FERRAGAMO								
MUSEO ZOOLOGICO								
OPIFICIO DELL PIETRE DURE				Closed.		Closed.	Closed.	Closed.
ORSANMICHELE								
ORTO BOTANICO	Closed Oct-Mar.	Closed Oct-Mar.						
PALAZZO DAVANZATI		Closed.		Closed.		Closed.	Closed 2nd and 4th of the month.	Closed.
PALAZZO MEDICI								
PALAZZO PITTI								
PALAZZO VECCHIO		Closed.						
SANTA CROCE							Closed.	
SANTA MARIA DEL CARMINE							Closed.	
SANTA TRINITA								Closed.
SANTISSIMA ANNUNZIATA								
SANTO SPIRITO								
SYNAGOGUE				Closed.	Closed.	Closed.		
UFFIZI								

BRUNELLESCHI'S DOME. The problem of building the enormous cupola of St. Maria del Fiore was not addressed until the early 15th century, when the nave was finally stable enough for construction of the dome to begin. Dozens of proposals were brought before the wool guild, some of them ludicrous to modern audiences. One architect proposed that the city fill the cathedral with soil until it reached the level of the dome, and when he could not think of a way to get the soil out again, a guild member mockingly suggested that they hide gold in the dirt—then every man in the city would be willing to take out a wheelbarrow-full! However, the honor of constructing the dome went to Filippo Brunelleschi, who, after studying Classical methods of sculpture, devised the ingenious techniques needed to construct a dome large enough for the nave. For the Duomo's sublime crown, now known simply as **Brunelleschi's Dome,** the architect designed a revolutionary, double-shelled structure that incorporated self-supporting, interlocking bricks. However, Brunelleschi was nearly the undoing of his own brilliance. Jealously secretive of his plans (he sometimes made his models from turnips so that at day's end he could boil and eat them), he refused to reveal to the council exactly *how* his model would stay

SIGHTS

upright. Legend has it that, enraged by their lack of faith in him, he called for an egg and snarled that any man with wit enough to make the egg stand on one end could also construct the dome. When member after member failed to keep the egg upright, Brunelleschi snatched it up, cracked it at the base, and thereby stood it on the table. The committee complained that they could have done as much, had they known they were allowed to, and Brunelleschi retorted that so too could they have known how to build the dome if they knew his plans.

Luckily, they were impressed enough by his earlier work with domes to award him the commission, but his secrecy worried them. And so, in a move that was probably in no small part a punishment for his arrogance, they assigned him a co-*capomaestro*: Lorenzo Ghiberti, his hated rival from the Baptistery doors fiasco (p. 119). Brunelleschi was infuriated by the selection of Ghiberti, who was a brilliant bronzeworker but had very little architectural experience. Though he had never been a man to take things lying down, he made an exception this one time and did just that: for week and weeks, he lay in bed playing sick. Ghiberti was clearly unable to continue the project without him, since only Brunelleschi knew the plans for the dome, and when the council told Brunelleschi of Ghiberti's trouble with building the project on his own, Brunelleschi answered that *he* would have no such trouble with a solo job. The council took the hint and Ghiberti gradually moved on to other projects, leaving Brunelleschi to build on his own. During construction, Brunelleschi built kitchens, sleeping rooms, and lavatories between the two walls of the cupola so the masons would never have to descend. Brunelleschi intended for a gallery to crown the top of the cupola, and in 1507 there was a contest to determine who would get to build it. However, winner Baccio d'Agnolo halted building in 1519 when Michelangelo told him it looked like a "cricket cage." The **Museo dell'Opera del Duomo** (p. 120) chronicles the mechanics of Brunelleschi's engineering feats in an in-depth exhibit. Today, visitors can climb the 463 steps inside the dome to Michelangelo's lantern for an expansive view of the city from the external gallery. Halfway up, visitors can enjoy a view of the dome's frescoed interior from just inches away. *(Entrance on southern side of the Duomo. ☎055 23 02 885. Open M-F 8:30am-7pm, Sa 8:30am-5:40pm. €8. Cash only.)*

THE UGLY AMERICAN. Going to Mass may seem like a quick way to get into the Duomo without waiting in line, but other people's religious ceremonies are not your tourist attraction. Be aware that Mass is only in English on Saturdays; if you go on Sunday, you'll be hearing the ceremony in Italian or Latin. And foreigners who leave early, snapping a shot on the way out, are seen as the lowest species of insensitive vermin on the tourist ladder. So either sit through the ceremony or don't come in at all. Leaving during the consecration of the host, when the priest lifts the Eucharist above the altar, is the most offensive.

CRYPT OF ST. REPARATA. Low-ceilinged, musty, and more than 2½m below the floor of the cathedral, this archaeological potluck has yielded everything from a Roman mask to Brunelleschi's tomb. Pre-Roman remains, early medieval artifacts, Renaissance frescoes—they're all found here. While little is known about how pre-Roman peoples used this space, the Christian church of St. Reparata can be traced to at least the fifth century, when it was consecrated to St. Reparata as thanks for the Christian victory over Radagasius, king of the Goths, in 405. As you wander through this maze of stone staircases to nowhere, you won't be wowed by the beauty of what you see, but you'll be amazed at just how many different cultures were drawn to this spot. Be sure to check out Brunelleschi's tomb and the crumbling bronze sword and spurs from a Medici family burial. (*Entrance in the floor of the Duomo. Open M-F 10am-5pm, Sa 10am-4:45pm, 1st Sa of the month 10am-3:30pm. €3. Tomb free.*)

GETTING SCHOOLED. Sadly, capital letters at most museums in Florence remind visitors that there are **NO STUDENT DISCOUNTS.** The price of a ticket should not keep anyone from seeing the best Renaissance art collections in the world. Choose carefully and plan to spend a few hours at each landmark. Since most labels are in Italian, consider investing in cheap English-language audio tours, as their descriptions provide a valuable context for understanding the works. In the summer, ask at the tourist office about **Sere al Museo,** evenings when certain museums are free 7-10pm.

OTHER SIGHTS

BATTISTERO. Though built between the fifth and ninth centuries, the octagonal *battistero* was thought in Dante's time to have originally been a Roman temple dedicated to Mars, the god of war. Later Christians re-dedicated it to God and his son, the Prince of Peace, a symbolic conversion that pleased the Florentines. The building's exterior has the same green- and white-marble patterning as the Duomo, and the interior contains magnificent 13th-century Byzantine-style mosaics. Dante was christened here, and later gained inspiration for his *Inferno* from the murals of damnation. The glittering depiction of the Last Judgment that crowns the ceiling is backed with real gold and covered in thousands of tiny beads of glass. Christ sits in the center of the picture, condemning the damned souls on his left (the viewer's right) to Hell, and welcoming the saved on his right to glory. His arms are extended in what is ostensibly the position he assumed on the cross, but a closer look reveals that while his right hand is opened in welcome, he is actually shooting a "talk to the hand" gesture at the damned. Florentine artists competed fiercely for the commission to create the famous **bronze doors,** which depict scenes from the Bible in exquisite detail. In 1330, the winner, Andrea Pisano, left Pisa to cast the first set of doors, which now guard the southern entrance (facing the river). In 1401, the cloth guild announced a competition to choose an artist for the remaining two sets. Two young artists, Brunelleschi and Ghiberti, were asked to work in partnership to enter the competition, but the uncompromising Brunelleschi left in an arrogant huff, allowing Ghiberti to complete the project alone. Their separate entries into the competition are displayed side by side in the **Bargello** (p. 142). Ghiberti's project, completed in 1425, was so admired that he immediately received the commission to forge the final set of doors. The **Gates of Paradise,** as Michelangelo reportedly called them, are nothing like Pisano's earlier portals. Originally intended for the northern side, they so impressed the Florentines that they were moved to their current eastern position facing the Duomo. Best admired in the morning or late evening after the tourist crowds have thinned, the doors are truly a masterpiece, each panel a work of art itself. Even Leonardo da Vinci assumed a role in the structure's execution, finishing the terra-cotta models. (*Opposite the Duomo. ☎055 23 02 885. Open M-Sa 12:15-6:30pm, Su and 1st Sa of the month 8:30am-2:30pm. €4. Audio tour €2.*)

CAMPANILE. Also called "Giotto's Tower," the 82m bell tower next to the Duomo has a marble exterior that matches neighboring monuments. Three great Renaissance minds contributed to its construction: Giotto drew the design and laid the foundation in 1334, Andrea Pisano added two stories, and

Francesco Talenti completed construction in 1359. Pisano altered Giotto's original plans, adding all the Gothic elements, naves, and statues. The reliefs and statues trace man's moral and intellectual progression, from Adam on the lower level to the Renaissance man to the prophets on the second floor. The 414 steps to the top offer stunning views of the Duomo, baptistery, and city. The best time to make the trek is in the early morning, to avoid the smog. (☎ 055 23 02 885. Open Nov.-May daily 8:30am-6:50pm; June-Oct. 1st M-Th and Su 8:30am-6:50pm, F-Sa 8:30am-10:20pm. €6.)

MUSEO DELL' OPERA DEL DUOMO. Most of the original art from the Duomo and Baptistery resides in this less crowded, modern museum. The pieces have been moved here to preserve them: the three statues whose replicas are now over the Baptistery were damaged by acid rain, and the Gates of Paradise, torn off their door by the Flood of 1966, have to be kept in a nitrogen environment to prevent further damage. However, Arnolfo di Cambio's statue **Madonna with the Glass Eyes,** on the ground floor, was put into the Opera's storage room because the popular devotion to it was so intense that Church leaders feared they were encouraging superstition by keeping it in the cathedral. The museum's most famous work is a late **Pietà** by Michelangelo, up the first flight of stairs. He began working on it in his early 70s, and the soft curves and flowing lines of the marble and the limpness of Christ's body are said to reflect the artist's conception of his own mortality. He also used his own face as the model for the man cradling Christ, the biblical figure of Nicodemus. Despite his personal investment in the statue, Michelangelo smashed the statue's left arm with a hammer in a fit of frustration with the marble's imperfections. An over-eager apprentice touched up the work soon after, leaving lines visible on Mary Magdalene's head. Also in the museum's collection are Donatello's achingly realistic *St. Mary Magdalene* (1455) and his beardless *Prophet* (supposedly based on Brunelleschi's face), Donatello and Luca della Robbia's *cantorie* (choir balconies with bas-reliefs of cavorting children), and the gold frames from the baptistery's original Gates of Paradise. The statues that remain from Arnolfo di Cambio's original facade are also here, along with a wooden model of what it probably looked like.

Check out the huge statues of the four Evangelists on the first floor. They were originally commissioned in a competition in 1408, with three artists each assigned one Evangelist. Whoever carved the best sculpture would receive the fourth, St. Matthew. Due to time constraints, however, the Opera assigned St. Matthew to Bernardo di Piero Ciuffagni in 1410. Apparently someone didn't get the memo that the competition was over, though: Donatello, one of the original three, boarded up his workshop in July 1410, ostensibly to protect his statue of St. John from the eyes of his competitors. But it was Ciuffagni he should have been worried about, because when he unveiled his *St. Matthew*, the Evangelist was seated in the exact same pose as Donatello's *St. John*! The Opera has kindly placed the two statues beside one another, out of chronological order, so that the visitor can compare. A huge wall displays all of the paintings submitted by architects in the 1870 competition for the Duomo's facade. (P. del Duomo 9, behind the Duomo. ☎ 055 23 02 885. Open M-Sa 9am-6:50pm, Su 9am-1pm. €6. Audio tour €4. Cash only.)

BORGO DEGLI ALBIZI. This wonderful street runs from V. del Proconsolo to V. Pietrapiana, named for a wealthy 14th-century Florentine family, whose palaces are among those lining both sides of the street. At the intersection with V. del Proconsolo are **Palazzo Pazzi** and **Palazzo Nonfinito.** The former is attributed to Giuliano da Maiano (15th century) and was built for the Pazzi, an old Florentine banking clan. In 1478, Francesco de' Pazzi killed Giuliano de' Medici, brother of Lorenzo il Magnifico, as part of an anti-Medici conspiracy. Francesco hid here after the deed, but was soon snatched up by a mob and hung from a window of the Palazzo Vecchio. Palazzo Nonfinito has a less bloody history, perhaps because it was—spoiler alert—never finished. It was begun by Buontalenti in 1593 and is still a remarkable sight. Opposite the Pazzi homestead are two palaces attributed to Bartolomeo Ammanati (late 1500s), **Palazzo Vitali** and **Palazzo Matteucci Ramirez di Montalvio.** No. 18 on the street, **Palazzo Altoviti,** is also called *"dei Visacci"* for the portraits of 16th-century Florentine citizens in marble on the facade. The gigantic **Palazzo Albizi** is No. 12, and the artist Canova had his studio in No. 15, the **Palazzo degli Alessandri.**

PIAZZA DELLA SIGNORIA

ORSANMICHELE. A grain market was built here in 1284 over the site of the ninth-century church of **San Michele ad Hortum.** In the early 14th century, after a great fire convinced city officials to move grain operations outside of the city, the building was transformed into a church. Florence's powerful craft and trade guilds used the chapel and, late in the 14th century, the city told these groups to ornament the facades of the church with statues of their patron saints. Naturally, the guilds fought it out to get the best artists of the day to represent their standing. Of the statues lining the church walls, many are those of Ghiberti: *St. John the Baptist* (1412-16), for the cloth merchants, on V. dei Calzaiuoli; *St. Matthew* (1419-22), for the banking guild, on V. Arte della Lana; and *St. Stephen* (1428), for the wool guild, on the same street. On V. Orsanmichele are Donatello's *St. George* (a copy—the original is in the **Bargello,** p. 142) for the armory guild and Brunelleschi's *St. Peter* for the butchers' guild. The interior of the church contains 14th-century frescoes and the magnificent tabernacle by Andrea Orcagna (1355-59), which depicts tales from the life of the Virgin Mary with marble, colored glass, and reliefs. *(V. Arte della Lana, off V. de Calzaiuoli, between the Duomo and P. della Signoria. ☎ 055 28 49 44. Open Tu-Su 10am-5pm. Free.)*

PIAZZA DELLA SIGNORIA. With the turreted **Palazzo Vecchio** to the west and the Uffizi Gallery to the south, this 13th-century *piazza* is now one of the city's most touristed areas. You can enjoy the statues outside of Palazzo Vecchio, like the copy of Michelangelo's **David,** and the 14th-century stone **Loggia della Signoria,** outside the confines of a traditional museum with gelato in hand. The palace's location, said to have been chosen to avoid the "damned" house of the Ghibellines, made the *piazza* into an L shape and encouraged the square to blossom into Florence's cultural and political center. In 1497, religious zealot Girolamo Savonarola convinced Florentines to light the Bonfire of the Vanities in the *piazza,* barbecuing some of Florence's best art, including (according to legend) all of Botticelli's secular works held in public collections. A year later, disillusioned citizens sent Savonarola up in smoke on the same spot, marked today by a comparatively discreet commemorative disc near the **Fountain of Neptune.** The fountain, to the left of the Palazzo Vecchio, so revolted Michelangelo that he decried the artist: "Oh, Ammanato, Ammanato, what lovely marble you have ruined!" The Loggia, once used for civic orators, is now one of the best places in Florence to see world-class sculpture for free, including Giambologna's spiraling composition of ▧**The Rape of the Sabines.**

THE PONTE VECCHIO. Built in 1345, Florence's oldest bridge played host in the 1500s to butchers and tanners, a group that lined the bridge to dump pig's blood and intestines into the river Arno. The resulting smell understandably offended the powerful bankers who crossed the Arno on the way to the office.

LOCAL LEGEND

BEAUTY AND THE BOAR

The famous bronze boar at Mercato Nuovo now serves as an excellent leaning-post for gelato eaters, but according to legend, this metal pig was once alive and oinking.

According to the myth, the boar was the ill-gotten offspring of a rich lord and his barren wife. The wife, longing for a child, saw a litter of piglets and wished aloud to be as fertile as the mother pig. Lo and behold, the lord's wife gave birth to a living and breathing boar. This newborn could speak because he was human on the inside.

Poor boar-man fell madly in love with a peasant girl, who agreed to marry him because he was charming and rich. Luckily for him, on their wedding night, the hog's pigskin fell away to reveal quite the human stud. Now that he was no longer a bachelor, he could assume his person form at night with his wife, but would remain pig-like during the day. If his new wife ever revealed what occurred after dark, she would be transformed into a frog and he would remain a boar for the rest of eternity. As any good wife would do, she didn't tell a soul about her husband's secret sexiness, except for her mother, sisters, cousins, and friends. Within hours, the whole town knew, and the consequences duly dealt; the wife was indeed turned into a frog and the boar was doomed to remain his porky little self forever.

Don't you just love a good happy ending?

In an effort improve the area, the Medici clan—themselves originally bankers—kicked out the lower-class shopkeepers, making room for goldsmiths and diamond-cutters. Today, their descendants line the street in medieval-looking boutiques, and the bridge glitters with rows of gold necklaces, brooches, and charms. While technically open to vehicles, it is chiefly pedestrians who swamp the roadway. The historical position of the bridge has helped preserve it throughout the years. During WWII, Ponte Vecchio was the only Florentine bridge to escape the German bombs. A German commander who led his retreating army across the river in 1944 couldn't bear to destroy it, choosing instead to make it impassable by toppling nearby buildings. From the neighboring **Ponte alle Grazie,** the heart-melting ◼**sunset view** of Ponte Vecchio showcases its glowing buildings and the shimmering Arno River beneath.

BADIA. Founded in AD 978, the Badia was the site of medieval Florence's richest monastery and the parish church of Dante's love, Beatrice Portinari; in fact, it is supposedly where he saw her for the first time. The building was so much a part of daily Florentine life that the bell's tolling set time for the city and is mentioned in the Divine Comedy (*Paradiso*, XV). The church's simple facade belies the treasures within. Filippino Lippi's stunning *Apparition of the Virgin to St. Bernard,* one of the most acclaimed paintings of the late 15th century, hangs in eerie gloom to the left of the church. Note the beautiful frescoes and Corinthian pilasters, and be sure to glance at the intricately carved dark wood ceiling by Felice Gamberai. Visitors are asked to walk silently among the white-robed monks. (*Entrance on V. Dante Alighieri, off V. Proconsolo. ☎055 26 44 02. Officially open to tourists M 3-6pm, but respectful visitors can walk through the church at any time.*)

PIAZZA DELLA REPUBBLICA. The largest open space in Florence, this *piazza* teems with crowds and street performers at night. An enormous arch filling in the gap over V. Strozzi marks the square's western edge. Overpriced cafes, restaurants, and gelaterie line the rest of the *piazza*. In 1890, the *piazza* replaced the Mercato Vecchio as the site of the city market, but has since traded market stalls for high-fashion ware. The inscription *"Antico centro della città, da secolare squalore, a vita nuova restituito"* ("the ancient center of the city, squalid for centuries, restored to new life") makes a derogatory reference to the fact that the *piazza* is the site of the old Jewish ghetto. When the "liberation of the Jews" of Italy in the 1860s allowed

Jews to live elsewhere, the ghetto slowly fell apart. An ill-advised plan to demolish the *centro*'s historical buildings and remodel Florence destroyed the Old Market, but an international campaign successfully thwarted the razing of the entire ghetto, leaving the present-day gathering space as a vibrant center for city life. Today, the *piazza* has returned to its commercial roots, though it is still a wonderful place to relax. A small-lighted carousel decorated with frescoes in the style of the Renaissance masters sits in the center of the *piazza*, providing enjoyment to partakers of all ages.

COMPLESSO DI SAN FIRENZE. Half of this late baroque complex—the **Chiesa di San Firenze**—is worth a peek if you're in the area. The other half might be better to avoid; the former Oratory is now the location of the city's primary court of law. The entire complex grew from a gift from Pope Urban VIII, which included the P. San Firenze and stretches from Borgo dei Greci to V. dell' Anguilara and V. Filippina. The original church had been there since 1174, and the Oratorians, the recipients of the Pope's gift, wished to create an entire complex—including a convent, oratory, and church—which would have been dedicated to St. Philip Neri, the Florentine founder of the order. Their original design by Pietro da Cortona was a bit unrealistic given the funds that they had—even with a generous donation from Giuliano Serragli upon his death in 1648—and eventually the project was given to Pier Francesco Silvani in 1667. After his death, Ferdinando Ruggieri oversaw the work of the facade, which was built in 1715, in honey-colored *pietra forte*. The oratory of San Firenze Vecchio was not in accordance with the Congregation's custom of keeping the oratory separate from the Church, so the old building was demolished in 1772 and a new one was built. The entire complex was given a Baroque facade, and though his gift had not been enough to get the Oratorians what they really wanted, Serragli's coat of arms was placed on the outside, signaling his position as the order's principal benefactor. Inside, Camillo Sagrestani's *Glory of St. Philip Neri* (1715) sits as the centerpiece of the ornate ceiling. On the other side, in the former oratory, the benches of the court fill the former nave. Above, the galleries supported by Ionic columns, had once been for the singers of the former auditorium for sacred music. (*In P. San Firenze, near the Bargello. ☎ 055 29 08 32. Church open daily for respectful visitors. Free.*)

PALAZZO GONDI. The Gondi family had many ties to the French, but their hearts remained firmly in Florence. **Giuliano Gondi,** the wealthy merchant who commissioned the palace, famously denied payment for his services from King Ferdinando of Naples, believing that no member of a free republic should accept money from a foreign monarch. The stately home that he asked Giuliano da Sangallo—whom he coincidentally met in Naples—to build for him reflects his hometown pride. Begun in 1490 and finished in 1501, the facade of this typically Florentine palace is made of rusticated stone blocks, which become flatter as they near the top. Inside, the artist used the courtyard to regulate the irregular shape of the property across from the Complesso di San Firenze. The staircase, ornately done with carvings of animals and foliage, is said to be one of the finest things Sangallo ever created. Upstairs, the mantle of the fireplace shows the triumph of Neptune and statues of Hercules and Samson. Additional figures have now taken up residence in the palace, in the form of shops and restaurants occupying the ground level. (*In P. San Firenze, across from Complesso di San Firenze.*)

SIGHTS

MERCATO NUOVO. Under their Corinthian-columned splendor, the *loggias* of the New Market have housed gold and silk traders since 1547. Today, gold falsely glints among the wares of vendors selling leather purses, belts, journals, and pashminas. In exchange for the convenience of accepting credit cards, the goods in the market are up to 50% more expensive than in the Mercato de San Lorenzo or from other vendors. Pietro Tacca's pleasantly plump statue, *Il Porcellino* (The Little Pig—actually a wild boar; 1612), appeared some 50 years after the market opened. Rub its snout and put a coin in the pig's mouth; if the coin drops neatly into the grate below, your luck is golden. *(Off V. Porta Rossa, between P. della Repubblica and the Ponte Vecchio. Vendors hawk wares from dawn to dusk.)*

SANTA MARIA NOVELLA

BASILICA DI SANTA MARIA NOVELLA. The first incarnation of the basilica, Santa Maria delle Vigne, was built in 1094 on the site of a c. 9th-century chapel. The property was given to the Dominicans—called Domini Canes, Hounds of the Lord, because they took a bite out of sin and corruption—in 1221, building began in 1246, and was completed by Fra' Jacopo Talenti in the mid-14th century. He was also responsible for the bottom of the intricately crafted Romano-Gothic facade that is considered one of the greatest masterpieces of early Renaissance architecture. The top was executed in the 15th century by Leon Battista Alberti. Made from Florentine marble, this geometrically pure complex of perfectly aligned squares and painstakingly traced circles is a precursor to the Classical revival of the high Renaissance (see **Life and Times**, p. 50). Inlaid friezes show the emblems of the Rucellai (one of the church's benefactors) and Medici, to honor the wedding of Bernardo Rucellai and Nanni di Medici in 1461. The arcades to the right house the family vaults of Florentine nobles; they lead to the old cemetery, where Domenico Ghirlandaio is buried.

Thirteenth-century frescoes covered the interior until the Medicis commissioned Vasari to paint new ones. Vasari spared Masaccio's powerful *Fresco of the Trinity and the Virgin and St. John the Evangelist* (c. 1428), the first painting to use geometric perspective. It's on the north side of the church (left, if you're facing the altar). The vast, vaulted ceiling is made of striated dark *pietra serena*. For the most part, though, the church's notable works lie in the many family chapels.

In the **Rucellai chapel** are a statue of the Madonna and Child by Nino Pisano and the tomb of the Dominican Francesco Lionardo Dati by Ghiberti. The 13th-century frescoes in the **Cappella dei Bardi** have been attributed (tentatively) to Cimabue. The **Cappella di Filippo Strozzi,** to the right of the high altar, contains unusually antiquity-influenced frescoes by Filippo Lippi, including a cartoonish Adam, a woolly Abraham, and an excruciating *Martyrdom of St. John the Evangelist*. Lippi also designed the stained-glass windows and the trompe l'oeil frescoes of the altar wall. Filippo Strozzi's tomb is the work of Benedetto di Maiano. Boccaccio's *Decameron* features the chapel as a meeting place for some of his protagonists.

In the sanctuary are frescoes by Ghirlandaio and his assistants (including, possibly, a young Michelangelo); their Biblical scenes contain many portraits of medieval Florentines. Brunelleschi's crucifix in the **Gondi Chapel** is a response to Donatello's crucifix in Santa Croce, (p. 129) which Brunelleschi thought was too full of "vigorous naturalism." The horror. The vault fresco fragments in the same chapel date from the late 13th century, depicting the Evangelists. The **Cappella Strozzi** (another one) houses beautiful frescoes by Nardo di Gione (mid-14th century) showing Thomas Aquinas, the Last Judgment, Paradise, and Inferno (after Dante). Nardo's brother, Andrea, painted the altarpiece.

Outside the church, in the **Chiostro Verde**, are 15th-century frescoes by Paolo Uccello which, though damaged, can still be made out to depict some Genesis stories. Adjoing the cloister is the **Cappella dei Spagnuoli** (Spanish Chapel), used by the Spanish members of Duchess Eleonora of Toledo's entourage, adorned with bright frescoes by Andrea di Bonauioto and assistants (14th century). Finally, the Museo di Arte Sacra houses frescoes and statues (some by Andrea Orcagna) in the old **refectory**. *(Piazza di Santa Maria Novella. ☎ 055 21 59 18. Open M-Th and Sa 9am-5pm, F and Su 1-5pm. €2.50)*

CHIESA DI SANTA TRINITÀ. Hoping to spend eternity as they had lived—in elite company—the most fashionable *palazzo* owners commissioned family chapels in this church, built in the 11th century by Vallombrosian monks and expanded through 1405. The stone facade, designed by Bernardo Buontalenti in the 16th century, is an exquisite example of late Renaissance architecture, while the interior boasts 14th-century Gothic style. Scenes from Ghirlandaio's *Life of St. Francis* (1486) decorate the **Sassetti Chapel.** The scene above the altar shows Pope Honorius giving St. Francis the Rule of the Order in P. della Signoria; the audience includes the figures of Lorenzo il Magnifico and Sassetti, the merchant who commissioned the cycle. In the scene of *The Miracle of the Boy Brought Back to Life*, you can see P. Santa Trinità and the church with its original facade. In the second chapel left of the altar is Luca della Robbia's tomb of Benozzo Federighi, with the enameled terra cotta for which his family's workshop was famous. *(In P. di Santa Trinità. ☎ 055 21 69 12. Open M-Sa 7am-noon and 4-6pm, Su 7am-noon. Free.)*

CHIESA DI SAN SALVATORE AD OGNISSANTI. This church was originally part of the complex founded in 1251 by the Umiliati, a monastic order devoted to physical labor rather than to alms-giving and asceticism. Frescoed with false architecture in soft grays and yellows, this peaceful church doubles as Botticelli's final resting place. His tomb is located directly to the right of the high altar, in the right-hand chapel down the corridor behind the piano. Marked by a yellow lion on a blue shield, the small stone bears his real name, Mariano Filipepi. The church is not merely home to Botticelli's body but also his body of work: between the third and fourth altars hangs his portrait of *St. Augustine.* Directly across the nave, Ghirlandaio's *St. Jerome* honors another scholar of the Church. *(P. Ognissanti 42. ☎ 055 23 96 802. Open M-Sa 7am-12:30pm and 4-8pm, Su 4-6pm. Free.)*

IL CENACOLO DI 'FULIGNO.' When it was originally rediscovered in 1843, this version of **The Last Supper** was believed to be a once-lost masterpiece by Raphael. The fact that Raphael himself had lauded it as a work of a genius apparently didn't strike anyone as oddly arrogant—Raphael did, after all, spend a lot of time in Florence—and so it wasn't until much later that historians correctly identified the artist as Pietro Perugino. Though less well-known than his fellow Umbrian, Perugino was no less influential on Renaissance art. Visitors to the Cenacolo can compare the works by his imitators and admirers to his masterpiece on the back wall. In this depiction, the traitor Judas has his purse of 30 silver coins clutched under the table, and he looks out at the viewer with a weary, unreadable expression. Above the supper itself, the *Agony in the Garden* plays out on a hillside. *(V. Faenza 40. Open Tu, Th, Sa 9am-noon. Free.)*

SAN LORENZO

BASILICA DI SAN LORENZO. Built on the site of an early church consecrated in 393 by St. Ambrose of Milan, the Basilica di San Lorenzo claims to be Florence's first cathedral. In 1418, leading Renaissance architect Filippo Brunelleschi redesigned the original Romanesque building. The financial burden for the project was shared by the Church and the Medici family, who wished to turn the basilica into their familial crypt. Changes were slow, and by 1440, only the Old Sacristy had been done. Brunelleschi soon died, and the basilica was "completed" in 1461 by Antonio Manetti, though many portions still remained unfinished. Michelangelo designed the church's exterior, but, disgusted by the corruption of Florentine politics, he abandoned the project to study architecture in Rome, which accounts for the basilica's still unadorned brown-stone facade. Today, the church continues to hold a regular mass every morning at 9:30am with additional services on Sunday at 11am and 6:30pm.

The family cleverly placed **Cosimo de' Medici's grave** in front of the high altar (underneath the dome, marked by grilles in the floor and the Medici arms), making the entire church his personal mausoleum. The church also houses the craftsmanship of some of the greatest Renaissance masters. Donatello created two bronze pulpits, one for each aisle; they were completed c.1460 and are his last works. Their fine engravings depict the last days of Christ, including scenes such as the *Agony in the Garden, Christ Before Pilate, the Crucifixion* (north pulpit), *the Marys at the Sepulchre*, and *the Resurrection* (south pulpit). Also by Donatello, the *Martelli Sarcophagus* in the left transept takes the form of a wicker basket woven in marble.

The **Old Sacristy,** to the left when facing the altar, was the first part of the church to be rebuilt (1420-29). Decorative details on the vault are by Donatello; the sarcophagus in the center is by Buggiano and holds Giovanni Bicci de' Medici and Piccarda Bueri (parents of Cosimo il Vecchio). The porphyry and bronze sarcophagus placed on the wall is that of Giovanni and Piero de'Medici (Cosimo il Vecchio's sons), commissioned from Verocchio by Lorenzo il Magnifico in 1472.

A small **chapel** near the entrance to the cloister has an *Annunciation* by Filippo Lippi; the beautiful cloister is by Manetti (1457-62). (☎055 26 45 184. Open Mar.-Oct. M-Sa 10am-5pm, Su 1:30-5pm; Nov.-Feb. M-Sa 10am-5pm. €3.50. Basilica and the Laurentian Library €6.)

THE CAPPELLE DEI MEDICI (MEDICI CHAPELS). These chapels consist of dual design contributions by Matteo Nigetti and Michelangelo. Michelangelo created and sculpted the entire **New Sacristy**—architecture, tombs, and statues—in a mature, careful style that reflects his study of Brunelleschi. Designed to house the bodies of four of the Medicis, the room contains two impressive tombs for Medici Dukes Lorenzo of Urbino and Giuliano of Nemours. Lounging on the tomb of the military-minded Lorenzo are the smooth, minutely rendered female *Night* and the muscle-bound male *Day*, both left provocatively "unfinished," but considered to be among his greatest works. Michelangelo rendered the hazier *Dawn* and *Dusk* with more androgynous figures for the milder-mannered Giuliano's tomb, which is closer to the entrance. Some of the artist's sketches can be found in the basement. Plans for even more statues by Michelangelo had been made, but the only other one by the master in this chapel is the Madonna and Child, the last Madonna Michelangelo sculpted.

The large **Cappella dei Principi** (Chapel of the Princes) was designed by Giovanni de'Medici, Cosimo I's illegitimate son, and exhibits some stunning pietre dure craftsmanship. Buried here are (right to left): Ferdinando II, Cosimo II, Ferdinando I, Cosimo I, Francesco I, and Cosimo III. (Walk around to the back entrance in P. Madonna degli Aldobrandini, behind the Basilica di San Lorenzo. ☎055 23 88 602. Open daily 8:15am-5pm. Closed 1st, 2nd, and 5th M and 2nd and 4th Su of each month. €9).

LAURENTIAN LIBRARY. This adjacent building was built to signify the Medici entrance into intellectual society and now contains over 11,000 manuscripts, including those from the private library of the Medici family. Construction began in 1525, but the library did not open until 1571. Michelangelo's famous entrance **portico** confirms his virtuosity; the *pietra serena* sandstone staircase is one of his most innovative architectural designs. (☎ *055 21 07 60. Open daily 8:30am-1:30pm. Free with entrance to San Lorenzo.)*

CHIESA DI SAN BARNABA. On June 11, 1289, the feast day of Saint Barnabus, the Florentine Guelphs triumphed over a Ghibelline army from Arezzo. This church was built in 1322 in honor of the victory and the saint to whom it was attributed. The **Guild of the Medici and Speziali** (Doctors and Apothecaries) took over the patronage of the church in 1335, but the religious care of the building passed through many caretakers, first under the Augustinians in 1350, the Carmelites in the 16th century Reformation, and later the sisters of that order. The Doctors and Apothecaries commissioned the *Madonna and Child* by Giovanni della Robbia, having already paved her way in 1377 to be the only "holy" woman standing at the corner of Via Guelfa when they legally prohibited prostitutes from coming within 50m of the church. *(Corner of V. Panicale and V. Guelfa.)*

MERCATO CENTRALE. When the Old Market was destroyed to make room for P. della Repubblica, this indoor market was built to take its place. Occupying an entire block since 1874, the building has housed dozens of stalls and counters on two levels, running the gamut of cheeses, meats, fruits, breads, vegetables, and *vino*. Watch fresh pasta being made at one station and then pick some up for €6-12 per kg. Choose from local wine, oils, and sausages. Grab a bite to eat or a drink at one of the drop-by bars or get some other prepared food. Many counters accept credit cards, but it varies, so bring cash just in case. *(V. dell'Ariento. Open M-F 7am-2pm and Sa 7am-5pm.)*

PALAZZO MEDICI. It's surprisingly easy to walk right by this great stone palace, located between Basilica di San Lorenzo and the Duomo, but that was Cosimo de' Medici's intention when he had it built between 1445 and 1460. The reserved nature of the building's exterior was due to the Medicis' wish to keep a low profile when they returned to Florence after being thrown out by the city's people. Despite this, the palace stills serves as a symbol of the Medici's financial strength, and the entire structure is permeated—as are all things Medici—by the work of many Renaissance greats. One of Cosimo's favorite architects, Michelozzo di Bartolomeo, under the influence of Brunelleschi, designed the palace; he also had hand in the redesign of Palazzo Vecchio. The windows on the ground floor were designed by Michelangelo, and Luca Giordano completed the palace in 1682 by creating the frescoes on the ceiling of the Great Hall which pay tribute to the greatness of the Medici family. *(V. Camillo Cavour 1, on the corner of V. de Goir and V. Cavour. ☎ 055 27 60 340; www. palazzo-medici.it. Open M-Tu and Th-Su 9am-7pm. €7, groups of over 15 and members of the armed forces €4. W 3-7pm free. Last entry 30min. before closing.)*

SAN MARCO

BASILICA DELLA SANTISSIMA ANNUNZIATA. This entirely uncrowded church was once one of the most venerated shrines to the Virgin Mary in Florence. Its prominence stemmed from a 14th-century incident involving Fra Bartolomeo. While working on his *Annunciation*, the artist found himself unable to paint the Virgin's face; after hours of fruitless attempts, he fell asleep beside the fresco. When he awoke the next morning, he discovered that "angelic hands" had finished the painting for him. This reportedly miraculous painting is still on display in the church in the Chapel of the Most Holy Annunciate, located to the left of the entrance. In the small oratory beside the chapel, there is a portrait of the *Holy Face* by Andrea del Sarto. The highlight is the nave of the church, a gloriously ornate ceiling of wrought (some might say overwrought) gold. Closer to the ground, more than ten 17th- and 18th-century Baroque chapels radiate out from the nave. One up from the Chapel of the Most Holy Annunciate on the left is the **Feroni Chapel,** containing Andrea del Castagno's fresco of St. Julian. If you leave the church by the door at the end of the left side of the nave, you'll see the **Cloister of the Dead.** Turn around once you've entered to see *Madonna del Sacco* (1525), by Castagno, above the door. *(P. della Santissima Annunziata. ☎ 055 26 61 81. Open daily 7:30am-12:30pm and 4-6:30pm. Free.)*

CIMITERO DEI PROTESTANTI (DEGLI INGLESI). Completely encircled by three lanes of high-speed traffic, this cemetery is one sight which inadvertently invites some audience participation. Once you've made your way safely through the whizzing traffic of Piazzale Donatello, you will find the surprisingly serene resting place of such famous foreigners as poet Elizabeth Barrett Browning, writer Walter Savage Landor, sculptor Hiram Powers, and abolitionist Theodore Parker. Although popular convention has dubbed this the cemetery "of the English," it was actually built in 1828 for Florence's Swiss community. Protestants, the Swiss could not be buried in Catholic cemeteries, so the city provided them with their own burial ground. The cemetery eventually came to inter Protestant ex-pats from sixteen different countries; when Florence was redesigned to better manage its traffic, it became an elevated "island of the dead," looming as a sort of morbid reminder to reckless Florentine drivers. Arnold Böcklin's painting *The Island of the Dead* was inspired by this sight. *(In the center of Ple. Donatello. Take bus #8. The crossing from V. Vittorio Alfieri, to the right of Borgo Pinti if you're coming from the centro, is the only relatively safe, direct path to the cemetery's entrance. Open daily 9am-noon and 3pm-6pm. Free.)*

CENACOLO DI SANT'APOLLONIA. This small museum, dedicated mostly to the work of Andrea del Castagno, was once the refectory of the Observant Benedictines of Saint Apollonia. On the right wall of the second room you'll find Castagno's dark, disturbing version of the *Last Supper.* Painted in a menacing mixture of reds and blacks, the fresco's creepy incarnation of Judas hovers ominously beside Christ and the sleeping St. John, a knife in his hand. The entire scene seems awry. Christ is difficult to locate, pushed to the left of his usual central location by the sleeping body of St. John, his halo no larger than those of the apostles. Your eye is only drawn to the cluster of Christ, Judas, and St. John because the swirling red-and-black panel above them pops out like a psychedelic bad omen. Above the *Last Supper,* the remnants of Castagno's *Crucifixion, Resurrection, and Deposition* triptych have been restored, but are a poor, faded shell of the original. They weren't rediscovered until 1871, at which point they were so badly damaged that they had to be cut down in order to be preserved. You can still see the cuts running through the fresco. During the removal process, the restorers discovered the original drawings on top of which Castagno had begun his fresco. These gigantic sketches are now displayed on the wall opposite that of the restored fresco so that the visitor can compare the two. *(Open daily 8:30am-1:50pm. Closed the 2nd and 4th Monday and the 1st, 3rd, and 5th Su of the month. Free.)*

CHIOSTRO DELLO SCALZO. This cloister takes its name from the Lay Penitents who once owned it; dedicated to St. John the Baptist or the Passion of the Christ, they dictated that the member who carried the cross in procession should go barefoot (*scalzo*). The cloister is famous, however, because of the painter who frescoed its interior. Andrea del Sarto returned to this cycle, *Life of St. John the Baptist*, over a period of thirteen years in the early 16th century, and his unique, quasi-monochrome result carries out twelve scenes from the saint's life and four depictions of the virtues Faith, Hope, Charity, and Justice in shades of cream and tan. Under the soft lighting of a skylight above, the cloister invites slow, peaceful enjoyment of del Sarto's art. To follow the panels in narrative order, begin on the wall to your right as you enter, at the personification of Faith holding a Communion wafer and cross. *(V. Camillo Cavour 69. ☎055 23 88 604. Open M, Th, Sa 8:15am-1:50pm. Free.)*

ORTO BOTANICO. This shady, sun-speckled *giardino*, known as the "Garden of Simplicity," is an exception to all things Florentine. Not only is it cool, green, and quiet, but it is also quite content with second place. The uber-competitive Florentines may have built the widest nave and tallest dome in Tuscany, but they can only boast the region's second-oldest botanic gardens (Pisa dedicated its garden two years earlier, in 1543). It's not a very large complex, and activity in the surrounding buildings can occasionally disturb your walk, but the overall experience is very calming and ideal in the heat of high noon. Potted palms and ferns line the pathways, arching oaks shade the grass, and a fountain crowns the center of the outdoor complex. Don't confine yourself to the outdoors—in the rooms that line the entrance building, you'll find a reconstructed rainforest of towering tropical plants and vines. *(Entrance at V. Pier Antonio Micheli 3. ☎055 2346760; www.msn.unifi.it. Open from April 1st to mid-Oct. 15th M-Tu and Th-Su 10am-7pm, from mid-Oct. to Mar. M and Sa-Su 10am-5pm. €6.)*

SANTA CROCE

▧BASILICA DI SANTA CROCE. Ascetic as they may have been, the Franciscans produced what is arguably the city's most magnificent church with a unique Egyptian cross layout, far to the east of their Dominican rivals at Santa Maria Novella. Architect Arnolfo di Cambio decided to change things up a bit, designing the splendid Basilica that was established in 1294. Breathtaking marble sculptures adorn the grand tombs of Florentine luminaries on both sides of the main aisle, frozen in expressions of grief and mourning. The Renaissance greats buried here include Michelangelo, who rests near the beginning of the right aisle; Galileo, directly opposite in the left aisle; and Machiavelli, farther down and on the right. Michelangelo chose his final resting spot with the hope that he would rise out of his tomb on Judgment Day to view the great Duomo through Santa Croce's front entrance; he'll have to take a glance at the grave Vasari built for him first, though, since his body is actually buried under the floor and slightly to the left of his monument. Beside him, the empty tomb of Italy's greatest poet stands as a tribute to Dante Alighieri, who was banished from the city in 1321. Although Dante was forgiven posthumously, his body never made it out of the hands of the literary necrophiles in Ravenna, where he died.

In the **Cappella Bardi di Vernio,** the first to the left of the transept, is Donatello's *Crucifix* (1412-13). The frescoes that adorn the chapels also showcase the work of some of the great precursors to the Renaissance. In the central **Cappella Maggiore,** the frescoes of Agnolo Gaddi are undergoing restoration, while next door once can still pick out the work of Giotto's school. **Cappella Peruzzi** features scenes from the life of St. John the Baptist, while **Cappella Bardi** has six scenes from the life of St. Francis,. Once you enter the courtyard, run the gauntlet past the tombs and busts of those long dead through the barely lit **Galleria dei Monumenti Funebri,** to the right of the bottom of the stairs. At the end of the cloister next to the church is Brunelleschi's **Cappella Pazzi,** a modest marvel of perfect proportions. Construction continued after his death in 1446, but work on the nearly completed chapel halted in 1478, when Pazzi's involvement in the assassination of Lorenzo the Magnificent's brother Giuliano led to the family's ruin. Luca della Robbia created the glazed terra-cotta medallions depicting the *Twelve Apostles*, and the four medallions showing the *Four Evangelists* are attributed to Brunelleschi himself. **The Museo dell'Opera** contains a collection of fresco remnants and artwork either removed from the church during renovations or relocated after the Napoleonic invasions. While wandering the church and the museum, note the water mark about eight feet up the walls—an enduring reminder of the devastating effects of the flood of 1966. Santa Croce is located in a dip below the level of the Arno River, and during the flood, the waters rose to over 13 ft at some points. (☎ *055 24 66 105 or 055 23 02 885. Open M-Sa 9:30am-5:30pm, Su and holidays 1-5:30pm. Last entrance at 5pm. €5, ages 11-17 €3. Cash only.)*

SYNAGOGUE OF FLORENCE. The relationship between the Jewish community of Florence and the rest of the city was tense in the centuries before the Synagogue's construction. The area around Piazza della Repubblica marks the location of the old Jewish ghetto, where Jews had been required to live since 1570, at the command of Cosimo I. The community was finally permitted to live and work outside of the ghetto in 1848, and when wealthy Jewish businessman and president of the Hebrew University David Levi died in 1870, he left his fortune for the construction of "a monumental temple worthy of Florence." The main design, created by architect Marco Treves with the assistance of Mariano Falcini and Vincenzo Micheli, is now situated behind a hefty iron gate among the Renaissance creations that dominate the city. During WWII, the Nazis used the Synagogue as a parking garage when they occupied Florence in 1943. Before leaving, they planted bombs throughout the Synagogue, but only destroyed the upper left women's gallery. The only temple in Florence also houses the **Museo del Tempio Israelitico,** which showcases a small collection of Jewish ritualistic items, like a beautiful 19th-century circumcision dress. (☎ *055 23 46 654. Open M-Th and Su 10am-6pm, F 10am-1:30pm. Cash only.)*

BIBLIOTECA NAZIONALE CENTRALE. If after the artwork and architecture you're still not convinced that the Tuscans were good with their hands, then ruffle through the collection of Italian literary works at the largest library in Europe. Born in 1714 when Italian scholar Antonio Magliabechi donated his entire 30,000-volume collection to the city of Florence, the library grew in 1743 with the order that every published Tuscan work be included. It was opened to the public in 1747 and gained its current name in 1885. Cesare Bazzaniu and Via Mazzei designed the building, which has held the collections since 1935, beside the Arno River. This location may have seemed like prime real estate at the time, but when the river flooded in 1966, the waters destroyed nearly a third of the library's collections. Today, the library is difficult to enter without a card, though you may be let in to see the small, usually Italian-language exhibitions that are sometimes held. (*P. dei Cavalleggeri 1.* ☎ *055 24 11 31; www.bncf.firenze.sbn.it. Open M-F 8:15am-7pm and Sa 8:15am-1:30pm. Free.)*

CHIESA DI SANT'AMBROGIO. Originally built in the seventh century as a chapel for Benedictine nuns, the current church has been standing since the 11th century. It was built on the spot where St. Ambrose, its namesake, stopped during his visit to Florence in 393. The works inside were badly damaged during the Flood of 1966, but after some restoration, they were returned to the church. Among the frescoes displayed are *Madonna del latte* (Mary breast-feeding) on a throne with St. John the Baptist and St. Bartholomew by Andrea Orcagna's school, in the second area on the right as you walk in. Also present is the *Martyrdom of St. Sebastian*, attributed to Agnolo Gaddi, in the first arched area on the left. Other works attributed to artists like Mino de Fiesole, Botticelli, and Verrocchio live behind the old, plain facade, but fresher faces spend most of their church time on the front steps; P. del Sant'Ambrogio is a popular nightlife spot for locals. *(P. Sant'Ambrogio. ☎ 055 24 01 04. Open daily for respectful visitors. Free.)*

PIAZZA DEI CIOMPI. This quiet square near P. di Sant'Ambrogio contains two main attractions. The **Loggia del Pesce,** built in 1567 and designed by Vasari, originally located in the Old Market of P. della Repubblica, the *loggia* was dismantled in the late 19th century when the *piazza* was restructured, and in 1956 it was decided that it should be reassembled in P. dei Ciompi. The *loggia* bears the combined coats of arms of Cosimo de Medici and Eleonora of Toledo. Today, a local bar uses it for outdoor seating. The second attraction, just behind the *loggia*, is the **antique market.** Covered in vines, the small shops of the market offer a jumble of jewelry, knick-knacks, and books. A 1378 revolt by an organization of clothmakers gives this square its name. Ghiberti lived in a house here (look for the small plaque), and Cimabue lived just south on Borgo Allegri.

WEST OLTRARNO

The churches of the Southwest Oltrarno are smaller than some of the attention-grabbers on the other side of the river, but their size allows a fuller appreciation of the important and often spectacular work housed within them.

CHIESA DI SANTA MARIA DEL CARMINE. Originally built in 1268 as part of a Carmelite convent, this Oltrarno church was enlarged in 1328 and 1464, but damaged by a fire in 1771. Though much of it needed to be rebuilt internally, the fire fortunately spared the greatest attraction of the church, the **Brancacci Chapel,** ("The Sistine Chapel of the Early Renaissance") which features famous frescoes by Masaccio and Masolino da Panicale. The chapel itself was begun in 1386, commissioned by Pietro Brancacci, and the pictorial embellishments were financed by his relative, Felice, who hired Masolino and his young student Masaccio to do the honors. However, Masolino left for Hungary in the middle of the project, leaving it to his pupil, and upon his return, found himself learning from his talented former student. Masaccio was then called to Rome before he could complete his task, and died there at the age of 27. This left Filippino Lippi to complete the unfinished portions of the chapel. Among the most famous works is Masaccio's *Expulsion from the Garden of Eden*, the first fresco on the upper part of the left side facing the chapel, which captures the emotional distress of Adam and Eve as they are forced to leave Paradise. Michelangelo is said to have imitated Masaccio's work in the chapel as practice for his own. *(P. del Carmine. Church ☎ 055 212331. Chapel ☎ 055 2382195. Church open M-Tu and Th-F 9am-noon, W and Sa 10am-noon. Chapel open M and W-Sa 10-5pm. Church free. Chapel €4, with combined Palazzo Vecchio ticket €8.)*

CHIESA DI SANTO SPIRITO. Possibly one of the least publicized beauties of the Florentine churches, construction on this Augustinian building did not begin until 1443, nearly 200 years after the decision was made to create the complex. The plan for the church was supplied in 1434 by Filippo Brunelleschi, the architect of the great Duomo in the city's center, and the work was not finished until 1481, 35 years after his death. Externally, the rough stone of the church's facade was plastered over in the 18th century, giving it the tan, smooth look it has today. Internally, 38 niche chapels hold some of the most interesting examples of religious artwork in Florence. In the **Nerli chapel** on the far side of the right transept, one can find Filippino Lippi's *Madonna and Child with the Infant, St. John, St. Martin, and St. Catherine* (1493-1494). In **Cappella Segni**, find Raffaellino del Garbo's *Madonna with the Baby among Saints Giovanni Evangelista, Lorenzo, Stefano, and Bernardo* (1505); notice the devil in the lower right hand corner and how the halo of the saint above him is faded—very risky stuff, this. The most noticeably magnificent part of this church is the center **high altar,** a glorious marble Eucharistic tribute by Giovanni Caccini that some accuse of spoiling Brunelleschi's interior. Locked behind the friar's quarters in the sacristy is a **Crucifix** created by Michelangelo. *(Open daily M-Tu and Th-Su 9:30am-12:30pm and 4-5:30pm. Free.)*

TIP **SWEET TALKING.** If you ask the guard humbly and respectfully to see Michelangelo's *Crucifix,* he may escort you through the friar's quarters to where it is located in the back. Don't take this privilege for granted, though: the friars often use the cloister for praying and confession, making a visit impossible.

CENACOLO DI SANTO SPIRITO. Located beside the Chiesa di Santo Spirito, this Gothic building was built in the 14th century as part of the convent and weathered the fire of 1471. Eremite friars now house the collection of sculptures, artwork, and ruins of antiquarian Salvatore Romano. Within one large, high-ceilinged room, you'll primarily find decorative sculptures from the 13th through 16th centuries. Check out *A Blessed Franciscan,* which has been attributed to Veronese, and the large, fading 14th-century fresco by Orcagna on the right as you walk through the door. The lower portion depicts the Last Supper, though only three of the characters—their faces highly expressive— now remain. The animated apostles are believed to be Thaddeus and Matthew, while the Augustinian friar at the far right has been identified as St. Augustine Novello. *(P. di Santo Spirito 29. Open Apr.-Oct. daily 9am-5pm; Nov.-March Sa 10:30am-1:30pm. €2.20, ages 18-25 €1.70, 3-17 €0.60.)*

CHIESA DI SAN FELICE. Though it sits right between Ponte Vecchio and Palazzo Pitti, this fairly inconspicuous 18th-century church possesses a concealed history: excavations have revealed the remaining foundations and epigraphs of an earlier fifth-century church. A Romanesque church was built in the 11th century, and additions to this include the Brunelleschi's sacristy from 1473, Taddeo Gaddi's 14th century *Madonna with Child and Saints,* and the Barbadori chapel, designed by Brunelleschi and decorated by Pontormo. In 1565, Cosimo I decided to build the corridor that would connect Palazzo Vecchio to Palazzo Pitti, passing through the church; from the corridor, the Medicis could watch mass undetected. With the modernization of the Counter Reformation came the construction of a new church in 1735, which now contains Antonio Ciseri's *Martyrdom of the Maccabees* (1863) in the third chapel on the right and Volterrano's *Assumption of the Virgin with Saints* (1677) at the end of the left transept. *(P. di San Felice 7. Open daily for respectful visitors. Free.)*

CASA GUIDI. The perfect location for a Victorian-era episode of *Cribs,* this is where the magic happened for poets Elizabeth and Robert Browning. Restored to its 19th-century beauty, visitors can walk through the bedroom, sitting room, dining room, and drawing room of the apartment, which housed the couple from 1847 until Elizabeth's death in 1861. Walk into the small room off the left of the main dining area to find a cast of the two poets, bound forever in bronze, or take a break on the luxurious 19th century loveseats. For those who really want to engage with the residence, it is available for rent (p. 94) through **The Landmark Trust,** which is responsible for the administrative details of the apartment; the proceeds go toward continued restoration. *(P. San Felice 8. Go past Palazzo Pitti; P. San Felice is the 1st fork on the right. Open Apr.-Nov. M, W, F 3-6pm. Free.)*

PORTA SAN FREDIANO. The surrounding walls were built by the commune in 1284-1333 and demolished in the 19th century; the gate itself was built in 1324, possibly by Andrea Pisano. Its function was to guard the road between Florence and Pisa. Today, its strong medieval look stands out incongruously from its neighboring Florentine architecture, though it is somewhat reflected in the brick facade of the neighboring **Chiesa di San Frediano in Cestello.**

VIA MAGGIO. The name is an abbreviation of "Via Maggiore," quite appropriate considering the importance of this thoroughfare when it opened in the mid-13th century. Once the Medici moved into Palazzo Pitti in the 1500s, this became a very fashionable residential street and still contains a number of beautiful palaces. No. 7 is **Palazzo Ricasoli,** the biggest on the street. The **Palazzo di Bianca Cappello,** No. 26, was built by the grand-duke Francesco I for the eponymous Venetian beauty who was his mistress and, later, wife. **Palazzo Ridolfi,** No. 13, is attributed to Santi di Tito. The street ends in P. San Felice, where you can find **Casa Guidi** (see p. 132).

EAST OLTRARNO

PIAZZALE MICHELANGELO. Though the *piazzale* itself is a bit of an eyesore, the romantic view it affords is well worth a visit. At sunset, waning light casts a warm glow over the city. Make the challenging uphill trek at around 8:30pm during the summer to arrive in time for sunset. The large *piazza* doubles as a parking lot, hosting convoys of tour buses on summer days and occasional concerts. *(Cross Ponte Vecchio and turn left. Walk through the piazza and turn right on V. dei Bardi. Follow it uphill as it becomes V. del Monte alle Croci, where a staircase to the left heads to the piazzale. Or take bus #13 or #12 from Santa Maria Novella or any other point along the way.)*

SAN MINIATO AL MONTE. One of Florence's oldest churches, San Miniato looks out over the charming greenery south of Florence, and is ringed by a large cemetery that contains the grave of Florentine Carlo Collodi, author of *Pinocchio*. The church itself is fronted with a marble facade and 13th-century mosaics that hint at the incredible interior. The floor inside is patterned with lions, doves, and astrological signs, but don't stare at your feet the entire time—the crazy ceiling is a maze of medieval pattern paintings. The **Chapel of the Cardinal of Portugal** houses a collection of superb terra-cotta pieces by Luca della Robbia. *(Take bus #13 from the station or climb stairs from Ple. Michelangelo. ☎ 055 23 42 731. Open daily Mar.-Oct. 8am-7pm; Nov.-Feb 8am-1pm and 2:30-6pm. Free.)*

Adventure in Europe?

Do it by rail

With a Eurail Global or Select Pass you zoom fast from country to country, from city centre to city centre. So you can soak up hip street scenes. Shop till you drop. Explore the nightlife and meet cool people.

Why wait? Go to www.adventure-europe.com or contact your local travel agent now!

EuRail®
Your Pass. Your Europe.

MUSEUMS

Some cities have museums; Florence, on the other hand, is one living, breathing, inescapable museum. This incontrovertible assertion was made official by the UN, who surely paled at the Herculean task of determining exactly what in the city could be a World Heritage Site—they just decided to give the honor to the great city itself. But two images are iconic whenever Florence comes to mind: *David*'s glistening curves, and the teeming entrance line that snakes around the Uffizi. Florence really is home to some of the best galleries and museums in the world, but this also carries the curse of hosting some equally notable galleries that get lost in the shuffle. Remember that there is more to Florence than just the Renaissance—and also that much of the city's best art can be found outside museum walls, in the city's many churches. On the other hand, the building that houses a museum is often a work of art in itself.

For these reasons, the line between Sights and Museums is a fuzzy one; for our purposes, we have tried to list the establishments that fit the traditional idea of a museum in the following chapter; whenever a major church has an accompanying museum that houses some of its works, we have left those together in the Sights chapter. Be prepared; Florentine museums may have inconvenient hours and galleries that close inexplicably; some are not handicapped-accessible. Many museums retain the 19th-century presentation of their collections (thirty paintings to a wall is not uncommon), and labels range from highly informative, multi-lingual placards to none at all. But who really needs any of that? The art will speak for itself. For comprehensive listings on museum openings, check out www.firenzeturismo.it. To avoid interminable waits for Florence's most renowned attractions, make phone reservations by calling Firenze Musei. (☎055 29 48 83; www.firenzemusei.it. Open M-F 8:30am-6:30pm, Sa 8:30am-12:30pm.)

PIAZZA DELLA SIGNORIA

▇UFFIZI GALLERY

Off P. della Signoria. ☎055 29 48 83; www.polomuseale.firenze.it. Open Tu-Su 8:15am-6:35pm. €10; EU citizens 18-25 €5; EU citizens under 18 or over 65, EU student groups, and archaeology students in American programs free. Visit website for details. Proof of eligibility required. Reserve a ticket ahead of time and avoid lines with an extra €4 fee. Audio tours (1½hr.) €5.50.

When the end of the Medici bloodline fell to Anna Maria Luisa de' Medici, so did the family's magnificent art collection. Unsuccessful attempts at producing heirs by the remaining Medici siblings meant that other arrangements had to be made, not only for the future of Tuscany, but also for the thousands of historically invaluable works. Anna Maria Luisa astutely negotiated the transfer of the collection to the next ruler in 1737 with the **Patto di Famiglia** (Family Pact). The agreement ensured that the dynasty's treasures would remain forever in Florence "for the ornamentation of the State, the use of the public, and to attract the curiosity of foreigners." Appropriately, Anna Maria Luisa's portrait now greets hundreds of visitors from around world as they visit the collection's primary home in the Uffizi Gallery, so named for its original use as the offices *(uffizi)* of the Medici administration. Furthermore, the overwhelmingly large acquisitions of the family also hold prominent positions in many of Florence's other museums.

Construction of the palace itself began in 1560 by **Giorgio Vasari** for **Cosimo I de' Medici.** Two long corridors face away from the River Arno, connected by a corridor on the second floor from which visitors can view the river to the South and the row of caricaturists, street performers, and vendors that occupy the courtyard. Administrative offices, the Tribunal, and the state archive coexisted for many years alongside a selection of the Medici masterpieces. After the signing of the Family Pact and the demise of the family's power, however, the gallery was transformed into one of the first modern museums, open to the public since 1765. Since the 19th century, the niches on the Uffizi's facade have contained the statues of some of Italy's greatest personalities. Play "spot the Renaissance man" and pick out the likenesses of such greats as Leonardo da Vinci, Machiavelli, Petrarch, and Vespucci. Or just head straight for the line; the museum only lets in a group about every 20min. Spend more time looking at the works inside rather than at your watch in a line outside by reserving a ticket in advance. If you don't, approximately 50 rooms containing over 1550 priceless works within a venue that is itself a work of art make the Uffizi well worth your wait.

Before even reaching the ticket station, busts from the AD early centuries welcome visitors and provide a context for the pieces found within, which primarily drew from Classical influences. Throughout the city and lining the corridors of the museum, the stereotypically opposing fields of sport and art join forces in statues that personify the strength of athletes, gods, and the Florentine people; precursors to these works lead you up the stairs toward the main gallery. On the first landing in the flight of stairs, notice the first century Greek marble portrait of an athlete. Just head and shoulders, what makes him manlier than his peers? His swollen ears, which characterized athletes at this time. Additionally, his shoulders are draped with lion's skin, lending his image the nobility associated with gods.

Once on the first floor, stop to see the **Gabinetto dei Disegni e Stampe ("Cabinet of Prints and Drawings").** Painter Cennino Cennini considered drawing to be "the foundation of art." The Uffizi collection contains nearly 120,000 graphic works from the 14th century to the present, including sketches by Leonardo da Vinci, Michelangelo, Raphael, Andrea del Sarto, and many others; however, proper conservation techniques often keep these works hidden from laymen. As a result, it is recommended to begin the climb toward expertise with the scholarly notes accompanying the frequently changing displays in the Exhibition Room. Down the second corridor stairs on the first floor, you will find frequently changing temporary exhibitions as well as works by Caravaggio and his workshop. Caravaggio's painted *Medusa* on a disk and the awesome *Judith Slaying Holofernes* are available for view here.

Because the trek through the Uffizi could be a daytrip in itself, a **cafeteria** is available at the end of the second floor table. Even if you're not hungry, make a journey to the outdoor terrace located here to get up-close and personal with the **Palazzo Vecchio's turret.**

By planning ahead you may also visit the **Vasarian Corridor,** which connects Palazzo Vecchio with the Medici's **Palazzo Pitti** on the other side of the Arno. Reservations must be made in advance (☎055 26 54 321; €6.50 plus an obligatory €4 booking charge).

MAIN GALLERY. No red carpets are rolled out to escort you into the main gallery, but you receive a royal welcome nonetheless; the ascent up the great set of wide, sun-soaked stairs past modestly mint-colored walls is indicative of the entire museum's grace, and the grandiosity of the gallery's design is more awe-inspiring than overwhelming. Two wide corridors serve to make the intimidating collection of art and history a more manageable foray through Western art.

READY. SET.

LET'S GO

www.letsgo.com

THE STUDENT TRAVEL GUIDE

ROOM 2. Beginning in Room 2, the museum sets the mood with a high, peaked ceiling of wood designed in the 20th century to recall the atmosphere of the Tuscan churches of the 14th. Containing works from the Byzantine tradition, the main attractions are the three magnificent depictions of Madonna Enthroned, the holy mother surrounded by angels and saints as she holds the Christ child. Though the version created by **Cimabue** exhibits a remarkable degree of plastic strength and Duccio's suggests the move from the classic to the Gothic, it is **Giotto**'s *Ognissanti Madonna*, named for the church in which it originally sat, that holds center stage. Commissioned by the recently instituted order of the Humiliati, the painting exhibits the perspective-conscious techniques of Giotto and conveys the humility so important to the order through an unconventional depiction of the mother and child. The tunic draped over the Madonna outlines her breasts and knees, and the child's hand draws attention to these curves, while the mother's hand similarly draws the eye to the child's groin and his manhood. By stressing the mortal aspects of these iconic figures, Giotto was likely stressing their humanity, and thereby humility. At the time, however, such emphasis was both revolutionary and scandalous.

ROOM 3. Developing alongside Giotto's influence and emphasis on plasticity in Florence were the painters in Siena, whose attention was more often given to line and color. In Room 3 are Sienese paintings from the 14th century, including Simone Martini's *Annunciation* (1333), depicting the famous scene of the angel Gabriel's appearance to the Virgin Mary. His words, *"Ave gratia plena Dominus tecum"* ("Hail, full of grace, the Lord is with thee"), are literally enunciated in the direction of Mary who shies away, surprised (Luke 1:28).

ROOM 4. The Sienese and Florentine traditions can be seen melded in the panel by the Master of Saint Cecilia in Room 4, which contains 14th century Florentine works. The artist, unidentified except by the painting of the Saint that had hung in the Church of Saint Cecilia, demonstrates Sienese influence in its arrangement but the presence of Giotto in its style. The works of Taddeo Gaddi shown here also illustrate the guidance of Giotto, in whose workshop he often worked.

ROOMS 5-6. Despite the concern with the International Gothic style in Rooms 5 and 6, actually one room, the focus remains with Italian perspective. Giovanni di Paolo of Siena, Jacopo Bellini of Venice, and Gentile da Fabriano all contribute works that married a decorative use of line with an analytic approach to nature, objects, animals, and other material subjects. Among the Florentine works featured, the *Coronation of the Virgin* by Lorenzo Monaco stands out as the only work signed by the artist.

ROOM 7. With Room 7 comes works from the early Renaissance. The movement came to life during a period characterized by an interest in humanist studies, the political balance between secular and ecclesiastical branches, and relative economic well-being. The room includes examples of the attention to detail that would come to define the period. Take note of Paolo Uccello's *The Battle of San Romano*. With the precision brought by his additional occupation as a mathematician, Uccello is said to have spent late nights studying the exact vanishing point; when his wife called him to bed, he would reply "Oh! What a lovely thing this perspective is!" His scene from the battle is actually one of three in a set: the others can be found in the National Gallery in London and the Louvre in Paris. Meant to be hung on different heights, the perspective is adjusted in each painting to reflect the inconsistencies.

ROOM 8. The moment between the first and second halves of the 15th century and what could be said to mark the end of the early Renaissance is captured in Room 8. This room is dedicated to the Florentine friar **Filippo Lippi.** His penchant for earthly pleasures was manifested in his social life when he fell in love with a young nun, **Lucrezia Buti,** and received special permission from the Pope to marry her. His concern with secular materials is evident in his attention to fabrics and his particular depiction of objects. Notice in *Madonna and Child with Two Angels* (1465) the attention paid to the positioning of shadows on the Virgin's face. In keeping with the humanizing approach of Renaissance art, the interaction between mother and child is more realistic: the Madonna captures her baby's adoration, and that of Lippi and the viewer, with her appearance. The model for this most holy lady is said to have been Lippi's love Lucrezia. Also in this room is Piero della Francesca's detailed diptych portraying Federico da Montefeltro, Duchess of Urbino, and his late wife Battista Sforza. Commissioned after the death of Battista, Piero's piece portrays the two forms with honest detail. The Duke's crooked nose, the result of a jousting accident, is highlighted. Facing him on an opposing panel is Battista, pale and somewhat lifeless, but eternally joined in conversation with her husband.

ROOM 9. Move onto the second phase of the Renaissance in Room 9, which primarily contains the works of brothers **Antonio** and **Piero del Pollaiolo.** The attention to anatomy in their subjects is one of their greatest contributions to the artistic movement. One of their collaborative efforts, *The Saints Vincent, James, and Eustace,* can be found in this room, in addition to seven panels portraying the Virtues. Six of them were painted by Piero; the seventh, *Fortitude,* was created by a young **Botticelli,** a student of Antonio's, one of his first documented works.

ROOMS 10-14. These rooms pay tribute to a pupil who surpassed his instructor. **Botticelli's** two most famous works can be found here: *Primavera* and *The Birth of Venus.* Both paintings, depicting the goddess Venus, were painted for Lorenzo di Pierfrancesco de' Medici's villa at Costello. They both achieve a distinctly pagan effect, especially after the long tradition of Roman Catholic themes. The flowing nature of the characters is unique at a time when figures were painted with as much realism as possible. *Primavera* marks Botticelli's golden age. Venus stands in the center as Cupid takes aim at the Three Graces, who are dancing a rondel. Mercury, in a red cloak and winged shoes, stands as the guard of the garden. On the opposite side of the work, the goddess of spring, Flora, scatters flowers while Zephyrus, god of the winds, pursues the nymph Chloris. The *Birth of Venus* was inspired by ancient Greek descriptions of the event. Also in this room is the *Portinari Triptych* by **Hugo van der Goes.** Depicting the adoration of the shepherds, the three panels use as its models the figures of the Portinari family, who commissioned the work. By placing both Botticelli and Van der Goes in the same room, one may view the two trajectories of the Renaissance: the Tuscan perspective-focused approach and the Flemish naturalist approach.

ROOM 15. Leaving the high-ceilinged Botticelli room, you enter Room 15 to find works by the master **Leonardo da Vinci,** who received his early artistic training in Verrocchio's workshop. Leonardo's *Annunciation* found here is said to have inspired disappointment in his teacher, who found himself surpassed by his student. Indeed, the rich draping of Mary's robes already proclaim the artist's great talent and her smile anticipates that of *Mona Lisa.* Further witness to his development is the remarkable *Adoration of the Magi,* left unfinished when the artist left for Milan bearing a horse-head shaped lyre as a gift for the Duke of Milan, seeking to secure peace after Leonardo had been charged and acquitted of sodomy two years earlier.

ROOMS 16-19. Off the Leonardo da Vinci room is **Room 16,** which was once a room dedicated to the cartographical representation of Old Florence, but is now only opened periodically. A more impressive collection of maps can be found in the Palazzo Vecchio. The "Stanzino delle Matematiche," **Room 17** does not permit entry, but guests may peer through the doorway into the small area that was commissioned by Grand Duke Ferdinando I to hold scientific instruments; it now contains small modern bronzes placed into the niches in the wall. "The Tribune," **Room 18,** was commissioned to **Buontalenti** by Grand Duke Francesco I to become the *sancta sanctorum* (Holy of Holies) of the Medici collection. The great domed ceiling is inlaid with mother-of-pearl, capping a collection of portraits, most notably **Bronzino's** *Bia dei Medici*, **Vasari's** *Lorenzo Il Magnifico*, and **del Sarto's** *Woman with the Petrarchino.* Formerly part of the Armory, **Room 19** holds works by **Perugino,** such as his *Portrait of Francesco delle Opere*, and two medallions by **Luca Signorelli** depicting the Allegory of Fecundity and Abundance.

ROOM 20. Room 20 contains the work of German painter **Albrecht Dürer,** "the Master of Nuremberg." *The Portrait of the Artist's Father* stands as a testament to the man who taught him the basics of drawing and encouraged the boy's talent; Dürer's father ignored his own wish for the boy to follow his footsteps as a goldsmith and apprenticed him to Michael Wolgemut in 1486, when Dürer was 15. While you're here, admire Lucas Cranach's large panels of *Adam and Eve.*

ROOM 21. This room is dedicated to Giambellino and Giorgione, displaying major works from the 15th- and 16th-century Venetian school, including the work of Emilian artists **Cosmè Tura** and **Lorenzo Costa. Giovanni Bellini's** presence in the room includes the captivating, monochromatic *Lamentation over the Dead Christ.* His spiritually enigmatic *Sacred Allegory*, also found here, continues to draw various interpretations.

ROOMS 22-23. Exploration of contemporary Northern European painting continues in **Room 22** with the work of German and Flemish artists such as **Albrecht Altdorfer, Hans Holbein,** and **Hans Memling.** Overhead, a battle plays out in the scenes created in the late 16th century by **Ludovico Buti,** who also adorned the ceiling in **Room 23.** This room dedicates its space to the Renaissance painters of northern Italy between the 15th and 16th centuries, among them **Andrea Mantegna** and **Coreggio.**

ROOM 24. Completing the display rooms of the first corridor is Room 24, The Room of Miniatures. Also called "Madame's Room," this space once held the jewels of the Grand Duchess of Tuscany, Christina of Lorraine. The frescoed, domed room currently holds examples of the most exquisite pieces of the Uffizi's collection of small portraits, most no larger than a playing card. The museum's entire collection is the second largest in the world, impressive in both the quality of the pieces and the span of time that they cover.

ROOMS 25-26. The second corridor begins with **Room 25,** which features the work of Florentines and **Michelangelo's** only oil painting, the *Tondo Doni.* The bright range of colors inspired the Mannerist tradition and the figures echo the artist's sculptural work, while the naked figures in the background of the work itself allude to the pagan world before grace. Following this is **Room 26,**

dedicated to **Raphael.** Admire his *Madonna of the Goldfinch,* inspired by the compositional approach of Leonardo. Further works from the artist's mature period and from **Andrea del Sarto** are also shown here.

ROOMS 27-28. These rooms explore the early decades of the 16th century. The former documents the period in Florence, with **Pontormo's** personal style found in the *Supper at Emmaus.* The latter captures the work of Venetian giant **Titian,** including pieces from his earlier period and the great *Venus of Urbino.*

ROOMS 29-32. In the following **Rooms 29** and **30,** the study of the first half of the century continues with the Emilian school and **Parmigianino's** *Madonna of the Long Neck,* named for obvious reasons. Also notice **Giorgione's** *Witchcraft of Allegory of Hercules,* the purpose of which is not so clear, though it may have been intended to betray some of the questionable behaviors of courtly gentlemen. The Venetian master **Veronese** can be found in **Room 31,** concluding the exploration of Renaissance Venice. In **Room 32** are the works of **Tintoretto.** Admire his depiction of the myth of Leda and the Swan, but also notice the monotony of the colors, symptomatic of the artistic fatigue he felt in his maturity.

ROOM 33. Room 33, misleadingly designated, is actually a corridor. The space contains on its walls the work of the always captivating **El Greco** in the form of *Saint John the Evangelist* and *St. Francis,* a number of pieces by Tuscan artists, and *The Appearance of Jesus to Magdalene* by **Lavinia Fontana,** the first female artist to be displayed in the Uffizi.

ROOMS 34-35. The works of the Lombard masters are located in **Room 34,** which is dominated by the **Girolamo Figino** altarpiece *Madonna and Child with St. Margaret and Mary Magdalene,* an early example of the Counter Reformation. This segues nicely to **Room 35,** which contains **Barocci** and the Tuscan Counter-Reformation painters.

ROOMS 36-38. Another misnomer is found in **Rooms 36, 37,** and **38** (Antiquity Hall), as they actually occupy the landing near the Second Corridor staircase and contain Roman sculptures and funerary altars from the first century.

ROOM 41-42. Room 41 is dedicated to **Rubens,** but also features the work of **Van Dyke** and **Velasquez.** The exploration of 17th-century painting is interrupted by **Room 42,** the great **Room of Niobe. This** domed hall, beautifully detailed in gold, was built in 1781 to house a group of ancient sculptures that depicted the myth of Niobe, whose attitude toward the mother of Apollo and Diana resulted in the deaths of her seven beautiful children. The sculptures cower and reach their hands toward the sky as though protecting themselves against a force much greater than they.

ROOMS 43-45. The tour of the second floor finishes in **Rooms 43-45.** The works of **Rembrandt** and other 17th and 18th century Italian and European painters indicate that the Medici family wished to enrich the collection with the newest European trends.

OTHER MUSEUMS

🖼PALAZZO DAVANZATI. The 14th-century palace fell into the hands of the merchant and scholar Bernardo Davanzati in 1578 and belonged to his family until the early 20th century; it was eventually purchased by the Italian state in 1951 and turned into a museum designed to showcase the life of a Florentine merchant in the 15th-17th centuries. Renaissance furniture adorns the rooms, and the painted walls are the highlights. Check out the bedroom on the second

THE HIDDEN DEAL

VIEW FROM THE TOP

If you're a sucker for a view, then be sure to make your way to the cathedral of Florence, Basilica di Santa Maria del Fiore, also known as the famous Duomo.

While everyone fights the lines and crowds to get inside the cathedral to climb to the top of the dome, head over to the *campanile*, the bell-tower of the cathedral just to the right of the Duomo.

The *campanile*, always less crowded than the Duomo, also invites ambitious view-seekers to climb to its top, which is almost as tall as the dome of the cathedral itself. Many strangely fail to realize that when standing on the top of the dome, a masterpiece of the Renaissance architect Filippo Brunelleschi, it is impossible to see the dome itself (they took down the full-length mirror a few years ago).

This problem is easily circumvented by climbing the *campanile*, which offers similarly breathtaking views of the city, as well as an opportunity to get up close and personal with Brunelleschi's dome. Florentine building codes stipulate that all roofs must be made of red brick, resulting in a spectacular sea of red that only a birds-eye view can provide.

floor with the 17th-century bed and the painting *Madonna Adoring the Christ Child with Young Saint John*, from Filippino Lippi's workshop of the late 15th century. Also of particular interest are the vibrant wall paintings in the **Sala dei Pappagalli** (Room of the Parrots). (*V. Porta Rossa 13. ☎ 055 23 88 610. Open daily 8:50am-1:50pm. Closed 1st, 3rd, 5th M and 2nd and 4th Su of each month. Free.*)

THE BARGELLO. In the heart of medieval Florence, this 13th-century brick fortress was once the residence of Florence's chief magistrate. Later, it became a brutal prison with public executions held in its courtyard, but when the death sentence was abolished in 1786, the torture materials were burned in the same space. In the 19th century, Bargello's former elegance was restored, and it now gracefully hosts the quiet **Museo Nazionale,** a treasury of Florentine sculpture and the "minor arts" gathered from the Medici collection and other generous donors. On the ground floor, a room displays the work of Michelangelo and his students. Michelangelo created *Bacchus* on his first visit to Rome in 1497 for banker Jacopo Galli, and it was later bought by the Medici. Other works on display by the hometown hero are the *Tondo of Madonna and Child* (1503-05) and the intense bust of *Brutus* (1539), the only bust Michelangelo ever made—it was supposedly sculpted after the murder of Duke Alessandro de' Medici, in honor of the Republican victory over Medici tyranny. In the second part of the room, a group of works by Cellini attract particular attention. On the same floor, the Gothic cortile is lined with 16th-century sculpture; off the courtyard is the **Sala del Trecento** with 14th-century statues, many from Orsanmichele and the Badia. Works by Donatello and his contemporaries occupy the rooms on the first floor, the most famous being his bronze *David* (c. 1430) in the **Salone del Consiglio Generale,** the first free-standing nude since antiquity. This "nude" still poses in hat and boots. David's playful expression and youthful posture contrast with Michelangelo's perfectly chiseled David in the Accademia Gallery. On the right, two bronze panels of the *Sacrifice of Isaac* submitted by Ghiberti and Brunelleschi to the Duomo's baptistery door contest compete for attention. Also of note are the works by Luca della Robbia and his students, who carefully guarded their secret method of enameled terra cotta sculptures. Other rooms on the floor house collections of Islamic art and Byzantine jewelry. Make a stop in the old **armory,** which has a collection of arms and armor, some used by the Medicis themselves. *(V. del Proconsolo 4, between the Duomo and P. della Signoria.* ☎ *055 23 88 606. Open daily 8:15am-6pm. Closed 2nd and 4th M of each month. €7. Audio tour €5.50.)*

PALAZZO VECCHIO. The "Old" Palace was constructed in 1299 from a design attributed to Arnolfo di Cambio, but after the election of Cosimo I de' Medici as Duke in 1537, the palace underwent a complete overhaul, leaving only the structure as a reminder of its medieval design in favor of a more resplendent interior. During the republican era of the 15th century when the Medicis were expelled, the interior was altered to create, among other things, the **Sala dei Cinquecento** to house the new regime's legislative body. Once the Medicis made a comeback, the inside was redone again—although the Medicis did not enjoy it for long, leaving this side of the river for the **Palazzo Pitti** (p. 149). The asymmetrical structure of the building is a result of the medieval ban on building on the land belonging to the treasonous Uberti family. Today, the palace has preserved its original grandeur, and now houses the mayor's office and administrative office. Much of the palace was dedicated to proclaiming the glory of Florence; the entrance wall of the Sala dei Cinquecento portrays the Florentine conquest of Pisa, while the opposing side shows the conquest of Siena. On the ceiling, the center fresco depicts Cosimo I being crowned by the city of Florence in honor of his wedding to Joanna of Austria. Leonardo da Vinci and Michelangelo were both commissioned to do frescoes for the room, but both left before the works were anywhere near done. The current incarnation was designed by Vasari. Upstairs, wander through the various rooms once occupied by the early Medici rulers, including the **Green Room,** named for the landscape scenes that once covered the walls in the room adjacent to the chapel of Eleonora of Toledo, wife of Cosimo I. Eleonora so wanted a garden that Palazzo Pitti was built outside of the city walls to create her desired haven, and a door from her Green Room opens to the palace across the Arno. In the **Room of the Maps,** giant cabinets once held clothes, tapestries, and detailed ancient maps. The **Sala dei Gigli** has a fresco by Ghirlandaio of St. Zenobius and lunettes depicting the heroes of ancient Rome. The rooms on the second floor also offer beautiful views of the city from their windows. *(☎ 055 27 68 465. Open M-W and F-Su 9am-7pm, Th 9am-2pm. Palazzo €6, ages 18-25 €4.50. Courtyard free. Combined ticket with Cappella Brancacci €8/6.)*

MUSEO DI STORIA DELLA SCIENZA. This impressive and unique collection presents the history of ancient science, with hundreds of artifacts spanning centuries. Quadrants and sundials dominate the first portion of rooms, while **Room 4** is a small Galileo museum. Here you'll find the lens used to observe the moons of Jupiter for the first time in 1610 and the instruments Galileo used in his study of magnetism. Within a glass egg on a marble stand is Galileo's embalmed middle finger. **Room 7** is notable for its collection of spheres and globes from different time periods; note how the image of the world has changed. Antique telescopes, clocks, and other instruments of measurement are found in the rest of the museum. Detailed English guides are available at the ticket office. *(P. dei Giudici 1, behind Palazzo Vecchio and the Uffizi. ☎ 055 26 53 11. Open M and W-F 9:30am-5 pm, Tu and Sa 9:30-1pm; also open 2nd Su of each month Oct.-May 10am-1pm. €6.50, under 18 €4.)*

CASA DI DANTE. This residence, reputedly identical to Dante's original home, traces the poet's life from youth to exile in its displays, and pays homage to the *Divine Comedy* that immortalized him. Wooden representations of Florentine family crests line the hallway and stairwell, accompanied by English descriptions. Unfortunately, the more interesting objects in this small museum, like the replicas of medical instruments that may have been used by Dante, remain without English explanations. *(Corner of V. Dante Alighieri and V. Santa Margherita, 1 block from the Bargello. ☎ 055 21 94 16. Open Tu-Su 10am-5pm. €4, groups over 15 €2 per person.)*

SANTA MARIA NOVELLA

MUSEO NAZIONALE ALINARI DELLA FOTOGRAFIA. This museum spans over 160 years of the history of photography through seven separate exhibits. Drawing from the massive Alinari collections, the MNAF displays black-and-whites from the birth of photography, transparencies and negatives, avant-garde images, and even some inappropriate shots from 18th-century optic boxes. Other exhibits are dedicated to the wider world of photography, and cover topics like photo albums and the cameras themselves. An extensive, comprehensive itinerary for the blind runs through more than half of the museum, complete with plaques in Braille and 3D textured versions of the displayed photographs. Temporary installations immediately after the entrance highlight modern masters of the art. *(P. Santa Maria Novella 14a, across from the church facade. ☎ 055 21 63 10; www.alinarifondazione.it. Open M-Tu, and Th-Su 10:30am-1:30pm and 4-9pm. Last entry 30min. before closing. €6, students and guests using the audio guide €5. Audio guide €4.)*

PALAZZO STROZZI. Construction began in 1489 on this great merchant's palace, built of massive stone blocks and rusticated external walls. Its worn but grand appearance stands out amongst the high-end stores with which it now stands. No fan of the Medicis, Filippo Strozzi had a family with a history of exile for their opposition to the dynasty's rule. Since WWII, the palace has been Florence's largest temporary exhibition space, housing extraordinarily popular shows such as 2004's *Botticelli and Filippo Lippi* and *Cézanne in Florence* in 2007. The sunny courtyard hosts temporary installations, while in "La Strozzina," the **Centre of Contemporary Culture Strozzino** hosts exhibits of contemporary art. The primary exhibition space also holds exhibits and the cafe located under the *loggia* decorates according to the theme. *(P. degli Strozzi, 1 block from P. della Repubblica. ☎ 055 277 64 61; www.palazzostrozzi.org. Prices and hours vary for each exhibition; check website for details.)*

MUSEO SALVATORE FERRAGAMO. The Accademia of the fashionista, Museo Salvatore Ferragamo celebrates the innovation and artistry of a man who once wrote, "I was born to be a shoemaker." Scores of custom-made shoes line the display cases. Simple models are sculpted from suede, silk, cork, or leather; more exotic numbers are shaped from strange hides like sea leopard, fish skin, or antelope. Of course, the clientele is nearly as impressive as the craftsmanship. One case exhibits receipts from famous customers like John Wayne and Ginger Rogers; another holds models made for Hollywood hotshots like Audrey Hepburn, Bette Davis, and Sophia Loren. The museum even contains a pair of heels owned and worn by Marilyn Monroe. Exhibitions rotate every two years in order to give each of the collection's over 10,000 pairs of shoes a chance to enjoy life at eye level. However, one exhibit is permanent: the **Pozzo di Beatrice,** a well named for its proximity to Dante and Beatrice's first meeting at the Ponte Santa Trìnita, is located in the rear of the museum. *(Entrance at P. Santa Trìnita 5r, in Palazzo Spini Feroni. ☎ 055 33 60 456; www.ferragamo.com. Open M and W-Su 10am-6pm. Free audio guides in English, French, Italian, and Japanese. €5.)*

MUSEO MARINO MARINI. This museum is dedicated to the work of a single artist: Marino Marini, born in nearby Pistoia and raised in Tuscany. Fascinated by ancient Etruscan art, his rough bronzes, plasters, and terra-cotta pieces evoke their style and themes. Marini returns again and again to the image of the rider astride his horse, and you can explore the different incarnations of this image throughout the museum. Also on display are a small number of ink sketches, oil paintings, and lithographs. (*☎055 21 94 32; www.museomarinomarini.it. Open M and W-Sa 10am-5pm. €4, students with ISIC €2. Cash only.)*

SAN LORENZO

MACCHINE DI LEONARDO. This interactive exhibit invites visitors to try out more than 50 models constructed from Leonardo da Vinci's codices. Experiment with pulleys, cogwheels, column hoists, and dozens of other simple machines that have made the modern world possible, or marvel at Leonardo's models for forward-thinking innovations like the tank, parachute, and life buoy. Even his more ambitious designs—the flying machine, the air screw, and a rotating 16-cannon deck for naval warfare—are incredible for their ingenious employment of simple science as a solution to complex problems. A fourth room details Leonardo's study of the human anatomy. Free videos on the artist-inventor's life run with English subtitles throughout the day. *(V. Cavour 21, inside the Galleria Michelangiolo. ☎055 29 52 64; www.macchinedileonardo.com. Open daily 9:30am-7:30pm. €6, students with ISIC €5.)*

SAN MARCO

ACCADEMIA. In 1784, Pietro Leopoldo I gave a group of paintings to the Academy of Fine Arts (Accademia di Belle Arti) for study purposes, and in 1873 the **David** and other statues by Michelangelo wended their way into the collection, solidifying its eternal fame. No matter how many pictures of Michelangelo's triumphant sculpture you've seen, seeing *David* in the marble flesh will blow you away. From five feet away, Michelangelo's painstaking attention to detail—like the veins in David's hands and at the backs of his knees—bring the statue to life. The sheer size of the work, and the fact that Michelangelo used a 4.1m block of marble from the Museo dell'Opera del Duomo that was discarded by artists including Leonardo da Vinci, give new appreciation to Michelangelo's genius. He carved it when he was 29. The statue's base was struck by lighting in 1512, damaged by anti-Medici riots in 1527, and finally moved here from P. della Signoria after a stone hurled during a riot broke David's wrist in two places. However, even the move couldn't save David from accidents: in 1991, a vandal splintered his left foot with a stone, though the damage has now been undone with restoration. If this real David seems a bit different from the copy in front of the Palazzo Vecchio, there's a reason: Michelangelo intended him to be positioned on a high pedestal and therefore exaggerated his head and torso to correct for distortion from viewing far below; in the Accademia, the statue stands on a relatively high pedestal and appears less top-heavy. Here, the statue is housed in a special room built for it in 1882.

If you can manage to pull your eyes from David, look for Michelangelo's four **Slaves** (1520), also called *Prisoners*, lining the hall. Even today, it is hotly debated whether the statues were meant to appear unfinished. Chipping away only enough to show the figures emerging from the marble, Michelangelo left his cramped, struggling subjects half-lodged in their stone prisons, creating an effect that truly embodied his theories on "releasing" statues from the living stone. Also worth a look are Botticelli's paintings of the Madonna, as well as works by Uccello. Two panel paintings, Lippi's *Deposition* (1504) and

Perugino's *Assumption* (1504), sit in the room just in front of the rotunda. The Serviti family, who commissioned the two-sided panel, disliked Perugino's depiction so much that they only displayed Lippi's portion in their church.

Past the rotunda, down the corridor to the left, you can get a glimpse of what they learned back when the Accademia was actually an academy. This room, the **Gallery of Plaster Casts,** is literally stacked with plaster models made by two of the Accademia's master teachers, Lorenzo Bartolini and Luigi Pampaloni. You'll notice that all the molds are dotted with what appear to be black freckles. These are actually from iron staples, which were inserted into the molds as reference points of distance and height so that the assistants could do a better job in transferring the mold to marble. Upstairs, in the **Sala del Tardo Trecento,** there is an extraordinary piece of Florentine textile work from 1336. *The Coronation of the Virgin Among Eight Angels and Fourteen Saints,* embroidered by Jacopo di Cambio, is so intricately sewn that you'll think it's a painting at first glance. In the **stairwell,** the museum houses the highlights of its Russian icons collection, the oldest in the world outside of Eastern Europe. *(V. Ricasoli 60, between the churches of San Marco and the Santa Annunziata. Line for entrance without reservation begins at V. Ricasoli 58. The line is shortest early in the day. ☎ 055 23 88 609. Open June-Aug. Tu-Th and Sa-Su 8:15am-6:50pm, F 8:15am-10pm; Sept.-May Tu-Su 8:15am-6:50pm. Last entry 45min. before close. Most areas wheelchair-accessible. €10, with reservation €14. Audio guide €5.50.)*

MUSEO ARCHEOLOGICO. The unassuming archaeological museum holds a surprisingly diverse collection behind its bland plaster facade. Its rooms teem with the statues, sarcophagi, and bronzes of the ancient Greeks, Etruscans, and Egyptians. As the home of both the **Florence Egyptian Museum** and Italy's most important collection of Etruscan bronzes, this museum would be a major cultural highlight in almost any other city in the world—but in Florence it is uncrowded and unfortunately understaffed. The Egyptian collection is especially extensive, spanning eleven rooms and containing some 15,000 objects; **Room 13** alone has four mummies. Since a large portion of the collection was retrieved during a joint French-Italian expedition to Egypt, many of the pieces have a twin in the Louvre. The second-floor exhibits—focused on Etruscan bronzes, Greco-Roman sculpture, and Greek attic pottery—are usually open to explore, but when the museum is understaffed for the day (a particular problem in the summer), they are only accessible through a guided visit every hour or so. Don't miss the *Chimera d'Arezzo,* a bronze sculpture from the late fifth century BC in **Room 14.** One of the most interesting and least accessible areas of the museum is the **Monumental Garden,** where visitors can wander among Etruscan tombs rebuilt here with their original materials. It is usually open on Saturday mornings, but call ahead to be sure that you won't miss out on this unique open-air museum. *(V. della Colonna 38. The museum is located in the P. della Santissima Annunziata, at the corner of V. Gino Capponi and V. della Colonna. ☎ 055 23 57 50. Open M 2-7pm, Tu and Th 8:30am-7pm, W and F-Su 8:30am-2pm. €4, EU citizens under 26 €2.)*

MUSEO DI SAN MARCO. Remarkable works by Fra Angelico adorn the Museo di San Marco, one of the most peaceful places in Florence. The **Pilgrim's Hospice,** located to the right on the entrance wall, contains all of the artist's panel paintings, whose bright and brazen grandeur is so different from the pious simplicity of his more famous frescoes on the second floor. Coming back into the courtyard, turn right into the **Lavabo Room** to see a terra-cotta piece by Luca della Robbia and a *Last Judgment* by Fra Bartolomeo. To the left of the Lavabo Room is the **Fra Bartolomeo Room,** a salute to San Marco's other famous Dominican friar. Inside are Bartolomeo's two famous portraits of Savonarola. The one in which Savonarola is bleeding from the skull, painted in 1508, was actually a secret salute to the preacher disguised as a painting of St. Peter the Martyr. At the time of the portrait, Savonarola had already been tortured and burned at the stake, but his popularity was still so dangerous that any memorial to him was forbidden. Fra Bartolomeo, who had actually joined the Dominican order because of Savonarola's preaching, masked his tribute as a regular hagiographic painting.

The highlight of the museum is the second floor, which houses Angelico's famous fresco cycle and the monks' quarters. At the top of the staircase is his most famous *Annunciation*, and each cell in the hallway contains its own Fra Angelico fresco. Each is painted in flat colors and sparse detail to facilitate the monks' somber meditation. Important works include *Noli me tangere*, in **Cell 1,** and a second, less famous *Annunciation* in **Cell 3. Cells 15-21** all contain variations on the same theme: St. Dominic worshiping the Crucifix. To the right of the stairwell, **Michelozzo's library,** based on Michelangelo's work in San Lorenzo, is a simple space for reflection that houses a collection of mid-15th-century antiphonaries and missals. In **Cells 17** and **22,** underground artwork peeks through a glass floor, excavated in the medieval period. Look also for Savonarola's cells, at the end of the northwest corridor, which display some of his relics. **Cells 38-39,** reserved for Cosimo de' Medici's spiritual retreats, are at the end of the other corridor. On the way out, the **Museo di Firenze Antica of Florence** is worth a quick visit. These two rooms showcase numerous archaeological fragments, mostly pieces of stonework from Etruscan and Roman buildings in the area. Be sure to peek into the church itself, next door to the museum, to admire the elaborate altar and vaulted ceiling. *(Enter at P. di San Marco 3. ☎ 055 23 88 608; www.polomuseale.firenze.it. Open M-Th 8:15am-1:50pm, F 8:15am-6pm, Sa and Su 8:15am-7pm. Ticket office closes 30min. before closing. Closed on the 1st, 3rd, 5th Su and 2nd and 4th M of each month. €4, EU citizens ages 18-15 €2.)*

MUSEUM OF THE OPIFICIO DELLE PIETRE DURE. Unlike its neighbor the Accademia, the Opificio has no dramatic focal points or high masterpieces of Renaissance art. Instead, this glittering gallery of intricately crafted trinkets, tables, and tableaux from the late Medici, Lorraine, and even Napoleonic courts of Italy serves as a tribute to a lesser-known fine craftsmanship. The Opificio, founded in 1588, was famous for its "paintings of stone," a type of sharply detailed mosaic that is

only distinguishable from actual paintings by the shine of the semi-precious stones from which it is cut. Here in the museum, visitors can directly compare original oil paintings to the "paintings of stone" which copied them. The Opificio reproduced everything from landscapes to portraits to still-life in polychrome marble and semi-precious stone. The shading and clarity achieved by this ducal workshop is sometimes breathtaking, sometimes boring—but at only €2 a ticket, these almost unbelievably ornate pieces of Medici lifestyle are certainly worth the price. The upstairs display recreates an Opificio workshop with a display case of the over 600 semi-precious stones kept in stock for their projects and a set of crude worktables that will really increase your appreciation of the final product. *(V. degli Alfani 78. ☎ 055 26 51 11. Open M-W and F-Sa 8:15am-2pm, Th 8:15am-7pm. €2.)*

MUSEO DEGLI INNOCENTI. In 1419, the Florentine Silk Merchants' Guild *(Arte della Seta)* began construction of a new *spedale*, or hospital, for the expanding city's ever-increasing population of orphans and abandoned children. Filippo Brunelleschi, the genius of Duomo fame and a Guild member, provided the designs for the new building, breaking with medieval conceptions of civic architecture and creating a network of courtyards and quarters that was practically a miniature city. The complex was finally opened in 1445, and in the first three years alone, over 260 babies were dropped off at the "Wheel of the Innocents." The "wheel"—a rotating circular stone—is still intact, located on the far left of the front portico. It is ringed by a waist-high metal fence that was originally intended to keep mothers from dropping off older children, and is surmounted by a fresco of cherubs that reads *"Pater et mater dereliquerunt nos. Dominus autem assimpsit"* ("Father and mother forsook us; God, however, took us up"). Boys were taught to read and write and then placed in one of the many artisan workshops in the city. Girls worked principally for the Silk Workers' Guild; the majority either married (with dowries supplied by the institution) or became nuns. Others stayed on and worked at the hospital themselves. But the children were also somewhat at the mercy of the rulers. In the 1570s, the Grand Duke Francesco ordered the hospital to send him boys to row the galleys in the warships. Although the wheel was closed in 1875, the *Spedale degli Innocenti* still functions as an orphanage and a UNICEF child research center today.

The museum itself is only two rooms long, but due to popular demand, some notable works of art made it into the building. To the right of the door that leads to the second room is the *Madonna and Child* (1464-1465) painted by the young Botticelli while he was still an assistant in Filippo Lippi's shop. As you enter the second room, the glazed white statue of *Madonna and Child* by Luca della Robbia to your left is considered one of his late masterpieces, an example of Classical beauty and serenity. For the historians out there, the first room houses eight mid-14th and early-15th century books, including Missals, an Antiphony, and a Vesperal—all with either illuminated initials or incredibly detailed miniatures. As you enter the front portico, the entrance is on the far right. *(P. della Santissima Annunziata 12. ☎ 055 2037308. Open M-Sa 8.30am-7pm, Su 8.30am– 2pm. €4, EU citizens ages 18-25 €2.)*

SANTA CROCE

MUSEO HORNE. Like many of the museums in Florence, the items in this one came primarily from the collection of a private enthusiast, Herbert Percy Horne. His appreciation for the city and the art it inspired led him to bequeath his entire lot to the Italian state in his will, under the condition that a founda-

M
U
S
E
U
M
S

tion in his name be established. In contrast to the vast collections gathered by wealthy investors, Horne's collection grew despite his limited resources as an art critic and writer, mostly due to his scholarly artistic background and honed aesthetic sense. Among his luckier acquisitions were the wooden **statues** of St. Paul that he found in an antique store, which he attributed to—and scholars later confirmed as the work of—Lorenzo Vecchietta, and the 18th century *Visitation*, beneath which he uncovered a *St. Jerome* by Piero di Cosimo. The building which houses the museum was built in the 1350s, and over the years passed through many hands, including those of the merchant Luigi di Jacopo Corsi, before Horne bought it in 1911. The **ground floor** holds an exhibition of coins, medals, and seals, dating from as early as the third century BC. The primary room of the museum, however, is a large one on the **second floor.** Once the banquet room, this area now holds works by a number of masters. **Dosso Dossi's** *Allegory of Music* captures the mythical figure of Tubalcain, founder of art and music, and the images of sacred and profane music, the two female components. You will also find the aforementioned *St. Jerome* and two small panels by Bernardo Daddi, *Madonna and Child* and *The Crucifixion.* On the table is Giambologna's terra-cotta model for *Kneeling Venus.* The two smaller rooms on the floor, the bedrooms, are connected by a door, which would allow husband and wife to pass through their respective rooms privately. The third floor has another bedroom, this one including a 15th-century day bed and Beccafumi's *Putti Holding a Tondo Depicting the Drunkenness of Noah* (1522-23). *(V. de' Benci 6, between Chiesa di Santa Croce and the Arno. ☎ 055 24 46 61; www.museohorne.it. Open M-Sa 9am-1pm. €5, students €3. Cash only.)*

CASA BUONARROTI. Once Michelangelo made it big, he decided to celebrate and bought three houses, including this one, on the same street. Though the master never actually lived here, it is now a small museum and holds selections from the collection of the Buonarroti family: Michelangelo's sketches and early work as well as examples of art directly influenced by him. On the ground floor, check out the exhibit of tiny first-century statuettes in the **Archeological Room** and then find Da Vinci's studies of horses in movement. Upstairs, two of Michelangelo's earliest works from when he was just 16 years old, hold the museum's place of honor. The first, *Madonna of the Steps*, is a carved panel that demonstrates the artist's study of Donatello, while *The Battle of the Centaurs*, a subject said to have been suggested to Michelangelo in the court of Lorenzo the Magnificent by poet Agnolo Firenzuola, shows the artist's passion for ancient art. Another room is covered floor to ceiling with paintings dedicated to scenes from Michelangelo's own life. *(V. Ghibellina 70. ☎ 055 25 17 52. From P. Santa Croce, follow V. dei Pepi and turn right on V. Ghibellina. Open M-Th and Su 9:30am-4pm. €6.50, students and groups over 10 people €4.50.)*

THE OLTRARNO

PALAZZO PITTI

Ticket office is on the right before the palazzo. ☎ 055 29 48 83. Gardens ☎ 055 29 48 83. Galleria d'Arte Moderna ☎ 055 23 88 616. Gallerie and Appartamenti open Tu-Su 8:15am-6:50pm. Gardens open daily Oct. 8:15am-5:30pm; Nov.-Feb. 8:15am-4:30pm; Mar.-May 8:15am-6:30pm; June-Aug. 8:15am-7:30pm. Museo degli Argenti and Museo della Porcellana open daily 8:15am-6:50pm. Closed 1st and last M and 1st, 3rd, and 5th Su of each month. Last entry 1hr. before closing. Combined ticket for Palatine Gallery, Royal Apartments, and Modern Art Gallery €8.50, EU students €4.25. Combined ticket for all 5 sights €10, EU students €4. Cash only.

Luca Pitti, a 15th-century banker, built his *palazzo* east of Santo Spirito against the Boboli Hill. The Medici family acquired the *palazzo* and the hill in 1550 and rebuilt everything on a grand scale. Today, the Palazzo Pitti is fronted with a vast, uninhabited *piazza* and houses a gallery and four museums, providing enough diversions for an unhurried visit.

GALLERIA PALATINA. The Galleria Palatina was one of only a few public galleries when it opened in 1833. Today, it houses Florence's most important collection after the Uffizi. Typically, the itinerary begins in the **Galleria delle Statue,** where first- and second-century Roman statues from the Villa Medici in Rome line the hallway. The *galleria* leads into the **Castagnoli Room,** named for the artist who painted its walls and ceiling, where you'll find a second century statue of Augustus Caesar. To the right of the Castagnoli room is the **Volterrano wing,** which opens with the **Allegories Room,** named for Volterrano's ceiling frescoes of the Virtues. The Allegories room leads into the **Sala delle Belle Arti,** yet another room named for its ceilings; this collection is vaulted with a depiction of Jove sending the Arts to earth. On the wall across from the entrance is Cigoli's masterpiece, *The Martyrdom of St. Stephen.* Continue through several rooms into the **Berenice Room,** where *The Tooth Puller,* controversially attributed to Caravaggio, is displayed on the wall to your right. Having taken a quick look at the two rooms which branch off of Berenice—the **Psyche Room** and the **Room of Fame**—you can now turn around and pass into the **Sala de Ark** (the door to your far right as you return move away from Berenice).

If the Volterrano wing is closed during your visit, you'll pass directly from the Castagnoli Room into the **Music Room.** Luigi Ademello was commissioned to paint a cycle entitled *Glory of the House of Hapsburg* in 1814, a triumphant personification of Austria. When Italy was unified in 1860, however, the Savoy family changed the picture. They redressed the personification of Austria to make her the personification of Italy, draping her in a blue cloak, Savoy crown, and Italian flag. Straight through the Poccetti Corridor is the **Prometheus Room.** The long, rectangular piece at the base of the entrance wall to the right is Pontormo's *Adoration of the Magi* (1520), a recently restored work including a self-portrait of the artist. Past Pontormo is Botticelli's *Madonna and Child with St. John* (1505) on the right wall. On the next wall, that opposite the entrance wall, hangs Filippo Lippi's famous, circular *Virgin and Child with Scenes from the Life of St. Anne* (1450).This work is a unique transition piece, drawing on both the medieval tradition of bringing multiple scenes into the same painting and the Renaissance innovation of perspective. In the **Ulysses Room** are works by Raphael, Andrea del Sarto, Filippo Lippi, and Cigoli. As you continue toward the **Education of Jupiter Room,** you'll pass by Napoleon's tiny bathtub on your right. In the Education of Jupiter Room is Cristofano Allori's *Judith Holding the Head of Holofernes.* In this version of the Biblical tale, the dead man's head is Allori's self-portrait, while the woman who cut it off, Judith, is his mistress Mazzafirra. After this room, exit out onto the stairwell and turn left to re-enter the gallery through a set of glass doors. This will bring you to the **Iliad** and **Saturn Rooms,** which have handfuls of Renaissance masters: del Sarto, Peter Paul Rubens, Raphael, Tintoretto, and Titian.

APPARTAMENTI REALI. The Royal Apartments, at the end of the *galleria,* are lavish reminders of the *palazzo*'s historical function as the Royal House of Savoy's living quarters. The apartments hold a few Renaissance and Baroque greats, but visitors mostly come to soak in the gold-garnished luxury.

GALLERIA D'ARTE MODERNA. For a change of pace, check out this gallery, one of the rare art exhibits in Florence without a single piece from before 1600. The gallery's rooms travel from the emergence of neo-classicism in Tuscany to the birth of the Italian avant-garde. For an epic experience, check out Amos Cassioli's floor-to-ceiling *The Battle of Legnano* (1870) in Room 5. Other highlights include the proto-Impressionist works of the Macchiaioli group, a rebellious crowd of young painters who met and conspired against the establishment in Florence's cafes.

GALLERIA DEL COSTUME. Find out if the clothes make the Medici in this gallery, where rotating exhibits of the collection's over 6,000 pieces share the floor with a permanent display of the restored and excavated burial clothes of Cosimo I de' Medici, his wife, and his son. The only museum in Italy dedicated to the history of fashion, the Costume Gallery is usually worth a visit, depending on which pieces are on display.

MUSEO DEGLI ARGENTI. Officially dedicated to the Medici family treasures—including cases of precious gems, ivory, silver, and Lorenzo the Magnificent's famous vase collection—the museum is worth a visit for its frescoes alone. The false architecture on the ceilings will literally make you do a double-take: you'll think those columns are real. In the **Sala di San Giovanni,** play a game of Renaissance *Where's Waldo*: Lorenzo il Magnifico is seated in every panel of the wall frescoes. The cycle, which begins on the entrance wall to the far right of the door, gives a glorified history of Lorenzo's reign. It opens with the rise of Islam and Mohammed (an allegory of expanding power of the Turks) and continues with an image of blind Homer and the nine Muses fleeing Mount Parnassus, an allusion to the exodus of Greek scholars to Lorenzo's court after the Turkish invasion of 1453. *On the ground floor of the palace, to your left as you enter from the piazza.*

BOBOLI GARDENS. This sprawling stretch of arbor deserves half a day in itself. Coming from the palace, visitors enter through the large oval amphitheater, marked by an Egyptian obelisk. From here, the hill leads to the **Forcone Basin** and its bronze *Neptune.* Continuing up the hill along the right will take you to the **Knight's Garden,** a neat plateau with charming views of the surrounding hillside that houses the **Museo della Porcellana.** From the Knight's Garden, follow the path at the foot of Fort Belvedere to reach the **Kaffeehaus,** a red-and-white rotunda added in the 18th century as a resting place for the nobles during their taxing walks through the garden. In the other direction, labyrinthine avenues of cypress trees lead eager wanderers to the bubbling fountains and half-submerged statues in the **Vasca dell'Isola,** a manicured island accessible only in May and June. Once you've wound your way back to the palace, hook down the hill to the right to find the **Piazzale di Bacco,** where stands the famous fountain of portly Bacchus sitting astride a very strained turtle. This supposed "Bacchus" was modeled on the famous Florentine dwarf Morgante. Next to Bacchus is the **Grotta del Buontalenti,** the original home of Michelangelo's *Slaves/Prisoners* series (now in the Accademia). This knotty, encrusted grotto opens into vaulted chambers of paintings and statues. Unfortunately, the grotto is only open by guided visits every hour or so; ask at the ticket office for the day's schedule, or just check the sign.

GIARDINO BARDINI. Less expansive but more stylish than Boboli and without the accompanying crowds, Giardino Bardini is a small, neat slope of statuary and streams. The quick, steep climb to the villa yields lovely views of the Duomo and the city.

MUSEO DELLA PORCELLANA. Hidden behind the gardens and up a steep hill, this small and airy museum exhibits fine porcelain from the Medici, Lorraine, and Savoy collections.

OTHER MUSEUMS

CASA DI RODOLFO SIVIERO. The former residence of Italy's "007 of art," this kooky *casa* houses a remarkable hodgepodge of Italian art. Statues from the workshop of Luca della Robbia sit side-by-side with fourth-century Etruscan mirrors, papal bulls hang beside 17th-century landscapes, and Neapolitan rifles are flanked by cover designs for *Vogue* (by de Chirico) and tunic scraps from the Dark Ages. With altarpieces in the bedrooms and Neo-Baroque sketches in the kitchen, the Siviero house is an disorganized immersion in centuries of art. Siviero left the house and all its contents to the region of Tuscany in 1983 after a career of art collecting and espionage. Originally employed as a secret agent by the Military Intelligence Service of the Italian army, Siviero turned double-agent when the Fascists came to power and became the main contact point for Anglo-American Intelligence Forces in Florence. He dedicated the rest of his life to recovering art stolen from Italy by both the Nazis and traders on the black market. (*Lungarno Serristori 1-3, at the corner of P. Poggi and Lungarno Serristori. ☎ 055 23 45 219. Open Sept.-June M 10am-1pm, Sa 10am-6pm; July-Aug. 1st M 10am-1pm, Sa 10am-2pm and 3pm-7pm, Su 10am-1pm. Free.*)

MUSEO ZOOLOGICO This 200-year-old public museum is stuffed with stuffed animals. Its over 5,000 specimens hail from six continents and four oceans, with representatives from nearly every exotic species you could imagine— ostriches, anteaters, crocodiles, lions, and two giant Galapagos turtles are all on show. There's even a 300-year-old hippo from the seventeenth-century Boboli garden menagerie. Whoever designed the primate room had quite the sense of humor. As you enter the room, a mirror across from the doorway shoots your reflection back at you—providing a look at the one major modern primate missing from the display cases: *Homo sapiens*. The other ten rooms are dedicated to anatomical waxes of chickens, cats, and human beings. Having refined your morbid sensibility among these displays of outpouring innards and split-open skulls, put your taste for viscera to the test with the wax scenes by Giulio Gaetano Zumbo, which include such cheerful works as *The Pestilence* and *The Corruption of the Flesh*. (*Entrance at V. Romana 17, past Palazzo Pitti. ☎ 055 22 88 251; www.msn.unifi.it. Open daily 9:30am-4:30pm. Closed the 1st and last M of each month. Last entry 4pm. €6. Cash only.*)

Lost and Found: The Florence Flood

The Arno River is Florence's most prominent geographical feature. Traversing the city on its route from the Apennine Mountains to the Ligurian Sea, it flows past the Uffizi Gallery and the Biblioteca Nazionale Centrale. But this seemingly benign waterway, the most important in Tuscany, has been a constant threat to Florentine masterpieces. On November 4, 1966, it nearly destroyed the city and all its artwork.

The problem began on November 3. After weeks of non-stop rains that culminated in a storm that dumped a third of the region's annual rainfall in two days, the Arno rose to its highest levels in years. Water jumped the banks of dams and began to pour downstream at the alarming rate of 2100 cubic meters per second. Basements in Santa Croce—site of the basilica that houses the tombs of Michelangelo, Machiavelli, and Galileo—were flooded to a depth of 1m. Water jets began to shoot out of manholes. The flood's first casualty—a workman—drowned at 3am while trying to stave off the collapse of the Roman aqueduct. Jewelers on the Ponte Vecchio rushed in to retrieve as many valuables as possible, only to abandon the effort when the water burst over bridge, sending the stock downstream.

At 4am, fearing that the Valdarno dam upriver would burst, engineers discharged a volume of water that channeled down paved roads toward Florence, arriving at speeds of up to 37 mph. The torrent overturned cars, ruptured oil tanks, and swept trees along its deadly course. Florentines awoke to a city cleft in two by mud and oily water. An embankment of the Arno had given way, causing huge landslides that blocked all access to the region. There was no electricity—clocks had stopped at 7:26 AM—and no way to move around. The water level reached heights of over 6m in places. Thirty people died and 50,000 families were left homeless.

The effect on the city's treasured art collections was catastrophic. Museum personnel rushed to remove works of art from the path of mud and water, but the flood swept through cultural institutions, inundating over one million rare books and historic documents from the Biblioteca Nazionale Centrale. The Uffizi fared better; nonetheless hundreds of its paintings, sculptures, and tapestries were also damaged. Every institution in the city was affected. In P. del Duomo, the muddy, tree-filled torrent tore Lorenzo Ghiberti's gilded bronze *Gates of Paradise* from their hinges and swept Donatello's painted wooden *Penitent Magdalene* into its path. Perhaps the greatest loss was at Santa Croce, where Giovanni Cimabue's 13th-century painted wooden *Crucifix* was so badly damaged that it became a symbol of the tragedy.

Even a catastrophe of this proportion has an upside. Volunteers, known as the Mud Angels, arrived from around the world to help rescue artworks. Supervised by trained conservators who also rushed to Florence, the Mud Angels salvaged books and artwork from the muck. The magni-

> ## "On November 4, 1966, [the Arno] nearly destroyed the city and all its artwork."

tude and complexity of the rescue effort resulted in new conservation methodologies that advanced the conservation field as a whole and led to the passing of cultural heritage protection laws around the world. Forty years later, many works are still awaiting conservation, but a vast majority of the most important pieces have been stabilized, if not restored. The tragedy in Florence was therefore a turning point in the history of preservation—not only for Florence, but also for art collections around the world.

Rosa Lowinger is an art conservator and writer based in Los Angeles. The 2009 Rome Prize fellow in Conservation, she is presently working on a book on art vandalism. She is the author of Tropicana Nights: The Life and Times of the Legendary Cuban Nightclub.

SHOPPING AND ENTERTAINMENT

🛍 SHOPPING

Florentines cook up some of the snazziest window displays you'll ever see—you'll be tempted to stop in nearly every store you pass. If you're going to be in the city for a while, wait for the sales. The best months for shopping in Florence are January and July. As retailers prepare for the August slump, when the city is nearly emptied as locals head for the seashore, they chop prices drastically. By the end of the first week in July, signs are springing up all over the Florence for sales and discounts, and by mid-month nearly everything for sale is 50% off or more. Mid-July is also the season of scorching temperatures, so you'll have more than one reason to stay inside the air-conditioned stores.

ENGLISH LANGUAGE BOOKSTORES

Feltrinelli International Bookstore, V. Cavour 12 (☎055 29 21 96). Open M-Sa 9am-7:30pm. V. de'Cerretani 30/32r (☎055 23 82 652). Open M-F 9:30am-8pm, Sa 10am-8pm, Su 10:30am-1:30pm and 3pm-6:30pm. A large chain with an equally large selection. MC/V.

Mel Bookstore, V. de' Cerretani 16r (☎055 28 73 39). Sizable English language selection and long hours make it the best bet for finding something other than a witty and irreverent travel guide to read on the train. Open M-F 9am–midnight, Su 10am–midnight.

Paperback Exchange, V. delle Oche 4r (☎055 28 73 39; www.papex.it). Probably the best selection of children's books in English. In addition to both fiction and nonfiction bestsellers, the store also has an eclectic, ever-changing selection of used books that's fun to hunt through. Trade-ins welcome. Open M-F 9am-7:30pm, Sa 10:30am-7:30pm.

Edison, P. della Repubblica 27r (☎055 21 31 10; www.libreriaedison.it). Long hours and a convenient location coupled with the usual selection of travel guides and fiction. Open M-Sa 9am-midnight, Su 10am-midnight.

BM, Borgo Ognissanti 4r (☎055 29 45 75). Unique guidebooks, tailored to special interests like shopping or cuisine, and a wide fiction selection that includes mysteries, sci-fi, and bestsellers. 20% discount on all books by American or English publishers. Open M-Sa 9:30am-7:30pm. AmEx/MC/V.

OPEN-AIR MARKETS

Though you'll doubtless be tempted by the window displays in Florence's shops, you're unlikely to encounter anything half as persuasive as the salesmen in its public markets. Whether they're aggressive, flirtatious, flattering, or argumentative, the vendors in the markets know how to convince you to buy. Never be afraid to barter; most customers begin with the classic opening question, "Is that the best price you can give me?" But don't expect miracles; there are plenty of tourists around to keep these guys in the green.

Le Cascine Market. Take bus 17c, which picks up on the hotel side of Piazza Dell'Unita Italiana, to the Cascine 5 stop. Look for the tents. Located at the far end of the public park, this gigantic maze of stalls is a bargain-hunter's bacchanalia, with everything from

MARBLEIZED PAPER

Marbleized paper in Florence might cost you a pretty penny, but don't worry, this is no Dunder Mifflin product.

The vivid paper, with rippling lines of color, is as precious and stunning as the expensive stone it resembles. Marbleized paper originated east of Italy; in China, paper would be pulled through colorful paste to create free-flowing patterns, while in Turkey, artisans shifted pigments on a lubricated surface to create a similar effect.

It is thought that the Silk Road brought the stone-like paper to Florence in the 16th and 17th centuries, when "Turkish paper" quickly became a must-have. Today, the paper is as ingrained within the city's identity as the writers whose books it decorates. In the best paper shops, the procedure is even handed down from one generation to the next. At **Giulio Giannini e Figlio,** 37/r P. Pitti (☎055 21 26 21), which produces some of city's finest paper, marbling skills have been passed down from father to son since 1856.

A marbled notebook from an artisan shop can run upwards of €30, but the wood pulp and pigment comes from centuries of craft. Put pen to this paper, and you've made your own small mark on Florentine history.

housewares to bedsheets to earrings on display for your consumption. Its remote location and somewhat inconvenient hours keep most tourists at bay. Here, the best deals to be had are the clothes and shoes, both of which can be found in abundance. As with San Lorenzo, the merchandise here can be cheap (both senses of the word), so shop around and examine everything closely. Open Tu 9am-1pm.

Mercato Centrale. While the official, indoor market is full of foodstuffs and olive oil, the ring of tents that surrounds the central building is crammed with T-shirts and souvenirs. Essentially an offshoot of the San Lorenzo market, the Mercato Centrale sells the same goods as its larger counterpart with smaller crowds and a bit less haggling. Open daily 9am-dusk.

Mercato Nuovo (Mercato del Porcellino). From P. della Signoria, take V. Vacche Reccia; from Ponte Vecchio, follow V. Santa Maria toward the Duomo. Sometimes called the "Mercato del Porcellino" in honor of the bronze boar that sits inside the *loggia,* this *piazza* has hosted vendors since the 11th century. Close to the tourist crowds at Ponte Vecchio, it is also generally pricier than San Lorenzo but with the same assortment of goods. More of the merchants here are willing to accept credit cards. Some of the price hikes reflect a legitimate increase in quality, but others are simply a rip-off. If you're considering something particularly popular, such as a pashmina (€5 in San Lorenzo, €8 in Mercato Nuovo) your best bet is probably San Lorenzo, but unique or suspect items (like leather) can be better here. Open daily 9am-7pm.

Mercato delle Pulci, in P. dei Ciompi. A 2-faced flea market, the Mercato delle Pulci has two very different feels. The regular vendors, camped out in semi-permanent stalls complete with roofs and doors, are by and large open every weekday (some are closed M). They hawk bric-a-brac and old furniture, kitschy junk, and chunky jewelry. On the last Su of the month, the market is transformed into a large antiques fair with a huge selection of authentic items. Open M-Sa 9am-1pm and 4-7pm. Large market last Su of every month.

San Lorenzo. The most popular, most touristed of Florence's open-air markets, San Lorenzo is a loud, crowded mishmash of souvenirs, T-shirts, pashminas and leather goods. Most of the vendors here are open to haggling, but since they're not exactly desperate for customers, you usually won't be able to wrangle any fabulous discounts out of them. With a little savvy and a good poker face, however, you should be able to take 10-20% off any purchase that costs over €12. Both the prices and the quality in this market can be surprisingly high—they can also come surprisingly low, so be sure to shop around before shelling out. As with any packed area of Florence, watch your pockets and your purse, because pickpockets frequent the area. Open daily 9am-7pm.

CLOTHING

DEPARTMENT STORES

La Rinascente, entrances in P. della Repubblica and V. degli Speziali 17-19 (☎055 21 91 13). Designer tags like D&G on the racks. One of the earliest and best July sales in the city. Open M-Sa 9am-9pm, Su 10am-8pm.

COIN, V. dei Calzaiuoli 56r (☎055 28 05 31). Smaller and less upscale than La Rinascente but still pricey. Great choice for basics like socks and underwear. Open M-Sa 10am-8pm, Su 10:30am-8pm.

BOUTIQUES

All things high-end and haute couture can be found around **Piazza della Repubblica** and **Via de' Tornabuoni,** where the well-dressed and well-heeled come to pay their homage to the fashion gods of Italy and Europe. These names require no introduction, so we won't bore you with any, but for those not in the know—any purchase made at one of the below establishments would definitely qualify as a splurge. We've also listed a few lesser known (but still not cheap) Italian designers for your shopping pleasure. All accept major credit cards.

Burberry, V. de' Tornabuoni 27-29r (☎055 29 38 11). Open M-Sa 10am-7pm, Su 2-7pm.

Cartier, V. degli Strozzi 36r (☎055 29 23 47). Open Tu-Sa 10am-1:30pm and 3-7pm.

Christian Dior, V. de' Tornabuoni 57/59r (☎055 26 69 11). Open M-Sa 10am-7pm.

Diesel, V. Arte della Lana 16r (☎055 23 99 951). Open M-Sa 10am-7pm, Su 2-7pm.

Dolce & Gabbana, V. degli Strozzi 12/18r (☎055 28 10 03). Open M-Sa 10am-7pm.

Emilio Pucci, V. de' Tornabuoni 20-22r (☎055 26 58 082). Open M-Sa 10am-7pm, Su 2-7pm.

Emporio Armani, P. Strozzi 16r (☎055 28 43 15). Open M 10am-2pm and 3-7pm, Tu-Sa 10am-7pm.

Ermenegildo Zegna, V. de' Tornabuoni 3r (☎055 26 42 54). Open M-Sa 10am-7pm, Su 2-7pm.

Fendi, V. degli Strozzi 21r (☎055 21 23 05; www.fendi.com). Open Sept.-July daily M-Sa 10am-7pm, Su 2-7pm; Aug. M-Sa 10am-7pm.

Fornarina, P. San Giovanni 13 (☎055 29 05 45). Open M-Sa 10am-7pm, Su 2-7pm.

Giorgio Armani, V. de' Tornabuoni 48r (☎055 21 90 41; www.giorgioarmani.com). Open M-Sa 10am-7pm.

Gucci, V. de' Tornabuoni 73r (☎055 26 40 11; www.gucci.it). Open M-Sa 10am-7pm, Su 2-7pm.

Lacoste, V. della Vigna Nuova 33r (☎055 21 66 93). Open M-Sa 10am-7pm, Su 2-7pm.

Louis Vuitton, P. degli Strozzi 1 (☎055 26 69 81). Open M-Sa 10am-7pm, Su 2-7pm.

Max & Co., V. Calzaiuoli 89r (☎055 28 86 56). Open M-Sa 10am-7pm, Su 2-7pm.

Miss Sixty, V. Roma 18-22r (☎055 23 99 549). Open M-Sa 10am-7pm, Su 2-7pm.

Prada, V. de' Tornabuoni 67r (☎055 28 34 39; www.prada.it). Open M-Sa 10am-7pm.

Roberto Cavalli, V. de' Tornabuoni 83r (☎055 23 96 226). Open M-Sa 10am-7pm, Su 2-7pm.

Salvatore Ferragamo, V. de' Tornabuoni 4r-14r (☎055 29 21 23). Don't forget to check out the Ferragamo museum (p. 144). Open M-Sa 10am-7pm, Su 2-7pm.

Valentino, V. dei Tosinghi 52r (☎055 29 31 42). Open M-Sa 10am-7pm, Su 2-7pm.

Versace, V. de' Tornabuoni 13r (☎055 23 96 167). Open M-Sa 10am-7pm, Su 2-7pm.

OUTLETS

If a piece from this season's stock is just too expensive, but you're still itching for your piece of Prada or Gucci, consider a trip outside of the city to one of the area outlets. These bargain emporiums are insanely popular among the tourist crowds. In fact, they've become so popular that companies even run tours of the outlets; ask at the tourist office (p. 79) for a list of those on offer. It is best to visit the shops before the weekend rush; by the time the Friday crowd has had its pick, the selection is severely reduced. Also be sure to ask about tax-free shopping—customers who aren't EU citizens often qualify for a VAT refund (see **Essentials,** p. 16). When you're dropping serious euro, that's no small consideration.

The Mall, V. Europa 8 in Leccio (☎055 86 57 775; www.themall.it.) A 30min. drive from Florence via the A1 highway (toward Rome); get off at the Incisa exit and drive straight through Pontassieve to Leccio. Autolinee Chianti Valdarno also runs buses from the SITA station near Santa Maria Novella (1hr.; M-Sa 6 per day, Su 3 per day; €3.10, round-trip €6.20). Last bus back to Florence leaves the mall at 7:23pm M-Sa, at 7:05pm Su.) By far the largest and most popular outlet in the area. It's easy to understand the appeal of this classy complex once you've arrived: the names here include Gucci, Fendi, Giorgio Armani, Yves Saint Laurent, Burberry, Salvatore Ferragamo, and Valentino. If you're planning for a long day of shopping, be sure to bring some snacks of your own: most of the food available here is pricey. July sales are particularly great. Open daily 10am-7pm.

McArthurGlen Barberino Outlet, (☎055 84 21 61; www.mcarthurglen.it/barberino), in Barberino di Mugello, 30km from Florence. By car, take the A1 toward Bologna and get off at the Barberino di Mugello exit. A shuttle (2 per day) runs out of both Fortezza da Basso and Santa Maria Novella Station. Departures from Florence at 10am and 2:30pm (Fortezza) and 10:05am and 2:35pm (Santa Maria Novella). Return trips leave the outlets at 1:30pm and 6pm. Round-trip €12, €8 ages 14 to 16. Stretching along the banks of a river, this outlet has fewer big-bucks designers than The Mall, but it does boast The Mall's most obvious absentee: Prada. The other names are nothing to sneeze at, either. Options include D&G, Lacoste, Guess, Nautica, Puma, and United Colors of Benneton. Up to 70% off in July. Open Feb.-May and Oct.-Nov. Tu-F 10am-8pm and Sa-Su 10am-9pm; June-Sept. and Dec.-Jan. 1st M 2-8pm, Tu-F 10am-8pm and Sa-Su 10am-9pm.

Il Giglio, V. Borgo Ognissanti 86. Although the window displays for this stockhouse try to lure you with clothing, head here for the shoes. The hit-or-miss shoe section holds some real gems. most of the items have designer tags on them, so shoes are still expensive (€50-100), but are much cheaper than what the big names would go for in a regular store. Open daily 9:30am-1:30pm and 3:30-7:30pm. MC/V.

BARGAIN BABY! Even when prices are marked, don't hesitate to haggle. Start with half the price offered or at least feign a lack of interest and have a price in mind you are willing to pay. Brush up on your Italian shopping phrases, as vendors are more likely to lower the price for shoppers who "talk the talk." Bargain only if paying with cash.

SOUVENIRS

PAPER GOODS AND JOURNALS

Florence is famous for its beautiful paper goods, whether they're marbleized journals, thumbprint-sized copies of the *Inferno,* or hand-painted stationery. Cheap packets of *Carta di Firenze* (€5-8) can be found throughout the city in *tabacchi* and the stalls of San Lorenzo. Nicer, more original versions of this paper can be found for roughly the same price in the below stores.

Made in Tuscany, V. degli Alfani 129r. Well-priced journals, planners, and sketchbooks custom-made at no extra cost in your choice of leather color and cover stamp. Both marbleized and leather-bound volumes are available, and although the paper is not marbleized on location, the books themselves are all put together right there in the store. A budget way to have the artisan experience. Open M 2:30-7pm, Tu-Su 9:30am-2pm and 2:30-7pm. MC/V.

Il Papiro, V. Cavour 55r (☎055 215 262; www.ilpapirofirenze.it). A city-wide chain of paper stores that produces quality marbleized paper, journals, and pencils. Open M-Sa 9am-7:30pm, Su 10am-6pm. MC/V. Also in P. del Duomo 24r (☎055 28 16 28), P. Rucellai 8r (☎055 21 16 52), V. Porta Rossa 76r (☎055 21 65 93), and V. de'Tavolini 13r (☎055 21 38 23).

Fantasie Fiorentine, Borgo San Jacopo 50r, right beside the Hotel Lungarno in the Oltrarno. Exquisite, delicate bookmarks (from €1.50) and hand-painted paper crowd this tiny mom-and-pop shop. There is also a selection of marbleized paper journals, but the items in this store are generally more patterned and painted than marbleized. Open M-F 10:30am-1pm and 3-6pm. Cash only.

Giulio Giannini e Figlio, P. Pitti 36r (☎055 212 61). In business since 1856, this family-run establishment makes everything it sells. Their handmade paper (€22-30) is incredibly delicate, and the hand-stamped and painted boxes (€20-24) are unlike anything else for sale in the city. Notebooks €22-30. Bookmarks €2.50-5. Open M-Sa 10am-7pm, Su 11am-6:30pm. MC/V.

MASKS

They may be typically Venetian, but Italian carnival masks are all over Tuscany. As with every tourist good in Florence, a cheap imitation is readily available at San Lorenzo, but for the genuine article, try the shop below.

Alice's Masks Studio, V. Faenza 72 r (☎055 28 73 70; www.alicemasks.com). Look for the "Masks of Agostino Dessi" sign. Scores of handmade masks coat the walls, tables, and chairs of this cluttered treasure trove, where Professor Dessi and his daughter Alice craft all the masks on display. 5-lesson mask-making classes in the last week of every month €500. MC/V.

GOLD

Ponte Vecchio is the famous row of the goldsmiths, although one or two glovemakers have moved into this traditional jewelry territory. Prices are sky-high, but you can often get a discount by agreeing to forego your EU VAT refund (see **Essentials**, p. 16).

Santa Vaggi & Figli, Ponte Vecchio 2/6r and 20r (☎055 21 55 02; www.vaggi.it). Join the crowds here for a little relief from the high prices. Charms from €25. 18k gold earrings from €55. Open daily 9am-7:30pm. AmEx/MC/V.

LEATHER

Florence was once famous as Italy's bargain bin of quality leather, but sheer popularity has driven the costs up at most local leatherworks, and real deals are harder to come by nowadays. The quality is still there, however, and a little looking can still yield some great bargains. If the real deal is too expensive, you can always buy the imitation at San Lorenzo.

NOI, V. delle Terme 22r (☎055 21 03 19; www.noi-firenze.com). This store produces leather apparel of superb quality for a hotshot clientele of international designers, but they also carry some affordable goods, such as wallets (from €28) and bags (€80-200) made by other Italian designers. Jackets from €250. *Let's Go* discount 10%. Open daily 9:30am-7:30pm. AmEx/MC/V.

Santa Croce Leather School (☎055 24 45 33 or 24 45 34; www.leatherschool.com), in Chiesa di Santa Croce. Enter either through the church or on V. San Giuseppe 5r. This workshop offers first-rate products at reasonable prices, but the real attraction isn't the final product. Stop by and observe the craftsmen making bags and jackets. Open from mid-Mar. to mid-Nov. daily 9:30am-6pm; from mid-Nov. to mid-Mar. M-Sa 10am-12:30pm and 3-6pm. AmEx/MC/V.

Cellerini, V. del Sole 37r (055 28 25 33; www.cellerini.it). Some of the most beautiful leather pieces in the city. It's certainly pricey stuff, but that's probably part of its appeal with Florentines. Wallets €60-72. Purses from €400. Open M-F 9am-1pm and 3-7pm, Sa 9am-1pm. AmEx/MC/V.

ARTISAN GOODS

Most of the one-of-a-kind, exquisitely crafted goods in this section fall well out of the student price range, but that doesn't mean you can't come to watch the artists at work. The **Oltrarno** area is especially known for its artisans, and signs through the neighborhood will direct you to "more artisan shops." Usually, they don't mind if you're just stopping to admire their art.

Museo Bottega del Maestro Alessandro Dari, V. San Niccolo 115r (☎055 24 47 47; www.alessandrodari.com). The rings displayed in this combination shop and showroom are absolutely exquisite and almost unbelievably elaborate. They're more like miniature statues than rings, taking the shape of everything from unicorns to castles to the cupola of Brunelleschi. The master is usually at work when you enter, and he offers a great view of his workshop. Open M-Sa 9:30am-1pm and 4-7:30pm. AmEx/MC/V.

Stefano Bemer, showroom at V. Camaldoli 10r, workshop at V. San Frediano 143r (☎055 22 25 58; www.stefanobemer.it). **Daniel Day Lewis** once came to Florence to learn shoemaking from this master craftsman, whose handmade leather shoes can be ordered custom-fit or purchased from the selection in the showroom. Simply stop in to the workshop to see Stefano himself, or one of his employees, working on a new shoe. Open M-F 9am-1pm and 3-7pm, Sa 9am-1pm. AmEx/MC/V.

ENTERTAINMENT

CINEMA

Most international movies shown in Italy are dubbed in Italian; to find one shown in English, look for v.o. *(versione originale)* at the end of a listing.

Odeon CineHall, P. Strozzi (☎055 21 40 68; www.cinehall.it). Blockbuster movies in English with Italian subtitles. Generally 2 showings per day in the evening.

THEATER

The Florentine theater season usually runs from October to May, but most of these spaces feature some kind of spectacle throughout the year. Most performances are in Italian.

Teatro Verdi, V. Ghibbellina 99r (☎055 21 23 20; www.teatroverdifirenze.it). A full program of dance, theater, and music. Tickets can be purchased at the Box Office, at the theatre, or over the phone with credit card (☎055 210804, M-F 10am-6pm). Open in summer M-F 10am-7:30pm and Sa 10am-2pm, in winter M 3:30-7:30pm and T-Sa 10am-7:30pm.

Teatro della Pergola, V. della Pergola 18/32 (☎055 22 64 353; www.teatrodellapergola.com). Performances of theater, opera, and film. Recent works have been as varied as the films of Ingmar Bergman and the plays of Pirandello, Shakespeare, Brecht, and Ibsen. Performances tend to be in Italian. Tickets €15-29; €11-18 for those under 26. Box office open M-F 9:30am-6:45pm, Sa 9:30am-2pm.

Stazione Leopolda, Vle. Fratelli Rosselli 5 (☎055 21 25 51; www.stazione-leopolda. com). Founded by the Pitti Immagine company, this reclaimed train station hosts numerous performances of avant-garde theater, exhibitions, fairs, fashion shows, galas, and the like. Contact the Box Office or any tourist office for full info and schedules.

Teatro della Limonaia, V. Gramsci 426 (☎055 44 08 52; www.teatrodellalimonaia.it). Famous space for performances of new Italian theater. Also has live music, notably jazz and Latin big band. Tickets €8-13.

LIVE MUSIC

Jazz Club, V. Nuova de' Caccini 3 (☎0552479700; www.jazzclubfirenze.it). Tu and W house band and jam session; otherwise a huge variety of music, from folk and Cuban to funk and soul. Open Tu-Sa 9pm-2am.

Caruso Jazz Cafe, V. Lambertesca 15/16r (☎055 26 70 207; www.carusojazzcafe.it). Mellow space to enjoy live shows. F-Sa beginning from 9:15pm.

Viper, V. Pistoiese (☎055 31 82 31; www.viperclub.eu) and **Flog,** V. Mercati Michele 24b (☎055 47 79 78 or 48 71 45; www.flog.it). Rock concerts and other entertainment. Check their websites for upcoming acts by local and internationally-recognized performers.

SPECTATOR SPORTS

SOCCER

Every June, the origins of the favorite Florentine sport are reenacted when the various *quartieri* turn out in costume to play their own medieval version, known as **calcio storico.** Two teams chase a wooden ball in *piazze* around the city; unsurprisingly, matches often blur the boundary between athletic contest and riot. Check newspapers or the tourist office for the exact dates and locations of historical or modern *calcio,* and always book tickets ahead. In 2007, the event was suspended due to rowdiness in previous years; check with the tourist office for the most updated information. To watch the modern version of soccer, go to the **stadio,** north of the *centro* (Vle. M. Fanti 4/6; ☎055 587 858; www.fiorentina.it) to cheer on Florence's team, La Fiorentina. Tickets are sold at the Box Office for about €20. Or take the bus from the station to the **Giardini del Drago** for a pick-up game of futból.

NIGHTLIFE

After being denied a student discount at yet another pricey museum just because you're not an EU citizen, the last thing you need is to shell out for an expensive cocktail just to unwind. Fortunately, Florentine nightlife is extremely student-friendly—nay, just friendly all around. Sure, there are the super-clubs frequented by the glamorous and the wannabe teenyboppers who wish they were, as well as the ubiquitous faux-Irish pubs that always seem to be full of Americans. However, Florence has mastered two extremely important areas of nightlife: the *aperitivo con buffet* and the *piazza* block party. For the simple price of one drink at the former, you can often scrounge up a pretty decent meal from buffet offerings. And at the latter, which are prevalent around **Santa Croce** and the **Oltrarno**, you can grab a beer and just enjoy the night air along with Florentine families and youths.

Of course, there are also the less easily categorized establishments, such as internet cafes with cocktails and gelaterie that turn into impromptu nightclubs. Basically, the same divide-and-conquer attitude that will only get you a severe case of Stendhal syndrome when sightseeing during the day will prevent you from enjoying the true beauty of the city at night; just grab a Peroni and see where the evening takes you.

THE DUOMO

Piazza del Duomo's steaming, teeming mass of tourists evaporates after nightfall, and the city's most packed *piazza* becomes a near-deserted hangout for drunk study-abroad students and lounging locals. Options in this area are mostly in the central *piazza* or along **Via del Corso, Via degli Albizi,** and **Via de' Pandolfini.** The nightlife here is low-key; head to Santa Croce (p. 167) for more action.

Astor Caffè, P. del Duomo 20r (☎055 28 43 05). Come after 11:30pm to join American students in this 2-tiered club. Drinks and socializing at the street-level bar, dancing downstairs. Beer €4-5.50. Mixed drinks €7. €1 table charge. Open daily 10pm-3am. MC/V.

Lion's Fountain, Borgo Albizi 34r (www.thelionsfountain.com). A student-friendly pub. Most drop by for a peaceful drink outside. Beer on tap €3.50 per ½-pint, €5.20-5.50 per pint. Mixed drinks €6.50. Shots €3. Free Wi-Fi. MC/V over €10.

May Day Lounge, V. Dante Alighieri 16r (☎055 23 81 290; www.maydayclub.it). An eclectic club covered in old electronics. Spend the whole night reading poetry, looking at original artwork, and conversing with other socially-conscious partiers. A different theme every night of the week with special mixed drinks—on "Bizarre Night" they slip in "aphrodisiac" herbal extracts. Organic wine €5. Local microbrew beer €7. Mixed drinks €7. Happy hour 8-10pm, €3 beers. Open Sept.-July M-Sa 8pm-2am. Cash only.

The Fiddler's Elbow, P. Santa Maria Novella 7r (☎055 21 50 56). Expat bartenders serve beer (€5 per pint) to convivial foreigners. Don't be surprised if impromptu karaoke breaks out in the wee hours. Happy hour noon-9pm. Open daily 11am-1am. MC/V.

Eby's Latin Bar, V. dell'Oriuolo 5r (☎055 33 86 50 89 59). Listen to Latin music on the palm-covered patio while sipping fresh-fruit mixed drinks blended with seasonal ingredients. Fantastic nachos, burritos, and sangria. Beer €1.40-4.50. Mixed drinks €5.50-7. Lunch special (burrito and drink) €4.50. Happy hour M-F 6-10pm, drinks €3.50. Open Sept.-July M-Sa 11am-3am.

Public House 27, V. del Proconsolo 27-29r (☎339 30 22 330; www.publichouse27.com). A Christmas light-ringed temple to the rock-gods, this pub is full of regulars, students, and large but docile dogs. Come the weekend, it gets crowded at happy hour and stays that way until closing. ½-pints €2.50, pints €4. Mixed drinks €5. Happy hour daily until 9:30pm. Open M-W 5pm-2am, Th-F 5pm-5am, Sa 4pm-3am, Su 2:30pm-2am. Cash only.

Caffè Bigallo, V. del Proconsolo 73r (☎055 29 14 03). Despite its rustic Tuscan decor, Bigallo shoots for the student crowd with its late-night drinking specials and blaring American pop music. You and your friends can usually have the place to yourselves if you come before midnight. Students get 3 drinks for €10 every night from 11pm on. Mixed drinks €4. Shots €2. Beers €4.

Old Stove Duomo, P. San Giovanni 4r (☎055 28 02 60; www.jjcathedral.com). "Old" World atmosphere in 2 senses of the word—the exposed bricks walls and dark wood may hearken back to an earlier era, but many of the patrons here were born in that era. The specials are tailored for a spry crowd of American alcoholics. Pints €5. Mixed drinks €8. Happy hour daily 6-10pm; drink 8 pints and get 1 free or pay for your drinks in dollars. Th mixed drinks and beers €4 for women. Open 11:30pm-2am.

Bar-Café "Rum Pera," V. del Proconsolo 2r. This tiny bar-cafe doesn't draw large, hard-partying crowds, but it's got the perfect ambience for a small group of tipsy friends in the mood for munchies and a few more cheap drinks. Waffles €3.50-4. Mixed drinks €4.50-5. Small beer €3, large beer €5. Open daily until midnight or 1am. MC/V.

Bar-Enoteca Coquinarius, V. delle Oche 15r (☎055 230 2153). A packed former stable that's always thrumming with conversation, Coquinarius keeps the snobby on the wine list and out of the atmosphere. Still, expect a line if you arrive without a reservation. Squeeze into one of the long tables to get the wine-and-cheese experience without feeling out of place. Wine from €6. Cheese and salami platters €16. MC/V.

PIAZZA DELLA SIGNORIA

Nightlife is sparse in P. della Signoria, with most clubs located in nearby Santa Croce. Tabasco Gay Bar, just outside of the P. della Signoria, is one of the few gay-friendly nightlife locations in the city. Like most things in this neighborhood, the other nightlife establishments tend to be high-end.

Angie's Pub, V. de Neri 33 (☎055 28 37 64). 4 nights a week, a DJ brings a mix of European and American music to this anime-inspired bar, but you likely won't find much dancing. The crowd here mingles to a different drum than those of many other nightclubs in the area. Beer €3-5. Sangria €3. Open daily 4pm-2am. Cash only.

Twice, V. Giuseppe Verdi 57r (☎055 24 76 356). Glittering white walls give the impression that this club is made of ice. Populated by students and older couples alike. Trendy bar, smoking lounge, and dance floor are definite pluses. Come early (7-11pm) for the happy hour and *aperitivo* buffet (€5), or dance late to the daily disco theme, like Tu International Students Night. Beer €6. Mixed drinks €8. Shots €4. Open daily 7pm-4am. AmEx/MC/V.

Noir, Lungarno Corsini 12/14r (☎055 21 07 51; www.noirfirenze.com). Don't let the all-black furniture and walls fool you; the vibe is light and friendly. Patrons flock to Noir M evenings to enjoy *aperitivi* (€9) and watch the glorious sunset. Open daily 6pm-3am. AmEx/MC/V.

Oibò, Borgo dei Greci 1 (☎055 26 38 611; www.oibo.net). Purple and orange glass chandeliers light this sophisticated bar, where old records serve as the only decorations on otherwise white walls. A disco ball twirls as a mix of local and foreign 20-somethings sip mixed drinks (€8). 1 themed party per month. Open daily 7pm-2am. AmEx/MC/V.

Slowly, V. Porta Rossa 63 (☎055 26 45 354). "Smoothly" may have been a more appropriate name for this wine bar near P. della Repubblica. Diverse music includes everything from remixed indie pop to techno. A glass tube in the middle of the room casts a color-changing glow on the furniture and adds to the whimsical decor. Wine €6-10 per glass, €35-300 per bottle. Open M-Sa 7pm-2am. AmEx/MC/V.

Tabasco Gay Bar, P. di Santa Cecilia 3r (☎055 21 30 00), in a tiny alley across P. della Signoria. This dark basement club features smoke machines, strobe lights, low-vaulted ceilings, and a special movie room. Caters to gay men. 18+. Beer €6. Mixed drinks €8. M-W and F-Su cover €13, after 1am €15; Th free, after 1am €10, including 1st drink. Open daily 11pm-6am. AmEx/MC/V.

Colle Bereto Lounge, V. degli Strozzi (☎055 28 31 56), next to Louis Vuitton and across from Armani. Where the sophisticated and beautiful come to play and the name of the game is "gothic chic." Red velvet curtains drape over large windows, red light illuminates the bottles of alcohol behind the bar, and red lamp shades adorn wooden chandeliers, adding color to the otherwise black interior. Most choose to sit in the lighter outdoor area. Don't expect to just people-watch, however; seating requires a drink purchase. Open daily 8am-3am. AmEx/MC/V.

Pasticceria Maioli, V. Guicciardini 43r. If you find yourself near Ponte Vecchio on a F or Sa evening with nothing to do and a strong urge to party like it's a 13-year-old's birthday, follow the blaring beats of The Village People pass the gelato and pastries downstairs up to the bar. If you're prone to seizures, watch out: there are strobe lights. If you're prone to awkward, don't worry: there are balloons. Bat them around and reflect on how fun junior high was. Beer €3.50-4.50. Wine €3.50-6. Mixed drinks €4. Open F-Sa 7pm-midnight. MC/V. [SWO]

SANTA MARIA NOVELLA

The after-hours scene in Santa Maria Novella is driven by an eclectic ensemble. A stroll down one of the main drags—**Borgo Ognissanti**, **Via Palazzuolo**, or **Via della Scala**—brings you past raucous biker bars, mellow pubs, raging discos, and exclusive *enoteche*. DJs and live acts are on offer alongside quiet conversation and mellow bars. Places that are hopping one night can be absolutely dead come the next night, so you're likely to spend some time shopping around.

Antico Caffè del Moro (Café des Artistes), V. del Moro 4r (☎055 28 76 61). A classy, candlelit place that specializes in coffee-based mixed drinks (€8.50) and fresh fruity beverages. Squeeze into a table or just lean on the bar during their crowded happy hour (6:30-9pm). Open daily 6:30pm-2am.

Central, V. del Fosso Macinante 2 (☎055 35 35 05), in Parco delle Cascine. Four open-air dance floors pulse with hip-hop, reggae, and Italian "dance rock." Favored by teens and university students. Well-dressed bouncers and management keep things under control. All drinks €10. Cover €20, foreign students €3 until 1am. Open in summer Tu-Su 8pm-3am. AmEx/MC/V.

Aquarama Meccanò, Vle. degli Olmi 1 (☎055 33 13 71), near Parco delle Cascine. One of Florence's most popular discos; caters to a slightly older crowd than Central. Open-air dance floors and sparkling grounds make for sophisticated fun. Drinks €10. Cover €10-16; includes 1 drink. Open Tu-Sa 11pm-4am. AmEx/MC/V.

Joshua Tree, V. della Scala 41. A friendly barkeep and jolly mixed crowd make this Irish pub's weekend happy hour a great way to unwind. Pints €5, ½ pints €3. Happy hour daily 4-9pm; pints €3, ½ pints €3. Open daily 4pm-2am. Cash only.

Space Club Electronic, V. Palazzuolo 37 (☎055 29 30 82; www.spaceelectronic.net). Conveniently closer to the *centro* than Central and Meccanò, Space Club rocks out in a shamelessly themed, space-age atmosphere. Pleather, fog machines, orgies of neon—it's all here. Drunk Americans and Italian men cover the dancefloor on weekends. Mixed drinks and beer €6.50. Cover €16, €10 for foreign students; includes 1 drink. Open daily 10pm-4am.

San Carlo, Borgo Ognissanti 32/34r (☎055 21 68 79; www.sancarlofirenze.it). This funky hangout delivers chrome and cocktails (€7) to its young, local clientele, while tourists from every corner of the globe opt for the wines from every corner of Italy. It's most popular with small crowds of young Italians. Wine €7-9 per glass, €30-50 per bottle. Open M-Sa 7:30am-midnight. AmEx/MC/V.

Sei Divino, Borgo Ognissanti 42r (☎055 21 77 91; www.seidivino.com). A dark, candlelit storehouse of big-name Tuscan wines, Sei Divino would be incredibly romantic if it weren't incredibly popular. Come on a weeknight if you want the intimate ambience; weekends are full of chatty young Italians. Beer €4.50-5. Wine €5-10. Mixed drinks €8. Open daily noon-2am. AmEx/MC/V.

Il Trip Per Tre Pub, V. Borgo Ognissanti 144r (☎055 29 20 85). With rock gods on the walls and beer gods on tap, Il Trip has established a temple for the alternative crowd. Students and bikers flock here to jam, packing into wooden tables scrawled with heavy-metal anthems. Customers here like the music and the conversation loud, so sensitive ears be warned. Mixed drinks €6. Beer €3-5. Happy hour daily 1-9:30pm. Open Tu-Th and Su 1pm-2am, F and Sa 1pm-3am.

Pub Caffé Lo Stregatto, V. Il Prato 44r (www.lostregatto.it). A pub without a theme, Lo Stregatto (the Cheshire cat) keeps the whimsy of its Alice in Wonderland namesake with gears and wheels on the walls, plaid furniture, and a pair of slot machines. It's rarely crowded but always lively, and the staff is cheery and friendly. Beer €4.50 per pint. Wine €4. Mixed drinks €6.50. Open daily 6:30pm-2am.

La Cantinetta Wine Bar, V. della Scala 7r (☎055 26 18 77 70). A classy place catering to a quiet mix of 20-somethings and 60-somethings, La Cantinetta eschews the rustic aesthetic of its competition and aims for sophisticated fun. *Aperitivo con buffet* daily 6-11pm. Open daily 11am-3pm and 5-11pm. MC/V.

La Rotonda, V. il Prato 10/16 (☎055 26 54 644; www.larotondacecconi.it), on the round traffic island. The indoor pub hosts live music acts most Th and F nights, but more importantly, the kitchen stays open into the wee hours of the morning. Customers come here for late-night eats, usually paired with a few drinks. *Primi* €6.50-12. *Secondi* €12-30. Open Tu-Su until 1:30am. MC/V.

SAN LORENZO

San Lorenzo doesn't offer much in the way of nightlife—except for the shamelessly American college student-oriented Fish Pub. You'll have better luck finding a good time in any of the other neighborhoods, particularly Santa Croce.

Shot Café, V. De' Pucci 5A (☎055 28 20 93). Just 1 block from the Duomo, Shot Café has it all. The quirky wallpaper and leather couches match the whimsical decor, which includes brightly-painted windows and Cabbage Patch Dolls on the lamps. The staff will dish on the best places to visit in Florence. Enjoy a delicious coffee break during the day or drink mixed drink specials (€4) with locals and students at night. Free Wi-Fi. Open daily noon-2am. AmEx/MC/V.

Café Deluxée, V. XXVII Aprile 65r (☎055 48 57 49; www.cafedeluxee.com). Cafe by day and bar by night, Deluxée boasts a diverse mix of locals and students. Hip bartender Alessandro will engage in friendly conversation with you, while either a DJ or a live band plays. Free appetizer buffet with drink purchase. Wine €3.50-4. Beer on tap €3.50-5.50. Mixed drinks €7. Buy 3 shots for €2.50 and get 1 free. Open daily 6pm-4am. V.

Kitsch Pub, V. San Gallo 20r. Decorated with stained-glass windows, leather booths, and velvet paneling, this tavern playfully embraces medieval kitsch. With 4 rooms, shots like Orgasmo and Tequila bum bum (€3), and a dinner menu until 10pm, Kitsch is a merry place to start your evening with friends. Beer on tap and mixed drinks €7. *Aperitivi* €7. Open daily 6:30pm-2:30am. Cash only.

The Fish Pub, P. del Mercato Centrale 44r (☎055 26 82 90). Don't let the respectable bookshelf above the bar fool you; you're in for one big frat party. For American college students who want to visit Italy without leaving Tupac at home, the Fish Pub offers beer pong upstairs and a soundtrack of American rap and hip-hop music. With specials like a free drink just for showing up and 5 shots for €5, it's no wonder there are people dancing on the counter by the end of the night. As with any place that offers dizzying amounts of cheap alcohol, exercise caution and never accept drinks from strangers. Open 10pm-3am. Kitchen open 5-10pm. MC/V.

Dublin Pub, V. Faenza 27 (☎055 29 30 49). This Irish pub near the Basilica di San Lorenzo is a perfect place to watch sports or people-watch. Traditional Irish beers on tap like Guinness and Killarney, Irish coffee (€7), and vino (€3) keep the jovial crowd content. Open daily 7pm-2am. AmEx/MC/V over €10.

SAN MARCO

This slow, quiet area of Florence stays mellow well into the evening. Locals prefer a couch and a cocktail to a dance party, and even most of the pubs have a calm, conversational feel. With a few notable exceptions, San Marco's establishments center on tables where friends sit down for drinks.

Finnegan Irish Pub, V. San Gallo 123r (☎055 49 07 94; www.finneganpub.com). With its well-loved wall seats and a social scene centered on the TV, Finnegan feels more like your friend's living room than a Friday night slosh spot. You won't find much of a crowd here unless there's a good game on the screen, but American students and a small but dedicated local following make this a relaxing, inviting place to shout at your favorite sports team. ½-pint €3, pint €5. Mixed drinks €5-6.50. Th student night. Open M-Th 1pm-1:30am, F-Sa 1pm-1am, Su noon-1:30am. Cash only.

The Murphy's Pub II Fauno, V. Cavour 89 (☎055 46 27 176). A place built and maintained for the beer-guzzlers, whiskey shooters, and cocktail-chuggers of the student body, Il Fauno keeps the alcoholic challenges coming and hands out T-shirts to their American Idols of inebriation. Try snacks like popcorn (€1.50) and Mexican nachos (€5) before you start binging. 3 beers or 3 mixed drinks €10. Shots €3. Mixed drinks €7, 1L €10. Small beer €3, medium beer €4.50. 5L Heineken €45. Open daily 5pm-2am.

Nobilis, V. Pietrapiana 82r (☎055 23 45 696; www.nobilisfirenze.com). Minimalist both in decor and physical size, this bar provides inexpensive drinks and meals in a candlelit setting. Check out the meal of the day at lunch, which comes with *primo, secondo,* water, and coffee (meat €10, seafood €15), or wait for *aperitivo con buffet* (daily 6-9pm; €5). Not hungry? Opt for a drink and get a free shot. *Primi* €6-10. *Secondi* €8.50-14. Beer, mixed drinks, and wine €5. Open noon-midnight. Cash only.

SANTA CROCE

Ask any local where the nightlife happens, and they'll direct you here. The row of bars and clubs on Via de' Benci close to the city's center fill the street every night with people looking for—and finding—a good time. Farther into the neighborhood, **Piazza Sant'Ambrogio** and **Piazza Ghiberti** are each sustained by a solitary bar, which manage to accommodate hundreds of locals.

⬛ Mago Merlino Tea House, V. Pilastri 31r (☎055 24 29 70). Always ready to share his wisdom, expert Rocco serves steaming cups of sophisticated tea in his Moroccan-inspired cafe. Choose from a variety of specialty brews (€7-9 a pot) containing everything from amber and saffron to homemade orange water and fresh mint. Take your shoes off and lounge among the floor pillows in the back room, or hit the hookah (€15 per group) in the small courtyard. Come during Happy hour (6:30-9pm) and have organic vegetarian food as you sip on a tea cocktail (€5); Rocco will make it with absinthe if you ask. Open daily 6:30pm-2am. Cash only.

Las Palmas, P. Ghiberti (☎347 27 60 033). Each summer, P. Ghiberti is transformed into a neighborhood block party with the help of Las Palmas. Drinks, live music, and an outdoor dance floor ensure fun-filled nights. Serves tasty dishes. Tables fill quickly, so make reservations. Happy hour 6:30-9pm; drinks €4. Beer €4. Mixed drinks €7. Shots €3. Open daily from the 2nd week of May to the 2nd week of Aug. 6:30pm-1:30am.

Moyo, V. de' Benci 23r (☎055 24 79 738; www.moyo.it). With a vibe like a classy terra cotta cafe, this restaurant becomes a hip spot at night. Outdoor seating, yummy *aperitivi*, and W night sushi draw crowds. Order a fruity Striptease (€7), sit back, and enjoy. Happy hour daily 6-10pm; free *aperitivi*. Open daily 8:30am-2am. AmEx/MC/V.

Caffè Sant'Ambrogio, P. Sant'Ambrogio 7 (☎055 24 10 35). Hip red lights and pulsating techno pop. People begin pouring in for *aperitivi* 6-9pm, but during the rest of the night, most just come in to buy their drinks before heading back into the warm night air of the *piazza*. Wine €4-6. Beer €2.50-5. Open M-Sa 10am-2am, Su 6pm-2am. MC/V.

Red Garter, V. de' Benci 33 (☎055 23 44 904). Claims to be one of the oldest bars in Italy and attracts crowds of young Americans. If you can make it past the throngs of sweaty people grinding near the bar, a row of benches and dancing space is available in the back. Burgers (€7-9) and steak (€13-15) are available through the door at the adjacent House of Sizzle steakhouse. Tu-F karaoke. DJ or live music most nights. Tu beer pong, but sign up early because all 32 slots are usually filled before the 10pm deadline. Open daily 8pm-3pm. Cash only.

Piccolo Café, Borgo Santa Croce 23r. A colorful atmosphere and a colorful crowd frequent this club, which misses the typical college student clusters that occupy the row of Santa Croce clubs just a few steps away. Friendly staff and reasonable drink prices make this a welcoming stop on any night out. While you're waiting for your drink, occupy yourself by turning on the little man at the counter. Hint: he's a lamp. Beer €3-5. Mixed drinks €7. Shots €3. Open daily 6pm-2am. MC/V. [SC]

Kikuya, V. de' Benci 23r (☎055 23 44 879). Although Kikuya proudly calls itself "The English Pub," it also draws crowds of festive Italians. Classy decor in cherry hues. Offers British beers high in alcohol, like the 10% Dragon Strong (pint €5). Open daily 7pm-2am. MC/V.

Salamanca, V. Ghibellina 30r (☎055 23 45 452). Hot red walls set the tone in this Spanish-inspired tavern. Move your body to reggaeton on the dance floor—noticeably free of drunk American girls, a rarity in Florence. Open daily noon-2am. MC/V.

Lochness Lounge, V. de' Benci 19r (☎055 24 14 64; www.lochnessfirenze.com). Black, white, and red all over, this bar strives for a chic New York ambience, providing comfy leather seating for chatting. DJs play both techno and indie folk. Extensive selection of martinis, like the *Balsamic Martini* (martini bianco, gin, *crema di aceto balsamico;* €8). Mixed drinks €7-8. Open daily 5pm-3am. AmEx/MC/V.

PLAZ, V. Pietrapiana 36r (☎055 24 20 81), in P. dei Ciompi. Less community-oriented than the bar in nearby P. Sant'Ambrogio, this one attracts a 20-something crowd of more sophisticated Italians (read: they like to wear their button-ups undone at the top). Opt to take your drink away from the leather seats and red trim of the indoor area to enjoy it beneath the Loggia de Pesce right outside. Beer €3-4. Wine €2.50. Mixed drinks €6. Table charge €2. Open daily 10am-3am. AmEx/MC/V.

James Pub, V. della Mattonaia 20r (☎055 24 28 62). Hard Rock Café T-shirts serve as the primary decoration in this intimate English-style bar. Friendly but not rowdy, it offers a less crazed place to drink between the summer scenes in P. Sant'Ambrogio and P. Ghiberti. Beer €3-5. Wine €4-6. Mixed drinks €5-7. Open M-Sa 6:30pm-2am. Cash only.

Australiano, Borgo Santa Croce 31r (☎055 24 49 01). Coming from "down-under" takes on a different meaning in this bar, where the alternative crowd includes locals and American art school students. Go for the large sitting area and admire original artwork. Beer €3-5. Mixed drinks €6. Shots €3, 5 for €5. Open Tu-Su 9pm-2am. AmEx/MC/V.

WEST OLTRARNO

As with other, more residential areas of Florence, the nightlife in this section of Florence focuses around a particular square, **Piazza Santo Spirito,** where hundreds of locals gather every night to enjoy the warm air and cool drinks from one of the surrounding bars. Other nearby bars with their own attitudes allow most people to find what they're looking for—unless you're in the mood for dancing; then you'll have to go elsewhere.

The Friends' Pub, Borgo San Jacopo 51r (☎055 29 49 30). The atmosphere in this English-style bar is extremely (wait for it) friendly. Lively chatter passes between strangers and friends against the all-wooden layout. Watch the game on TV or take advantage of the free internet. MC/V.

Pop Café, P. Santo Spirito 18r (☎055 21 38 52). Original artwork and a soundtrack ranging from Radiohead to reggae draws a somewhat alternative crowd to the all-white walls of this small bar. Wine €3. Beer €5. Mixed drinks €5. Shots €2.50. Open M-Tu 5pm-2am, W-Su noon-2am. Cash only.

Cabiria, P. Santo Spirito 4r (☎055 21 57 32). Pop culture meets pop art on the walls of this Santo Spirito watering hole, where colorful paintings of Jack Nicholson, David Bowie, and Steve Urkel keep watch over the generally sparse indoor seating area. Sunnily yellow, it doesn't gather much of a crowd, as most people head from the bar back to the outdoor tables and the lively plaza. *Aperitivi* 7-9pm; min. €4 drink purchase. Wine €3.50. Long drinks €6. Open M and W-Su 10am-1:30am. AmEx/MC/V.

La Dolce Vita, P. del Carmine (☎055 28 45 95). Pricier drinks (beer €6-8, mixed drinks €10) gather a slightly older crowd to this popular Oltrarno bar, but the color-splattered floor and relaxed atmosphere welcome students, too. Comfortable outdoor seating on pastel chairs and fruity summertime Su *aperitivi* add extra freshness. Open M-F 8:30am-2am, Sa-Su 5pm-2am. Closed 3rd week in Aug. MC/V.

La Cité, Borgo San Frediano 20r (☎055 21 03 87; www.acitelibreria.info). Part coffee shop, part library, this cool spot offers comfortable, colorful seating and free Wi-Fi to help you feel like a real hip, bookish student. *Caffe* €0.80. Cappuccino €1.20. Beer €2.50-4. Wine €2.50-5. Shot €2.50. Open Sept.-July daily 5pm-1am. Cash only.

Cavalli Club, P. del Carmine 7r (☎055 21 16 50; www.cavalliclub.com). Only for those who are willing to break out the Benjamins for a crunk night. If the recession hasn't hit you and animal rights isn't too high up on your list of priorities, check out the leopard-skin print seats in this club, where the drinks are pricey and the chrome well-shined. Beer, wine, and mixed drinks €10. Shots €5. Open from late July to early Sept. T-Su 7pm-2am. AmEx/MC/V.

EAST OLTRARNO

This quarter of the city likes the sort of nightlife that comes with side dishes. Arnoside establishments from Ponte Vecchio to Lungarno Ferrucci are littered with locals in search of *aperitivi*, and though you won't find the party-hard pubs and dance-happy discos popular near the *centro*, you might find a bar where the only English you hear is the word "buffet." **Piazza Giuseppe Poggi** may be the most popular nightlife destination in the Oltrarno. If you're looking to rub elbows (literally) with the locals, just follow the noise and the motos along Lungarno B. Cellini.

NIGHTLIFE

Enoteca Bevo, V. San Niccolo 59r. A welcoming neighborhood *enoteca* where customers feel free to sit on the sidewalks and gossip with the barkeeps. If you don't know what you'd like to drink, ask the helpful and opinionated staff for some suggestions. GLBT-friendly. Wine €4.50-9 per glass. Open daily 11am-1am. MC/V.

Kitsch the Bar, Vle. Gramsci 1-5r (☎055 23 43 890; www.kitsch-bar.com), in P. Beccaria. Despite its location in the outskirts, this popular companion to the *centro* pub overflows with young Italians chatting in leopard-print booths. A great spot on the north side of the river to stop for drinks on your way to the nightlife near Ponte San Niccolò. *Aperitivo con buffet* daily 6:30-10pm. Beer €4-6. Mixed drinks €7. Open daily 6pm-2am. Cash only.

James Joyce Pub, Lungarno B. Cellini 1r (☎055 65 80 856). A warm, literary vibe saturates the old-fashioned interior of this "Books and Beer" pub while the huge outdoor patio hosts chain-smoking Italians and foosball. A window on the back wall of the bar opens onto the outdoor area, so you can enjoy the night air without even moving. ½-pints €3.50, pints €5. Mixed drinks €7-8. Open daily 4pm-2:30am. AmEx/MC/V.

Il Kioskino, P. Giuseppe Poggi. The seats by Il Kioskino provide the cheapest riverside view in the city. Cheap drinks power the dull roar in the *piazza.* Beer €4. Wine €2 per glass, €10 per bottle. Open M-Sa 8:30pm-1:30am. Cash only.

Easy Living, P. Giuseppe Poggi. Though most of the mob is happy to stand in circles, a quick jaunt down the ramp by Easy Living will bring you to a hut-dotted sandbar on the bank of the Arno where you can sit and sip. Mixed drinks €6. Open daily 10am-1am. Cash only.

Flò, Ple. Michelangelo 84 (☎055 65 07 91; www.flofirenze.com). "Standing room only" would be an exaggeration of the space available in this insanely popular open-air lounge bar. Locals of all ages are willing to wait in a quick-moving but winding line for their chance to chat beneath the green-lit greenery of Vle. Michelangelo. Pay for drinks at the cash register by the door first and use your receipt to order at the bar. Beer €6. Mixed drinks €8. Open daily 7pm-late. V.

Zoe, V. de Renai 13r (☎055 24 31 11; www.zoebar.it). An ultra-modern black and white bar whose unusually tasty buffet even includes some hot dishes (but get 'em fast). Sleek techno music and a young crowd keep this scene cool long past aperitifs. *Aperitivo con buffet* (€5-8) 5pm-10pm. Beer and wine €4-6. Mixed drinks €7. Open daily 8am-late. MC/V.

Negroni, V. de Renai 17r (☎055 24 36 47; www.negronibar.com). Though the menu draws its inspiration from the principle of so-called "alcoholic alchemy," Negroni's warm lighting, light-colored wood, and small interior is more suited to conversation than bacchanalia. Most popular when the DJ is there. *Aperitivo con buffet* (€8) 7pm-11pm. Open M-Sa 8am-2am, Su 6:30pm-2am. AmEx/MC/V.

Montecarla, V. dei Bardi 2 (☎055 23 40 259). A jungle-themed joint stashed away on the more remote end of V. dei Bardi; nothing else in this area is quite like it. There's snake skin on the stairs, coloring books and Connect Four on the tables, and an upside-down alligator hanging from the rafters. The low-ceilinged 2nd floor is covered in comfy cushions and seats so long that you can lie down on them. Drinks €8. Open Tu-Su 10pm-3am or later. Cash only.

Caffè la Torre, Lungarno B. Cellini 65r (☎055 68 06 43). A sleek, mellow spot popular with the quieter aperitif crowd. Most customers choose to sit streetside at the open-air tables, but the indoor area gets busy when the cafe becomes a cocktail bar later on. *Aperitivo con buffet* daily 6:30-10:30pm. Wine and beer €6. Mixed drinks €7. Open M-Sa 10:30am-3am. Cash only.

LungArno 23, Lungarno Torrigiani 23 (☎055 234 5957; www.lungarno23.it). A wide, well-lit lounge that grills delicious Chianina beef hamburgers (€10-12) in the evening and stacks its long tables with happy crowds after the kitchen's closed. Regardless of the hour, the atmosphere is always friendly and fun. Beer €4-7. Mixed drinks €8. Open 9am-late. Kitchen open 7-10:30pm. MC/V.

GoldenView Ocafé, V. De' Bardi, 54/56r (☎055 21 45 02; www.goldenviewopenbar.com). Consciously cool young couples sip their drinks in this posh world of glass windows and glossy tables, where the buffet is gourmet and the art is ultra-modern. Come after sunset to enjoy an Arno view, when the darkness lends the ordinarily murky river some romance. Drinks €10. Open daily 11:30am-1am. MC/V.

Rifrullo Caffe Ristorante, V. San Niccolo 55r (☎055 234 26 21; www.ilrifrullo.com). The young aperitif crowd here is usually overflowing, and even if you don't see any Rifrullo customers on the sidewalk, you'll certainly hear them. Join this chatty, cheery group for a great start to your night out. Check the website or call for information on the popular monthly events, like full beach parties. *Aperitivo con buffet* daily 7-10pm; €7. MC/V.

Il Giardino del BuonVino, in the green area between Lungarno Serristori and V. de Renai, in front of Zoe and Negroni. An outdoor wine bar operated by Zoe and Negroni, this *giardino* has a smaller crowd and a greener atmosphere than its 2 older siblings. Enjoy the elegance of the backlit statuary behind the bar or snag a sunset spot at one of the tables for a great view of the red-gold river. €2 glass deposit. Open in summer noon-midnight. Cash only.

Checkpoint, on the traffic island in P. Ferrucci. With a location and size akin to a gas station, this pint-sized pitstop serves as the refueling station for Florentine partiers. Most customers won't spend the entire night here, but you'll always find a few clusters of locals and tourists in the outdoor seating area. *Aperitivo con buffet* daily 7-10pm; €6. Mixed drinks €6. Open daily 7pm-3am. Cash only.

High Bar, V. dei Renai 27a (☎055 23 47 082). The tiny crowd at this quaint and quiet bar is clearly dwarfed by the throngs at Zoe and Negroni, but regulars enjoy its small size and old-fashioned atmosphere. The jeans-and-T-shirt dress code is perfect for a foosball match in the back room, and your group is guaranteed to have room for a table together in the outdoor seating. House wine €3 per glass. Happy hour 3-7pm. Open 8:30am-late. MC/V.

NIGHTLIFE

TUSCANY

Tuscany is the stuff of Italian dreams—and more than one romantic Brits-in-Italy movie. Gazing out over rolling hills, fields of sunflowers, and inviting cobblestone streets, it's hard not to wax poetic. Tuscany's Renaissance culture became Italy's heritage, and its regional dialect— the language of Dante, Petrarch, and Machiavelli—became today's textbook Italian. The subtle variations in Tuscan cuisine give you an excuse to have a meal and a bottle of wine in every single town.

Though cut from similar cloth, each Tuscan city has its own fierce heritage and unique characteristics; after all, they did spend centuries trying to conquer each other. The land from Chianti's vineyards to Viareggio's beaches has something for everyone, served with a dose of quaint small-town Italian charm.

FIESOLE   ☎055

Fiesole (FEE-yeh-SOH leh; pop. 14,000) is the site of the ancient Etruscan settlement that later extended down the hill to become Florence. Fiesole's clean, cool breezes have long been a welcome escape from the sweltering summer heat of the Arno Valley and this spot on the hill, with its awesome views of the city below, has been a source of inspiration for many a famous figure: Alexandre Dumas, Anatole France, Paul Klee, Marcel Proust, Frank Lloyd Wright, and Gertrude Stein. Leonardo da Vinci once used the town as a testing ground for his famed flying machine.

🚍 TRANSPORTATION. From Florence, catch the ATAF city **bus** #7 from the train station (30min., every 30min., €1.20); it stops in the *centro* at P. Mino da Fiesole. Purchase return tickets at the newsstand beside the bus stop.

📊🛈 ORIENTATION AND PRACTICAL INFORMATION. The **tourist office**, V. Portigiani 3, is next to the Teatro Romano. Cross the street from the bus stop, go down V. Giovanni Dupre, and take the first right; the office is on the left. The office provides a free map with museum and sights listings. (☎055 59 87 20; www.comune.fiesole.fi.it. Open Easter to Oct. M-F 9:30am-6:30pm, Sa-Su 10am-1pm and 2-6pm; Nov. to Easter M-F 10am-6pm, Sa-Su 10am-4pm.

🏠 ACCOMMODATIONS AND FOOD. Accommodations in Fiesole are expensive, so a daytrip can be more budget-friendly. Take in Arno Valley views over coffee (from €0.80) or gelato (from €1.60) at **Blu Bar ❶**, P. Mino 39. (☎055 59 363. Pizza €3.50. Crepes €6. Mixed drinks €10.50. Open daily Feb.-Dec. 9am-11pm. AmEx/MC/V.)

🔲 SIGHTS. Begin your exploration by facing away from the bus stop, walking across P. Mino da Fiesole, and down V. Dupre to the entrance of the Teatro Romano, V. Portigiani 1. One ticket provides admission to three associated attractions: Museo Civico Archeologico, Museo Bandini, and the Teatro Romano within the archeological area. The **archaeological area** includes the perfectly rectangular foundations of Etruscan thermal baths and the toppled columns and sturdy archways of temple ruins. The well-preserved **Teatro Romano** still retains the components of an ancient Roman amphitheater, though it is now occasionally gussied up with modern sound equipment and spotlights for summer concerts. On the right, after entering the archeological grounds, the

TUSCANY

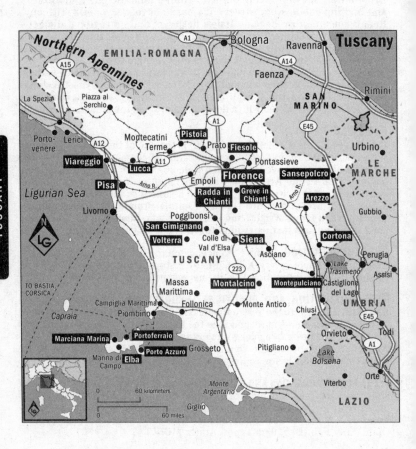

Tuscany

EMILIA-ROMAGNA
Northern Apennines

Bologna
Ravenna
Faenza
Rimini

SAN MARINO

A1
A15
A14
E45
La Spezia
Piazza al Serchio
Urbino
LE MARCHE
Porto-venere
Lerici
A12
Montecatini Terme
Pistoia
Prato
Fiesole
Pontassieve
Sansepolcro
Viareggio
Lucca
A11
Florence
Empoli
Gubbio
Pisa
Arno R.
Radda in Chianti
Greve in Chianti
Arezzo
Arno R.
A1
Ligurian Sea
Livorno
Poggibonsi
San Gimignano
Colle di Val d'Elsa
Cortona
Volterra
Siena
Perugia
Asciano
Lake Trasimeno
TUSCANY
Assisi
223
TO BASTIA, CORSICA
Massa Marittima
Montalcino
Montepulciano
Castiglione del Lago
Capraia
Campiglia Marittima
Follonica
Monte Antico
Chiusi
UMBRIA
Piombino
Todi
Marciana Marina
Portoferraio
E45
Porto Azzurro
Grosseto
Orvieto
A1
Marina di Campo
Elba
Pitigliano
Lake Bolsena
Orte
N
LG
Monte Argentario
Viterbo
LAZIO
Giglio
0   60 kilometers
0   60 miles

Museo Civico Archeologico houses an extensive collection of Etruscan artifacts (most gathered from Fiesole and its territory), well-preserved Grecian urns, a reconstructed tomb with a skeleton, and vases from Magna Graecia (southern Italy, once part of the Greek Empire). Cross the street to breeze through **Museo Bandini**, V. Dupre 1, which holds the collection of 18th-century intellectual Canonical Angelo Maria Bandini. Within the museum, you'll find Italian works from the 13th through 15th centuries, including works by Cortona's Signorelli, Giotto, the della Robbias, Gaddi, and Botticelli. (☎055 59 61 293. Open Apr.-Sept. M and W-Su 10am-7pm.; Oct. M and W-F 10am-6pm; Nov.-Feb. M and Th-Su 10am-4pm; Mar. M and W-Su 10am-6pm. Last entry 30min. before closing. €12, students and over 65 €8, families €24. MC/V.)

A short, steep walk uphill to the left of the bus stop takes you past the **public gardens.** The entrance to the gardens is on the left side of the path. These small areas provide stunning views of Florence. The panorama of the valley below is perhaps the only context in which Florence's massive duomo appears small. At the end of the path is the **Chiesa di San Francesco.** Take the stairs through the door to the right of the main entrance to experience the eerie quiet of the small rooms of study. The church itself contains 15th- and 16th-century Tuscan paintings, such as Piero di Cosimo's *Immaculate Conception.* Go through the door on the right side of the church to check out the **Museo Etnografico.** Housing Etruscan and Roman archeological findings and materials gathered by Franciscan missionaries in ancient China and Egypt, the museum's collection features Chinese pottery, jade figurines, and even an Egyptian mummy. (Open Tu-F 10am-noon and 3-7pm. Free) Live performances bring new life to the Roman theater from June through September, when **Estate Fiesolana** sponsors concerts, opera, theater, and film (www.estatefiesolana.it).

GREVE IN CHIANTI ☎055

Welcome to Chianti country, where the cheese and olive oil are exquisite and the wine is even better. The tiny town of Greve (GREV-ay; pop. 12,855), is the hub of it all. To find out what that *Chianti Classico* (key-AN-tee CLAS-see-ko) is all about, get your taste buds ready and sip with the best.

◪ **TRANSPORTATION.** SITA **buses** run to Greve from Florence (1hr., every hr. 7am-8pm, €3.10; reduced service Su and holidays). There are 2 stops in Greve; get off at the first at P. Trento. P. Trento is not clearly labeled, so be sure to ask the bus driver to alert you when the bus arrives there.

◪◪ **ORIENTATION AND PRACTICAL INFORMATION.** From P. Trento, continue to walk in the direction of the bus on Vle. Vittorio Veneto, turning right at the first stop light on V. Battisti, leading to the main square, P. Matteotti. For a list of local vineyards and help booking accommodations, head to the building shared by the **tourist office** and **Chianti Slow Travel Agency,** P. Matteotti 11. (☎055 85 46 299. Open M-F 9:30am-1pm and 2-6pm, Sa 2pm-6pm.) **Officina Marco Ramuzzi,** V. Italo Stecchi 23, offers scooter and mountain bike rentals. (☎055 85 30 37; www.ramuzzi.com. Bikes €20 per day, €120 per week. Scooters €30-55/175-290.)

◪◪ **ACCOMMODATIONS AND FOOD.** Accommodations in the *centro* are scarce and many nearby villas are not easily accessible by public transportation.

However, **Albergo del Chianti ❶**, P. Matteotti 86, belies this generalization at a price. Located in the main *piazza*, the hotel offers 16 clean, comfortable rooms, each with bath, mini-bar, phone, air conditioning, and TV. The rustic lobby and adjoining bar open onto an outdoor oasis: a lovely patio, garden, and swimming pool. (☎055 85 37 63; www.albergodelchianti.it. Breakfast included. Singles €75; doubles €100.) For a truly Tuscan meal, the well-known **Mangiando, Mangiando ❸**, P. Matteotti 80, will do the job with traditional plates such as *cinta senese* (a type of pig native to Tuscany) under a wood-beamed ceiling or under outdoor umbrellas. (☎055 85 46 372. *Primi* €6.50-11. *Secondi* €12-25. Open Tu-Su in summer 11am-11pm, in winter noon-3pm and 7-10:30pm. MC/V.) For fresh, local goods, **Macelleria**, P. Matteotti 69-71, is as authentic as it gets. Choose from the wide array of meats and cheeses or pop into the back room to taste several varieties for free. Wine tastings start at €10.20. (Open M-Sa 8am-1pm and 3:30-7:30pm, Su 10am-1pm and 3-7:15pm. AmEx/MC/V.) Dirt cheap picnic eats can be found at **Coop,** Vle. Vittorio Veneto 76. (☎055 85 30 53. Open M-Sa 8am1pm and 4-7:45pm. MC/V.) Pick up fresh bread and sweets (from €1.50) at **Forno,** P. Matteotti 89. (Open daily in summer 7am-1pm and 5-8pm, in winter 5-8pm. Cash only.)

🄖 **SIGHTS.** Just down Vle. Vittorio Veneto and on the right in P. delle Cantine, a wine lover's paradise awaits at 🄖**Le Cantine di Greve in Chianti,** P. delle Cantine 2, which is part wine museum, part *enoteca*. Opened in 2000, the Cantine use a new technology for wine tasting where the bottles rest in vacuum-valves that enable over 150 bottles to be tasted at once, including a wide range of local *Chianti Classico* and *Supertuscan*. They also stock *Nobile, Brunello,* and *Bolgheri,* wines from other Tuscan towns. Grab a tasting card in denominations of €10, €15, €20, or €25, and insert the card above the wine you wish to taste; tastes start around €0.60, depending on the type of wine. Helpful staff will help you navigate the stands that pack the brick-arched, stone-walled basement. (☎055 85 46 404; www.lecantine.it. Open daily 10am-7pm. Free. AmEx/MC/V.) Many other *enoteche* in town offer free wine tastings of 3-5 wines in the hopes that you'll whip out the wallet. The selection at **Enoteca del Chianti Classico,** P. San Croce 8, is especially impressive. (☎055 85 32 97; www.chianticlassico.it Open daily in summer 9:30am-7:30pm, in winter 9:30am-12:30pm and 3:30-7:30pm. AmEx/MC/V.)

SIENA ☎05 77

Siena's (see-EH-na; pop. 50,000) vibrant character and local energy make it a distinctly Tuscan city. Locals are fiercely proud of their town's history, which dates back to the 13th century. The city's vehement (and still palpable) rivalry with Florence resulted in grandiose Gothic architecture and soaring towers, though the arrival of the Black Death briefly put a halt to the architectural one-upmanship. These days, the Sienese celebrate their heritage with festivals like the semi-annual *Palio*, a riotous display of pageantry in which jockeys race bareback horses around the central square. In the heart of the Tuscan wine country, Siena is also an ideal base for exploring local vineyards and vintages.

▐ TRANSPORTATION

Trains: P. Rosselli, 15min. from the *centro* by bus #3, 4, 7, 9, 10, 17, or 77. Buy tickets from vending machines by the station entrance or at the ticket office (€1). Ticket office

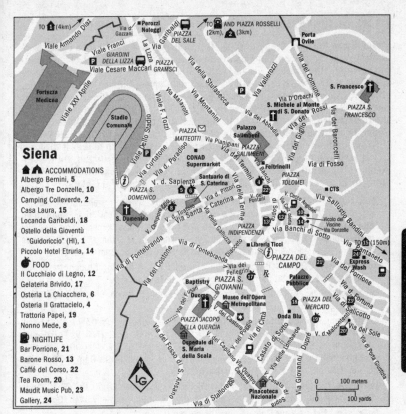

Siena

🏕️🏠 **ACCOMMODATIONS**
Albergo Bernini, **5**
Albergo Tre Donzelle, **10**
Camping Colleverde, **2**
Casa Laura, **15**
Locanda Garibaldi, **18**
Ostello della Gioventù
  "Guidoriccio" (HI), **1**
Piccolo Hotel Etruria, **14**

🍎 **FOOD**
Il Cucchiaio di Legno, **12**
Gelateria Brivido, **17**
Osteria La Chiacchera, **6**
Osteria Il Grattacielo, **4**
Trattoria Papei, **19**
Nonno Mede, **8**

🍷 **NIGHTLIFE**
Bar Porrione, **21**
Barone Rosso, **13**
Caffé del Corso, **22**
Tea Room, **20**
Maudit Music Pub, **23**
Gallery, **24**

TUSCANY

open daily 6:30am-1:10pm and 1:40-8:10pm. To **Florence** (1¼hr., 21 per day 5:50am-9:18pm, €6.10) and **Rome** (3hr., 19 per day 5:45am-8:19pm, €13) via **Chiusi.**

Buses: TRA-IN/SITA (☎05 77 20 42 46; www.trainspa.it). Some intercity buses leave from P. Gramsci, but most leave from the train station. Ticket offices in the underground terminal in P. Gramsci (open daily 7am-7pm) and at the train station (open M-Sa 6:15am-8:15pm, Su 7:30am-12:30pm and 2:30-6:30pm). To reach the train station from P. Gramsci, take bus 3, 9, or 10 to Ferrovia. Tickets can be purchased at the underground ticket office or at the local *tabaccheria* (€0.95). To: **Arezzo** (7 per day, €5.20); **Florence** (every hr., €6.80); **Montalcino** (7 per day, €3.30); **Montepulciano** (4 per day, €4.70) via **Buonconvento** or **Torrenieri; San Gimignano** (31 per day, €5.30) via **Poggibonsi.** TRA-IN also runs buses within Siena. Buy tickets (valid 1hr., €0.95) at the office in P. Gramsci or a vendor that displays a TRA-IN sign. Reduced bus service Su.

Taxis: RadioTaxi (☎05 77 49 222), in P. Indipendenza and P. Matteotti.

Car Rental: Siena Perozzi Rental, V. dei Gazzani 16 (☎05 77 28 83 87) and V. del Romitorio 5 (☎05 77 28 08 39; www.perozzi.it), off P. la Lizza. Cars €50-115 per day. Mountain bikes €10 per day, €50 per week. Scooters €26-52 per day, €150-260 per week. Rates include insurance. Valid license required. €300 deposit or credit card number required. Open M-Sa 9am-7pm and Su 9am-1pm. AmEx/MC/V.

⚜ ⁊ ORIENTATION AND PRACTICAL INFORMATION

From **Piazza Gramsci**, the main bus stop, follow **Via Malavolti** into **Piazza Matteotti**. Cross the *piazza* and continue straight on **Via Banchi di Sopra**, heading through the heart of town. Continuing downhill, pass through one of the several archways that lead to **Piazza del Campo**, Siena's *centro storico*, also known as **Il Campo**. The **Palazzo Pubblico**, the tourist office, and the best people-watching in the town are located here. To get to the *centro* from the **train station**, cross the street to the mall and take one of the buses listed above from the underground terminal. These buses stop in **Piazza del Sale** or P. Gramsci. Some buses stop just before P. Gramsci, which makes it difficult to know where to get off; ask the bus driver. From either *piazza*, follow the signs to Il Campo. From the bus station in **Piazza San Domenico**, follow the signs to P. del Campo. **Piazza del Duomo** lies 100m west of Il Campo.

Tourist Office: APT, P. del Campo 56 (☎05 77 28 05 51; www.terresiena.it). Knowledgeable staff offers brochures, some at a nominal fee. Open daily 9am-7pm. **Prenotazioni Alberghi e Ristoranti** (☎05 77 28 80 84 or 84 80), in P. San Domenico, makes hotel reservations (€2). Books reservations for 2hr. walking tours of Siena (M-F 11am, reserve by 10am; €20) and San Gimignano. Open M-Sa 9am-7pm, Su 9am-noon.

Budget Travel: CTS, V. Sallustio Bandini 21 (☎05 77 28 50 08). Student travel services. Open M-F and Su 9am-12:30pm and 3:30-7pm. MC/V.

Luggage Storage: At TRA-IN ticket office beneath P. Gramsci. €3 per 6hr., €5.50 per 12hr. No overnight storage. Open daily 7am-7pm. Cash only.

English-Language Bookstore: Libreria Ticci, V. delle Terme 5-7 (☎05 77 28 00 10). Fairly extensive selection. Open M-Sa 9am-7:30pm. AmEx/MC/V. **Feltrinelli**, V. Banchi di Sopra 52 and 64 (☎05 77 27 12 04 or 27 44 009). Classics, popular fiction, and English-language magazines. Open M-Sa 9am-7:30pm, Su 11am-1:30pm and 3:30-7:30pm. AmEx/MC/V.

Laundromat: Express Wash, V. Pantaneto 38. Self-service. Wash €3.50. Dry €3.50. **Onda Blu**, V. Casato di Sotto 17. Wash €3 per 7kg, dry €3. Both open daily 8am-10pm.

Police: (☎112), on V. del Castoro near the *duomo*.

Pharmacy: Farmacia del Campo, P. del Campo 26. Open M-F 9am-7:30pm. Posts late-night rotations. AmEx/MC/V.

Hospital: V. Le Scotte 14 (☎05 77 58 51 11). Take bus #3 or 77 from P. Gramsci.

Internet Access: Cafe Internet/International Call Center, V. Cecco Angiolieri 16 (☎05 77 41 521). €2 per hr. Open M-Sa 8:30am-11pm, Su 9am-11pm. Cash only. **Internet Train**, V. di Città 121 (☎05 77 22 63 66). €4 per hr. Wi-Fi. Open M-F 10am-8pm, Sa noon-8pm, Su 3-7pm. AmEx/MC/V. **Netrunner**, V. Pantaneto 132. €4 per hr. Discounts for return customers. Open M-F 10am-11pm, Sa 10am-8pm, Su 3-8pm. MC/V.

Post Office: P. Matteotti 36. Open M-F 8:15am-7pm, Sa 8:15am-1:30pm. **Postal Code:** 53100.

⌂ ACCOMMODATIONS

Finding a room in the center of Siena can be difficult and expensive in the summer. Book months in advance for the Palio (p. 183). For visits over a week, *affittacamere* (room rentals) are a popular option. Tourist offices (see above) can provide a list of these private rooms and help with booking.

Casa Laura, V. Roma 3 (☎05 77 22 60 61), 10min. from Il Campo in the university area. Ring 3rd doorbell down, labeled *"Bencini Valentini."* Sacrifice immediate access to downtown Siena for spacious, well-priced rooms with TVs, some with baths. Kitchen available. Singles €55; doubles €70; triples €70; quads €90. MC/V. ❸

Piccolo Hotel Etruria, V. Donzelle 3 (☎05 77 28 80 88; www.hoteletruria.com). A stone's throw from Il Campo. Small, family-run establishment maintains 20 immaculate rooms, each with phone, TV, telephone, safe box, and hair dryer. Breakfast €6. Curfew 1am. Singles €50, with bath €55; doubles €90-110; triples €117. Extra bed €28. AmEx/MC/V. ❸

Ostello della Gioventù "Guidoriccio" (HI), V. Fiorentina 89 (☎05 77 52 212), in Località Lo Stellino, a 10-20min. bus ride from town. Take bus #10, 17, 15, or 36 from P. Gramsci. Buses #15 and #36 stop at front door. For buses #10 and 17, continue from the stop in the bus's direction and take the first right; it's another 50m down. Mostly 2- to 4-person rooms in this 100-bed hostel. Breakfast included; dinner €10. Wi-Fi €3 per day. Lockout 9:30am-3pm. Reservations recommended. Dorms €20. Cash only. ❶

Albergo Tre Donzelle, V. Donzelle 5 (☎05 77 28 03 58). Close to Il Campo. Basic rooms have simple wood furnishings and lots of space. Curfew 1am. Singles €38; doubles €49, with bath €60; triples €70/85; quads €120. AmEx/MC/V. ❷

Albergo Bernini, V. della Sapienza 15 (☎05 77 28 90 47; www.albergobernini.com). 9 antique-laden rooms, some with A/C, have picture-perfect views of the *duomo*. Outdoor patio is lined with plants, the perfect setting for a serenade by the accordion-playing owner. Breakfast €5.50-7. Free Wi-Fi. Curfew midnight. Singles €50, with bath €75; doubles €65/85; triples €115, with shared bath €135. Extra bed €15. Cash only. ❸

Hotel Alma Domus, V. Camporeggio 37 (☎05 77 44 177), next to Santuario di Santa Caterina and Chiesa San Domenico. Though quieter during the day, 2 nearby restaurants may prevent an uninterrupted night's sleep. Run by nuns. Bare, spotless rooms have baths and A/C. Ask ahead of time for a *duomo* view. Curfew 1:30am. Singles €42, with breakfast €45; doubles €65/75; triples €80; quads €95. Cash only. ❷

▐▌ FOOD

Siena specializes in rich pastries. The most famous is *panforte*, a concoction of honey, almonds, and citron that was once baked as a trail mix for the Crusaders. For something a little less military and little more sugary, try *ricciarelli*, soft almond cookies topped with a thick coating of powdered sugar. Sample either (€2.20 per 100g) at the **Bar/Pasticceria Nannini,** V. Banchi di Sopra 22-24, Siena's oldest *pasticceria*, now a chain. (Open M-Sa 7:30am-9pm, Su 8am-9pm. AmEx/MC/V.) The local meat specialty, *cinta senese,* and the region's trademark thick spaghetti, *pici*, are also popular. Siena's **open-air market** fills P. La Lizza each Wednesday (8am-1pm). For groceries, head to **Conad,** in the Galleria Metropolitan in P. Matteotti (open M-Sa 8:30am-8:30pm, Su 9am-1pm and 4-8pm; MC/V), or **Pam,** in the mall across from the train station. (Open M-Sa 8:30am-9:30pm, Su 9am-9pm. AmEx/MC/V.)

▨ Trattoria Papei, P. del Mercato 6 (☎05 77 28 08 94), on the far side of Palazzo Pubblico from Il Campo. Despite the large capacity, the outdoor tables and stone-arched dining room at this popular *trattoria* can get crowded and noisy, but the company's always cheerful. Vast range of homemade pasta dishes, including scrumptious *pici alla cardinale* (spaghetti with tomato-pepper sauce and pancetta; €7), and traditional meat dishes. Cover €2. Open Tu-Su noon-3pm and 7-10:30pm. AmEx/MC/V. ❷

Osteria La Chiacchera, Costa di San Antonio 4 (☎05 77 28 06 31), next to Santuario di Santa Caterina. Frequented by young Italians and savvy tourists. Delicious Italian

TUSCANY

staples at low prices in a casual and lively atmosphere. *Primi* €5.50-6.50. *Secondi* €6.50-12. Open M and W-Su noon-3pm and 7-10pm. MC/V. ❷

Nonno Mede, V. Camporeggio 21 (☎05 77 24 79 66), down the hill to the left of Chiesa San Domenico. Expansive outdoor seating area with great views of the *duomo* and picturesque Siena rooftops. Extensive pizza menu, along with everything from mixed vegetables to stuffed rabbit. Pizza €4.50-7. *Primi* €6-7.50. *Secondi* €10-15. Cover €1.60. Open daily noon-3:30pm and 7pm-1:30am. MC/V. ❶

Osteria Il Grattacielo, V. dei Pontani 8 (☎05 77 33 46 31 14 60), between V. dei Termini and V. Banchi di Sopra. The perfect place to enjoy native culinary delights, including baby artichokes, olives, sun-dried tomatoes in oil, and hunks of salami and *pecorino*. Half the fun here is ordering—add ingredients by pointing at jars of food to create your dream lunch. Full lunch with wine €11. Open M-Sa noon-2:45pm and 7:30-10pm. Cash only. ❷

Gelateria Brivido, V. dei Pellegrini 1-3 (☎05 77 28 00 58). Gelato in flavors like kiwi and watermelon, presented in spiraling towers. Standing-room only. Cones (€2-5.50) come plain or chocolate-dipped. Open daily 10am-midnight. Cash only. ❶

🔅 SIGHTS

The "My name is Duccio" all-inclusive ticket (€10) includes the Duomo, the Museo dell'Opera and *facciatone*, the Cripta, the Battistero, and the Oratorio di San Bernardino. It can be purchased from the ticket office of any of the participating sights.

█IL CAMPO. Siena radiates from the **Piazza del Campo,** a shell-shaped square designed for civic events and affectionately referred to as "Il Campo." The *piazza*'s brick paving is divided into nine sections, representing the city's medieval Council of Nine. Dante's *Inferno* referred to the square in the account of the real-life drama of Provenzan Salvani, a heroic Sienese merchant who panhandled in Il Campo to pay a friend's ransom. Later Sienese mystics used the *piazza* as a public auditorium. Today, Il Campo is framed by restaurants and cafes overlooking the monstrous clock tower, and it provides a perfect hangout. Twice each summer, the **Palio** (p. 183) morphs the mellow Campo into a chaotic arena as horses race around its edge. At the top of the slope is the **Fonte Gaia,** a rectangular marble fountain nestled into the slanted *piazza*. The water here emerges from the same 25km aqueduct that has refreshed Siena since the 14th century. Standing at the bottom of the *piazza* is the imposing **Palazzo Pubblico** and its looming *campanile*, the **Torre del Mangia.** In front of the *palazzo* is the **Cappella di Piazza,** which was started in 1348 but took 100 years to complete due to the arrival of the Black Death.

PALAZZO PUBBLICO. This impressive medieval building was home to Siena's Council of Nine in the Middle Ages, and it still houses city government offices today. However, the main draw is its **Museo Civico.** While the Sienese art pieces here range from medieval triptychs to 18th-century landscapes, the greatest treasure is the collection of late-medieval to early-Renaissance painting from the distinctive Sienese school. The large and airy **Sala del Mappamondo,** named for a lost series of astronomical frescoes, displays Simone Martini's *Maestà*, which combines religious overtones with civic and literary awareness. The Christ child is depicted holding a parchment inscribed with the city's Horatian motto, *"Expertus fidelem"* ("having found him faithful"), and the steps of the canopied throne are engraved with two stanzas from Dante's *Divine Comedy*. In the next room, the **Sala dei Nove** holds Ambrogio Lorenzetti's famous frescoes, the *Allegories of Good and Bad Government and their Effects on Town* *and Country*, with opposing visions of Hell on Earth and utopia on the right and left walls. (☎05 77 29 26 14. *Open daily from mid-Mar. to Oct. 10am-7pm; from Nov. to mid-Mar. 10am-6pm. Last entry 45min. before closing. €7.50, students €4.50, under 11 free. Combined ticket for tower and Museo €12. Cash only.*)

The Palazzo Pubblico's other star attraction is the **Torre del Mangia,** named for the gluttonous bell-ringer Giovanni di Duccio, also called *"Mangiaguadagni"* ("Eat-the-profits"). At 102m, Italy's tallest secular medieval monument is Siena's equivalent of the North Star. Lost tourists need only search for the tower's ornate top to orient themselves. After 500 dizzying and narrow steps, persistence pays off underneath the tower's highest bell: from the top, Siena's tiled rooftops, farmlands, and vineyard hills form an enchanting mosaic. Arrive early, as it gets crowded in the afternoon. (*Open daily from mid-Mar. to Oct. 10am-7pm; from Nov. to mid-Mar. 10am-6pm. €7.50, students €4.50. Cash only.*)

DUOMO. Atop one of the city's seven hills, the *duomo* is one of few completely Gothic cathedrals south of the Alps. Construction began in 1229, and the entire structure was completed over a hundred years later. The dome was built in 1263, the bell tower by 1313. The huge arch of the *facciatone*, part of a striped wall facing the front of the cathedral, is the sole remnant of Siena's 1339 plan to construct a new nave, which would have made this *duomo* the largest church in all Christendom. The effort ended when the Black Plague decimated the working population in 1348. One of the *duomo's* side aisles has been enclosed and turned into the **Museo dell'Opera Metropolitana.** Statues of philosophers, sibyls, and prophets by Giovanni Pisano stand guard beneath impressive spires.

The bronze sun on the *duomo's* facade was the creation of San Bernardino of Siena, who wanted the feuding Sienese to relinquish their emblems of nobility and unite under this symbol of the risen Christ. Alas, his efforts were in vain—the Sienese continue to identify with the animal symbols of their *contrade* (districts). The marble floor, like the rest of the *duomo*, is ornate, depicting diverse and often violent themes like the *Slaughter of the Innocents*. Michelangelo, Donatello, Pinturicchio, and Bernini are just a few of the many renowned artists who worked on the floor, called "the Unveiled Floor" because it is only open to the public from mid-August to October. Halfway up the left aisle is the **Piccolomini Altar,** designed by Andrea Bregno in 1503. The statue was built to host a very special holy relic: St. John's right arm. The lavish **Libreria Piccolomini,** commissioned by Pope Pius III in 1492, houses elaborately illustrated books of his uncle, Pius II. On the right, the **Papal Chapel of Madonna del Voto** houses two Bernini statues. (*Open daily from mid-Mar. to Sept. 10:30am-8pm; Oct. and 1st 2 weeks of Mar. 10:30am-7:30pm; Nov.-Feb. 10:30am-6:30pm. Open holidays Mar.-Sept. 1:30-6pm and Nov.-Feb. 1:30-5:30pm. Modest dress required. €4-5.50. Cash only.*)

Outside and downhill lies the 14th-century **baptistery.** Inside, lavish fifteenth-century frescoes depict the lives of Christ and St. Anthony. The central part of the ceiling, painted by Vecchietta, illustrates the ideas and important events from the Apostles' Creed . The baptistery's centerpiece is the hexagonal Renaissance baptismal font, made of marble, bronze, and enamel. Panels include Ghiberti's *Baptism of Christ* and Donatello's *Il Battista davanti a Erode*. (*Open daily from mid-Mar. to Sept. 9:30am-7:30pm; first 2 weeks in Mar. and all of Oct. 9:30am-7:30pm; Nov.-Feb. 10am-5pm. Modest dress required. €3. Cash only.*)

TUSCANY

PALIO PANIC

When the cops first shooed me off the road and into the *piazza,* I thought everything was normal. Then they locked me in. It was three days before the Palio and suddenly all the tourists in Il Campo had been jostled into the center of the *piazza* and locked behind a gate. At first I was calm: this was probably just a strike—the Italian national specialty.

Then hordes of Sienese children and their parents came marching into the *piazza,* screaming in Italian and whipping their *contrada* scarves in angry spirals over their heads. The men were shaking and pumping their fists; the children were shrieking the contrada theme songs at each other. This was quickly starting to look like a modern version of the gladiatorial games, except with me in the pit.

More shouting men brought horses into the *piazza.* So it was to be death by trampling. And then, I saw that the jockeys were wearing colorful pajamas, and I realized that this was the Palio pre-lim. For two days before the actual event, the jockeys run a practice race around the course to accustom the horses and themselves to the experience. If you want to experience the Palio without braving the crowds and the waits, consider heading to Siena a few days early. You'll still get to catch all the contrada drama and watch the takeoff without fellow travelers obstructing your view. Just get ready to run in case they bring the lions out.

—Marykate Jasper

X MARKS THE SPOT. If you look closely, you'll notice a small cross two-thirds of the way up the stairs that lead from P. San Giovanni to the entrance of the *duomo.* This mark is neither a trick of the pavement nor graffiti. Legend has it that this step is where St. Catherine of Siena tripped and fell down the stairs in the 14th century, supposedly pushed by the devil. Despite the steepness and severity of the marble steps, she walked away without a scratch—*un miracolo* worthy only of a saint, as any Sienese will tell you.

CRIPTA. Recently rediscovered in 1999, the 700-year-old "crypt" was actually a series of underground rooms where pilgrims would prepare themselves for entering the *duomo;* they're called the *cripta* only because that's what the archaeologists who discovered them originally thought they were. The 13th-century depictions of the Old and New Testament episodes are attributed to the pre-Duccio Sienese painters, including Diotisalvi di Speme, Guido da Siena, and Guido di Graziano. Due to the absence of light, climactic instability, or human intervention, the colors remain vibrant and detailed. (*In P. del Duomo. Entrance halfway down the stairs, to the left of the baptistery. Open daily from mid-Mar. to Sept. 9:30am-8pm; Nov.-Feb. 10am-5pm; Oct. and 1st 2 weeks of Mar. 9am-7:30pm. €6. Audio guide in English, French, German, or Italian included. Cash only.*)

MUSEO DELL'OPERA METROPOLITANA. This museum, feeling spurned, holds all the art that won't fit in the *duomo.* It shouldn't: the first floor contains some of the foremost Gothic statuary in Italy, all of it by Giovanni Pisano. Upstairs, the 700-year-old *Maestà,* by Duccio di Buoninsegna, originally served as a screen for the cathedral's altar. Other notable works are the Byzantine *Madonna dagli Occhi Grossi,* paintings by Lorenzetti, and two altarpieces by Matteo di Giovanni. Follow signs for the **Panorama dal Facciatone,** in Room 4, to a balcony over the nave. A very narrow spiral staircase leads to a tiny tower for a beautiful, unadvertised view of the entire city. (*Entrance outside of duomo; exit portals and turn left. Open daily from mid-Mar. to Sept. 9:30am-7:30pm; Oct. and 1st 2 weeks of Mar. 9:30am-7pm; Nov.-Feb. 10am-5pm. €6. Cash only.*)

OSPEDALE DI SANTA MARIA DELLA SCALA. Built as a hospital in the 13th century, the *ospedale* is now a museum displaying its original frescoes, chapels, and vaults. The **Sala del Pellegrinaio,** or the

Pilgrims' Hall, used as a ward until the late 20th century, contains an expressive fresco cycle by Vecchietta that tells the history of the hospital's construction. The **Sagrestia Vecchia,** or *Cappello del Sacro Chiodo,* houses masterful 15th-century Sienese frescoes. On the way downstairs, duck into the dim underground chapels and vaults, sites of rituals and "acts of piety for the dead" performed by various *contrada.* One level down is the entrance to the **Museo Archeologico,** included in admission to the *ospedale.* Established in 1933 to preserve Etruscan artifacts from the Siena area, the museum is now almost entirely housed in the eerie, medieval, underground waterworks of the city. Signs point the way through dank, labyrinthine passageways before emerging into rooms with well-lit displays of Etruscan pottery and coins. *(Opposite the duomo. Open daily 10:30am-6:30pm. Last entry 30min. before closing. €6, students €3.50, under 11 free. Cash only.)*

PINACOTECA NAZIONALE. Siena's superb art gallery displays works by every major artist of the highly stylized Sienese school. Masters represented include seven followers of Duccio—Simone Martini, the Lorenzetti brothers, Bartolo di Fredi, Bartolomeo Bulgarini, Sano di Pietro, and Il Sodoma. The museum is refreshingly free of tourist crowds, though the collection is geared toward art-lovers. *(V. San Pietro 29, in the Palazzo Buonsignori, down V. del Capitano from the duomo. Open M 8:30am-1:30pm, Tu-Sa 8:15am-7:15pm, Su 8:15am-1:15pm. €4, EU citizens and students 18-26 €2, EU citizens under 18 or over 65 free. Cash only.)*

SANTUARIO DI SANTA CATERINA. This sanctuary honors St. Catherine of Siena, who had a miraculous vision of a ring-bearing Christ proposing marriage to her. Known for her outspoken manner, Saint Catherine persuaded Pope Gregory XI to return to Rome from Avignon in 1377; in 1939 she was proclaimed one of Italy's patron saints. The brick buildings and airy courtyards, converted into a Renaissance *loggia,* branch into Baroque chapels. The **Chiesa del Crocefisso,** on the right, is impressive, but don't overlook the beautiful but smaller **Oratorio della Cucina** on the left. *(Entrance at the intersection of Costa di San Antonio and V. dei Pittori, down from P. San Domenico on V. della Sapienza. Open daily 9am-12:30pm and 3-6pm. Free.)*

OTHER SIGHTS. Siena's Franciscan and Dominican basilicas rival each other from opposite ends of town. The **Basilica Caterinana di San Domenico** contains Andrea Vanni's portrait of Saint Catherine and several other dramatic frescoes that illustrate her miraculous acts. The exquisite chapel inside, dedicated to St. Catherine, was built in 1460 to store her preserved head and half of one of her fingers, still on display today for the curious and non-squeamish. *(In P. San Domenico. Open daily May-Oct. 7am-1pm and 3-7pm; Nov.-Apr. 9am-1pm and 3-5:30pm. Modest dress required. Free.)* Those interested in the Palio may enjoy one of Siena's 17 **contrada museums.** Each neighborhood organization maintains its own collection of costumes, banners, and icons. *(Most require an appointment at least 1 week in advance; inquire at the tourist office for information.)* Take a break from sightseeing for a stroll within the brick walls of the **Fortezza Medicea,** filled with fountains and towers. *(Just north of P. Gramsci on Vle. Cesare Maccari. Open from dawn to dusk. Free.)*

🎵 🎭 ENTERTAINMENT AND NIGHTLIFE

Siena's ▦**Palio,** hands-down the highlight of the town's entertainment, overtakes the city twice each summer, transforming Siena into an exciting frenzy as people pack Il Campo to watch the bareback horse race. Even when it isn't fueled by primitive racing, Siena's nightlife keeps booming, thanks to the large population of local and foreign students. A great place to sample regional wines is **Enoteca Italiana,** in the Fortezza Medicea near the entrance off Vle. Cesare Maccari, where fine wines are sold by the bottle or by the glass. (☎05 77 22 88 13.

THE HIDDEN DEAL

FREE FIESOLE

If the very idea of a room with a view (let alone a terrace) is wreaking havoc on your wallet, take to the hills—literally. The town of Fiesole, overlooking the towering Duomo and an endless expanse of tiled rooftops, offers refreshingly cool breezes and makes a classic escape from city's crowds. Pack some bread and a bottle of wine to make a day of it, relaxing on Fiesole's shaded terraces. Fiesole boasts an impressive Roman amphitheater and baths, but the real draw is its clear, fresh air. If you're really scrounging for gelato funds, skip the return bus and enjoy a leisurely walk back down to Florence.

On the way, stop in San Domenico, halfway down the hill. Home to the **European University Institute,** the hamlet allows you a peek at the halls of international academia, complete with lounge chairs, breathtaking views, and the student-run Bar Fiasco. Pack *A Room with a View* (or maybe something a bit less cliché) as a conversation starter, find the bar, and mingle with Europe's best and brightest. With a drink in hand, enjoy the magnificent Florentine views—room not included.

On the way back down, take a right on V. dei Roccettini just before the San Domenico bus stop to reach the EUI. You'll soon hit Badia Fiesolana, the EUI's main building.

Wine from €3.50. Open Apr.-Sept. M noon-8pm, Tu-Sa noon-1am; Oct.-Mar. M-W noon-8pm, Th-Sa noon-1am. AmEx/MC/V.)

☒ **Caffè del Corso,** V. Bancha di Sopra 25 (☎0566 22 66 56; www.caffedelcor sosiena.it.) Cheap eats like pizza upstairs; bar downstairs that doubles as an outdoor dance floor in summer. Beer €3-4.50. Mixed drinks €5. 3-shot specials €5. Open daily 8am-3am.

☒ **Gallery,** V. Pantaneto 16-22 (☎05 77 34 05 73 16 32). A centrally located bar serving a variety of drink specials. Pounding music, fluorescent lights, and a young crowd make this bar popular. The crowd is best after midnight. Beer €4.50. Mixed drinks €5-6. Open Tu and Th-Sa 11pm-3am.

Barone Rosso, V. dei Termini 9 (☎05 77 28 66 86; www.barone-rosso.com). A study-abroad crowd sprinkled with locals. Lively themed parties. F-Sa live music. W reduced prices for international students W. Open daily 9pm-3am. AmEx/MC/V.

Bar Porrione, V. Porrione 44, off P. del Campo. Huge bar and floor, but limited indoor and outdoor seating. Plays contemporary American music but sells traditional Italian drinks, including *Negroni* (€3.50). If drinking and mingling with locals gets tiring, there's more Americana—arcade games—in back. Open daily 10am-3am.

Maudit Music Pub, V. della Manna 25 (☎05 77 46 818). Follow V. Salicotto, the left center street leading off P. il Campo facing the clock tower, and turn left onto V. della Manna. A mostly teenage crowd hangs out at this pub, known for its great pizza (€4.50), cheap drinks, and live music. Pints €5. Mixed drinks €5. Open daily 8pm-2am.

⚑ DAYTRIPS FROM SIENA

RADDA IN CHIANTI

Buses connect Siena to Radda in Chianti (1hr., 4 per day, round-trip €5.80). Buses leave from Siena's train station. Take bus 9 to the station from P. Gramsci. Buses also connect Radda to Florence (1hr., 3 per day), though schedules are sporadic; call ☎800 37 37 60 for info. In the morning, buses arrive at and depart from V. XX Settembre. In the afternoon, return buses to Florence and Siena usually leave from a stop across the street about 100m down, but sometimes don't, so ask at the tourist office. Stand in front of the orange sign and flag down the bus as it approaches.

Siena lies within easy reach of the Chianti region, a harmonious landscape of green hills, ancient castles, tiny villages, and of course, uninterrupted expanses of vineyards. In the Middle Ages, the small countryside towns of Castellina, Radda, and Gaiole formed a military alliance against French and Spanish invaders, adopting the black rooster as their symbol. Today, the rooster adorns bottles of Chianti, which are famous throughout the world. Peaceful **Radda in Chianti** (RAD-da; pop. 1668), just 30km from Siena, makes a great base for exploring the surrounding countryside. Every year on the 2nd of June, the town comes together for **Radda in the Glass.** For this one-day event, the *enoteche* provide ample bottles of Chianti on outdoor tables along V. Roma as rosy-cheeked citizens and lucky visitors make frequent stops with glasses in hand. If you can get out of town, most wineries in the area give free tastings, though a stroll down V. Roma also reveals numerous *enoteche* willing to let you try free samples. Cellar tours often require reservations—tourist offices provide bookings.

Located in the center of town, the outgoing staff at **La Bottega di Giovannino ❷,** V. Roma 37, serves filling plates on a breezy outdoor patio or in a wine-bottle laden dining room. Pair pasta with a glass of *Chianti classico* (from €3). The Bernardoni family lovingly maintains their restaurant and also offers transportation and tours for groups of seven or fewer to local wineries. (☎05 77 73 80 56; www.labottegadigiovannino.it. *Primi* €6. *Secondi* €6-9. Open M and W-Sa 8:32am-10:03pm, Su 11:30am-8:03pm. MC/V.) After a rigorous day of wine-tasting, relax in the public gardens outside the city walls, near P. IV Novembre. Inside the reputable **Porciatti Alimentari,** P. IV Novembre 1-3, master butchers sell handmade salami, pork sausages, and cheeses that are available for tastings or as fillings for a delicious *panino.* They also sell bus tickets. (☎05 77 73 80 55; www.casaporciatti.it. Open in summer M-Sa 8am-1pm and 4-8pm, Su 8am-1pm; in winter M-Tu and Th-Sa 8am-1pm and 4-8pm, W and Su 8am-1pm. AmEx/MC/V.) Across the street and down Camminamento Medievale, a medieval passageway from the 14th century, is **Casa Porciatti,** run by the same owners. Savor the free samples of wine, *grappa,* and olive oil, or schedule a tasting with a larger group (6-8 people) for €8-12. (☎05 77 73 80 55; www.casaporciatti.it. Open from mid-Mar. to Oct. M-Sa 10:30am-7pm, Su 10:30am-12:30pm and 3-7pm. MC/V.) The cheapest place to pick up wine is the **Coop** supermarket, V. Primo Maggio 32, which stocks bottles from €1.50. (www.e-coop.it. Open M-Sa 8:30am-1pm and 4-8pm. AmEx/MC/V.)

Check at the **tourist office** for bus and train information, directions, free brochures, or help scheduling wine tastings and tours. The office is located in P. Castello, off V. Roma. Turn off V. Roma onto Sdrucciolo di Castello. Follow the street to P. Castello, and the office will be on your left. (☎05 77 73 84 94. Open M-Sa 10am-1pm and 3:15-7pm, Su 10:30am-12:30pm.) For maps, and for more info on touring nearby wineries, vacation rentals, and excursions to the countryside, inquire at **A Bit of Tuscany,** V. Roma 39, next to Camere di Giovannino and housed in a real estate office. Private tours begin at €60 for 5hr. Larger, public tours are more economical, if slightly less revealing. (☎05 77 73 89 48. Open M-F 10am-1pm and 2:30-6pm.)

> **VINTAGE TIMING.** Many hotels in the Tuscan wine country consider September and October to be their high season (instead of the typical July and August tourist peak in Italy) because of the grape harvest. Prices can jump to €10-30 per night. Of course, you may not care so much after a couple of glasses of bubbly.

MONTEPULCIANO

Buses are the easiest way to reach Montepulciano; the train station is 10km out of town, with no reliable bus linking it to the city. A TRA-IN bus connects Siena to Montepulciano (1½hr., M-Sa 4 per day, €4.70), some via Buonconvento.

TUSCANY

Situated atop a limestone ridge, this small, medieval hamlet is Tuscany's highest hill town. Sixteenth-century *palazzi* and *piazze* grace Montepulciano's (Mohn-teh-pool-CHYA-no; pop. 5,000) narrow streets and walkways. After centuries of neglect following the Renaissance, this walled town is now wealthy and heavily touristed, largely as a result of its traditional *Vino Nobile* and its famous red wine industry. Visitors busy themselves browsing the wine stores and tasting free samples. Enjoy a few sips at the shop at **Porta di Bacco,** on the left immediately inside the city gates. (Open daily 9am-8pm.)

To get to **Tempio di San Biagio** from P. Grande, follow V. Ricci to V. della Mercezia. Turn left down the sloped street before Piazzetta di San Francesco. Follow signs through the city walls and along V. di San Biagio. The temple, built on a wide, grassy plateau, is a stunning example of high-Renaissance symmetry. The cavernous interior was redone in the 17th century in overwrought Baroque, but the simplicity of the original still shines through. The surrounding area has stunning views of the rolling Tuscan hills and the houses poised in between. (Open daily 9am-1pm and 3:30-7pm. Free.) Montepulciano's main square, **Piazza Grande,** is surrounded by the **Palazzo Tarugi** to the north, an unfinished *duomo* to the south, the **Palazzo Contucci** to the east, and the 14th-century **Palazzo Comunale** to the west. The exterior of the *duomo*, Santa Maria Assunta (1594-1680), is somber, with simple, bare walls that contrast with several great oil paintings. Note the Sienese master Taddeo di Bartolo's joyful *Assumption of the Virgin* above the altar. (Open daily 9am-12:30pm and 2:30-6:30pm. Free.)

Since most lodgings in Montepulciano are pricey three- or four-star hotels, *affittacamere* (rooms for rent) are the best option if you absolutely must spend the night. *Alimentari* selling local Tuscan products line V. Gracciano nel Corso. For a delicious selection of typical Tuscan food, visit **Osteria Acquacheta ❷,** V. del Teatro 22, off V. di Voltaia nel Corso, where you can savor a platter of *pecorino fresco al tartufo* (soft pecorino cheese with truffles; €3.10) while chatting up fellow diners. (*Primi* €5.20-7.50. *Secondi* €3 per 100g. Open M and W-Su 12:30-3pm and 7:30-10:30pm. MC/V.) Try the *pollo e coniglio all'Etrusca* (Etruscan-style chicken and rabbit; €10.40) at **Il Cantuccio ❸,** V. delle Cantine 1-2, where tuxedo-clad waiters serve elegant dishes under dim lights. (☎0578 75 78 70; www.ristoranteilcantuccio.com. *Primi* €7.50-10. *Secondi* €9-16. Open Tu-Su 12:30-2:30pm and 7:30-11pm. MC/V.) **Ristorante ai Quattro Venti ❷,** P. Grande 2, in the heart of the central *piazza*, provides outdoor seating overlooking the *duomo*. Try the heavenly *ribollita* (€8), a vegetable soup with fresh bread. (☎0578 71 72 31. *Primi* €7.30-8.50. *Secondi* €8.50-15. Open M and W-Su 12:30-2:30pm and 7:30-10:30pm. MC/V.) The **open-air market** is every Thursday in P. del Mercato, in parking lot #5 off V. delle Lettere. For cheap groceries head to **Conad,** V. Bernabei 4/A, 50m downhill from Chiesa Sant'Agnese. (☎0578 71 67 31. Open M-Sa 8:30am-8pm. MC/V.)

The **Ufficio delle Strade del Vino,** P. Grande 7, provides maps and bus schedules, makes free arrangements for hotels and nearby affittacamere, and sells tickets for wine and olive oil tours. (☎0578 71 74 84; www.stradavinonobile.it. Open M-F 10am-1pm and 3-6pm.) The **tourist office** in P. Don Minzoni, off V. Sangallo, sells city maps (€0.50) and provides free brochures. (☎0578 75 73 41; www.prolocomontepulciano.it. Internet available. Open M-Sa 9:30am-12:30pm and 3-7pm, Su and holidays 9:30am-12:30pm.)

BUSING YOUR CHOPS. On its way to Siena, the southbound bus stops twice in Montepulciano. The 1st stop is at V. dell'Oriolo, in a parking lot at the higher end of the city. From the bus stop, climb the stairs along V. delle Mura to arrive at V. dell'Opio nel Corso. The 2nd stop is at the bus station at the bottom of the hill. Before entering Montepulciano, know which stop you want. While the trek offers great views, hiking with a gargantuan backpack is never fun.

SAN GIMIGNANO ☎ 05 77

The hilltop village of San Gimignano (san jee-meen-YA-no; pop. 7000) looks like an illustration from a medieval manuscript. Its fourteen famous towers, all that remain of the original 72, loom above the city walls beside a host of spire-capped churches. The impressive towers date back to a period when prosperous families used the town square as their personal battlefield, and the towers were used during sieges—mostly to dump boiling oil on attacking enemies. After WWII, the skyline began to lure tourists, whose tastes and wallets resuscitated production of the golden *Vernaccia* wine. Despite herds of daytrippers and an infestation of souvenir shops, the fortress-top sunsets, nighttime gelato strolls, and ample spots for lounging on *piazza* steps make an overnight stay worthwhile.

TRANSPORTATION

Trains: The nearest station is in Poggibonsi. **MiniBuses** go from the station to Ple. Martiri Montemaggio (20min.; M-F every 30min. 6:05am-8:35pm, Sa-Su every hr. 7:35am-8:20pm; €1.80).

Buses: TRA-IN, Ple. Martiri Montemaggio (☎800 57 05 30 or 20 42 46; www.sienamobilita.it), outside Pta. San Giovanni. Tickets are available at Caffè Combattente, V. San Giovanni 124, on the left after entering the city gates; at *tabaccheri;* or at the tourist office. Schedules at the tourist office. Change at Poggibonsi for **Florence** (1hr., every hr., €6). Buses also run to **Siena** (1hr., every 1-2hr., €5.40), departing from Poggibonsi and in Ple. Martiri Montemaggio, across from the bottom of V. San Giovanni.

Bike and Car Rental: Bruno Bellini, V. Roma 41 (☎05 77 94 02 01; www.bellinibruno.com). Bikes €7-11 per hr., €15-21 per day. Scooters €31-51 per day. Cars from €62 per day. Open M-F 9am-1pm and 3-7:30pm. AmEx/MC/V.

ORIENTATION AND PRACTICAL INFORMATION

Buses to San Gimignano stop in **Piazzale Martiri Montemaggio,** just outside the city walls. To reach the *centro,* pass through **Porta San Matte,** climb the hill, and follow **Via San Giovanni** to **Piazza della Cisterna,** which merges with **Piazza del Duomo.** The town's other main street, **Via San Matteo,** extends from the other side of P. del Duomo. Addresses in San Gimignano are marked in both black stencil and etched clay tiles; most establishments go by the black addresses; accordingly, *Let's Go* lists these.

Tourist Office: Ufficio Informazioni Turistiche, P. del Duomo 1 (☎05 77 94 00 08; www.sangimignano.com). *Affittacamere* listings and bus tickets. Free maps and help with hotel bookings. Tu and Th 5pm 2hr. tours of wineries with tastings (€18, with transportation €20); reserve by noon the day before. Open daily in summer 10:30am-1pm and 3-6pm, in winter 10:30am-1pm and 2-6pm.

Accommodations Services: Associazione Strutture Extralberghiere, P. della Cisterna 6 (☎/fax 0577 94 31 90). Head for the building with the "Protur" sign above the door. Patient staff makes free reservations for private rooms. Call a week ahead to stay in the countryside; the *centro* is easier to book. Open daily 10am-1pm and 3-6pm. MC/V.

Currency Exchange: Protur and the post office offer best rates. **ATMs** scattered along V. San Giovanni, V. degli Innocenti, and P. della Cisterna.

Police: (☎05 77 94 03 13), in P. Martiri.

Pharmacy: P. della Cisterna 8 (☎05 77 99 03 69; at night ☎34 80 02 17 10), on the far left coming from V. San Giovanni. Open M-Sa in summer 9am-1pm and 4:30-8pm, in winter 4-7:30pm. AmEx/MC/V.

Internet Access: Edicola La Tuscia, V. Garibaldi 2, outside the gates to the right of Pta. San Matteo. €4.50 per hr. Open daily 7am-1pm and 2:30-7:30pm. Cash only.

Post Office: P. delle Erbe 8, behind the *duomo*. Open M-F 8:15am-1:30pm, Sa 8:15am-12:30pm. **Postal Code:** 53037.

ACCOMMODATIONS

San Gimignano caters to wealthy tourists, and most accommodations are well beyond budget range. *Affittacamere* provide an alternative to over-priced hotels, with most doubles with bath from €70. An abundance of signs for "Camere/Rooms/Zimmer" hang in souvenir shops, restaurants, and other storefront windows along main streets. The tourist office and the Associazione Strutture Extralberghiere have lists of budget rooms; the tourist office also has photos of the rooms to help you choose.

Camere Cennini Gianni, V. San Giovanni 21 (☎05 77 94 19 62; www.sangiapartments.com). Enter through Pta. San Giovanni. Reception is at the *pasticceria* at V. San Giovanni 88. Each room is lovingly decorated by the young English-speaking owner, with large baths and scenic views of the surrounding vineyards. Kitchen use €15. Reservations recommended. Singles €45; doubles €55-60; triples €70; quads €85. MC/V. ❷

Albergo Il Pino, V. Cellolese 4 (☎/fax 05 77 94 04 15), just off V. San Matteo before exiting Pta. San Matteo. 7 spacious rooms owned by the restaurant downstairs have hand-sewn comforters, antique furnishings, comfy sofa chairs, and TV. Reservations recommended. Singles €45; doubles €55. AmEx/MC/V. ❷

Hotel La Cisterna, P. della Cisterna 23 (☎05 77 94 03 28; www.hotelcisterna.it). Panoramic views of San Gimignano from atop a hill in a central *piazza*. All 49 large rooms have baths, A/C, and satellite TVs; some have terraces. Breakfast included. Free Wi-Fi in lobby. Singles €62-80; doubles €87-100, with view €100-118, with balcony €107-140. Extra bed €25-28. AmEx/MC/V. ❹

FOOD

San Gimignano specializes in *cinghiale* (boar) and other wild game, though it also caters to less daring palates with mainstream Tuscan dishes at high prices. A weekly **open-air market** is in P. del Duomo and P. della Cisterna (open Th 8am-1pm). Purchase the famous *Vernaccia di San Gimignano*, a light, sweet white wine, from **La Buca,** V. San Giovanni 16, for around €4.50 per bottle. This cooperative also offers tastes of terrific sausages and meats produced on its own farm. The boar sausage *al pignoli* (with pine nuts; €2.07 per 100g) and the satisfying *salame con mirto* (salami with blueberry) are delicious. (☎05 77 94 04 07. Open daily 9am-8pm. AmEx/MC/V.)

Trattoria Chiribiri, P. della Madonna 1 (☎05 77 94 19 48). From the bus stop, take the 1st left off V. San Giovanni and climb a short staircase or follow your nose down the sidestreet. Unusually affordable local fare. *Primi* €5.50-7.50. *Secondi* €8-15. Open M-Tu and Th-Su Mar.-Oct. 11am-11pm; Nov.-Feb. noon-2pm and 7-10pm. Cash only. ❷

⌗ **Pluripremiata Gelateria,** P. della Cisterna 4 (☎05 77 94 22 44), to the immediate left after the hill. Visitors and locals pack in around 3 counters that hide award-winning gelato flavors. Try the *champelmo,* a mix of champagne and grapefruit, or the *Vernaccia,* a gelato version of the region's famous wine. Cups from €1.70. 3 flavors in a chocolate-lined cone €2.50. Open daily 9am-midnight. Cash only. ❶

Ristorante Perucà, V. Capassi 16 (☎05 77 94 31 36; www.peruca.eu). Behind V. San Matteo. Charming benches, lanterns, and a cheery staff welcome diners to a quiet spot hidden from the tourist bustle. The menu varies seasonally, but is always heavy with secret family recipes that fuse traditional Tuscan fare with atypical spices and ingredients. *Primi* €5-9. *Secondi* €10-18. Cover €2. Open daily noon-2:30pm and 7-10:30pm. MC/V. ❸

La Stella, V. San Matteo 77 (☎05 77 94 04 44). Food made with produce from the restaurant's own farm and served in the long, narrow dining room. Extensive wine list includes *Vernaccia* and other local favorites. *Primi* €6-9.50. *Secondi* €8-14. Cover €2. Open M-Tu and Th-Su Apr.-Oct. noon-3pm and 7-10pm; Nov.-Mar. noon-2pm and 7-9pm. AmEx/MC/V. ❸

👁 SIGHTS

Famous as the *Città delle Belle Torri* (City of the Beautiful Towers), San Gimignano has always appealed to artists. During the Renaissance, they came in droves, and the collection of their works complements San Gimignano's cityscape. It's hard not to be impressed by the proud towers and the humble, winding streets caught in their shadows.

▨ PIAZZA DELLA CISTERNA AND PIAZZA DEL DUOMO. P. della Cisterna (1237), surrounded by towers and palaces, is the center of life in San Gimignano. You'll find visitors cuddled up beside the central *cisterna* with a cup of gelato well into the night, and street musicians often give free concerts in the evening. P. della Cisterna neighbors P. del Duomo, site of the impressive tower of the **Palazzo del Podestà.** To the left, tunnels and intricate *loggias* fill the Palazzo del Popolo. To the right of the *palazzo* rises the Torre Grossa, the town's highest tower and the only one visitors can climb. Also in the *piazza* are the twin towers of the Ardinghelli, truncated due to a medieval zoning ordinance that regulated tower envy by prohibiting structures higher than the

Torre Grossa. A perch on one of the steps in either *piazza* offers opportunities to people-watch and soak up the atmosphere.

PALAZZO COMUNALE. A frescoed medieval courtyard leads to the entrance of the **Museo Civico** on the second floor. The first room of the museum is the **Sala di Dante,** where the bard spoke on May 8, 1300, in an attempt to convince San Gimignano to side with the Florentines in their ongoing wars with Siena. On the walls, Lippo Memmi's sparkling *Maestà* overwhelms the accompanying 14th-century scenes of hunting and tournament pageantry. Up the stairs, Taddeo di Bartolo's altarpiece, *The Story of San Gimignano,* tells the tale of the city's namesake saint, originally a bishop of Modena. Within the museum lies the entrance to the 218-step climb up ▨**Torre Grossa.** While the final steps are precarious (watch your head on the low ceiling at the top), they are well worth the climb, as the tower offers views of half a dozen of San Gimignano's towers, the ancient fortress, several *piazze,* and the Tuscan landscape stretching to the horizon in all directions. *(Palazzo del Popolo, Museo Civico, and Tower open M and Su 9am-1pm, Tu-Sa 10am-6pm. €5, students €4. Cash only.)*

BASILICA DI SANTA MARIA ASSUNTA. The bare facade of this 12th-century church seems unfit to shelter such an exceptionally frescoed interior. Off the right aisle, the **Cappella di Santa Fina** is covered in Ghirlandaio's frescoes of the life of Santa Fina, the town's ascetic saint who was stricken with a fatal disease at the age of 10. *(In P. del Duomo. Open Apr.-Oct. M-F 10:30am-7:30pm, Sa 10:30am-5pm, Su 1-5pm; Nov.-Mar. M-Sa 10:30am-5pm, Su 12:30-5pm. €3.50, under 18 €1.50. Cash only.)*

FORTEZZA AND MUSEO DEL VINO. Follow the signs past the Basilica di Collegiata from P. del Duomo to this tiny, crumbling fortress. The courtyard has a small cafe and outdoor seating on the turret, and offers a beautiful view of the countryside. Park benches enclosed by trees make for a great picnic or lounge spot when visitors clear out in the evening. There are weekly screenings of movies in the courtyard at night from June to August. Pop into the modest wine museum to brush up on your knowledge of *Chianti Classico* and *Vernaccia.* *(Fortezza open dawn-dusk. Museo del Vino ☎ 05 77 94 03 59. Open daily Mar.-Oct. 11:30am-7:30pm; closed W afternoon. Free. Movies €6, children €4; schedule at the tourist office.)*

MUSEO PENA DI MORTE AND MUSEO DELLA TORTURA. The Museum of Torture is filled with ancient instruments of castigation, including the medieval version of the electric chair. Admire the pain that must have been felt before human rights laws and lethal injection, and have fun with interactive displays; a head in a guillotine is almost always a great photo op. *(V. San Giovanni 15a and 123. ☎ 05 77 94 05 26. Open daily 9:30am-8pm. €10.)*

CORTONA   ☎ 0575

Though its quaint, tranquil streets may suggest otherwise, the ancient town of Cortona (cor-TOH-na; pop. 23,600) once rivaled Perugia, Arezzo, and even Florence in power and military dominance. After Naples appropriated it in 1411, Cortona was sold to the rival Florentines, and citizens of Cortona enjoyed peace and prosperity. Impressive art collections include works by Fra Angelico and Luca Signorelli, and architecture from this period of grandeur lingers within the small city's walls.

TRANSPORTATION

Trains: Camucia-Cortona station. Trains depart to **Florence** (every hr., €7.20) and **Rome** (2hr., every 2hr., €9.40). Coming from Florence, Cortona is usually a stop on the Florence-Rome line, but check with one of the TrenItalia employees before boarding. **LFI buses** (☎0575 30 07 48) run to Cortona's P. Garibaldi from this station (15min., €1) and from **Terontola train station** (30min., every hr.). Be warned that they come very infrequently on Su.

Buses: Stop in P. Garibaldi from Arezzo (1hr., 12 per day, €2.70). Buy LFI bus tickets from the tourist office or *tabaccherie*.

Taxis: ☎335 81 96 313.

ORIENTATION AND PRACTICAL INFORMATION

Buses stop at **Piazza Garibaldi** at the base of the city. Enter the city by following **Via Nazionale**, which leads to **Piazza della Repubblica**. Follow the road at the far right side of the *piazza* to reach **Piazza Signorelli**, Cortona's main square.

Tourist Office: V. Nazionale 42 (☎05 75 63 03 52; www.apt.arezzo.it.), alongside Monte dei Paschi. Provides maps, bus schedules, and bus, train, and tour tickets. Open from May 17 to Sept. 27 M-Sa 9am-1pm and 3-6pm, Su 9am-1pm; in winter M-F 9am-1pm and 3-8pm, Sa 9am-1pm.

Currency Exchange: Banca Etruria, V. Santa Margherita 5. **24hr. ATM.** Open M-F 8:20am-1:20pm and 2:35-3:35pm, Sa 8:20-11:50am.

Bookstore: Nocentrini Libri, V. Nazionale 32. Stocks books in English, including classics, bestsellers, and travel guides. Open daily 9am-1pm and 3-8pm. AmEx/MC/V.

Police: V. Dardano 9 (☎05 75 60 77 00).

Pharmacy: Farmacia Centrale, V. Nazionale 38 (☎05 75 60 32 06). Open M-Sa in summer 9am-1pm and 4:30-8pm, in winter 9am-1pm and 4-7:30pm. AmEx/MC/V.

Hospital: ☎0575 63 91.

Internet Access: Lamentini Internet, V. Nazionale 33 (☎05 75 62 588). Wi-Fi available. Internet €4 per hr. Open daily 10am-8pm. AmEx/MC/V.

Post Office: V. Benedetti 2 (☎05 75 60 15 11), uphill from P. della Repubblica. Open M-F and Su 8:15am-1:30pm, Sa 8:15am-12:30pm. **Postal Code:** 52044.

ACCOMMODATIONS

Ostello San Marco (HI), V. Maffei 57 (☎05 75 60 13 92; www.cortonahostel.com). From the bus stop, walk 5min. uphill on V. Santa Margherita and follow signs curving left to the hostel. A stone, wood-beamed, medieval lobby lends amiable cheer to this clean, well-kept hostel. Breakfast and linens included. Open to individuals from mid-Mar. to Nov., to groups year-round. Dorms €18; singles €20. Cash only. ❶

Casa Betania, V. Gino Severini 50 (☎/fax 05 75 63 04 23; www.casaperferiebetania. com), downhill from P. Garibaldi. Cross Vle. Cesare Battisti and take an immediate right through the gates. Large windows admit glorious amounts of Tuscan sunshine into these airy and altogether charming rooms. Kitchen access. Breakfast €4 per person. Wi-Fi €7 per day. Singles €32, with bath €42; doubles €48; triples €60; quads €80. MC/V. ❷

Hotel San Luca, P. Garibaldi 1 (☎05 75 63 05 04). Take in spectacular views of the Chiana Valley from your private terrace. Richly decorated rooms—each with A/C, bath, minibar, phone, safe, and TV—are meticulously maintained. Singles €70-78; doubles €100-120; triples €143; quads €140-160; quints €188. AmEx/MC/V. ❺

LOCAL LEGEND

THREE'S COMPANY

In the Catholic canon, it is very common for a single saint to be the patron of multiple causes, but the reverse is not true; it's uncommon for a single city to have multiple patron saints. Florence, however, has never considered itself "typical"—it has three.

St. John the Baptist is the official patron saint of the city, the San Giovanni of the P. de San Giovanni (P. del Duomo), on which Florence is centered. On his feast day (June 24th), the city clambers to the rooftops to watch a spectacular fireworks display.

St. Reparata is remembered for her part in the 405 Christian victory over the Goths. She appeared in the sky, and the Christian army proceeded to vanquish the heathens. The church that once stood where the Duomo is today was dedicated to her.

St. Zenobius, the first bishop of Florence, is the third popular saint in the city. As his body was carried to its tomb, the coffin brushed a dead elm tree in the *piazza,* and the tree was resurrected. His powers of revival don't end there; he supposedly brought a small boy who had run over by a cart back to life.

Istituto Santa Margherita, V. Cesare Battisti 15 (☎05 75 63 03 36), on the corner of V. C. Battisti, downhill on V. G. Severini from P. Garibaldi. A former college, with antique furniture, wide hallways, and large baths as immaculate as the Conception. Run by nuns. Wheelchair-accessible rooms available. Breakfast €4. Singles €40; doubles €54; triples €70; quads €80. Unmarried couples must get 2 twin beds. Cash only. ❷

◪ FOOD

You won't have to search long for a bustling, home-style Tuscan *trattoria* in Cortona; tables spill onto the streets surrounding the town's main *piazze.* The best beef in Tuscany is raised in the surrounding valleys, so consider making a modest splurge on *bistecca alla Fiorentina.* Complement dinner with the fine, local white wine, *Bianco Vergine di Valdichiana.* Penny-pinchers can pick up a €2.50 bottle at **Despar,** P. della Repubblica 23, which also stocks basic groceries and picnic supplies, including cheap *panini.* (☎05 75 63 06 66. Open M-Sa 7am-1:30pm and 4-8pm, Su 9am-1pm. AmEx/MC/V.) On Saturday, P. Signorelli hosts an open-air **market** (open 8am-1pm).

Trattoria Dardano, V. Dardano 24 (☎05 75 60 19 44; www.trattoriadardano.com). Follow the succulent smells to lively conversation that carries down the street. Simple, filling dishes include a variety of affordable steaks (€3 per 100g). *Primi* €5-7. *Secondi* €5-8. Open M-Tu and Th-Su noon-2:45pm and 7:15-9:45pm. Cash only. ❷

Fufluns, V. Ghibellina 3 (☎0575 60 41 40; www.fufluns.net), off P. della Repubblica. The pizza may be the most popular option in this bustling eatery, but it's also the most generic. If you're up for an experience, opt instead for one of Fufluns' creative pasta dishes, whose unusual ingredients (blueberry!) will take your palette to new places. Try the gooey, godlike chocolate cake (€5). Pizza €4-9. *Primi* €6-9. *Secondi* €7-18. Open M and W-Su 12:15-2:30pm and 7:15-10:30pm. MC/V. ❷

Ristorante Preludio, V. Guelfa 11 (☎05 75 63 01 04; www.ilpreudio.net). Chandeliers and candlelit tables provide an elegant environment in which to enjoy upscale dishes like stuffed *crespelle* (crepes; €9) with duck and spicy tomato. *Primi* €8-10. *Secondi* €13-14. Open Tu-Su 12:30-3pm and 7:30-10:30pm. AmEx/MC/V. ❸

Gelateria Snoopy, P. Signorelli 29. Themed *gelateria* in the heart of Cortona, complete with Charlie Brown and Snoopy pictures on the wall. Generous 🍦**4 scoops** for €2.50, 5 for €3. Open daily 10am-midnight. Cash only. ❶

🔵 SIGHTS

MUSEO DELL'ACCADEMIA ETRUSCA E DELLA CITTA DI CORTONA. Perfectly preserved Egyptian sarcophagi and mummies, Roman coins, and golden altarpieces are displayed to fantastic effect in this extravagant collection. Also check out oil paintings by native sons Luca Signorelli and Pietro Berrettini (known as Pietro da Cortona), as well as those of Futurist Gino Severini. The first floor's main hall houses an unusual fourth-century BC Etruscan chandelier decorated with intricate allegorical carvings. The **Galleria,** lined with coats of arms, holds two 1714 globes by Silvestro Moroncelli; one depicts the "Isola di California" floating in the Pacific; the other sports vivid illustrations of all the constellations. *(P. Signorelli, inside the courtyard of Palazzo Casali, at the far right of P. della Repubblica. ☎ 05 75 63 72 35 or 63 04 15; www.cortonamaec.org. Open Apr.-Oct. daily 10am-7pm, Nov.-Mar. Tu-Su 10am-5pm. Guided tours available by reservation only. €8, groups of over 15 €4 per person. Combination ticket for MAEC and Museo Diocesano €10. Cash only.)*

MUSEO DIOCESANO. This humble museum manages to pack some of the Italian Renaissance's greats in a very small space. Admire the grace of the golden wings in Fra Angelico's stunning *Annunciation* (c. 1436) in **Room 3** of the upstairs gallery. Luca Signorelli's masterpiece, *The Deposition* (1502), which combines classical Roman and medieval detail, hangs in **Room 1.** Works by the Sienese Pietro Lorenzetti, such as his fresco *The Way to Calvary* in **Room 2** and his meticulously rendered *Crucifix* in **Room 3,** are also impressive. Severini's modern version of the Stations of the Cross lines the stairwell. *(From P. della Repubblica, pass through P. Signorelli and follow the signs. ☎ 05 75 62 830. Open Apr.-Oct. daily 10am-7pm; Nov.-Mar. daily 10am-5pm. €5, children under 12 and groups of over 15 people €3. Audio tours in English, French, German, Italian, and Spanish €3. Cash only.)*

FORTEZZA MEDICEA. As the highest point in Cortona, the *fortezza* offers unrivaled views of the Val di Chiana and Lake Trasimeno. The courtyard and bastions contain temporary art installations and shrines decorated with mosaics based on Severini's series in the Museo Diocesano. On the way, the unassuming white marble facade of the **Basilica di Santa Margherita** bursts into bold combinations of primary colors—blue ceilings are fancifully dotted with gold stars. The body of Santa Margherita (1247-1297) rests in a glass coffin at the center of the altarpiece. *(Trek to the top of V. Santa Margherita from P. Garibaldi. To reach the fortress, take a right out of the church and climb the small uphill road. ☎ 05 75 60 37 93 or 60 14 10 to reserve guided tours. Fortress open daily Sept. and from Mar. 22 to June 10am-1:50pm and 2:30-6pm; July-Aug. 10am-1:30pm and 2:30-7pm. Modest dress required. €3, under 12 €1.50. Cash only.)*

PALAZZI AND PIAZZE. In P. della Repubblica, the 13th-century **Palazzo Comunale** serves as a bold backdrop for the surrounding shops and cafes. At night, people gather on the steps to enjoy their gelato and watch the show at P. Signorelli's outdoor theater. **Palazzo Casali,** to the right and behind the Palazzo del Comune, dominates P. Signorelli. Only the courtyard walls lined with coats of arms remain from the original structure; the facade and interlocking staircase are 17th-century additions. **Piazza del Duomo** lies to the right and downhill from the Palazzo Casali. The simple, 16th-century **Cattedrale di Santa Maria** houses paintings by Signorelli and del Sarto as well as an impressive Baroque-canopied high altar and a rich, dark-wood pulpit built in 1524. *(Open daily Mar.-Oct. 7:30am-1pm and 3-6:30pm, Nov.-Mar. 8am-12:30pm and 3-5:30pm. Free.)*

❄ FESTIVALS

Relax in the gardens or enjoy a *passeggiata* in the park, which screens **movies** in their original language (usually English) weekly from mid-June through September. (Visit www.teatrosignorelli.com for lists of films and info. Films start 9:45pm. In bad weather, screenings in Teatro Signorelli. €5.)

Giostra Dell'Archidado, in early June. A crossbow challenge in which participants compete for the *verretta d'oro* (golden dart). This, along with period dress and other festivities, commemorates a local nobleman's 1397 marriage.

Umbria Jazz Festival, in July. Musical and theatrical events dominate July, when Cortona absorbs the spillover from the nearby festival.

Sagra della Bistecca, the week of Aug. 14th. Italian cows start to tremble for Steakfest, the most important town festival, when the populace shares superb steak in the public gardens behind the church of San Domenico.

Festa dei Porcini, on the 3rd weekend of Aug. Mushroom-lovers flock for tastings in Cortona's last culinary extravaganza. Tickets are sold at the garden entrance.

AREZZO   ☎ 05 75

Michelangelo once said, "Any talent I have is a result of the fine air of your town, Arezzo." Indeed, for its size, Arezzo (ah-RET-so; pop. 92,000) has seen a parade of influential artists and thinkers pass through. In addition to Michelangelo, the town was home to Renaissance titan Piero della Francesca, the poet Petrarch, the humanist Leonardo Bruni, and the artist and historian Giorgio Vasari. It's also the hometown of Roberto Benigni, director and star of the Oscar-winning *La Vita è Bella* (*Life is Beautiful*; 1997), who shot much of the film in the surrounding countryside. Escape the busy *centro* with a stroll outside the eastern portion of the medieval city walls, where you can catch striking views of the countryside and glimpses of backyard olive trees, vegetable gardens, and flowerbeds.

▐ TRANSPORTATION

Trains: In P. della Repubblica. Ticket booth open M-Sa 5:50am-8:50pm; self-service ticket machines open 24hr. To **Florence** (1hr., 2 per hr. 4:30am-9:50pm, €5.70) and **Rome** (2hr., every 1-2hr. 6:30am-10:10pm, €11.50-11.70).

Buses: ATAM ticket office (☎0575 800 38 17 30), in front and to the left of train station exit across from the bus depot. Open daily 5:50am-8:50pm. **TRA-IN, SITA,** and **LFI** run to **Sansepolcro** (1hr., every hr., €3.50) and **Siena** (1hr., 4 per day, €5.20). Call ☎0575 38 26 51 for more info.

Taxis: RadioTaxi (☎0575 38 26 26). 24hr.

Car Rental: Autonoleggi Royal, V. Marco Perrenio 21 (☎05 75 35 35 70). 21+. Manual and automatic available. Open M-F 8:30am-12:30pm and 3:30-7:30pm, Sa 8:30am-12:30pm.

▐▌ ORIENTATION AND PRACTICAL INFORMATION

Via Guido Monaco, which begins directly across from the **train station** at **Piazza della Repubblica,** parallels **Corso Italia;** together they form the backbone of the commercial district. To get to the *centro storico,* follow V. G. Monaco from the station to the traffic circle at **Piazza Guido Monaco.** Turn right on **Via Roma** and then turn left on the pedestrian walkway C. Italia, which leads to the old city. **Piazza Grande** lies to the right, 250m up C. Italia.

Tourist Office: Centro Servizi Turistici, P. Emiciclo Giovanni Paolo II (☎05 75 18 22 770; www.arezzoturismo.it) is located on the opposite side of town from the train station. Facing the entrance to the *duomo,* turn left and enter the adjacent building. Walk through the short hallway to the right, down the escalator, and the office is on the right. Services include hotel, airline and tour bookings, free **luggage storage,** and **internet** access (€1.50 per 15min.). Open daily 9am-7pm. **APT,** P. della Repubblica 28 (☎05 75 20 839; www.apt.arezzo.it). Turn right after exiting the train station. Free maps and brochures of the town and nearby valleys. Open in summer daily 9am-1pm and 3-7pm; in winter M-Sa and the 1st Su of the month 10am-1pm and 3-6pm, other Su 9am-1pm.

Budget Travel: CTS, V. V. Veneto 18 (☎05 75 90 78 08). Sells Eurail passes and plane tickets. Open M-F 9am-7:30pm, Sa 9am-1pm.

Bank: Line V. G. Monaco between the train station and P. G. Monaco. **Banca Nazionale del Lavoro,** V. G. Monaco 74. **Currency exchange** and **24hr. ATM.** Open M-F 8:20am-1:35pm and 2:50-4:05pm.

Police: V. Leone Leoni 16 (☎05 75 90 66 67).

Pharmacy: Farmacia Comunale, Campo di Marte 7 (☎05 75 90 24 66), next to Conad supermarket on V. V. Veneto. Front doors open daily 8am-11pm. For 24hr. service, ring the bell outside of the "Servizio notturno" at Campo di Marte 6.

Hospital: Ospedale Civico, V. Pietronenni (☎05 75 25 51).

Internet: InformaGiovani, P. G. Monaco 2 (☎05 75 37 78 68). 30min. free for customers living in Arezzo (including students studying abroad). Otherwise, €1 per 30min. Open M-F 10:30am-7:30pm, Sa 10:30am-12:30pm.

Post Office: V. G. Monaco 34 (☎05 75 33 24 11). **Currency exchange;** €0.50 commission. Open M-F 8:15am-7pm, Sa 8:15am-1:30pm. **Postal Code:** 52100.

ACCOMMODATIONS

Hotels fill to capacity the first weekend of every month due to the **Fiera Antiquaria** (Antique Fair). Finding a cheap room can pose a challenge given the expensive chain hotels that crowd Arezzo.

Foresteria San Pier Piccolo, V. Bicchieraja 32 (☎05 75 32 42 19). In the old city, a short walk from Arezzo's main sights. Rooms in this 14th-century Benedictine convent have changed little over the years. Thankfully, spartan stone walls and wooden furniture have been supplemented with electricity, renovated baths, and TVs. Breakfast €3. Reception 7am-11pm. Curfew 11pm. Singles €24, with bath €35; doubles with bath €75; triples with bath €95. Cash only. ❶

Albergo Cecco, C. Italia 215 (☎05 75 20 986). Follow V. G. Monaco from the train station, turn right on V. Roma, and right again on C. Italia. The no-frills rooms are great for the budget-minded who care about location. Breakfast €3. Singles €32, with bath €42; doubles €64-70; triples €80; quads €95. AmEx/MC/V. ❷

FOOD

An open-air **market** takes place in P. Sant'Agostino on weekdays until 1pm. Head to **La Mozzarella,** V. Spinello 25, to the right and across the street from the train station, for a great variety of cheeses. (Open M-F 8am-1pm and 4-8pm, Sa 8am-1pm. Cash only.) **Eurospar,** V. G. Monaco 82, carries basic groceries. (Open M-Sa 8am-10pm, 1st Su of the month 9am-1pm. MC/V.)

PUZZLING PANE. No, that bread isn't stale, just unsalted. Traditional Tuscan bread is made without salt because, historically, salt was so valuable it was used as currency. Before you dig into that breadbasket, know that Tuscan bread is best enjoyed with other dishes and sauces. If you're in a grocery store buying bread and want the salted kind, ask for *pane salato*.

Antica Osteria L'Agania, V. Mazzini 10 (☎05 75 29 53 81; www.agania.com). Sample wine from local vineyards (€4 per bottle) in an *osteria* that feels like a family kitchen. *Primi* and *secondi* €5-7. Open Tu-Su noon-3pm and 7-11pm. AmEx/MC/V. ❶

Trattoria Il Saraceno, V. Mazzini 6/a (☎05 75 27 644; www.ilsaraceno.com), off C. Italia. *Arezzese* specialties like duck and *pecorino* cheese in honey (€10). Pizza €6-8. *Primi* €7-8. *Secondi* €8-12. Cover €2. Open M-Tu and Th-Su noon-3:10pm and 7-9:30pm. AmEx/MC/V. ❷

Osteria del Borghicciolo, Corso Italia 34/35 (☎05 75 24 488). The staff swears the only secret to its great-tasting eats is authentic Italian extra virgin olive oil. 4-course meal for 2 €18. Cover €2. Open daily noon-3:30pm and from 7pm-late. ❷

Paradiso di Stelle, V. G. Monaco 58c (☎05 75 27 048). Great homemade gelato (from €1.70) and even better crepes (from €2). Open daily 11am-11pm. Cash only. ❶

SIGHTS

BASILICA DI SAN FRANCESCO. This extraordinary 13th-century basilica houses elaborate 15th-century frescoes like Piero della Francesca's ◪**Leggenda della Vera Croce** *(Legend of the True Cross)* in the *Bacci* chapel behind the main altar. It tells the story of the first crucifix and its role in early Christianity. The narrative begins with the death of Adam and proceeds to major events such as Emperor Constantine's conversion in the fourth century. St. Francis kneels at the foot of the cross. *(Walk up V. G. Monaco from train station and turn right into P. San Francesco. Basilica open daily 8:30am-noon and 2-7pm. Chapel containing della Francesca's frescoes open Apr.-Oct. M-F 9am6:30pm, Sa 9am-5:30pm, Su 1-5:30pm; Nov.-Mar. M-F 9am-5:30pm, Sa 9am-5pm, Su 1-5pm. Groups of 25 admitted every 30min. Last entry 30min. before closing. Reservation required. Call ☎05 75 29 90 71 or 35 27 27, or visit the office to the right of the church. Basilica free. Church €6, EU students 18-25 €4, art history students or EU citizens under 18 €2. Cash only.)*

CASA VASARI. Colors swirl on the elaborate ceilings of the Casa Vasari, built by the artist and historian himself. Vibrant portrait-frescoes by Michelangelo and del Sarto cover the walls. In one room, Vasari's depictions of the Muses crown the ceiling; one is a likeness of his fiancée, Niccolosa. He even painted himself taking in the view from one of the *casa*'s windows. *(V. XX Settembre 55, just off V. San Domenico. Ring bell to enter. ☎05 75 40 90 40. Open M and W-Sa 8:30am-7:30pm, Su 8:30am-1:30pm. Last entry 30min. before closing. €2, EU students €1. Cash only.)*

PIAZZA GRANDE (PIAZZA VASARI). This *piazza*, which surrounds a small fountain decorated by the garden club of Arezzo, contains the **Chiesa di Santa Maria della Pieve**, a spectacular Romanesque church built in the 12th century. Elegant columns and rounded arches frame a 13th-century portico. On the elevated presbytery sits Pietro Lorenzetti's brilliantly restored *Annunciation* and *Madonna and Child*. Below lies the 11th-century church upon which the Pieve was built. The adjoining pock-marked **tower** is known appropriately as the "Tower of 100 Holes." Surrounding *palazzi* enclose P. Grande with pleasing proportionality. The 14th-century Romanesque **Palazzo della Fraternità** and 16th-century Baroque **Palazzo delle Logge Vasariane** recall past eras. For a livelier version of history, attend the monthly **antique fair** or the semi-annual **Giostra del Saracino** each summer. To reach **Parco "Il Prato,"** a grassy retreat of flowers, picnic areas, and ancient statues, follow C. Italia to V. dei Pileati. *(Tower open M-Sa 8am-noon and 3-7pm, Su 8:30am-noon and 4-7pm. Park open daily until dusk. Free.)*

DUOMO. The massive 13th-century *duomo* sits high on the hill of Arezzo. Built in the Tuscan Gothic style, the cathedral houses Arezzo native Piero della Francesca's *Maddalena* and Bishop Guido Tarlati's tomb on the left side of the nave near the altar. Carved reliefs relate stories of the iconoclastic bishop's unconventional life. The seven elaborate stained-glass windows were designed by French artist Guillaume de Marcillat. The *Cappella della Madonna del Conforto*, off the austere nave, holds a notable terra-cotta *Crucifixion* by Andrea della Robbia. *(Up V. Andrea Cesalpino from P. San Francesco. ☎ 05 75 23 991. Open daily 7am-12:30pm and 3-6:30pm. Modest dress required. Free.)*

CHIESA DI SAN DOMENICO. The church's true gem is Cimabue's **crucifix** (1265-70), which hangs over the main altar. It is the artist's oldest and best preserved work. Other significant pieces in the simple, wood-timbered interior include Spinello Aretino's *Annunciation* and a Marcillat rose window depicting St. Augustine. *(Take V. A. Celaspino from P. San Francesco, turn left at P. Libertà on V. Ricasorli, then right on V. di Sassoverde. Open daily 8:30am-1pm and 3:30-7pm. Hours may vary. Closed to public during mass. Free.)*

FESTIVALS

Whether you're up for haggling or merely wish to browse, Arezzo's **antique fairs,** which take place in and around P. Grande on the first weekend of every month, paint a living portrait of the town's history and variety. Furniture and religious paraphernalia would be tough to lug through customs, though sundry bric-a-brac can make for unique souvenirs.

> **Giostra del Saracino** (☎0575 37 74 62; www.giostradelsaracino.arezzo.it), on the 3rd Sa of June and the 1st Su of Sept. Flags begin to plaster uncovered surfaces and celebrations engulf the town for the entire week before the medieval joust. In a Crusade-era ritual, knights representing the 4 quarters of the town charge a wooden effigy of a Saracen heathen with lances drawn.

PISA
☎050

Millions of tourists arrive in Pisa (PEE-zah; pop. 85,379) each year to marvel at the famous "Leaning Tower," forming a photo-snapping mire of awkward poses. Though worn around the edges, the heart of Pisa is still alive as a haven for the exuberant, opinionated students that attend the city's three universities. After that inevitable Kodak moment, take some time to wander through the alleys of P. dei Cavalieri and P. Dante, decorated with impassioned political graffiti in the sprawling university neighborhood, or along the Arno in the evening to take in the lively local nightlife.

TRANSPORTATION

> **Flights: Galileo Galilei Airport** (☎050 84 93 00; www.pisa-airport.com). Trains make the 5min. trip (€1.10) between the train station and the airport every 30 min., departing from track 14 (find access at the end of platform 1). Not a major Italian airport.

TUSCANY

Bus **LAM ROSSA** (red line) runs between the airport, train station, the Tower, and other points in Pisa and its environs (every 20min., €1.10).

Trains: Pisa Centrale, P. della Stazione (☎050 413 85), at the southern end of town. Ticket booth open 6am-9pm; self-service ticket machines available 24hr. MC/V. To **Florence** (1hr., every 30min. 4:15am-10:30pm, €5.60); **Livorno** (15min., every 30min., €1.80); **Rome** (4hr., every 2hr. 5:45am-7pm, €18-36). Regional trains to **Lucca** (30min., 2 per hr. 6:20am-9:50pm, €2.40) also stop at Pisa's **San Rossore** (€1.10), close to the *duomo* and Tower. If leaving from San Rossore, buy tickets from *tabaccherie*.

Buses: Lazzi (☎058 358 48 76; www.lazzi.it) and **CPT** (☎050 50 55 11; www.cpt.pisa) in P. Sant'Antonio. Ticket office open daily 7am-8:15pm. To: **Florence** (2hr., every hr., €6.10) via **Lucca** (every 40min., €2); **Livorno** (every hr., €2); **Volterra** (1hr., €5.20) via **Pondeterra.**

Taxis: RadioTaxi (☎050 54 16 00).

Car Rental: A number of companies have rentals available at the airport. **Avis** (☎050 42 028). **Budget** (☎050 50 37 56). **Europcar** (☎050 41 081). **Hertz** (☎050 43 220). **Thrifty** (☎050 45 490). Book in advance to ensure availability.

▌ ? ORIENTATION AND PRACTICAL INFORMATION

Pisa lies near the mouth of the **Arno River,** which splits the town. Most sights lie to the north of the Arno; the main **train station** is to the south. To reach **Piazza Duomo** from the station, take the bus marked LAM ROSSA going toward San Jacopo; it leaves from across the station, in front of Hotel Cavalieri. The plaza can also be reached by foot in 30min.—head straight from the station down **Viale Gramsci** to **Piazza Vittorio Emanuele II.** From there you can take the more direct route by walking around the plaza on the left, taking the first left into **P. Sant'Antonio,** near the bus station, and then heading right up **V. Francesco Crispi,** which will lead you over **Ponte Solferino** onto **Via Roma** and straight to P. Duomo. Alternatively, from P. Emanuele take the store-lined **Corso Italia** and once across **Ponte Mezzo,** walk along the river until you reach Ponte Solferino and turn right onto V. Roma.

Tourist Office: P. V. Emanuele II 13 (☎050 42 291). Open M-F 9am-7pm, Sa 9am-1:30pm. At P. Duomo in Museo dell'Opera del Duomo on the Arno side of the tower. (☎050 56 04 64). Open daily in summer 10am-7pm, in winter 10am-5pm. At the airport (☎050 50 37 00). Open daily 11am-11pm.

Budget Travel:New Taurus Viaggi, V. Francesco Crispi 25/27 (☎050 50 20 90), sells international tickets. Open M-F 9am-12:30pm and 3:30-7:30pm, Sa 9am-12:30pm. AmEx/MC/V.

Banks: Deutsche Bank, on the corner of V. Giusue Carducci and V. San Lorenzo, between P. Cavalieri and P. Martiri della Libertà. **24hr. ATMs.**

Luggage Storage: At the train station, on the left at the end of Platform #1. Self-service lockers available for small pieces. €3 per bag for 12hr. €2 for each successive 12hr. period. Open 6am-9pm. Cash only.

English-Language Bookstore: La Feltrinelli, C. Italia 50, has a small section of English books. Open M-Sa 9am-8pm, Su 10am-1pm and 4-8pm. AmEx/MC/V.

Laundromat: Lavenderia, V. Carmine 20. Wash €4, dry €4. Includes detergent. Open daily 7am-11pm.

Police: (☎050 58 35 11). For emergencies ☎113.

Pharmacy: Farmacia, Lugarno Mediceo 51 (☎050 54 40 02). Open 24hr.

Hospital: Santa Chiara (☎050 99 21 11) on V. Bonanno near P. del Duomo.

Internet Access: Internet Surf, V. Giusue Carducci 5. €2.50 per hr. Students €2 per hr. Open daily 9am-10pm.

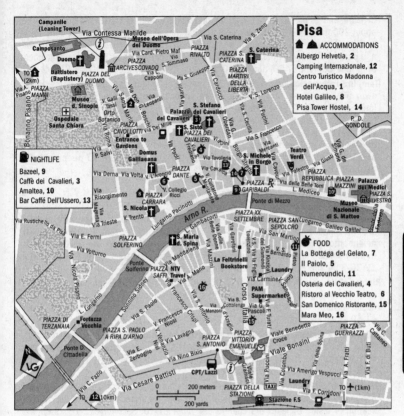

Pisa

🏠 ⛺ ACCOMMODATIONS
Albergo Helvetia, **2**
Camping Internazionale, **12**
Centro Turistico Madonna
dell'Acqua, **1**
Hotel Galileo, **8**
Pisa Tower Hostel, **14**

🌙 NIGHTLIFE
Bazeel, **9**
Caffè dei Cavalieri, **3**
Amaltea, **10**
Bar Caffé Dell'Ussero, **13**

🍴 FOOD
La Bottega del Gelato, **7**
Il Paiolo, **5**
Numeroundici, **11**
Osteria dei Cavalieri, **4**
Ristoro al Vecchio Teatro, **6**
San Domenico Ristorante, **15**
Mara Meo, **16**

TUSCANY

Post Office: P.V. Emanuele II 8 (☎050 51 95 15), near the station on the right of the *piazza*. Open M-F 8:15am-7pm, Sa 8:15am-1:30pm. **Postal Code:** 56125.

🏠 🏕 ACCOMMODATIONS AND CAMPING

Albergo Helvetia, V. Don G. Boschi 31 (☎050 55 30 84), off P. Arcivescovado. These rooms offer little in the way of style, but their location near major sights is convenient. Equipped with TV, fans, and phones. Shared and private baths available. Reception 8am-midnight. Breakfast €5. Singles €35, with bath €50; doubles €45/60. Extra bed €15. Cash only. ❷

Hotel Galileo, V. Santa Maria 12 (☎050 40 621; hotelgalileo@pisaonline.it). Stellar rooms in the university district, all with frescoed ceilings, minifridges, and TV. Shared bath is well-kept. Single €40, with bath €45; doubles €48/60; triples €63/75. MC/V. ❷

Pisa Tower Hostel, P. Garibaldi 9 (☎331 788 68 59). Taking a cue from the *gelateria* next door, these sherbert-colored rooms come with a few sweet deals, including free drop-off at the airport, internet, and kitchen facilities. Female-only dorms €25; private rooms available. ❶

Camping Village Torre Pendente, V. delle Cascine (☎050 56 17 04; www.campingtor-rependente.it). From P. del Duomo, go through the arch on the west side into P. Manin. Take V. Pisano right to the intersection next to the Pam Supermarket, take a left onto V.

Cascine, and go all the way through the underpass tunnel; at the end campsite will be about 200m on the right. An easy walk to the towers, this campsite provides dorm beds in close quarters, bungalow rental, and sites for campers and tents. On-site market, bar, and outdoor swimming pool. Dorms in bungalows offer bathrooms and kitchen facilities. April-June €8, tent €7.50, dorms €20. July-Aug. €9.50/14/25. MC/V over €10. ❶

Camping Internazionale (☎050 35 211; www.campeggiointernazionale.com), 10km away at V. Litoranea 7 in Marina di Pisa, across from its private beach. Take CPT intercity bus from P. Sant'Antonio to Marina di Pisa (20min., €1.80). Leaning trees (sorry, no towers) provide shade to small sites with baths shared with the campers and insects around you. While children on bikes whiz by on the dirt roads, head to the on-site bar or market or cross the street to the camp's private beach. Best for those who are satisfied seeing Pisa's sights as a daytrip. Open May-Sept. €7 per person, €6 per child; €9 per tent. July-Aug. prices increase by €1-5. MC/V. ❶

FOOD

Il Paiolo, V. Curtatone e Montanara 9 (☎050 42 528). Great music and original artwork hanging on the yolk-yellow walls set the mood for this popular university neighborhood restaurant where students fill the benches and the waitstaff adds friendly service to the fun atmosphere. *Primi* and *secondi* €6-9. Cover €1. Open M-F 12:30-3pm and 8pm-2am, Sa-Su 8pm-2am. MC/V. ❷

Ristoro al Vecchio Teatro, P. Dante (☎050 202 10). Enjoy fresh Pisan cuisine *al fresco* or in the dining room of one of the city's oldest buildings. Try the *risotto di verdure miste*, a butter dish with artichoke, garlic, and peppers. *Primi* and *secondi* €8. Cover €1.50. Open M-Sa noon-3pm and 7:30-10pm. AmEx/MC/V. ❷

Osteria dei Cavalieri, V. San Frediano 16 (☎050 58 08 58; www.osteriacavalieri.pisa.it). Relax after a busy day and sample traditional *spaghetti all'arrabbiata* (spicy pasta with tomato and herbs). *Primi* €8-9. *Secondi* €11-15. Open M-F 12:30-4pm and 7:45-10pm, Sa 7:45-10pm. MC/V. ❷

Galileo, V. San Martino 6 (☎050 28 287; www.ristorantegalileo.com). Crisp, white decor dominates this classy yet family-friendly dinner spot. Sit under the cover of the outdoor seating or inside beneath the chandeliers. *Primi* €7-10. *Secondi* €12-18. Cover €2. Open daily 12:30-2:30pm and 7:30-11pm. MC/V. ❷

La Bottega del Gelato, P. Garibaldi 11, right off of Ponte di Mezzo. Get generous scoops of homemade gelato and take it for a walk along the nearby Arno. Try the mascarpone. Cones and cups from €1.50. ❶

San Domenico Ristorante, C. Italia 139 (☎050 50 33 24), through the alcove to the right at Corte San Domenico 2. *Primi* €6-7. *Secondi* €9-15. Hot chocolate, pastries and karaoke Th-Sa after dinner. Open Sept.-May M-W 7:30am-7:30pm, Th-Sa 7:30am-11:30pm; June-July M 8am-7:30pm, Tu-F 8am-11:30pm, Sa 4:30-11:30pm, Su 8-11:30pm. ❷

🜂 SIGHTS

For sights in P. del Duomo, purchase all of your tickets at the booth behind the tower or at the Museo delle Sinopie, on the opposite side of the street from the *duomo*.

◼LEANING TOWER. The white stone buildings of the **Piazza del Duomo,** aptly renamed Campo dei Miracoli (Field of Miracles) by poet Gabriele d'Annunzio, stretch across the well-maintained greens of the *piazza*, which houses the Leaning Tower, *duomo*, baptistery, and *Camposanto* (cemetery). Look closely: all of the buildings lean at different angles, thanks to the mischievous, shifty soil. No matter how many postcards you see of the Tower, nothing quite compares to witnessing the 5.5° tilt in person. Bonanno Pisano began building the tower in 1173, and construction was repeatedly delayed as the soil shifted and the building began to lean. The tilt intensified after WWII, and thanks to tourist traffic, it continues to slip 1-2mm every year. In June 2001, the steel safety cables and iron girdles that imprisoned the Tower during years of stabilization efforts were finally removed. One year later, the Tower reopened, albeit on a tightly regulated schedule: once every 30min., guided groups of 30 visitors are permitted to ascend. *(Make reservations at the ticket offices in the Museo del Duomo, online, or next to the tourist info office. Tours depart daily June-Aug. 8:30am-10pm; Sept.-May 8:30am-8:30pm. Groups meet beside the tower 10min. before scheduled entry. Bags not allowed. Free storage for small bags, but not backpacks, so plan accordingly. Children under 8 not permitted, under 18 must be accompanied by an adult. €15. MC/V.)*

> **TIP**
>
> **LUNAR LEANER.** The wait to climb the Leaning Tower can sometimes take hours out of your day. To escape the crowds, save the ascent until after sundown; the tower is open during the summer until 11pm. You'll get a unique view of the city illuminated by moonlight.

 BATTISTERO. The baptistery, an enormous barrel of a building unfairly overshadowed by the all-too-famous leaning legend, was begun in 1153 by a man known as Diotisalvi ("God save you"), its design inspired by the church of the Holy Sepulchre in Jerusalem. Blending architectural styles, it incorporates Tuscan-Romanesque stripes with a multi-tiered Gothic ensemble of gables, pinnacles, and statues. Guido Bigarelli's **fountain** (1246) dominates the center of the ground floor. Nicola Pisano's **pulpit** (1260) recaptures the dignity of classical antiquity and is one of the harbingers of Renaissance art in Italy. Each of the building's four portals face one of the cardinal directions. The dome's acoustics are astounding: a choir singing in the baptistery can be heard 2km away. A staircase embedded in the wall leads to a balcony just below the dome; farther up, a space between the interior and exterior of the dome yields views of the surrounding *piazza.* *(Open daily Apr.-Sept. 8am-8pm; Oct. 9am-7pm; Nov.-Feb 10am-5pm; Mar. 9am-6pm. Last entry 30min. before close. €5; combined ticket with 1 other Piazza del Duomo sight €6; with 4 other sights, excluding the tower, €10.)*

CAMPOSANTO. Built in 1277, this cloistered courtyard cemetery greets visitors with over 600 tombstones, covered with earth that Crusaders brought back from Golgotha, and Roman sarcophagi that date from the AD third century. The sarcophagi reliefs inspired Pisano's pulpit in the baptistery. Fragments of enormous frescoes shattered by WWII Allied bombs line the galleries. The **Cappella Ammannati** contains haunting frescoes of Florence succumbing to the plague; its unidentified, 14th-century creator is known as the "Master of the Triumph of Death." *(Next to the duomo. Open daily Apr.-Sept. 8am-8pm; Oct. 9am-7pm; Nov.-Feb 10am-5pm; Mar. 9am-6pm. Last entry 30min. before close. €5; combined ticket with 1 other Piazza del Duomo sight €6; with 4 other sights, excluding the tower, €10.)*

DUOMO. The *duomo's* dark green-and-white facade is the archetype of the Pisan-Romanesque style. Begun in 1064 by Buscheto (who is now entombed in the wall), the cathedral is the *campo's* oldest structure. Enter the five-aisled nave through Bonanno Pisano's richly decorated bronze doors. Although a 1595 fire destroyed most of the interior, the cathedral was masterfully restored; original paintings by Ghirlandaio hang on the right wall, Cimabue's spectacular gilded mosaic **Christ Pantocrator** graces the apse, and bits of intricately patterned marble Cosmati pavement remain. Giovanni Pisano's last and greatest **pulpit** (1311),

LOCAL LEGEND

WINDOW OF OPPORTUNITY

You might recall the Medicis and the Puccis, aristocratic Italian families who had been friendly for centuries (see Life and Times, p. 43). For Cosimo I de' Medici, life as Duke was fairly typical—a major war here, an architectural renaissance there—but things took a turn for the worse in 1560 when the Duke noticed the very unsubtle and ungentlemanly behavior of his pal Pandolfo Pucci. The Duke had no choice but to publicly shame Pucci and boot him from the Florentine high court.

Humiliated, Pucci hired two hitmen to get even. The Duke passed by the Palazzo Pucci on his way to church every day; the two cronies hid behind the shutters of a first-floor window, ready to pounce. But the Duke learned of the plot just in the nick of time, saving himself from certain death. Unfortunately Pucci did not fare so well: he was publicly executed shortly thereafter. From that day forward, passing the place of his near assassination made the Duke so nervous that he ordered the window to be walled in with stone.

If you're in the neighborhood, stop at the corner of V. de'Servi and look for the Pucci family crest on the side of the Palazzo. Beneath it, you'll find the concealed window, the relic of a failed assassination attempt and an aristocratic neurosis. And yes, Pandolfo Pucci is an ancient relative of the late Italian fashion designer Emilio Pucci.

designed to outdo his father's in the baptistery, sits regally in the center. *(Open Apr.-Sept. M-Sa 10am-7:30pm, Su 1-7:30pm; Oct. M-Sa 10am-5:30pm, Su 1-5:30; Nov.-Feb. M-Sa 10am-12:30pm and 3-4:30pm, Su 3-4:30pm; Mar. M-Sa 10-5:30pm, Su 1-5:30pm. Closed for religious ceremonies. €2; combined ticket with 1 other Piazza del Duomo sight €6; with 4 other sights, excluding the tower, €10.)*

PIAZZA DEI CAVALIERI. Designed by Vasari and built on the site of the Roman forum, this *piazza*, originally a home that belonged to the Knights of St. Stephen, is now the site of the **Scuola Normale Superiore**, one of Italy's premier universities. The ⬛**Palazzo della Carovana** displays a magnificent facade, intricately detailed with the coats of arms and zodiac signs of the Medici. To the right, the **Church of Santo Stefano dei Cavalieri,** dedicated to Order founder Cosimo, is capped with a wood ceiling carved by Bartolomeo Atticciati in 1606. The wrought-iron baskets on either end of the **Palazzo dell'Orologio** (Palace of the Clock) were once receptacles for the heads of delinquent Pisans. In the *palazzo*'s **tower,** Ugolino della Gherardesca was starved to death in 1208, along with his sons and grandsons, as punishment for treachery. This murky episode in Tuscan politics is commemorated in Shelley's *Tower of Famine*, as well as in Dante's *Inferno* with gruesome, cannibalistic innuendos.

MUSEO NAZIONALE DI SAN MATTEO. Thirty rooms hold an important collection of medieval art by Masaccio, Fra Angelico, and Simone Martini. Sculptures by the Pisanos and a bust by Donatello also grace this converted Benedictine convent. *(Off P. Mazzini on Lugarno Mediceo next to the Palazzo dei Medici. ☎390 50 54 18 65. Open Tu-Sa 8:30am-7:30pm, Su 8:30am-1:30pm. Last entry 30min. before close. €5, under 18 and over 65 €2.50. Cash only.)*

MUSEO DELL'OPERA DEL DUOMO. For more on the monuments of the *Campo dei Miracoli*, try the Museo dell'Opera del Duomo, which provides excellent historical detail on the art and construction of the famous buildings of P. del Duomo. Lots of Pisano family work is displayed, including the 13th-century sculpture *Madonna del Colloquio* (Madonna of the Conversation) by Giovanni, which was named for the expressive gazes exchanged between mother and child. The collection also includes Egyptian, Roman, and Etruscan art. *(Behind the Leaning Tower. ☎050 38 72 19. Open daily Apr.-Sept. 8am-7:20pm; Oct. 9am-5:20pm; Nov.-Feb. 9am-4:20pm; Mar. 9am-5:20pm. €5; combined ticket with 1 other Piazza del Duomo sight €6; with 4 others, excluding the tower, €10.)*

CHIESA DI SANTA MARIA DELLA SPINA. This tiny Gothic church on the south side of the Arno offers a glimpse at masterpieces by Andrea and Nino Pisano. Originally built between 1063 and 1230, the Church of Saint Mary of the Thorn later housed a reputed thorn from the Crown of Thorns in 1333. *(From the Campo dei Miracoli, walk down V. Santa Maria and over the bridge. Open June-Oct. M-F 10am-1pm and 3pm-6pm, Sa-Su 10am-1pm and 3pm-7pm; Nov.-Oct. M-F 10-2 and 3-6, Sa-Su 10am-2pm and 3-7pm. €2.)*

FESTIVALS AND NIGHTLIFE

The most up-to-date event information can be found at the tourist office, but a few annual festivals bring the city to life. And light. The night before the city's Saint Day, that of St. Nicholas, on June 16, the **Luminara di San Ranieri** brightens the city (including the tower) with 70,000 lights. On the last Saturday evening in June, the **Gioco del Ponte** revives the city's medieval pageantry tradition. Pisans divide into multiple teams, pledging their allegiance to their respective neighborhoods. Pairs of teams converge on the Ponte di Mezzo and joust until one side conquers the bridge, to the cheers of the hundreds that fill the street on either side of the Arno.

Three universities flood Pisa with lively students, but as summer approaches, the nightlife gradually dies down. During the school year, students reclaim the tourist-packed *centro* after the sun goes down. Bars and cafes line the north side of the Arno, and students turn every horizontal surface into seating.

Bazeel, P. Garibaldi, across from Ponte di Mezzo. Bass lines bounce into the street from this castle-like structure. Beer €3.50-4. Wine €3.50. Mixed drinks €4. Open M-Th 8pm-1am, F-Sa 8pm-2am.

Amaltea, P. Cairoli, on the Arno past Bazeel. Candlelit outdoor seating and wine for about €5 per glass. Open M-F 5pm-1am, Sa-Su 5pm-2am.

Caffè dei Cavalieri, V. Corsica 8A (☎050 55 39 25). Arrive during *aperitivi* (7-9pm) and get some snacks with your drinks or just relax at the outside tables. Wine €2-3.50; beer €2-3.50. Free Wi-Fi. Open M-Th and Su 9am-1am, F-Sa 9am-2am.

Il Covo Del Tapiro Pub, V. San Martino 61, on the south side of the river. Students chill out with cheap drinks, rock music, and foosball. Beer €2-4; wine €2-3; mixed drinks €4. Open M-Th 9pm-1am, F 9pm-2am, Sa-8pm-2am.

DAYTRIP FROM PISA

VIAREGGIO
Trains travel to Florence (1½hr, 1-2 per hr. 5:38am-10:11pm, €6.60), Lucca (18min., 1-2 per hr. 6:30am-10:11, €2.40), and Pisa (26min., 1-3 per hr. 5:38am-11:07pm, €5.50). There are 2 tourist offices in town. The one at the train station (☎058 44 63 82) is open July-Aug. M-Th and Su 9am-1pm, F-Sa 9am-1pm and 3-6; Sept.-June M-Sa 9am-1pm. The main one closer to the beach is located down V. Leonardo Da Vinci from the train station on the street opposite the beach at V. Carducci 10 (☎058 496 22 33; www.aptversilia.it). Open July-Aug. M-Sa 9am-2pm and 3-7pm, Su 9:30am-12:30pm and 3-6pm; Sept.-June M-Sa 9am-2pm and 3-7pm, Su 9am-1pm.

The resort town of Viareggio (vee-ah-REJ-yo) sits at the foot of the Riviera, and every morning packed trains of young Italians arrive to slather on oil and soak up the sun; however, they usually return to the inland cities by evening to avoid the costly accommodations. Most of Viareggio's shoreline has been roped off by private beach owners who charge between €20 and €40 per family per day for a spot on the beach. Walk to the left facing the water across the canal along Vle. Europa, 20min. from the bus station at P. D'Azeglio, to locate the **free beach** at the southern end of town. Or, from the train station, take city bus #9 and save precious tanning time. Bus #9 also makes the return trip from the beach to the train station. Farther down the shore is **La Lecciona.** With a street of discos near to the water, this area has a reputation as an unofficial gay beach. The beach itself is sandy and relatively clean, considering the numbers that occupy it on hot days, but for those with private transportation, you would be better off heading farther south to less crowded, more scenic territory. Every year people flock to celebrate **Carnevale** (☎0584 1840 750; www.viareggio.ilcarnevale.com) with colorful parades, hilarious performances, and riotous parties. The dates of the month-long festivities change each year, with the last day falling 40 days before Easter. Few budget accommodations exist in town, and travelers are better off finding a bed in nearby Pisa or Lucca. Viareggio's restaurants generally cater to a wealthy clientele and there are few supermarkets. Pasta dishes typically cost €10-16 and meat dishes €12-36; even *gelaterie* may charge you a cover upwards of €1.50. Instead, pack up some food and have a pleasant picnic set to the sound of the waves crashing against the beach.

LUCCA ☎05 83

Lucca (LOO-ka; pop. 9000) is a pleasant retreat from the sight-seeing frenzy of other Tuscan destinations, successfully dabbling in nearly every area of tourist activity. Bikers rattle through the town and along the 4km tree-lined promenade that runs atop the city's encircling medieval walls; the well-heeled take on the trendy boutiques along the main streets; and art lovers admire the Romanesque churches and elegant architecture of the *centro*. Picturesque *piazze* appear every few blocks, along with notice boards advertising concerts, often related in some way to the operas by Lucca's own Giacomo Puccini. Tranquil and compelling, Lucca is no party spot, but it is the ideal location if you're looking to get away from it all.

▍▊ TRANSPORTATION

Trains: Station in Ple. Ricasoli. Ticket office open daily 6:30am-8:10pm. To **Florence** (1½hr., every hr., €5); **Pisa** (30min.; 2 per hr. M-Sa 5:40am-9:30pm, Su 7:42am-9:30pm; €2.40); and **Viareggio** (16min.; every hr. M-Sa 6:19am-11:30pm, Su 7:59am-11:30pm). For other major cities, change in Pisa. For **Cinque Terre**, change in Viareggio.

Buses: Lazzi (☎0583 587 897; www.valibus.it), in Ple. Verdi. To **Florence** (1hr. 10min.; M-Sa 1-2 per hr. 6:25am-6:55pm, Su every 2hr. via Montecatini 9:45am-7:45pm; €5.10) and **Pisa** (50min.; M-Sa 1-2 per hr., Su every 2hr. 8am-8pm; €2.80).

Taxis: RadioTaxi (☎0583 333 434). Taxis pick up at 4 stands around the city. To call a taxi, enter the appropriate code for your desired pick-up point when prompted. For pick up at the train station 01, in P. Napoleone 02, in P. Santa Maria 03, in Ple. Verdi 04.

Bike Rental: Most rental locations have comparable fares and hours of operation. In general, basic bicycles are €2.50 per hr., €12.50 per day; mountain and racing bikes €3.50/17.50; tandem bikes €5.50 per hr. Most rental places are open daily 9am-7:30pm. **Chronò,** Corso Garibaldi 93 (☎0583 490 591). **Cicli Bizzarri,** P. Santa Maria 32 (☎0583 49 66 82; www.ciclibizarri.net). **Cicli Rai,** V. San Nicolao 66 (☎348 893 7119). **Poli Antonio Biciclette,** P. Santa Maria 42 (☎0583 493 787; www.biciclettepoli.com). **Promo Tourist,** Porta San Pietro (☎348 380 0126). Or from the **tourist office** in Ple. Verdi (☎0583 583 150; www.luccaitinera.it).

Car Rental: Autonoleggio Giglio, V. Orzali 391 (☎058 349 2698). **Avis,** in Ple. Italia (☎0583 317 283; www.avisautonoleggio.it). **Europe Car,** Vle. Castracani 110 (☎058

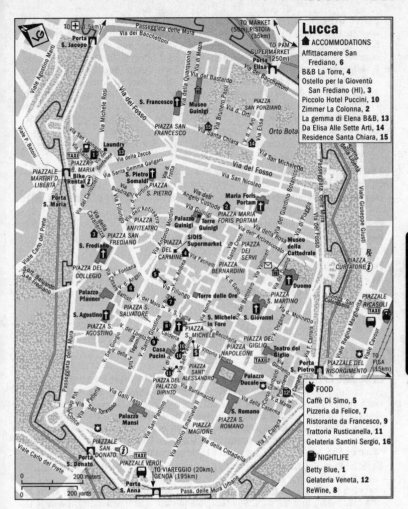

39 56 058; www.europecar.it). **Hertz,** V. Catalani 59 (☎058 350 5472; www.hertz.it).
Pittore, P. Santa Maria 34 (☎058 34 67 960). **Travel Car,** Vle. Puccini 82 (☎058 35 82 284).

ORIENTATION AND PRACTICAL INFORMATION

To reach the *centro storico* from the **train station,** cross the street and walk forward past **Piazza Ricasole** to take a left on **Viale Regina Margherita.** Enter the city through the arches to the right to of **Porta San Pietro.** Walk forward one block to take a left onto **Corso Garibaldi.** Turn right onto **Via Vittorio Veneto** and follow it one block to reach **Piazza Napoleone** (also called Piazza Grande). Continue walking on V. Veneto to reach to reach **Piazza San Michele** in the center of town. If arriving by bus, walk to the right through **Piazza Verdi,** follow **Via San Paolino** toward the center of town and P. San Michele, and turn right on V. Veneto to reach P. Napoleone.

Tourist Offices: Ufficio Regionale, P. Santa Maria 35 (☎0583 919931; www.luccaturismo.it). Includes an internet point, currency exchange, hotel booking, and tickets for Trenitalia. Open daily in winter 9am-1pm and 3-6pm, in summer 9am-8pm. **Ufficio Provinciale** (☎0583 91994) in Corile Carrara beside P. Napoleone. Open daily 10am-1pm and 2-6pm. **Centro Accoglienza Turistica** (☎0583 583150; www.luccaitinera.it), in Ple. Verdi, offers Wi-Fi for €2, scheduled guided tours (Sa 3pm, 2-3 hr., meets in P. San Michele under the Loggia of Palazzo Pretorio, €10), and self-guided audio tours (€9, €6 for every additional tour). Open daily 9am-6pm. 2nd branch near the train station in P. Curtatone on Vle. Guisti (☎0583 495 730). Open daily 10am-1:30pm and 2:30-5:30pm.

Currency Exchange: Ufficio Regionale, tourist office, in P. Santa Maria. Open daily in winter 9am-1pm and 3-6pm, in summer 9am-8pm.

24hr ATM: On corner of V. San Paolino, 50m away from the UniCredit Banca. Also on the corner of V. Fillungo and V. Mordini, beside Deutschebank.

Laundry: Lavanderia Niagara, V. Michele Rosi 26 (☎349 164 5084 or 328 675 4181). €4 per 7 kg. Open daily 7am-11pm.

Pharmacy: Farmacia Comunale, in P. Curtatone. Open 24hr.

Hospital: Campo di Marte (☎058 39 55 791), outside the wall in the Northeast corner on V. dell'Ospedale.

Police: ☎112 Carabinieri, ☎113 Police.

Internet: The tourist office in P. Verdi has Wi-Fi for €2 per hr. The other three have computers with internet. **Copesteria Paolini,** V. Paolini 63, has both. Internet €3 per hr.; Wi-Fi €2 per hr. Open M-F 8:30am-7:30pm, Sa 9am-1pm and 3:30-7:30pm.

Post Office: V. Vallisneri (☎058 34 34 51). Open M-F 8:15am-7pm, Sa 8:15am-1:30pm. **Postal Code:** 55100.

ACCOMMODATIONS

La Gemma di Elena Bed and Breakfast, V. della Zecca 33 (☎058 34 96 65; www.virtualica.it/gemma). Though the building is 450 years old, this B&B radiates with energy. The laid-back, friendly staff help make your stay even more comfortable in 1 of 6 plush and pretty rooms full of personality, some with fireplace and terrace. Shared and private baths. Common room and private parking available. Pets welcome. Breakfast included, served 8:30-10:30am. Check-out 11am. Singles €35; doubles €55, with bath €65. Extra bed €15, in room with bath €20. AmEx/MC/V. ❷

Ostello San Frediano (HI), V. della Cavallerizza 12 (☎058 34 69 957; www.ostellolucca.it), 15min. from P. Napoleone. Walk along V. Beccheria past P. San Michele as the street becomes V. Santa Lucia and then V. del Moro. At the road's end, turn left on V. San Giorgio and make an immediate right onto V. C. Battisti. When you reach the Basilica San Frediano, go right around the church, along the front, and straight onto V. Cavallerizza. Spacious rooms with hardwood bunk beds. Common spaces with high ceilings and plenty of couches. Internal and external baths, private and shared rooms available. Breakfast €3-5, lunch or dinner €11. Towels €1.50. Linens included. Reception 7:30am-10am and 1:30pm-midnight. Check-out 10am. Lockout 10am-3:30pm. 6- to 8- person dorms €18-20; 2- to 6-person rooms with bath €55-135. HI discount. Cash only. ❶

Bed and Breakfast La Torre, V. del Carmine 11 (☎058 39 57 044; www.roomlatorre.com). This family-run rest stop actually has 2 locations within a ½ a block of each other. At the reception portion, rooms are homey, with colorful bedspreads and family portraits on the walls. Though this first set of rooms is perfectly nice, ask to be placed in Torre 3 when booking. These doubles come with private bathrooms, kitchenettes, high ceilings, and antique furniture. Breakfast included. Free internet. Free pickup available; call ahead. Singles €35, with bath €50; doubles €50/80. Apartments with kitchen, parlor, and TVs for 2 people €80 per night, for 4 people €120 per night. MC/V. ❷

Zimmer La Colonna, V. dell'Angelo Custode 16 (☎058 34 40 170), off P. Maria Foris Portam. Colonnaded hallways lead to spacious rooms with TV and antique decor. Clean shared baths. Doubles €45, with bath €65. AmEx/MC/V. ❷

Da Elisa Alle Sette Arti, V. Elisa 25 (☎058 349 45 39). Antique beds and Art Deco furnishings in ornately-tiled *affitacamere*. Shared and private bath. Kitchen. Breakfast €6. Bike rental €2 per hr. June-Sept. singles €47, with bath €65; doubles €52/70, triples €67/77. Oct.-May singles €42/52; doubles €45/55; triples €57/62. ❸

Residence Santa Chiara, V. Santa Chiara 12 (☎058 34 91 349; www.residencesanta-chiara.com). Spacious rooms with tiled floors in a 16th-century building. Take breakfast in summer in the outdoor terrace; in the winter, have it brought to your room. Jan-Mar singles €50; doubles €65. Apr.-Dec. singles €65, doubles €90. AmEx/MC/V. ❹

Piccolo Hotel Puccini, V. di Poggio 9 (☎058 35 54 21; www.hotelpuccini.com). Named for the famous Luccan, the rooms of this 3-star hotel are decorated with framed playbills from Puccini's operas. Bath, TV with English channels, phone, and safe. Breakfast €3.50. Wi-Fi available. Singles €70; doubles €95; triples €115. AmEx/MC/V. ❹

🍴 FOOD

On Wednesday and Saturday mornings from 8am-1pm, an **open-air market** overtakes V. dei Bacchettoni on the east end of town. Within the city walls, **SIDIS,** P. del Carmine 2, stocks basic groceries. (Open M-Tu and Th-Su 8am-8pm, W 8am-1pm. MC/V.) Outside the north side of the city walls, **Esselunga** stocks a more extensive variety of supermarket goods.

Ristorante da Francesco, Corte Portici 13 (☎058 34 18 049), off V. Calderia between P. San Salvatore and P. San Michele. Ample patio seating. Ideal for a light but filling meal. Try the *zuppa di verdure* (vegetable soup; €6). *Primi* €6-7. *Secondi* €8-12. *Menù turistico* for lunch (*primo, secondo,* a glass of wine, and coffee) €15. Cover €1.50. Open Tu-Su noon-2:30pm and 7-10pm. MC/V. ❷

Da Leo, V. Tegrimi 1 (☎058 34 92 236; www.trattoriadaleo.it). Have a casual pasta meal at this local favorite. Reservations needed for outdoor seating. *Primi* €6-6.50. *Secondi* €9-11.50. Cover €1. ❷

Caffè Di Simo, V. Fillungo 58 (☎058 34 96 234; www.anticocaffedisimo.it). Amid a row of designer boutiques, the hardwood of this restaurant shines while mellow music plays in the background. Lunch buffet €10. *Primi* €7-9. *Secondi* €8.50-11. Open daily 12:30-3pm and 8-11:30pm. MC/V. ❷

Pizzeria da Felice, V. Buia 12 (☎058 34 94 986). Pizza *al taglio* (slices from €1.30) is a cheap and delicious meal option for hungry locals and tourists. Open M-Sa 10am-8:30pm. ❶

Gelateria Santini Sergio, P. Cittadella 1 (☎058 35 52 95). Has been wowing sweet-toothed passers-by since 1916 with flavors like *paciugo* (nougat, chocolate, cookies, and rum) and standard favorites. Cups and cones €1.50-3. Open daily July-Sept. 9am-midnight, Oct.-June 10am-8pm. AmEx/MC/V. ❶

🗺 SIGHTS

🏛**BALUARDI.** No tour of Lucca is complete and no journey into the city possible without passing the perfectly intact medieval city walls, or *baluardi* (battlements). The shaded 4km pedestrian path along the walls, which passes grassy parks and cool fountains, is perfect for a breezy, afternoon picnic or a sunset view. Rent a bike and try to master the Luccan art of simultaneously biking and chatting on your cell phone, or simply admire the city's layout as you stroll.

DUOMO DI SAN MARTINO. Though supposedly begun in the AD sixth century and rebuilt in 1070 by Pope Alexander II, the majority of the building that stands today is the result of another reconstruction, which took place between the 12th and 15th centuries. The multi-layered, arched facade of this asymmetrical *duomo* is the oldest feature of the present structure. The 13th-century reliefs that decorate the exterior of the *duomo* include Nicola Pisano's *Journey of the Magi and Deposition.* Matteo Civitali, Lucca's famous sculptor, designed the floor and contributed the San Martino statue to the right of the door. His prized *Colobium*, in the left aisle, houses the 11th-century **Volto Santo** (Holy Face). Reputedly carved by Nicodemus at Calvary, this wooden crucifix is said to depict a from-life image of Christ. Other highlights include Tintoretto's *Last Supper* (1590), the third painting on the right, and *Holy Conversation* by Ghirlandaio, in the sacristy off the right aisle. The **Museo della Cattedrale**, left of the *duomo*, houses religious objects from the *duomo*. *(P. San Martino. From P. Napoleone, take V. del Duomo past P. Giglio and P. San Giovanni. Duomo and sacristy open daily Apr.-Oct. 9:30am-5:45 pm; Nov-March 9:30am-5pm. Closed for Su mass 11am-noon. Duomo free. Sacristy €2. Museo della Cattedrale open from mid-March to Oct. daily 10am-6pm; from Nov. to mid-Mar. M-F 10:30am-2pm and Sa-Su 10am-5pm. €4; combined ticket for duomo, Sacristy, Museo della Cattedrale, and Chiesa di San Giovanni €6. Audio tour €1. Cash only.)*

CHIESA DI SAN MICHELE IN FORO. Given its current setting in a busy *piazza*, it's hard to tell that construction on this church actually began in the AD eighth century on the site of a Roman forum. Once inside, the church's large, stone interior holds beautiful and dramatic oil paintings, such as Lippi's bold *Saints Helen, Roch, Sebastian, and Jerome* toward the end of the right aisle, and Luca della Robbia's *Madonna and Child* near the front. Original religious statues were replaced in the 19th century with likenesses of prominent political figures: Cavour, Garibaldi, and Napoleon III. *(Open daily 8am-noon and 3-6pm. Closed during Su mass. Free.)*

CHIESA DI SAN GIOVANNI. The simple plaster dome of this unassuming church holds a recently excavated AD second-century Roman complex, complete with mosaic pavement, the ruins of a private house and bath (the church's foundations), a Longobard burial site, and a Paleochristian chapel, as well as a 10th- to 11th-century crypt. *(From P. Napoleone, follow V. del Duomo. Open from mid-Mar. to Oct. daily 10am-6pm; from Nov. to mid-Mar. Sa-Su 10am-5pm. Combined ticket with archeological area and baptistery €2.50; combined ticket valid for complete cathedral complex, including Museo della Cattedrale and Sacristy €6. Cash only.)*

TORRE GUINIGI AND TORRE DELL'ORE. These are two of the 15 remaining towers from medieval Lucca's original 250. Narrow **Torre Guinigi** rises above Lucca from the stone mass of Palazzo Guinigi, which is closed to the public. Crouch through a small door to reach a set of 227 stairs; seven little oak trees, called *"lecci,"* provide a shaded view of the city and the hills beyond. *(V. Sant'Andrea 41. From P. San Michele follow V. Roma 1 block, turn left on V. Fillungo and right on V. Sant'Andrea. ☎ 058 331 68 46. Open daily June-Sept. 9:30am-7:30pm; Oct.-May 9:30am-6:30pm. Last entry 20min. before close. €3.50, students and over 65 €2.50. Combined ticket for both towers €5/4. Cash only.)* For some more exercise, climb the 207 steps of the **Torre delle Ore** (Hour Towers/Clock Towers), where you can see the inner workings of the city's tallest timepiece. *(V. Fillungo 24. Open daily June-Sept. 9:30am-7:30pm; Oct.-May 9:30am-6:30pm. Last entry 20min. before close. €3.50, students and over 65 €2.50. Combined ticket for both towers €5/4. Cash only.)*

PIAZZA NAPOLEONE. Also called "Piazza Grande" by locals, this *piazza* is the town's administrative center. The 16th-century **Palazzo Ducale** now houses government offices. At night, *lucchese* pack the *piazza* for *passeggiate* (strolls).

PIAZZA ANFITEATRO. Closely packed buildings, three-star hotels, and upscale restaurants create a nearly seamless, oval wall around this *piazza*, originally an ancient Roman amphitheater. Though the ruins are now nearly 3m below the ground, some of the original arches are visible on the outer walls of the buildings. Locals and tourists mingle over coffee and conversation close to but free of the hyperactivity of Piazza Napoleone.

BASILICA DI SAN FREDIANO. Multiple additions led to San Frediano's proud, Romanesque structure. Originally constructed in the AD sixth century with the facade facing west, it was rebuilt in the first half of the 12th century with an eastward orientation. The gleaming Byzantine mosaic atop the facade is striking. *(Open M-Sa 9am-noon and 2:30pm-6pm, Su 9-noon and 2:30pm-5:30pm. Free.)*

PALAZZO PFANNER. Palazzo Pfanner's sumptuous garden oasis, complete with an octagonal fountain and statuary of mythical figures, was designed by Filippo Juvarra in the 18th century. While the view from the wall is free, sitting in the garden makes you feel like royalty. The *palazzo* now serves as a museum that showcases 18th- and 19th-century costumes and old medical instruments belonging to Dr. Pietro Pfanner, the surgeon who owned the *palazzo* and gave it his name. *(V. degli Asili 33. From the Basilica di San Frediano, take V. San Frediano to V. Cesare Battisti and turn left. Take a right onto V. degli Angeli to reach V. degli Asili. ☎ 340 923 30 85. Open daily Apr.-Oct. 10am-6pm. Palazzo €3.50, students €3; garden €3.50/3; both €5/4. €0.50 discount on all tickets in Apr. and Oct.)*

ORTO BOTANICO. For a change of pace, retreat to the calming paths of Lucca's botanical gardens. Created in 1820 by duchess Maria Luisa of Bourbon, the garden was originally linked to the Royal University of Lucca for scientific study. A broad main avenue leads to a pond and marshy plants before branching off into smaller, more isolated trails. *(In the southeast corner of the city. ☎ 058 344 21 60. Open daily from July to mid-Sept. 10am-7pm; from mid-Sept. to Oct. 10am-5pm; Nov-Dec. by reservation only M-Sa 9:30am-12:30pm; Mar. 20 to Apr. 30 10am-5pm; May-June 10am-6pm. Last entry 30min. before closing. €3.)*

🎵 🎭 ENTERTAINMENT AND NIGHTLIFE

Teatro Comunale del Giglio, Piazza del Giglio 13/15 (☎058 34 65 31; www.teatrodelgiglio.it), provides theater, opera, and dance performances year round.

Gelateria Veneta, V. V. Veneta 74 (☎058 34 70 37; www.gelateriaveneta.net.). For evidence that Lucca is a sleepy Tuscan town at its heart, look no further than

the epicenter of its nighttime activity. Delicious all-natural homemade flavors and outdoor seating. The whipped mousse flavors are sensational. Cones €1.90-3. Granita €1.90-2.70. Open daily Mar.-Oct. 10:30am-1am. MC/V over €10.

Betty Blue, V. del Gonfalone 16 (www.betty-blue.eu), slightly away from the *centro*. Internet cafe by day and buzzing bar by night, this mod-styled spot attracts a hip and friendly crowd. Wine €4. Beer €3-5. Long drinks €7 at table or €5 at the bar. Open M-Tu and Th-Su 11am-1am.

✳ FESTIVALS

Lucca's calendar is jam-packed with artistic and musical performances, especially in the summer.

Summer Festival (☎058 44 64 77; www.summerfestival.com), in July. Features performances by artists as various as Lenny Kravitz, Moby, and Dave Matthews Band.

Settembre Lucchese, Sept. 13-22. The king of Lucca's festivals—a lively jumble of artistic, athletic, and folkloric presentations.

Palio della Balestra, July 12. A crossbow competition dating from 1443 and revived for tourists in the early 1970s.

Lucca Comics and Games, November. Get your geek on at one of the largest comic conventions in Italy.

CINQUE TERRE   ☎01 87

Cinque Terre (CHEEN-kweh TEHR-reh; pop. 6000) is the outdoor enthusiast's Spring Break region. Though it's not actually in Tuscany, you don't want to miss this beautiful stretch of Liguria. An exorbitant number of American cliques crowd the area for beach-bumming and hiking. The tourist office claims strong hikers can cover all five villages in about 5hr., but the word on the cliff says 3½hr. will do. Both the speedy and slothful can find numerous opportunities for kayaking, cliff jumping, scuba diving, and horseback riding. Rather than rushing through, take time to wander through villages with tiny clusters of rainbow-colored houses amid hilly stretches of olive groves and vineyards. Each town has its own identity: Bustling Monterosso is the ideal destination for *gelaterie*, upscale Vernazza is the best swim-spot, Corniglia is a perfect rocky shore getaway, tiny Manarola maintains a steady stream of backpackers, and Riomaggiore offers stunning cliff views and wild nightlife. So reserve ahead, put on your hiking boots, and step away from the modern world for a few days.

 TERRE TRIPPING. The train stations and Cinque Terre National Park offices in each of the 5 towns sell 1-day (€8.50), 2-day (€14.70), 3-day (€19.50), and 7-day (€36.50) Cinque Terre Cards with unlimited train, bus, and path access among the 5 villages, La Spezia, and Levanto.

▐ TRANSPORTATION

Trains: The towns lie on the Genoa-La Spezia line. Find schedules at tourist offices. Most trains stop at **Monterosso** and **Riomaggiore,** making them the most accessible of the 5 towns. From the station on V. Fegina, trains run to: **Florence** (3hr., every hr., €9) via **Pisa** (2hr., €5.50); **Genoa** (1½hr., every 2hr. 4:55am-11:35pm, €5); **La Spezia** (20min., every 30min., €1.40);**Rome**(7hr., every 2hr., €24) via **Livorno**. Local trains connect the 5 towns (2-19min.; every 50min.; M-F €1.40, Sa-Su €1.50.).

Ferries: Monterosso can be reached by ferry from **La Spezia** (2hr., 4 per day, €12). Ferries from Monterosso also connect the towns. Navigazione Golfo dei Poeti (☎0187 81 84 40 or 73 29 87), in front of the IAT office at the port (in the old town; see **Practical Information**, below). To: **Manarola** (7 per day, €7); **Portovenere** (7 per day, €12); **Riomaggiore** (8 per day, €8.50); **Vernazza** (7 per day, €3).

Taxis: ☎01 87 33 56 16 58 42.

Boat Rental: Samba (☎01 87 33 96 81 22 65), across from the train station and along the beaches in Monterosso. 2-person canoes €25 per 3hr. Open daily 9am-6pm. Cash only. **Il Corsaro Rosso**(☎01 87 32 86 93 53 55), on the harbor in Riomaggiore. Kayaks and 3-person canoes €18 per hr. Snorkeling €10 per day. Snorkeling and boat tour €12. Cash only.

ORIENTATION AND PRACTICAL INFORMATION

The five villages string the coast between Levanto in the northwest and La Spezia in the southeast. They are connected by trains, roads—although cars are not allowed inside the towns—and inland and coastal footpaths that traverse the rocky shoreline. **Monterosso** is the largest and western-most town, followed from west to east by **Vernazza, Corniglia, Manarola,** and **Riomaggiore.**

Tourist Offices:

Cinque Terre National Park Office, P. Garibaldi 20, Monterosso (☎01 87 81 70 59 or 80 20 53; www.parconazionale5terre.it). Info on trails. **Cinque Terre Cards** available. Open daily 8am-8pm.

Pro Loco, V. Fegina 38 (☎/fax 01 87 81 75 06), below the Monterosso train station. Provides info on boats, hikes, and accommodations. Open daily 9am7pm.

Tourist Offices in the train stations of all 5 towns. Open daily June-Sept. 6:30am9pm. Tourist offices in Manarola, Riomaggiore, and Monterosso have **internet** access.

Tours: Navigazione 5 Terre Golfo dei Poeti (☎01 87 81 84 40; fax 73 03 36). Boat tours to **Vernazza**(€3, round-trip €5.50),**Manarola** (€7, round-trip €12), and **Riomaggiore** (€8.50, round-trip €13) from **Monterosso** (7 per day noon-6:30pm) and **Vernazza** (7 per day 10:40am-6pm). Round-trip boats also go to **Portovenere** (€20) and **Lerici** (€20). Dates and times vary seasonally.

First Aid: Doctor on call (☎01 87 338 853 0949) M-W and F-Su. **Carabinieri:** in Monterosso (☎01 87 81 75 24); in Riomaggiore (☎01 87 92 01 12).

Post Office: Main branch, V. Roma 73, Monterosso (☎01 87 81 83 94). Open M-F 8am1:15pm, Sa 8am12:30pm.**Postal Codes:** 19016 (Monterosso); 19017 (Manarola and Riomaggiore); 19018 (Corniglia and Vernazza).

> **TIP**
>
> **TREK THE TERRE.** If pressed for time, take the train (€1.40) to Monterosso or Corniglia and hike the 2 paths connecting those 2 towns. The better of the 4 trails along the Cinque Terre, the footpaths that connect Monterosso, Vernazza, and Corniglia, while strenuous, provide great vistas of the precariously positioned Cinque Terre towns.

MONTEROSSO ☎01 87

The largest and most developed of the five villages, Monterosso (Mohn-teh-ROS-so; pop.1600) lacks some of the natural wonders of the other towns, but

RIBOLLITA IN THE POT, NINE DAYS OLD

Minestrone soup is one of the cornerstones of Italian peasant cuisine. And, given that the typical minestrone spends hours on the stove, it's no wonder that Italian housewives made vast quantities at a time. Who has time to whip up small batches every day?

But while the cooks of Rome or Venice might serve the same soup day after day, the Florentines like to mix it up. The day of cooking results in a rich and brothy soup chock full of vegetables, but day two sees the leftovers layered with stale garlic bread, onions, and parmesan cheese and baked into a crunchy casserole. Day three, at long last, brings the ribollita, the true delight. Ribollita (Italian for "reboiled") involves mashing the (by now soggy) garlic bread into the underlying vegetables, and boiling the whole thing over again.

The resulting concoction is a heavenly mixture so thick you can eat it with a fork. Forget chili and stew—ribollita combines the garlicky zing (and healthy fresh vegetables) of the original minestrone with chunks of chewy bread and cheese. Guaranteed to fill you up, ribollita is also one of the most economical meals in town. Trust the Florentines to make leftovers the best part of the meal.

compensates with conveniences like multiple grocery stores, internet points, and endless strips of *gelaterie*. By day, visitors flood into town to take advantage of the free beach and shopping opportunities. By night, most retreat to other towns, leaving bustling Monterosso tranquil just in time for sunset.

ORIENTATION AND PRACTICAL INFORMATION

Descend the steps from the **train station** (where there is a **tourist office**) and turn left on **Lungomare di Fegina** through a tunnel into **Piazza Garibaldi**, the heart of town. From here, **Via Vittorio Emanuele** veers left; **Via Roma** veers right.

Currency Exchange: Cassa di Risparmio della Spezia, V. Roma 47. Open M-F 8:10am-1:10pm and 2:30-3:30pm, Su 8:1011:30am. **Banca Carige**, V. Roma 69. **ATM** outside. Open daily 8:05am-1:15pm and 2:30-3:45pm.

Laundromat: Laundry Matic, V. Molinelli 12 or the corner of V. Roma and V. Mazzini. Wash, detergent, and dry €12 per 5kg. Open daily 9am-1pm and 2-7pm. Cash only.

Pharmacy: V. Fegina 44 (☎01 87 18 18 394). Posts after-hours rotations outside. Open M-Sa 8:30am-12:30pm and 4-7:30pm, Su 9am-12:30pm and 4-7:30pm. Cash only.

Internet Access: Net, V. V. Emanuele 55 (☎01 87 81 72 88). €1 per 10min., €0.10 per min. thereafter; €10 per 2hr. Open daily 9:30am-12:30pm and 3:30-7:30pm. Cash only. **InNet**, Vcl. Martini 39, off V. V. Emanuele. €2.50 per 20min., €5 per hr. Wi-Fi available. Open daily 9am-10pm.

ACCOMMODATIONS

While most of Cinque Terre's hotels are in Monterosso, they generally fill up in early June. Inquire at the tourist office for help finding the more plentiful *affittacamere* (room rentals).

Hotel Souvenir, V. Gioberti 24 (☎/fax 01 87 81 75 95; hotel_souvenir@yahoo.com). Lively hotel popular with students. Bunk beds in comfortable rooms. The common areas and private garden are perfect for socializing. Breakfast €5. Rooms with shared bath for students €26; private rooms €44. Cash only. ❷

Alle 5 Terre, V. Molinelli 87(☎01 87 81 78 28 or 32 85 50 56 23). The friendly owners of nearby Cantina di Sciacchetrà also rent rooms here. 5 rooms with bath, TVs, and fridges; some have balconies. €25 per person. MC/V. ❷

Albergo La Pineta, V. Padre Semeria 3(☎01 87 82 90 29; hotel_lapineta@virgilio.it). Turn right from the train station, then right on V. Padre Semeria. The amiable owners keep a private beach and no-frills rooms with bath and TVs, some with sea views.

It's close enough to the *centro*, but out of earshot of nightlife noise. Breakfast included. Singles €42-52; doubles from €62. Cash only. ❹

FOOD

To avoid high prices, consider a picnic of items from the grocery store, **SuperConad Margherita**, P. Matteotti 9 (open June-Sept. M-Sa 8am1pm and 5-8pm, Su 8am-1pm; MC/V). Grab some pesto-spread focaccia and juicy local fruit, then wash it all down with a glass of light, dry *Cinque Terre bianco* or some *Sciacchetrà* dessert wine made from raisins.

- **Il Ciliegio**, Località Beo 2 (☎01 87 81 78 29). The restaurant is a 10min. drive from town; friendly management offers free shuttle service from V. Roma on request. Fantastic meals with ingredients fresh from the owner's gardens. Savor the exceptional *trofie al pesto* (pasta with pesto; €7.50) and *cozze ripiene* (stuffed mussels; €9) in the flowered garden overlooking the coastline. *Primi* €7-10.50. *Secondi* €8-15. Cover €2. Open Tu-Su 12:30-2:30pm and 7-11pm. AmEx/MC/V. ❷

- **Cantina di Sciacchetrà**, V. Roma 7 (☎01 87 81 78 28). Free tastings, delicious *antipasti*, deals on gourmet treats, and a patient English-speaking staff. *Cinque Terre bianco* €5-20 per bottle. *Sciacchetrà* €29 per bottle. Open Feb.-Dec. daily 9am-11pm. AmEx/MC/V. ❸

- **Ristorante Al Carugio**, V. San Pietro 9(☎/fax 01 87 81 73 67, in a narrow alley off V. Roma. Traditional Ligurian dishes. Share the excellent *risotto con frutti di mare* (seafood risotto; €9.50) with at least 2 people. *Primi* €7-11. *Secondi* €8-16. Open M-W and F-Su noon-2:30pm and 6-10:30pm. AmEx/MC/V. ❷

- **Focacceria Il Frantoio**, V. Gioberti 1 (☎01 87 81 83 33). Tasty *farinata* and hot focaccia stuffed with olives, onions, peppers, cheese, or herbs. Slices €1-3. Open M-W and F-Su 9am-2pm and 3:30-8pm. Cash only. ❶

- **Nuovo Eden Bar**, V. Fegina 7, above the beach. At night, grab a gelato (from €1.60) for a beachside stroll. Salad and pasta €5-7. Open daily 8am-midnight.

SIGHTS AND HIKES

Monterosso has Cinque Terre's largest **free beach**, surrounded by a cliff-cove in front of the *centro storico* to the left and down the stairs from the train station. Umbrella and chair rentals are available. About 200m to the right of the train station, **Il Gigante**, a craggy giant carved into the rocky cliff, watches over the sunbathers below. The 15th-century **Chiesa dei Cappuccini**, in the center of town, yields broad vistas of the five towns. In the chapel to the left is the 17th-century *Crucifixion* by Flemish master Anthony Van Dyck, who stayed here during his most productive years. (Open daily 9am-noon and 4-7pm. Free.)

MONTEROSSO-VERNAZZA. The hardest of the four town-linking treks, this 1hr. hike climbs steeply up a cliff-side staircase, winding past terraced vineyards and hillside cottages before the steep descent into Vernazza.

NIGHTLIFE

- **FAST,** V. Roma 13 (☎01 87 81 71 64). For a midnight snack, chow down on hot sandwiches named after American bands (from €4.50) and sip mixed drinks (€5.50) beneath hanging electric guitars and TVs broadcasting MTV. Beer €3-4, tap €2.80-8. Open in summer daily 8am-2am, in winter M-W and F-Su 8am-midnight. MC/V.

- **Il Casello,** V. Lungo Ferravia 70 (☎01 87 81 83 30 or 33 34 92 76 29. Enjoy seaside views from the patio over beer, liquor, and snacks. Mixed drinks €7-9. Open daily 11am-midnight. Cash only.

TUSCANY

▶ DAYTRIPS FROM MONTEROSSO

LEVANTO

A 2hr. hike connects Levanto and Monterosso. Trains run to Levanto from Monterosso (5min., every 30min. 4:46am-11:42pm, €1.40).

Sandy beaches and seaside promenades are the main attractions at this beach town, a busier and bigger alternative to the laid-back Cinque Terre towns, but with fewer tourists. The trek to Levanto (LE-van-toh) is more uncultivated and rugged than most of the hikes in Cinque Terre. The trail leaves Monterosso for a harsh 45min. climb to **Punta del Mesco**, a 19th-century lighthouse converted from the ruins of an Augustinian monastery. Before descending to Levanto, it wraps around cliffs and passes vineyards, orchards, and the remains of a 13th-century castle. Private and public beaches line the promenade.

Ostello Ospitalia del Mare ❷, V. San Nicolo 1, is the perfect option for an overnight stay and only a 5min. walk from the beach. The rooms are spacious and sunny. (☎01 87 80 25 62; www.ospitaliadelmare.it. Breakfast included. Internet access €5 per hr. Reception 8am-1pm, 4-8pm, and 9:30-11pm. Dorms €28; doubles with bath €30-32. MC/V.) Load up for a beach picnic at **La Focacceria Dome ❶**, V. Dante Alighieri 18, serving fresh focaccia, *farinata*, and pizza (€1-2) in heaping portions. (Open Sept.-Apr. daily 9am-9pm. Tu. Cash only.) Those staying for dinner shouldn't miss **Da Rino ❸**, V. Garibaldi 10, for a family-style Ligurian feast where the fish is always fresh. (☎01 87 32 83 89 03 50. *Primi* €6-10. *Secondi* €11-18. Cover €1.50. Open daily 7-10pm. Cash only.)

To reach the tourist office, P. Mazzini, cross the *piazza*, go down the stairs, cross a bridge, and take C. Roma. (☎01 87 80 81 25. Open M-Sa 9am-1pm and 3-6pm, Su 9am-1pm.)

VERNAZZA ☎01 87

Graced by a turquoise lagoon of multicolored motorboats surrounded by restaurant-filled *piazze* and a small but beautiful stretch of sandy beach, Vernazza (Vehr-NAT-sa; pop. 1000) is historically the wealthiest of the five Cinque Terre towns. Climb to the remains of the 11th-century Castello Doria, up a staircase on the left of P. Marconi, for great views of the other four towns.

TUNNEL VISION. Depending which train car you're in, stops in Cinque Terre stations—particularly Vernazza and Riomaggiore—are in tunnels. This may not appear to be the station stop, but it often is; ride in the center of the train and watch for your stop to be sure.

⬛▶ ORIENTATION AND PRACTICAL INFORMATION. Lined with shops and restaurants, **Via Ennio Quirino Visconti** runs from the station toward the sea and turns into **Via Roma** about halfway to the beach. **Piazza Marconi** overlooks the harbor at the end of V. Roma. There is a **tourist office** in the train station. Check email at **Internet Point,** V. Roma 32. (€0.15 per min. for the 1st 30min; €0.10 per min. thereafter. Wi-Fi available. Open daily 9am-1:30pm and 3-8pm.)

▶◖ ACCOMMODATIONS AND FOOD. Vernazza has some great hotels and private rooms. **Hotel Gianni Franzi ❸**, P. Marconi 1, has 23 rooms with antique decors, in several small rustic buildings at the top of the town. Some sport balconies with postcard views of the coast and Corniglia. The quiet private courtyard with manicured bright green grass makes an ideal relaxation spot. (☎01 87 82 10 03; www.giannifranzi.it. Singles €45, with bath €70; doubles €65/80, with balcony €100; triples with bath €120. AmEx/MC/V.) The friendly owners of **Albergo Barbara ❸**, P. Marconi 30, on the top floor, make their guests feel at home. The nine rooms are bright and some have views of the port. Attic rooms have wood-beamed ceiling and are located up multiple flights of stairs. (☎01 67 81 23 98; www. albergobarbara.it. Ring bell to enter. Doubles €50, with bath €60-65, with bath and view €100. Extra bed €10. Closed Dec.-Feb. Cash only.)

Reputedly home to the best restaurants in Cinque Terre, P. Marconi fills with hungry tourists each evening. The oldest *trattoria* in Vernazza, **Trattoria Gianni Franzi ❷**, P. Marconi 1, is famed for its pesto and friendly local charm. Dine casually in the roomy stone-walled interior or outside on the *piazza*. (☎01 87 82 10 03. Primi €5-12. Secondi €7-22. Open M-Tu and Th-Su noon-3pm and 7:30-9:30pm. AmEx/MC/V.) For a delicious splurge, visit **Gambero Rosso ❺**, P. Marconi 7. Touted by *vernazzesi*, the service is excellent and the food superb. (☎01 87 81 22 65. *Primi* €12-18. *Secondi* €16-26. Cover €3. Open Tu-Su noon-3:15pm and 7-10pm. AmEx/MC/V.) For a slice of pizza (€3), pop in to **Pizzeria Baja Saracena ❶**, P. Marconi 16, to enjoy a quick snack between rounds of hiking and sunbathing. Try the warm and tasty pesto lasagna (€9), available to go or to enjoy on terrace seating overlooking the ocean. (Open daily 10am-10:30pm. Cash only.) Fresh produce, and gourmet foods are available at **Salumi e Formaggi**, V. Visconti 19. (☎01 87 82 12 40. Open M-Sa 8am-2pm and 5:20-7:30pm, Su 8am-1:30pm. Cash only.) For groceries, visit **Coop**, V. Roma 25. (Open M and W-Su 8:15am-1pm and 5-8pm, Tu 5-8pm. AmEx/MC/V.)

🥾 **HIKING.** Geographic diversity and **unparalleled views** are the rewards along the 1hr. **Vernazza-Corniglia** hike. The trail climbs harshly from Vernazza, passing through vineyards and olive groves before curving through uncultivated landscape. Scents of rosemary, thyme, lemon, and lavender fill the summer air. At one point, the trail bends to reveal the secluded, clothing-optional **Guvano beach** hundreds of feet below, occupied largely by students and adventurous types willing to make the trek down the cliff, then get intimate. Corniglia, perched spectacularly in the distance, is in view for the duration of the hike.

FROM THE ROAD

IMMIGRATIONIZE ITALY

Walking down the street one day, I paused at a poster exclaiming "URGENT! APPEAL TO TOURISTS!" Its message was on behalf of immigrants, a demographic that has long been unwelcome in Italy. I admired that it hoped to shed some light on the less-than-picturesque realities of the country that attracts two types of foreigners: the art-hungry and the homeless and hungry.

In Tuscany, the predominantly center-left government has been working to address this problem, passing a new immigration law on June 1, 2009 to make the region more foreigner-friendly. Free access to healthcare, meals, beds, municipal cafeterias, and shelters are among the benefits, and though there is a delineated distinction between legal and illegal immigrants, this law is in stark contrast to others which try to control or prevent the migration of people from other countries.

The center-right is not going to take this laying down, however; the People of Freedom party has been collecting signatures to hold a referendum to counter the new law. And the Italian government plans to test the very constitutionality of the law, which opponents believe will make Tuscany the go-to place for illegal immigrants.

Tourists flocking to Italy may not heed the poster's cry to "Boycott it!" and hopefully, this new law will make it so that those looking for a European life won't have to either.

—Beryl Lipton

CORNIGLIA ☎01 87

Three hundred sixty-five steps and a 15min. climb from the station bring travelers to this colorful village on a seaside cliff. Without the beachside glitter of the Cinque Terra's other towns, Corniglia (cor-NEEL-ya; pop. 500) has a more peaceful ambience with considerably fewer tourists. A rocky strip of public beach beneath the tracks is a popular morning stop for local sunbathers, while more secluded beaches beckon hikers off the trail on the way to Vernazza.

◪ ORIENTATION. Via Alla Stazione begins at the top of the station steps and turns into **Via Fieschi** in the *centro*. To the right of the *centro*, down **Via Serra**, is the entrance to the trail from Vernazza. To reach the free beach beneath the station, walk down the stairs and turn left after the tunnel. Do not follow misleading signs that read "Spiaggia," as these refer to the distant **Guvana Beach**.

▟▙ ACCOMMODATIONS AND FOOD. Due to its small size and cliffside location, Corniglia is best as a daytrip. If you do plan to stay, private rooms are the way to go, as there are few hotels. See a list of available *affitacamere* in front of the stairs leading to the *centro storico* from the train station. **Ristorante Cecio ❹**, V. Serra 58, on the road from Corniglia to Vernazza, rents eight rooms above the restaurant with views of the sea and mountains, and eight rooms in the village with terraces. Seaside rooms all have bath. Request the corner room for more space and more windows. (☎01 87 81 20 43 or 33 43 50 66 37; www. cecio5terre.com. Singles €55; doubles €60; triples €80. Cash only.)

Pizzerie serve hungry hikers all over town. Follow your nose to **La Gata Flora ❶**, V. Fieschi 109, for delicious slices. Crispy *farinata* (€1.10) is also available. (☎018 7 82 12 18. Focaccia €1.20-2.10. Whole pizza €4.50-8, slice €2.60. Open Aug. daily 9:30am-4pm and 6-8:30pm, Sept.-July M and W-Su 9:30am-4pm and 6-8:30pm. Cash only.) To get to **La Posada ❸**, V. Alla Stazione 11, climb the staircase from the train station. Turn right on the road at the top; follow for about 50m. (*Primi* €6-8. *Secondi* €8-11. Cover €2. Open daily noon-3pm and 7-10:30pm. MC/V.) The cavernous **Cantina de Mananan ❸**, V. Fieschi 117, offers a cool setting in which to enjoy hearty homemade dishes like stuffed pasta, potato pasta, and spaghetti. (☎01 87 82 11 66. *Primi* €9-11. *Secondi* €12-16. Cover €1.80. Open M and W-Su 12:45-2:15pm and 7:45-9:15pm. Cash only.) Sip wine and twirl spaghetti on the terrace of **Ristorante Cecio ❸**, V. Serra 11. (☎01 87 81 20 43. *Primi* and *secondi* €8-22. Cover €2.50. Open Dec.-Oct. M-Tu and Th-Su noon-3pm and 7:30-10pm. MC/V.)

▧ HIKING. Take the stairs down to the station from V. Alla Stazione and turn left, following the path along the railroad tracks. The 1hr. **Corniglia-Manarola** trail begins just after the public beach. Though less picturesque than the hikes between the previous towns, the gentle trail to Manarola boasts an easier, flatter trek and has some sweeping, open-sea vistas. Experienced hikers can finish this portion of the trek in 30min.

MANAROLA ☎01 87

Two large swimming coves sheltered by rocky inlets attract swimmers and sunbathers to Manarola (ma-na-RO-la; pop. 900). Its laid-back pace and newly renovated hostel make this the ideal hangout for the backpacking crowd.

▣ ORIENTATION. From the train station, walk through the tunnel and emerge onto **Via Antonio Discovolo.** Turn left and cross **Piazza Dario Capellino,** after which **Via Birolli** runs to the sea, or turn right and head uphill for the hostel and stunning views.

▐▐ ACCOMMODATIONS AND FOOD. To reach the ▧**Ostello Cinque Terre ❶**, V. B. Riccobaldi 21, turn right from the train station, continue uphill 300m and turn left at the sign. Forty-eight beds, a bright dining room, a rooftop terrace with 360° of perfection, and a shelf full of board games contribute to the summer-camp atmosphere. Ask about kayaking, biking, and snorkeling equipment rental. (☎01 87 92 02 15; www.hostel5terre.com. Breakfast €4. 5min. shower and linens included. Laundry wash €4, dry €2 per 30min. Internet access €1.50 per 15min. Wheelchair-accessible. Lockout 10am-5pm. Curfew in summer 1am; in winter midnight. Reserve at least 1 week ahead. Dorms €20-23; double with bath €55-65; quad with bath €88-100. Closed Nov. 9-Feb. 28. Advanced payment of 1st night required. AmEx/MC/V.) The cheery **Bed and Breakfast La Torretta ❺**, Vico Volto 20, is filled with flowers. Canopied beds are spacious and rooms have balconies, TVs, and A/C in this fully staffed villa available for rent for a paltry €2000 per night. The terrace yields some of the town's best sea views. (☎01 87 92 03 27; www.torrettas.com. Breakfast included. Singles €100; doubles €120; quads €190. AmEx/MC/V.) The restaurant **Il Porticciolo ❷**, V. Renato Birolli 92, rents rooms with bath, TVs, and balconies. (☎/fax 01 87 92 00 83; www.ilporticciolo5terre.com. Breakfast €5. Singles €30; doubles €50-60. AmEx/MC/V.) **Da Paulin ❸**, V. Discovolo 126, offers rooms with quilted comforters, bath, hair dryers, balconies, Wi-Fi, and TV. (☎39 01 87 92 07 06; www.dapaulin.it. Doubles €60-75.)

At **Trattoria da Billy ❷**, V. Rollandi 122, get away from the town center and eat lunch with the locals. (☎01 87 92 068. *Primi* €6-8. *Secondi* €7-14. Open M-W and F-Su 12:30-2:30pm and 7-10:30pm. MC/V.) **Marina Piccola ❷**, V. lo Scalo 16, just off V. Renato Birolli, is a little place with big meals. Savor *risotto di frutta di mare* (with large pieces of shrimp on a plate lined with mussels) on the edge of a rocky cove. (☎01 87 92 09 23. *Primi* €8-16. *Secondi* €9-17. Open Jan.-July and Sept.-Dec. M and W-Su noon-2:30pm and 7pm-midnight. AmEx/MC/V.) **Trattoria Il Porticciolo ❷**,V. Renato Birolli 92, serves hearty meals in a casual ambience at a good value, such as excellent *gnocchi al pesto* (€6) and superb *torta di frutta e noci* (fruit and nut cake) for €4.50. (☎01 87 92 00 83. *Primi* €5-9. *Secondi* €7-16. Open M-Tu and Th-Su 7am-3:30pm and 5-11pm. AmEx/MC/V.)

▣ NIGHTLIFE. One of the quieter towns of the five, a night in Manarola is more likely to be a low-key evening than a bass-pumping rager, though a few times each summer, Manarola hosts disco parties in a *piazza*, advertised on posters around town with themes like "Havana Nights." **Bar Enrica,** on V. Renato Birolli in Punta Bonfiglio, serves gelato by day and mixed drinks by night. (☎01 87 92 02 77. *Bruschette* €3-5. Hot *panini* €4-4.50. Beer €2.50-5. Mixed drinks €5. Open daily 8:3011am and 8-11pm. Cash only.)

▣ HIKING. On the **Manarola-Riomaggiore** hike, **Via dell'Amore,** the most famous stretch of Cinque Terre hikes (20min.), passes through a stone tunnel of love decorated by romantic graffiti scenes and colorful mosaics. With elevators at its beginning and end, the slate-paved walk is almost wheelchair-accessible except for some steps in the middle, and is a good way to ease into the hikes and views the park provides for all its visitors.

TUSCANY

RIOMAGGIORE   ☎01 87

A castle crowns a cliff above the bright houses that cascade down the valley of Riomaggiore (REE-yo-ma-JO-reh; pop. 1736). Here, fishermen varnishing boat hulls are as common as sunbathers rubbing in lotion. There are rooms for rent around the harbor; Riomaggiore is the best bet to find last-minute lodging, and as a result, houses a busy population of young travelers and lively nightlife.

⚓ 🏛 ORIENTATION AND PRACTICAL INFORMATION. Turn right from the back of the **train station** and walk through a tunnel to the *centro*. Do not follow the train tracks, as that tunnel is not for pedestrians. The main street, **Via Cristoforo Colombo,** runs up the hill to the left. A **Pro Loco tourist office** in the train station provides info on trails, hotels, and excursions. (☎01 87 92 06 33. Open M-F 6:30am-8pm, Sa-Su 7am-9pm.) The **National Park Office** next to the station offers **Internet** access for €0.08 per min. and currency exchange. (☎01 87 76 05 15. Open daily 8am9:30pm.) You can also find currency exchange at **Banca Carige,** V. C. Colombo 215. (Open M-F8:20am-1:20pm and 2:30-4pm. AmEx/MC/V.) A 24hr. **ATM** can be found at the foot of V. C. Colombo. **Farmacia del Mare,** V. C. Colombo 182, posts a list of late-night pharmacies. (☎01 87 92 01 60. Open M-Sa 9am-noon and 4-8pm, Su 9am-noon. AmEx/MC/V.) **Wash and Dry Lavarapido** is at V. C. Colombo 109. (Wash €3.50 per 30min. Detergent €1. Open daily 8am-8pm. Cash only.) A **post office** is at V. Pecunia 7, up the stairs from V. C. Colombo and to the left. (☎01 87 80 31 60. Open M-F 8am-1pm, Sa 8am-noon.)

🛏 ACCOMMODATIONS. The clean and welcoming ▨**Mar-Mar ❷**, V. Malborghetto 4, rents dorms and rooms with bath, some with TVs and balconies. Apartments for two to six people are also available, and the community terrace lined with plastic furniture overlooks the harbor. (☎/fax 01 87 92 09 32; www.5terre-marmar.com. Dorms from Nov. to Easter €15-€20; doubles €60-80; apartments €65-120. Cash only.) **Hotel Ca Dei Duxi ❹**, V. C. Colombo 36, is pleasant and well situated, offering wood furnishings, tiled floors, and 60s-style floral bedspreads. Six rooms all have bath, TVs, A/C, and fridges; some have terraces. (☎01 87 92 00 36; www.duxi.it. Breakfast included. Doubles €60-90; triples €90-130. *Let's Go* discount. AmEx/MC/V.) At **5Terre Affitti ❹**, V. C. Colombo 97, Papa Bernardo rents rooms located mostly on the harbor with bath and satellite TV; some have balconies. (☎01 87 92 03 31; www.immobiliare5terre.com. Doubles €50-60; studios with kitchen and views for 2 or 3 people €65-75; quad with kitchen and terrace €90-120. Cash only.) **La Dolce Vita ❷**, V. C. Colombo 120, has a young, friendly staff that attract similar clientele. Rents doubles with bath and minibar, and four-person apartments. (☎01 87 76 00 44. Reception open 9:30am-7:30pm. Doubles €55-70; triples €80; quads €95-125. Cash only.)

🍴 FOOD. At popular **Trattoria La Lanterna ❸**, V. San Giacomo 46, off V. C. Colombo, enjoy delicious fresh fish or pasta and watch the fishing boats roll by. (☎01 87 92 01 20. Primi €7-9. Secondi €7-22. MC/V.) On a cliff above town, eat fried fish off chinaware at the glass-enclosed **Ripa del Sole ❸**, V. de Gasperi 282. The *gnocchi* with scampi and white truffles (€11.50) is excellent. (☎01 87 92 01 43. Primi €10-13. Secondi €12-24. Open Tu-Su noon2pm and 6:30-9:30pm. AmEx/MC/V.) For groceries, stop by one of the many *alimentari* lining V. C. Colombo, enticing backpackers with fresh fruit displays. Try **Alimentari della Franca,** V. C. Colombo 253. (☎01 87 92 09 29. Open daily 7:45am-1pm and 3-8pm. MC/V.)

⚠️📷 OUTDOOR ACTIVITIES AND NIGHTLIFE. Coopsub Cinqueterre Diving Center, on V. San Giacomo, conducts supervised dives off the coast, where dolphins frolic in June and September. Boat trips include stops to the natural waterfalls of nearby Caneto Beach. (☎01 87 92 00 11; www.5terrediving.com. Single kayak €7 per hr.; double kayak €12 per hr. Open daily from Easter to Sept. 8:30am-6pm. Cash only.) At night, groups of young tourists hang at the harbor. During the warmer months, restaurants with outdoor seating fill until late, and live performers serenade guests. The bar and outdoor patio at **Bar Centrale,** V. C. Colombo 144, fill up with young international backpackers. The energetic bartender serves a cold brew and turns up swingin' Motown. (☎01 87 92 02 08. Beer €3-5.50. Mixed drinks €5.50-7. Open daily 7:30am-1am. Cash only.) **A Pie de Ma, Bar and Vini,** with sweeping views of turquoise waters below on V. dell'Amore, is a hot spot to grab pre-dinner drinks. (☎01 87 92 10 37. Focaccia €3.50. Mixed drinks €5. Some F and Sa nights live music. Open daily 10am-midnight. Cash only.)

APPENDIX

CLIMATE

Geographically, Italy lies in a temperate zone and has a predominantly Mediterranean climate. Yet, due to the peninsula's length, temperatures and weather often vary drastically in different parts of the country, based on proximity to the coast or the mountains. Summers in the south near the coast are dry and hot, as the sea and beaches are baked by the warm *sicorro* wind blowing in from North Africa. Moving north and inland, summer temperatures remain hot, but in the absence of a sea breeze, excessive humidity gets added to the mix. Things cool down countrywide in the winter, but to varying degrees, ranging from mild temperatures in the south to freezing fog, frost, and snow in the northern valleys. As a general rule, average temperatures are lower at higher altitudes year-round, especially in the Italian Alps, and wet weather hits most areas of the country from April to June.

AVG. TEMP. (LOW/HIGH), PRECIP.	JANUARY			APRIL			JULY			OCTOBER		
	°C	°F	mm	°C	°F	mm	°C	°F	mm	°C	°F	mm
Brindisi	6/12	43/54	77	11/18	52/64	47	21/29	70/84	14	15/22	59/72	79
Cagliari	7/14	45/57	50	11/19	52/66	31	21/30	70/86	1	15/23	59/73	54
Florence	1/10	34/50	73	8/19	46/66	78	17/31	63/88	40	10/21	50/70	88
Milan	0/5	32/41	44	10/18	50/64	94	20/29	68/84	64	11/17	52/63	125
Naples	4/12	39/54	116	9/18	48/64	62	18/29	64/84	19	12/22	54/72	107
Palermo	8/16	46/61	71	11/20	52/68	49	21/30	70/86	2	16/25	61/77	77
Rome	5/11	41/52	71	10/18	50/66	51	20/30	68/86	15	13/22	55/72	99
Venice	1/6	34/43	37	10/17	50/63	78	19/27	66/81	52	11/19	52/66	77

To convert from degrees Fahrenheit to degrees Celsius, subtract 32 and multiply by 5/9. To convert from Celsius to Fahrenheit, multiply by 9/5 and add 32.

CELSIUS	-5	0	5	10	15	20	25	30	35	40
FAHRENHEIT	23	32	41	50	59	68	77	86	95	104

MEASUREMENTS

Like the rest of the rational world, Italy uses the metric system. The basic unit of length is the meter (m), which is divided into 100 centimeters (cm) or 1000 millimeters (mm). One thousand meters make up one kilometer (km). Fluids are measured in liters (L), each divided into 1000 milliliters (mL). A liter of pure water weighs one kilogram (kg), 1000 grams (g). One metric ton is 1000kg.

MEASUREMENT CONVERSIONS	
1 inch (in.) = 25.4mm	1 millimeter (mm) = 0.039 in.
1 foot (ft.) = 0.305m	1 meter (m) = 3.28 ft.
1 yard (yd.) = 0.914m	1 meter (m) = 1.094 yd.
1 mile (mi.) = 1.609km	1 kilometer (km) = 0.621 mi.

MEASUREMENT CONVERSIONS	
1 ounce (oz.) = 28.35g	1 gram (g) = 0.035 oz.
1 pound (lb.) = 0.454kg	1 kilogram (kg) = 2.205 lb.
1 fluid ounce (fl. oz.) = 29.57mL	1 milliliter (mL) = 0.034 fl. oz.
1 gallon (gal.) = 3.785L	1 liter (L) = 0.264 gal.

LANGUAGE

Italian is the official language of Italy, and if you plan to get anywhere in the country—physically or otherwise—you should brush up on the language before your trip. While the tourism-driven economy of urban areas has instilled locals with some English familiarity, ranging from knowledge of a few words to complete fluency, the likelihood of meeting an English-speaking Italian drops drastically the farther you travel from heavily touristed areas. In the south, on the islands, and in small towns to the north, tourists with no knowledge of Italian may have to rely entirely on hand gestures, a tactic that is naturally vulnerable to awkward misunderstandings. Be aware that spoken dialects vary greatly between different regions. To get in good with the locals wherever you may be, memorize a few Italian phrases to break the ice, and make sure to end any conversation with a polite "*grazie*" (GRAHT-see-yeh).

PRONUNCIATION

VOWELS

There are seven vowel sounds in standard Italian. **A, i,** and **u** each have one pronunciation. **E** and **o** each have two slightly different pronunciations, one open and one closed, depending on the vowel's placement in the word, the stress, and the regional accent. Below are approximate pronunciations.

VOWEL	PRONUNCIATION
a	"a" as in "father" *(casa)*
e (closed)	"ay" as in "gray" *(sera)*
e (open)	"eh" as in "wet" *(sette)*
i	"ee" as in "cheese" *(vino)*
o (closed)	"o" as in "bone" *(sono)*
o (open)	"aw" as in "ought" *(bocca)*
u	"oo" as in "moon" *(gusto)*

CONSONANTS

C and G: Before a, o, or u, **c** and **g** are hard, as in *candy* and *goose* or as in the Italian *colore* (koh-LOHR-eh; color) and *gatto* (GAHT-toh; cat). Italians soften c and g into **ch** and **j** sounds, respectively, when followed by i or e, as in *cheese* and *jeep* or the Italian *cibo* (CHEE-boh; food) and *gelato* (jeh-LAH-toh; ice cream).

Ch and Gh: H returns **c** and **g** to their "hard" sounds in front of i or e (see above): *chianti* (ky-AHN-tee), the Tuscan wine, and *spaghetti* (spah-GEHT-tee), the pasta.

Gn and Gli: Pronounce **gn** like the **ni** in *osnion*, or as in the Italian *bagno* (BAHN-yoh; bath). **Gli** is pronounced like the **lli** in *million*, or as in the Italian *sbagliato* (zbal-YAH-toh; wrong).

Sc and Sch: When followed by **a, o,** or **u**, sc is pronounced as **sk**. *Scusi* (excuse me) yields "SKOO-zee." When followed by an **e** or **i**, sc is pronounced **sh** as in *sciopero*

(SHOH-pair-oh; strike). The addition of the letter **h** returns **c** to its hard sound (sk) before **i** or **e**, as in *pesche* (PEHS-keh; peaches).

Double consonants: When you see a double consonant, stress the preceding vowel; failure to do so can lead to confusion. For example, *penne all'arrabbiata* is "short pasta in a spicy red sauce," whereas *pene all'arrabbiata* means "penis in a spicy red sauce."

STRESS

In Italian, the stress generally falls on the penultimate, or next-to-last, syllable. An accent usually indicates when it falls on a different syllable, such as with the word *città* (cheet-TAH; city).

GRAMMAR

GENDER AND PLURALS

Italian nouns fall into two genders, masculine and feminine. The singular masculine ending is usually **o**, as in *duomo*, and the feminine is usually **a**, as in *donna*. Words ending in an **o** in the singular usually end with an **i** in the plural: *conto* (KOHN-toh; bill) becomes *conti* (KOHN-tee). Words ending in an **a** in the singular end with an **e** in the plural: *mela* (MEH-lah; apple) becomes *mele* (MEH-leh). All words ending with **e** take an **i** in the plural: *cane* (KAH-neh; dog) becomes *cani* (KAH-nee). Words with a final accent, like *cittá*, and words that end in consonants, like *bar*, do not change in the plural. Adjectives, which come after the word they modify, agree with their noun in gender and number.

ARTICLES

In Italian, the gender and number of a noun determine the article that precedes it. **Definite articles** are **il, lo, l', la, i, gli,** and **le.** *Il* is used for most masculine singular nouns (*il gatto;* the cat), while those beginning with a vowel, z, or *s impura* (s plus any consonant) are preceded by the article *lo* (*lo zio;* the uncle; *lo stivale;* the boot). The article *la* is used with feminine singular nouns beginning with a consonant: *la capra* (the goat). For all singular nouns beginning with a vowel, *l'* is the appropriate article: *l'arte* (the art).

In the plural, the article *i* is used for most masculine plural nouns (*i libri;* the books), while *gli* is used with masculine nouns beginning with a vowel, z, or *s impura* (*gli stivali,* the boots; *gli aerei,* the airplanes). *Le* precedes all feminine nouns (*le scarpe;* the shoes).

Indefinite articles are **un, uno, una,** and **un'.** *Un* and *uno* behave like *il* and *lo,* respectively, except that *un* can precede a masculine noun beginning with a vowel: *un gatto* (a cat), *un uomo* (a man), *uno stivale* (a boot). For feminine nouns, *un'* is used before vowels and *una* is used everywhere else: *un'edicola* (a newsstand), *una ragazza* (a girl).

PHRASEBOOK

NUMBERS			
1	uno	8	otto
2	due	9	nove
3	tré	10	dieci
4	quattro	11	undici
5	cinque	12	dodici
6	sei	13	tredici
7	sette	14	quattordici

NUMBERS			
15	quindici	40	quaranta
16	sedici	50	cinquanta
17	diciassette	60	sessanta
18	diciotto	70	settanta
19	dicianove	80	ottanta
20	venti	90	novanta
30	trenta	100	cento

MONTHS			
January	gennaio	July	luglio
February	febbraio	August	agosto
March	marzo	September	settembre
April	aprile	October	ottobre
May	maggio	November	novembre
June	giugno	December	dicembre

DAYS OF THE WEEK	
Monday	lunedí
Tuesday	martedí
Wednesday	mercoledí
Thursday	giovedí
Friday	venerdí
Saturday	sabato
Sunday	domenica

*Note: In Italian, days of the week and months are not capitalized unless they come at the beginning of a sentence. *Domenica* (Sunday) is the only day of the week that is of the feminine gender.

GENERAL		
ENGLISH	**ITALIAN**	**PRONUNCIATION**
Hi/Bye (informal)	Ciao	chow
Good day/Hello	Buongiorno	bwohn-JOHR-noh
Good evening	Buonasera	bwoh-nah-SEH-rah
Good night	Buonanotte	bwoh-nah-NOHT-teh
Goodbye	Arrivederci/Arrivederla (formal)	ah-ree-veh-DEHR-chee/ah-ree-veh-DEHR-lah
Please	Per favore/Per piacere	pehr fah-VOH-reh/pehr pyah-CHEH-reh
Thank you	Grazie (formal/polite)	GRAHT-see-yeh
How are you?	Come stai/Come sta (formal)?	COH-meh STA-ee/stah
I am well	Sto bene	stoh BEH-neh
You're welcome/May I help you?/ Please	Prego	PREH-goh
Excuse me	Scusi (formal)/Scusa (informal)	SKOO-zee/-zah
I'm sorry	Mi dispiace	mee dees-PYAH-cheh
My name is	Mi chiamo	mee kee-YAH-moh
I'm on vacation	Sono qui in vacanza	SOH-noh qwee een vah-CAHN-zah
I'm American/British/Irish/Australian/New Zealander	Sono americano(a)/britannico(a)/irlandese/australiano(a)/neozelandese	SOH-noh ah-meh-ree-CAH-noh(nah)/bree-TAH-nee-coh(cah)/eer-lahn-DEH-seh/ah-oo-strah-LYAH-noh(nah)/neh-oh-zeh-lahn-DEH-seh
I live in	Abito a	AH-bee-toh ah
What's your name?	Come ti chiami? Come si chiama Lei (formal)?	COH-meh tee kee-YAH-mee/COH-meh see kee-YAH-mah lay
Yes/No/Maybe	Sì/No/Forse	see/no/FOHR-seh
I don't know	Non lo so	nohn loh soh
Could you repeat that?	Potrebbe ripetere?	poh-TREHB-beh ree-PEH-teh-reh

APPENDIX

GENERAL		
What does this mean?	Cosa vuol dire questo?	COH-za vwohl DEE-reh KWEH-stoh
I understand	Ho capito	oh kah-PEE-toh
I don't understand	Non capisco	nohn kah-PEES-koh
Do you speak English?	Parla inglese?	PAR-lah een-GLEH-zeh
Could you help me?	Potrebbe aiutarmi?	poh-TREHB-beh ah-yoo-TAHR-mee
How do you say?	Come si dice?	KOH-meh see DEE-cheh
What do you call this in Italian?	Come si chiama questo in italiano?	KOH-meh see kee-YAH-mah KWEH-stoh een ee-tahl-YAH-no
this/that	questo/quello	KWEH-sto/KWEHL-loh
more/less	più/meno	pyoo/MEH-noh
At what time?	A che ora?	ah keh OHR-ah
What time is it?	Che ore sono?	keh OHR-eh SOH-noh
What time does it open/close?	A che ora apre/chiude?	ah keh OHR-eh AH-preh/kee-OOH-deh
It's noon/midnight.	È mezzogiorno/mezzanotte	eh MEHD-zoh-DJOHR-noh/MEHD-zah-NOT-eh
now	adesso/ora	ah-DEHS-so/OH-rah
Let's go now.	andiamo adesso	ahn-dee-AH-moh ah-DEHS-so
tomorrow	domani	doh-MAH-nee
today	oggi	OHJ-jee
yesterday	ieri	ee-YEH-ree
right away	subito	SU-bee-toh
soon	fra poco/presto	frah POH-koh/PREHS-toh
after	dopo	DOH-poh
before	prima	PREE-mah
late/later	tardi/più tardi	TAHR-dee/pyoo TAHR-dee
early	presto	PREHS-toh
late (after scheduled arrival time)	in ritardo	een ree-TAHR-doh
daily	quotidiano	kwoh-tee-DYAH-no
weekly	settimanale	seht-tee-mah-NAH-leh
monthly	mensile	mehn-SEE-leh
vacation	le ferie	leh FEH-ree-eh

DIRECTIONS AND TRANSPORTATION		
ENGLISH	**ITALIAN**	**PRONUNCIATION**
there	lì/là	lee/lah
the street address	l'indirizzo	leen-dee-REET-soh
the telephone	il telefono	eel teh-LEH-foh-noh
street	strada, via, viale, vico, vicolo, corso	STRAH-dah, VEE-ah, vee-AH-le, VEE-koh, VEE-koh-loh, KOHR-soh
speed limit	limite di velocità	LEEH-mee-teh dee veh-loh-chee-TAH
to slow down	rallentare	rah-lehn-TAH-reh
one-way street	senso unico	SEHN-soh OOH-nee-coh
large, open square	piazzale	pee-yah-TZAH-leh
stairway	scalinata	scah-lee-NAH-tah
beach	spiaggia	spee-YAH-geeah
river	fiume	fee-YOO-meh
toilet, WC	gabinetto	gah-bee-NEHT-toh
What time does ... leave?	A che ora parte ... ?	ah keh OHR-ah PAHR-teh
From where does ... leave?	Da dove parte ... ?	dah DOH-veh PAHR-teh
the (city) bus	l'autobus	LAOW-toh-boos
the (intercity) bus	il pullman	eel POOL-mahn
the ferry	il traghetto	eel tra-GHEHT-toh
the hydrofoil	l'aliscafo	LA-lee-scah-foh
the plane	l'aereo	lah-EHR-reh-oh
the train	il treno	eel TREH-noh

| the ticket office | la biglietteria | lah beel-yeht-teh-REE-ah |
| How much does it cost? | Quanto costa? | KWAN-toh CO-stah |

DIRECTIONS AND TRANSPORTATION		
I would like to buy ...	Vorrei comprare ...	voh-RAY com-PRAH-reh
... a ticket	... un biglietto	... oon beel-YEHT-toh
... a pass (bus, etc.)	... una tessera	... OO-nah TEHS-seh-rah
one-way	solo andata	SO-lo ahn-DAH-tah
round-trip	andata e ritorno	ahn-DAH-tah eh ree-TOHR-noh
reduced price	ridotto	ree-DOHT-toh
student discount	lo sconto studentesco	loh SKOHN-toh stoo-dehn-TEHS-koh
the track/train platform	il binario	eel bee-NAH-ree-oh
the flight	il volo	eel VOH-loh
the reservation	la prenotazione	la preh-no-taht-see-YOH-neh
the entrance/exit	l'ingresso/l'uscita	leen-GREH-so/loo-SHEE-tah
I need to get off here	Devo scendere qui	DEH-vo SHEN-dehr-eh kwee

EMERGENCY		
I lost my passport/wallet	Ho perso il passaporto/portafoglio	oh PEHR-soh eel pahs-sah-POHR-toh/por-ta-FOH-lee-oh
I've been robbed	Sono stato derubato/a	SOH-noh STAH-toh deh-roo-BAH-toh/tah
Wait!	Aspetta!	ahs-PEHT-tah
Stop!	Ferma!	FEHR-mah
Help!	Aiuto!	ah-YOO-toh
Leave me alone!	Lasciami stare!/Mollami!	LAH-shah-mee STAH-reh/MOH-lah-MEE
Don't touch me!	Non mi toccare!	NOHN mee tohk-KAH-reh
I'm calling the police!	Telefono alla polizia!	tehl-LEH-foh-noh ah-lah poh-leet-SEE-ah
military police	carabinieri	CAH-rah-been-YEH-ree
Go away, moron!	Vattene, cretino!	VAH-teh-neh creh-TEE-noh

MEDICAL		
I have... allergies	Ho... delle allergie	OH ... DEHL-leh ahl-lair-JEE-eh
... a cold	... un raffreddore	oon rahf-freh-DOH-reh
... a cough	... una tosse	OO-nah TOHS-seh
... the flu	... l'influenza	linn-floo-ENT-sah
... a fever	... una febbre	OO-nah FEHB-breh
... a headache	... mal di testa	mahl dee TEHS-tah
My foot/arm hurts	Mi fa male il piede/braccio	mee fah MAH-le eel PYEH-deh/BRAH-cho
I'm on the Pill	Prendo la pillola	PREHN-doh lah PEE-loh-lah

RESTAURANTS		
food	il cibo	eel CHEE-boh
wine bar	l'enoteca	len-oh-TEK-ah
breakfast	la colazione	lah coh-laht-see-YO-neh
lunch	il pranzo	eel PRAHN-zoh
dinner	la cena	lah CHEH-nah
coffee	il caffè	eel kah-FEH
appetizer	l'antipasto	lahn-tee-PAH-stoh
first course	il primo	eel PREE-moh
second course	il secondo	eel seh-COHN-doh
side dish	il contorno	eel cohn-TOHR-noh
dessert	il dolce	eel DOHL-cheh
bottle	la bottiglia	lah boh-TEEL-yah
waiter/waitress	il/la cameriere/a	eel/lah kah-meh-ree-EH-reh/rah
the bill	il conto	eel COHN-toh
cover charge	il coperto	eel koh-PEHR-toh

RESTAURANTS		
tip	la mancia	lah MAHN-chyah

HOTEL AND HOSTEL RESERVATIONS		
hotel/hostel	albergo/ostello	al-BEHR-goh/os-TEHL-loh
I have a reservation	Ho una prenotazione	oh oo-nah preh-no-taht-see-YOH-neh
Could I reserve a single room/ double room (for the 2nd of August)?	Potrei prenotare una camera sin-gola/doppia (per il due agosto)?	poh-TREY preh-noh-TAH-reh oo-nah CAH-meh-rah SEEN-goh-lah/ DOH-pyah (pehr eel DOO-eh ah-GOH-stoh)
Is there a bed available tonight?	C'è un posto libero stasera?	cheh oon POHS-toh LEE-ber-oh sta-SAIR-ah
with bath/shower	con bagno/doccia	kohn BAHN-yo/DOH-cha
Is there a cheaper room without a bath/shower?	C'è una stanza più economica senza bagno/doccia?	cheh oo-nah STAN-zah pyoo eko-NOM-ika sen-zah BAHN-yo/ DOH-cha
open/closed	aperto/chiuso	ah-PEHR-toh/KYOO-zoh
sheets/linens	i lenzuoli	ee lehn-SUO-lee
the blanket	la coperta	lah koh-PEHR-tah
the bed	il letto	eel LEHT-toh
Is there heating?	C'è riscaldamento?	cheh ree-skahl-dah-MEHN-toh
Is there air conditioning?	C'è aria condizionata?	che AH-ree-ah con-deet-syon-AH-tah
How much is the room?	Quanto costa la camera?	KWAHN-toh KOHS-ta lah KAM-eh-rah
Is breakfast included?	È compresa la prima colazione?	eh com-PREH-sah la PREEH-mah coh-laht-see-YO-neh
I will arrive (at 2:30pm)	Arriverò (alle due e mezzo)	ah-ree-veh-ROH (ah-leh DOO-eh MED-zoh)
You'll have to send a deposit/ check	Bisogna mandare un anticipo/un assegno	bee-ZOHN-yah mahn-DAH-reh oon ahn-TEE-chee-poh/oon ahs-SEHN-yoh
What is that funny smell?	Che cos'è quest'odore strano?	keh kohz-EH kwest-oh-DOHR-eh STRAH-noh

AMORE		
I have a boyfriend/girlfriend	Ho un ragazzo/una ragazza	Oh oon rah-GAHT-soh/oo-nah rah-GAHT-sah
Let's get a room	Prendiamo una camera	prehn-DYAH-moh oo-nah CAH-meh-rah
Voluptuous!	Volutuoso/a!	VOL-oot-oo-OH-zhoh/zhah
To be in love with	Essere innamorato/a di	Eh-seh-reh een-am-mo-RAH-to/ ta dee
Just a kiss	Solo un bacio	SOH-loh oon BAH-chyoh
Are you single?	Sei nubile?	NOO-bee-leh
You're cute	Sei carino/a (bello/a)	SEY cah-REEN-oh/ah (BEHL-loh/ lah)
I love you, I swear	Ti amo, te lo giuro	tee AH-moh, teh loh DJOO-roh
I'm married	Sono sposato/a	SOH-noh spo-ZA-to/ta
I only have safe sex	Pratico solo sesso sicuro	PRAH-tee-coh sohl-oh SEHS-so see-COO-roh
Leave her alone, she's mine	Lasciala stare, è mia	LAH-shyah-lah STAH-reh, eh mee-ah
Leave right now!	Vai via subito!	vah-ee VEE-ah SOO-beet-oh
I'll never forget you	Non ti dimenticherò mai	nohn tee dee-men-tee-ker-OH mah-ee
The profound mystery of what you just said sets my soul on fire	Il profondo mistero di ciò che stai dicendo mi infuoca il cuore	eel pro-FOHN-doh mee-STEH-roh dee CHOE keh sty dee-CEN-doh mee een-FWOH-cah eel ku-WOR-eh

AMORE		
Not if you're the last man on earth	Neanche se lei fossi l'unico uomo sulla terra	neh-AHN-keh seh lay FOH-see LOO-nee-koh WOH-moh soo-LAH TEH-rah

AT THE BAR		
May I buy you a drink?	Posso offrirle qualcosa da bere?	POHS-soh ohf-FREER-leh kwahl-COHzah dah BEH-reh
a beer	una birra	oo-nah BEER-rah
glass of wine	un bicchiere di vino	bee-KYEH-reh dee VEE-noh
liter of wine	un litro di vino	LEE-troh dee VEE-noh
I'm drunk	Sono ubriaco/a	SOH-noh oo-BRYAH-coh/cah
Let's go!	Andiamo!	ahn-dee-AH-moh
I don't drink	Non bevo	nohn BEH-voh
Cheers!	Cin cin!	cheen cheen
Do you have a light?	Mi fai accendere?	mee fah-ee ah-CHEN-deh-reh
No thank you, I don't smoke	No grazie, non fumo	noh GRAH-zyeh, nohn FOO-moh
I was here first!	C'ero io prima!	CHEH-roh EE-oh PREE-mah

MENU READER

PRIMI (FIRST COURSE)	
pasta aglio e olio	in garlic and olive oil
pasta all'amatriciana	in a tangy tomato sauce with onions and bacon
pasta all'arabbiata	in a spicy tomato sauce
pasta alla bolognese	in a meat sauce
pasta alla boscaiola	egg pasta, served in a mushroom sauce with peas and cream
pasta alla carbonara	in a creamy sauce with egg, cured bacon, and cheese
pasta alla pizzaiola	tomato-based sauce with olive oil and red peppers
pasta alla puttanesca	in a tomato sauce with olives, capers, and anchovies
gnocchi	potato dumplings
ravioli	square-shaped and often stuffed with cheese or sometimes meat
tagliatelle	thin and flat, these are the northern version of fettuccini
pappardelle	wider and flatter than tagliatelle
polenta	deep-fried cornmeal
risotto	creamy rice dish, comes in nearly as many flavors as pasta sauce

PIZZA	
alla capricciosa	with ham, egg, artichoke, and more
con rucola	with arugula (rocket for Brits)
marinara	with red sauce and no cheese
margherita	plain ol' tomato, mozzarella, and basil
pancetta/speck	bacon
pepperoni	bell pepper; be careful not to confuse the Italian bell pepper with the American pepperoni meat, which doesn't exist in Italy!
polpette	meatballs
quattro formaggi	four cheeses
quattro stagioni	four seasons; a different topping for each quarter of the pizza, usually mushrooms, prosciutto crudo, artichoke, and tomato
salsiccia	sausage

SECONDI (SECOND COURSES)	
agnello	lamb
animelle alla griglia	grilled sweetbreads
asino	donkey (served in Sicily and Sardinia)
bistecca	steak
cavallo (sfilacci)	horse (served in Sicily and Sardinia)
cinghiale	wild boar

SECONDI (SECOND COURSES)

coniglio	rabbit
cotoletta	breaded veal cutlet with cheese
cozze	mussels
fégato	liver
gamberetti/gamberi	shrimps/prawns
granchi	crab
maiale	pork
manzo	beef
merluzzo/baccalà	cod/dried salted cod
osso buco	braised veal shank
ostriche	oysters
pesce spada	swordfish
pollo	chicken
polpo	octopus
prosciutto	smoked ham, available cured or cooked
salsiccia	sausage
saltimbocca alla romana	slices of veal and ham cooked together and topped with cheese
sarde	sardines
scaloppina	cutlet
seppia	cuttlefish, usually served grilled in its own ink
sogliola	sole
speck	smoked raw ham, lean but surrounded by a layer of fat
tonno	tuna
trippa	tripe (chopped, sautéed cow intestines, usually in a tomato sauce)
trota	trout
vitello	veal
vongole	clams

CONTORNI (SIDE DISHES)

carciofo/carciofini	artichoke/artichoke hearts
carote	carrots
cavolfiori	cauliflower
cavolo	cabbage
cetriolo	cucumber
cipolla	onion
fagioli	beans (usually white)
fagiolini	green beans
finocchio	fennel
funghi	mushrooms
insalata caprese	tomatoes with mozzarella cheese and basil, drizzled with olive oil
insalata mista	mixed salad with lettuce, cucumbers, and tomatoes
lattuga	lettuce
lenticchie	lentils
melanzana	eggplant
patate	potatoes
piselli	peas
pomodori	tomatoes
spinaci	spinach
tartufi	truffles

ANTIPASTI (APPETIZERS)

bresaola	thinly sliced dried beef, served with olive oil, lemon, and *parmigiano*
bruschetta	crisp slices of garlic-rubbed baked bread, often with raw tomatoes
caponata	mixed eggplant, olives, tomatoes, and anchovies
carpaccio	extremely thin slices of lean, raw beef

ANTIPASTI (APPETIZERS)	
crostini	small pieces of toasted bread usually served with chicken liver or mozzarella and anchovies, though other toppings are used
fiori di zucca	zucchini flowers filled with cheese, battered, and lightly fried
insalata di mare/riso	seafood/rice salad
insalata russa	salad of diced vegetables in mayonnaise
melanzane alla parmigiana	eggplant with tomato and parmesan cheese

FRUTTA (FRUIT)	
arancia	orange
ciliegia	cherry
fragola	strawberry
lampone	raspberry
mela	apple
pesca	peach
prugna	plum
uva	grape

DOLCI (DESSERTS)	
gelato	Italian-style ice cream
granita	ice-based fruit or coffee slushee
macedonia	fruit salad
panna cotta	flan
pasta	pastry
sfogliatelle	sugar-coated layers of flaky pastry filled with ricotta
tiramisù	cake-like dessert drenched in *espresso*, layered with *mascarpone*

BIBITE (DRINKS)	
acqua con gas/frizzante	soda water
acqua minerale	mineral water
aranciata	orange soda
bicchiere	glass
birra	beer
caffè	coffee
caraffa	carafe
cioccolata calda	hot chocolate
ghiaccio	ice
latte	milk
limonata	lemonade/lemon soda
spremuta	fresh fruit juice
spumante	sparkling wine
succo	concentrated fruit juice with sugar
tè	tea
tònica	tonic water
vino rosso/bianco/rosato/secco/dolce	red/wine/rosé/dry/sweet wine

PREPARATION	
al dente	firm to the bite (pasta)
al forno	baked
al sangue	rare
al punto	medium
al vino	in wine sauce
fritto/a	fried
ben cotto/a	well done
crudo/a	raw
fresco/a	fresh
fritto/a	fried
piccante	spicy

APPENDIX

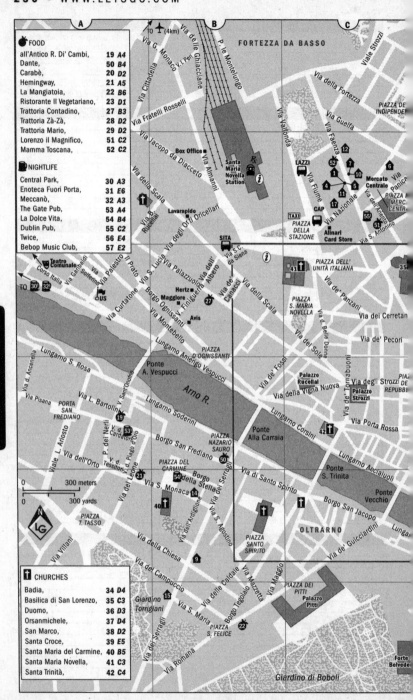

FOOD

all'Antico R. Di' Cambi,	19 A4
Dante,	50 B4
Carabè,	20 D2
Hemingway,	21 A5
La Mangiatoia,	22 B6
Ristorante Il Vegetariano,	23 D1
Trattoria Contadino,	27 B3
Trattoria Zà-Zà,	28 D2
Trattoria Mario,	29 D2
Lorenzo il Magnifico,	51 C2
Mamma Toscana,	52 C2

NIGHTLIFE

Central Park,	30 A3
Enoteca Fuori Porta,	31 E6
Meccanò,	32 A3
The Gate Pub,	53 A4
La Dolce Vita,	54 B4
Dublin Pub,	55 C2
Twice,	56 E4
Bebop Music Club,	57 E2

CHURCHES

Badia,	34 D4
Basilica di San Lorenzo,	35 C3
Duomo,	36 D3
Orsanmichele,	37 D4
San Marco,	38 D2
Santa Croce,	39 E5
Santa Maria del Carmine,	40 B5
Santa Maria Novella,	41 C3
Santa Trinità,	42 C4

APPENDIX

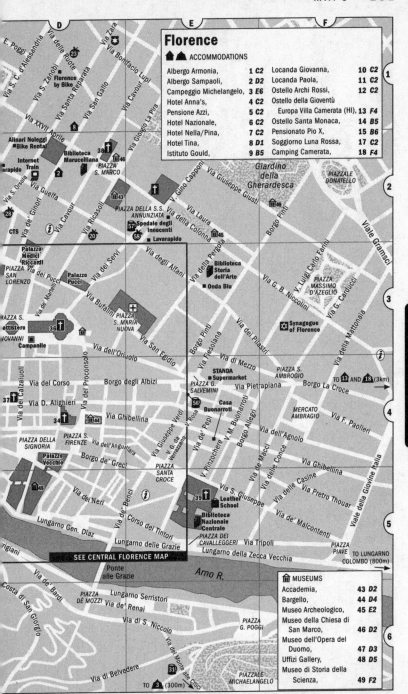

Florence

🏠🏠⛺ ACCOMMODATIONS

Albergo Armonia,	1 C2	Locanda Giovanna,	10 C2
Albergo Sampaoli,	2 D2	Locanda Paola,	11 C2
Campeggio Michelangelo,	3 E6	Ostello Archi Rossi,	12 C2
Hotel Anna's,	4 C2	Ostello della Gioventù	
Pensione Azzi,	5 C2	Europa Villa Camerata (HI),	13 F4
Hotel Nazionale,	6 C2	Ostello Santa Monaca,	14 B5
Hotel Nella/Pina,	7 C2	Pensionato Pio X,	15 B6
Hotel Tina,	8 D1	Soggiorno Luna Rossa,	17 C2
Istituto Gould,	9 B5	Camping Camerata,	18 F4

🏛 MUSEUMS

Accademia,	43 D2
Bargello,	44 D4
Museo Archeologico,	45 E2
Museo della Chiesa di San Marco,	46 D2
Museo dell'Opera del Duomo,	47 D3
Uffizi Gallery,	48 D5
Museo di Storia della Scienza,	49 F2

APPENDIX

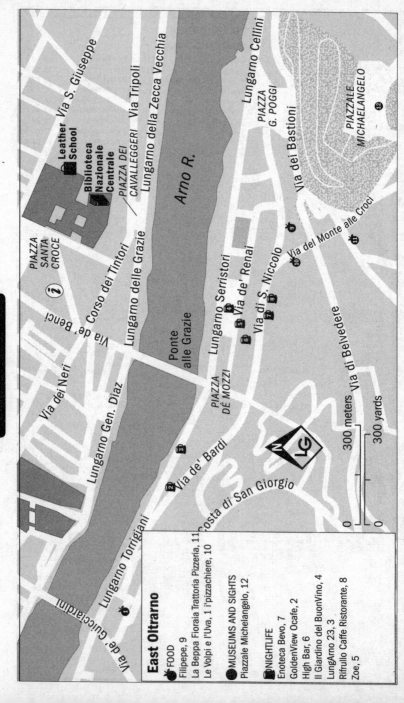

East Oltrarno

★ FOOD
Filipepe, 9
La Beppa Fioraia Trattoria Pizzeria, 11
Le Volpi e l'Uva, 1 i'pizzachiere, 10

● MUSEUMS AND SIGHTS
Piazzale Michelangelo, 12

▦ NIGHTLIFE
Enoteca Bevo, 7
GoldenView Ocafe, 2
High Bar, 6
Il Giardino del BuonVino, 4
LungArno 23, 3
Rifrullo Caffe Ristorante, 8
Zoe, 5

San Marco

FOOD
Snack Bar Lele, 5

MUSEUMS AND SIGHTS
Accademia, 6
Basilica della Santissima
  Annunziata, 7
Chiostro dello Scalzo, 1
Cimitero dei Protestanti, 4
Museo Archeologico, 9
Museo degli Innocenti, 8
Museo di San Marco, 3
Museum of the Opificio
  delle Pietre Dure, 10
Orto Botanico, 2

Via Marsilio Ficino
Via dei della Robbia
Via degli Artisti
Via Pier Capponi
Viale Giacomo Matteotti
Viale Gramsci
PIAZZALE DONATELLO
Via Farini
Borgo Pinti
Giardino della Gherardesca
Via Giuseppe Giusti
Via G. Modena
Via Venezia
Via A. Lamarmora
Via P. A. Micheli
V. Gino Capponi
Giardino dei Semplici
Via Cavour
Via Bonifacio Lupi
Via Zara
Via San Gallo
Via Cavour
Via Giorgio La Pira
Via Laura
Via della Colonna
PIAZZA DELLA S.S. ANNUNZIATA
PIAZZA S. MARCO
Via Ricasoli
Servi

APPENDIX

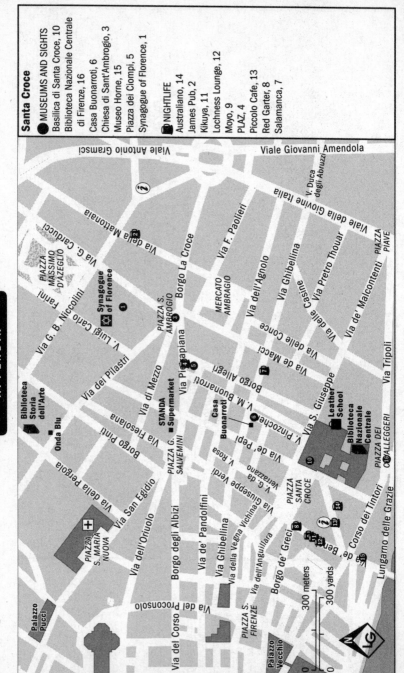

Santa Croce

MUSEUMS AND SIGHTS
Basilica di Santa Croce, 10
Biblioteca Nazionale Centrale di Firenze, 16
Casa Buonarroti, 6
Chiesa di Sant'Ambrogio, 3
Museo Horne, 15
Piazza dei Ciompi, 5
Synagogue of Florence, 1

NIGHTLIFE
Australiano, 14
James Pub, 2
Kikuya, 11
Lochness Lounge, 12
Moyo, 9
PLAZ, 4
Piccolo Cafe, 13
Red Garter, 8
Salamanca, 7

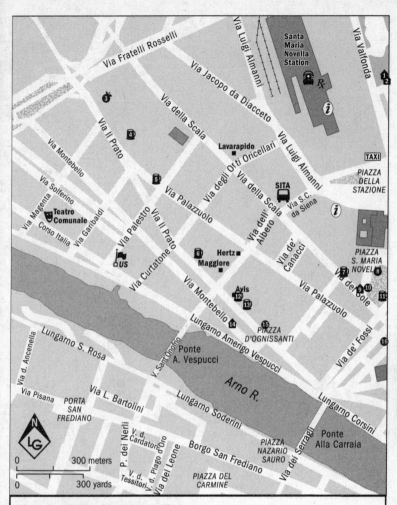

Santa Maria Novella

ACCOMODATIONS
Hotel Desiree, 1
Hotel Patrizia, 14
Hotel Serena, 2
Tourist House, 9
FOOD
Trattoria Baldini, 3
MUSEUMS AND SIGHTS
Chiesa di San Salvatore Ad Ognissanti, 15
Chiesa di Santa Maria Novella, 8
Museo Marino Marini, 16
Museo Nazionale Alinari della Fotografia, 10

NIGHTLIFE
Il Trip Per Tre Pub, 6
La Cantinetta Wine Bar, 7
La Rotonda, 5
Pub Caffe Lo Stregatto, 4
San Carlo, 13
Sei Divino, 12
The Fiddler's Elbow, 11

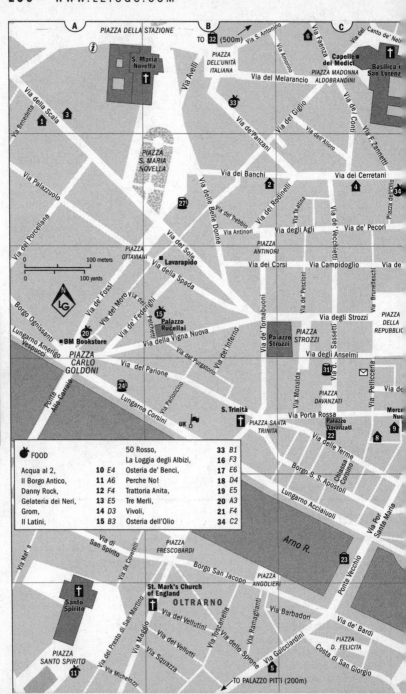

FOOD

Acqua al 2,	10	E4
Il Borgo Antico,	11	A6
Danny Rock,	12	F4
Gelateria dei Neri,	13	E5
Grom,	14	D3
Il Latini,	15	B3

50 Rosso,	33	B1
La Loggia degli Albizi,	16	F3
Osteria de' Benci,	17	E6
Perche No!	18	D4
Trattoria Anita,	19	E5
Tre Merli,	20	A3
Vivoli,	21	F4
Osteria dell'Olio	34	C2

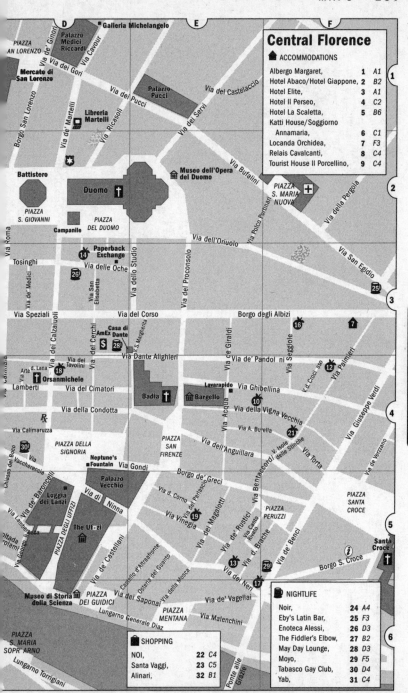

Central Florence

ACCOMMODATIONS

Albergo Margaret,	1	A1
Hotel Abaco/Hotel Giappone,	2	B2
Hotel Elite,	3	A1
Hotel Il Perseo,	4	C2
Hotel La Scaletta,	5	B6
Katti House/Soggiorno Annamaria,	6	C1
Locanda Orchidea,	7	F3
Relais Cavalcanti,	8	C4
Tourist House Il Porcellino,	9	C4

SHOPPING

NOI,	22	C4
Santa Vaggi,	23	C5
Alinari,	32	B1

NIGHTLIFE

Noir,	24	A4
Eby's Latin Bar,	25	F3
Enoteca Alessi,	26	D3
The Fiddler's Elbow,	27	B2
May Day Lounge,	28	D3
Moyo,	29	F5
Tabasco Gay Club,	30	D4
Yab,	31	C4

APPENDIX

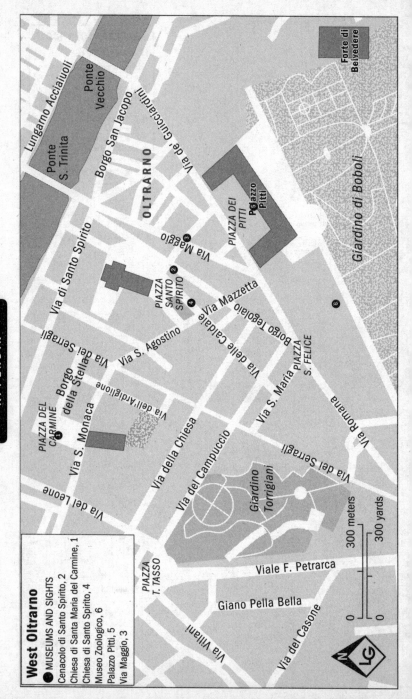

West Oltrarno

● **MUSEUMS AND SIGHTS**
Cenacolo di Santo Spirito, 2
Chiesa di Santa Maria del Carmine, 1
Chiesa di Santo Spirito, 4
Museo Zoologico, 6
Palazzo Pitti, 5
Via Maggio, 3

INDEX

Symbols

4 Leoni 109
5Terre Affitti, Riomaggiore 218
50 Rosso 102

A

A Bit of Tuscany, Radda in Chianti 185
A Casamia 107
Accademia 145
Accommodations 85
  East Oltrarno 95
  home exchanges and hospitality clubs 35
  long-term 35
  Piazza della Signoria 87
  San Lorenzo 89
  San Marco 92
  Santa Croce 93
  Santa Maria Novella 88
  The Duomo 86
  West Oltrarno 94
Acquacotta 107
agriturismo 34
airmail 32
Albergo Barbara, Vernazza 215
Albergo Bernini, Siena 179
Albergo Cecco, Arezzo 195
Albergo del Chianti, Greve in Chianti 176
Albergo Helvetia, Pisa 199
Albergo Il Pino, San Gimignano 188
Albergo La Pineta, Monterosso 212
Albergo Margaret 88
Albergo Merlini 91
Albergo Sampaoli 93
Albergo Tre Donzelle, Siena 179
Albergo Universo 89
Alekin Hostel 88
Alle 5 Terre, Monterosso 212
Amon Specialità e Panini Egiziani 102
Angels 99
Angie's Pub 164
Antica Gelateria Florentina 103
Antica Osteria L'Agania, Arezzo 196

Antico Caffè del Moro 165
Antico Noe 99
Appendix 220
  climate 220
  language 221
  measurements 220
  phrasebook 222
Aquarama Meccanò 165
Arezzo 194
art and architecture 47
artisan goods 160
art schools 72
Astor Caffè 163
au pair work 76
Australiano 169

B

Badia 122
Baluardi, Lucca 207
Bar Bano 105
Bar Cabras 104
Bar-Café "Rum Pera" 164
Bar Capitol 101
Bar-Enoteca Coquinarius 164
Bar Galli 105
Bargello 142
Barone Rosso, Siena 184
Baroque 52
Bar/Pasticceria Nannini, Siena 179
Bar Porrione, Siena 184
bars 163
Bar Sant'Agostino 110
Basilica della Santissima Annunziata 127
Basilica Di San Francesco, Arezzo 196
Basilica Di San Frediano, Lucca 209
Basilica di San Lorenzo 125
Basilica di Santa Croce 129
Basilica Di Santa Maria Assunta, San Gimignano 190
Basilica di Santa Maria Novella 124
Battistero 119

Battistero, Pisa 201
beaches
  Monterosso 213
  Vernazza 215
  Viareggio 203
Bed and Breakfast La Torre, Lucca 206
Bed and Breakfast La Torretta, Manarola 217
Beyond Tourism 67
  A Philosophy for Travelers 67
  Studying 70
  Volunteering 68
  Working 73
Biblioteca Nazionale Centrale 130
bike rentals 29, 81
Black Death 42
Blu Bar 173
Boboli Gardens 151
Boccaccio, Giovanni 57
Boccadama 108
bookstores 80, 155
border crossings 26
Borgo degli Albizi 120
boutiques 157
Brancacci Chapel 131
Brunelleschi, Filippo 50, 117, 124
Brunelleschi's Dome 117
Buongustai 100
buses 25

C

Cabiria 169
Café Deluxée 166
Café des Artistes 165
Caffè Astra 104
Caffè Bigallo 164
Caffè del Corso, Siena 184
Caffè Di Simo, Lucca 207
Caffe Landucci 105
Caffè la Torre 170
Caffelatte 107
Caffè Michelangiolo 104
Caffe Rosanó 106
Caffè Sant'Ambrogio 168
Caffetteria Raffaella 104

Caffè Vecchio Mercato 108
calling cards 31
Camere Cennini Gianni, San Gimignano 188
Cammillo 109
Campanile 119
Campeggio Michelangelo 95
Camping Internazionale, Pisa 200
Camping Village Torre Pendente, Pisa 199
Camposanto, Pisa 201
Cantina de Mananan, Corniglia 216
Cantina di Sciacchetrà, Monterosso 213
Cantinetta dei Verrazzano 100
Cappelle dei Medici 126
Cardillac Café 106
car rentals 81
Caruso Jazz Café 101
Casa Betania, Cortona 191
Casa Buonarroti 149
Casa di Dante 143
Casa di Rodolfo Siviero 152
Casa Guidi 94, 132
Casa Laura, Siena 178
Casa Porciatti, Radda in Chianti 185
Casa Vasari, Arezzo 196
Cattedrale di Santa Maria del Fiore 113
Cavalli Club 169
cell phones 31
Cenacolo di 'Fuligno' 125
Cenacolo di Sant'Apollonia 128
Cenacolo di Santo Spirito 132
Central 165
Checkpoint 171
Chiesa di San Barnaba 127
Chiesa di San Domenico, Arezzo 197
Chiesa di San Felice 132
Chiesa di San Firenze 123
Chiesa di San Francesco, Fiesole 175
Chiesa di San Giovanni, Lucca 208
Chiesa di San Michele In Foro, Lucca 208
Chiesa di San Salvatore ad

Ognissanti 125
Chiesa di Santa Maria del Carmine 131
Chiesa di Santa Maria Della Spina, Pisa 203
Chiesa di Sant'Ambrogio 130
Chiesa di Santa Trinità 125
Chiesa di Santo Spirito 131
Chiostro dello Scalzo 128
churches
  Badia 122
  Duomo 113
  Ognissanti 125
  Orsanmichele 121
  San Barnaba 127
  San Felice 132
  San Firenze 123
  San Lorenzo 125
  San Miniato al Monte 133
  Santa Croce 129
  Santa Maria del Carmine 131
  Santa Maria Novella 124
  Sant'Ambrogio 130
  Santa Trinità 125
  Santissima Annunziata 127
  Santo Spirito 131
Cimabue 48, 131, 138
Cimitero dei Protestanti 128
cinema 160
Cinque Terre 210
  Corniglia 216
  Levanto 214
  Manarola 216
  Monterosso 211
  Riomaggiore 218
  Vernazza 214
cinta senese 179
climate 1, 220
clubs 163
Colle Bereto Lounge 165
community service 69
Complesso di San Firenze 123
consular services 9
cooking schools 73
Cortona 190
credit cards 14
Crypt of St. Reparata 118
C.S.D.-Gould Institute 94
currency 13
customs and etiquette 63

D

Da Elisa Alle Sette Arti, Lucca 207
Da Leo, Lucca 207
dancing 163

Danny Rock 101
Dante 109
Dante Alighieri 56, 143
Da Paulin, Manarola 217
Da Rino, Levanto 214
della Robbia, Luca 50
department stores 157
dietary concerns 38
disabilities 37
Discover Florence 1
diving 219
drinking 163
driving permits 27
Dublin Pub 167
Duomo 113
Duomo, Arezzo 197
Duomo di San Martino, Lucca 208
Duomo, Pisa 201
Duomo, Siena 181

E

Easy Living 170
Eby's Latin Bar 163
ecotourism 36, 68
embassies 9
emergency numbers 83
Enoteca Bevo 170
Enoteca del Chianti Classico, Greve in Chianti 176
Entertainment 160
  cinema 160
  live music 161
  spectator sports 161
  theater 160
Essentials 9
  accommodations 33
  documents and formalities 10
  embassies and consulates 9
  getting around Florence 26
  getting to Florence 22
  keeping in touch 30
  money 13
  packing 16
  safety and health 17
  specific concerns 36
Etruscans 47

F

festivals 65
  Arezzo 197
  Cortona 194
  Lucca 210
  Pisa 203

INDEX

Fiesole 173
Filipepe 111
Finnegan Irish Pub 167
Fish Pub 167
flights 22
Flò 170
Florence Room Bed & Breakfast 89
Focacceria Il Frantoio, Monterosso 213
Food 97
  East Oltrarno 111
  Piazza della Signoria 100
  San Lorenzo 103
  San Marco 105
  Santa Croce 107
  Santa Maria Novella 102
  The Duomo 99
  West Oltrarno 109
football 161
Foresteria San Pier Piccolo, Arezzo 195
Fortezza And Museo Del Vino, San Gimignano 190
Fortezza Medicea, Cortona 193
Friends' Pub 169
Fufluns, Cortona 192
Futurism 54

G

Galileo, Pisa 200
Gallery, Siena 184
Gambero Rosso, Vernazza 215
Gattabuia 111
Gelateria Brivido, Siena 180
Gelateria del Neri 100
Gelateria La Carraia 109
Gelateria Pitti 110
Gelateria Santini Sergio, Lucca 207
Gelateria Snoopy, Cortona 192
Gelatissimo 108
Ghiberti, Lorenzo 50, 118
Giardino Bardini 151
GLBT resources 37, 82
gold 159
GoldenView Ocafé 171
Gran Caffè San Marco 105
Greve in Chianti 175
Grom 99
guilds 49

gyms 81

H

health 19
Hemingway 110
High Bar 171
hiking
  Cinque Terre 210
  Corniglia 216
  Manarola 217
  Monterosso 213
  Riomaggiore 217
  Vernazza 215
history 41
Holiday Rooms 90
holidays and festivals 65
hospitals 83
Hostel AF19 87
Hostelling International 33
hostels 33
Hostel Veronique 88
Hotel Abaco 88
Hotel Aldini 87
Hotel Alma Domus, Siena 179
Hotel Anna's 91
Hotel Ariston 94
Hotel Arizona 94
Hotel Armonia 91
Hotel Benvenuti 93
Hotel Bigallo 86
Hotel Bijou 89
Hotel Boboli 94
Hotel Bretagna 87
Hotel Ca Dei Duxi, Riomaggiore 218
Hotel Cimabue 93
Hotel Consigli 88
Hotel Crocini 88
Hotel Dali 87
Hotel Deco 92
Hotel Desirée 88
Hotel Duca D'Aosta 88
Hotel Etrusca 90
Hotel Galileo, Pisa 199
Hotel Garden 89
Hotel Gianni Franzi, Vernazza 214
Hotel Giappone 89
Hotel Gioia 93
Hotel Il Perseo 87
Hotel Jolì 89

Hotel La Cisterna, San Gimignano 188
Hotel La Scaletta 94
Hotel Leonardo da Vinci 89
Hotel Lombardia 92
Hotel Mario's 90
Hotel Medici 86
Hotel Monica 91
Hotel Montreal 89
Hotel Panorama 93
Hotel Patrizia 89
Hotel Porta Faenza 92
Hotel San Luca, Cortona 191
Hotel San Marco 92
Hotel Serena 89
Hotel Souvenir, Monterosso 212
Hotel Tina 92
Hotel Toscana 88
Hotel Varsavia 88
Hotel Villa Liberty 95

I

l'Brincello 104
l'brindellone 110
Il Campo, Siena 180
Il Cantuccio, Montepulciano 186
Il Ciliegio, Monterosso 213
Il Giardino del BuonVino 171
Il Giova 107
Il Kioskino 170
Il Latini 100
Il Paiolo, Pisa 200
Il Porcellino Tourist House 87
Il Porticciolo, Manarola 217
Il Principe 108
Il Ristoro dei Perditempo 110
Il Trip Per Tre Pub 166
immunizations 19
international calls 31
internet 30, 83
i'pizzachiere 111
Istituto Santa Margherita, Cortona 192
Italian grammar 222
Italian pronunciation 221

J

James Joyce Pub 170
James Pub 168

jazz 161
Joshua Tree 165

K

Kikuya 168
Kitsch Pub 166
Kitsch the Bar 170
kosher 39, 107

L

La Beppa Fioraia Trattoria Pizzeria 111
La Bottega del Gelato, Pisa 200
La Bottega di Giovannino, Radda in Chianti 185
La Cantinetta Wine Bar 166
La Casalinga 110
La Cité 169
La Dolce Vita 169
La Dolce Vita, Riomaggiore 218
La Focacceria Dome, Levanto 214
La Gata Flora, Corniglia 216
La Gemma di Elena Bed and Breakfast, Lucca 206
La Grotta di Leo 103
La Loggia degli Albizi 100
La Mescita 105
L'Angolo Della Pizza 108
language 221
language schools 72
La Pagnotta 108
La Posada, Corniglia 216
La Rotonda 166
Las Palmas 168
La Stella, San Gimignano 189
laundromats 80
Laurentian Library 127
Leaning Tower of Pisa 200
leather goods 159
Le Campane 108
Le Cantine di Greve in Chianti 176
Le Colonnine 108
Leonardo da Vinci 51, 139, 145
Leonardo House 88
Le Volpi e l'uva 111
libraries 81
Life and Times 41
  Art and Architecture 47

Culture 61
History 41
Holidays and Festivals 65
Literature 56
Music 59
Religion 60
Lion's Fountain 163
Lippi, Fra Filippo 50, 139
literature 56
live music 161
Locanda degli Artisti 91
Locanda Gallo 93
Locanda Giovanna 91
Locanda Orchidea 86
Lochness Lounge 168
Loggia del Pesce 131
lost property 79
Lucca 204
luggage storage 79
LungArno 23 170

M

Macchiaioli 54
Macchine di Leonardo 145
Macelleria, Greve in Chianti 176
Mago Merlino Tea House 167
mail 32
MaMMaMia 102
Mamma Toscana 104
Mangiando, Mangiando, Greve in Chianti 176
Mannerism 52
Marina Piccola, Manarola 217
markets 155
Mar-Mar, Riomaggiore 218
masks 159
Maudit Music Pub, Siena 184
May Day Lounge 163
measurements 220
medical services 83
Medici 43, 44, 125
Medici Chapels 126
Mercato Centrale 127
Mercato Nuovo 124
Michelangelo Buonarroti 51, 129, 140, 145, 149
minorities 38
Montecarla 170
Montepulciano 185
mopeds 30

movie theaters 160
Moyo 168
Mr. Kebab House 108
Murphy's Pub Il Fauno 167
Museo Archeologico 146
Museo Bandini, Fiesole 175
Museo Civico Archeologico, Fiesole 175
Museo degli Argenti 151
Museo degli Innocenti 148
Museo dell'Accademia Etrusca e della Citta di Cortona, Cortona 193
Museo della Porcellana 152
Museo dell'Opera del Duomo 120
Museo dell'Opera Del Duomo, Pisa 202
Museo dell'Opera Metropolitana, Siena 182
Museo del Tempio Israelitico 130
Museo di Firenze Antica of Florence 147
Museo Diocesano, Cortona 193
Museo di San Marco 146
Museo di Storia della Scienza 143
Museo Etnografico, Fiesole 175
Museo Horne 148
Museo Marino Marini 144
Museo Nazionale Alinari della Fotografia 144
Museo Nazionale di San Matteo, Pisa 202
Museo Pena di Morte and Museo della Tortura, San Gimignano 190
Museo Salvatore Ferragamo 144
Museo Zoologico 152
Museum of the Opificio delle Pietre Dure 147
Museums 135
  Oltrarno 149
  Piazza della Signoria 135
  San Lorenzo 145
  San Marco 145
  Santa Croce 148
  Santa Maria Novella 144
music 59

N

Nabucco Wine Bar 106
Negroni 170
neighborhoods 2

Neoclassicism 53
Nightlife 163
  East Oltrarno 169
  Piazza della Signoria 164
  San Lorenzo 166
  San Marco 167
  Santa Croce 167
  Santa Maria Novella 165
  The Duomo 163
  West Oltrarno 169
Ninna Nanna Bed & Breakfast 91
Nobilis 167
Noir 164
Nonno Mede, Siena 180
Nuovo Eden Bar, Monterosso 213

O

Oibò 164
Ok Bar 99
Old Stove Duomo 164
Opificio delle Pietre Dure 147
Orsanmichele 121
Orto Botanico 129
Orto Botanico, Lucca 209
Ospedale di Santa Maria della Scala, Siena 182
Ostello Archi Rossi 90
Ostello Cinque Terre, Manarola 217
Ostello della Gioventù "Guidoriccio" (HI), Siena 179
Ostello Ospitalia del Mare, Levanto 214
Ostello San Frediano (HI), Lucca 206
Ostello San Marco (HI), Cortona 191
Ostello Santa Monaca 94
Osteria Acquacheta, Montepulciano 186
Osteria de' Benci 101
Osteria dei Cavalieri, Pisa 200
Osteria del Borghicciolo, Arezzo 196
Osteria dell'Olio 100
Osteria il Gatto e la Volpe 99
Osteria Il Grattacielo, Siena 180
Osteria La Chiacchera, Siena 179
Osteria Pizzeria Zio Gigi 99
Osteria Santo Spirito 110
outlet stores 157

P

packing 16
Palazzo Comunale, San Gimignano 190
Palazzo Davanzati 141
Palazzo Gondi 123
Palazzo Medici 127
Palazzo Pfanner, Lucca 209
Palazzo Pitti 149
Palazzo Pubblico, Siena 180
Palazzo Strozzi 144
Palazzo Vecchio 143
Palio 183
panforte 179
paper goods 158
Paradiso di Stelle, Arezzo 196
passports 10
Pasticceria Maioli 165
Pensione Ferretti 87
Pensione La Scala 89
Pensione Maria Luisa de' Medici 87
Perché No! 101
Petrarch 57
pharmacies 83
phrasebook 222
Piazza Anfiteatro, Lucca 209
Piazza dei Cavalieri, Pisa 202
Piazza dei Ciompi 131
Piazza della Cisterna and Piazza del Duomo, San Gimignano 189
Piazza della Repubblica 122
Piazza della Signoria 121
Piazza Grande, Arezzo 196
Piazzale Michelangelo 133
Piazza Napoleone, Lucca 208
Piccolo Café 168
Piccolo Hotel Etruria, Siena 179
Piccolo Hotel Puccini, Lucca 207
pici 179
Pinacoteca Nazionale, Siena 183
Pisa 197
Pisa Tower Hostel, Pisa 199
Pizzeria and Ostaria Centopoveri 102
Pizzeria Baccus 103
Pizzeria Baja Saracena, Vernazza 215

Pizzeria da Felice, Lucca 207
PLAZ 168
Pluripremiata Gelateria, San Gimignano 189
police 83
Ponte Vecchio 121
Pop Café 169
Porciatti Alimentari, Radda in Chianti 185
Porta San Frediano 133
postmodernism 58
post office 83
Practical Information 79
  Emergency and Communications 83
  Local Services 79
  Tourist and Financial Services 79
Pub Caffé Lo Stregatto 166
Public House 27 164
public toilets 80
public transportation 26
pubs 163

R

Radda in Chianti 184
Red Garter 168
Relais Cavalcanti 87
religion 60
Renaissance 50, 57
rental cars 28, 81
Residence Santa Chiara, Lucca 207
Rifrullo Caffe Ristorante 171
Ripa del Sole, Riomaggiore 218
Ristorante Acqua al 2 99
Ristorante ai Quattro Venti, Montepulciano 186
Ristorante Al Carugio, Monterosso 213
Ristorante Cecio, Corniglia 216
Ristorante da Francesco, Lucca 207
Ristorante Da Mimmo 106
Ristorante del Faglioli 107
Ristorante Dioniso 105
Ristorante Il Paiolo 107
Ristorante Il Vegetariano 106
Ristorante La Spada 102
Ristorante Le Fonticine 104
Ristorante Perucà, San Gimignano 189

Ristorante Preludio, Cortona 192
Ristorante Self-Service
"Leonardo" 99
Ristoro al Vecchio Teatro,
Pisa 200
Rosticceria Alfio Beppe 106
Rosticceria Gastronomia II, Il
Pirata 102
Ruth's Kosher Vegetarian
Restaurant 107

S

Salamanca 168
Salumeria Verdi 108
Salumi e Formaggi, Vernazza 215
San Carlo 166
San Domenico Ristorante,
Pisa 200
San Gimignano 187
San Miniato al Monte 133
Santuario Di Santa Caterina,
Siena 183
Sei Divino 166
Seme d'uva 109
Semolina 108
Shopping 155
  bookstores 155
  clothing 157
  markets 155
  souvenirs 158
Shot Café 166
Siena 176
Sights 113
  East Oltrarno 133
  Piazza della Signoria 121
  San Lorenzo 125
  San Marco 127
  Santa Croce 129
  Santa Maria Novella 124
  The Duomo 113
  West Oltrarno 131
sights and museums closings 114
Slowly 164
Snack Bar Lele 106
soccer 161
Soggiorno Luna Rossa 90
Soggiorno Magliani 92
Soggiorno Prestipino 87
Sognando Firenze Bed and
Breakfast 95

souvenirs 158
Space Club Electronic 165
spectator sports 161
Steakfest 194
study abroad 70
sustainable travel 36
Synagogue of Florence 130

T

Tabasco Gay Bar 165
taxis 26
teaching English 75
Teatro del Sale 107
Teatro Romano, Fiesole 173
Tempio di San Biagio, Mon-
tepulciano 186
theater 160
The Fiddler's Elbow 163
The William 108
time differences 32
Torre Guinigi And Torre
Dell'Ore, Lucca 208
Tourist House 89
Tourist House Battistero 91
Tourist House Duomo 92
tourist offices 79
trains 25
transportation 22
Trattoria al Trebbio 103
Trattoria Anita 101
Trattoria Baldini 103
Trattoria Belle Donne 102
Trattoria Chiribiri, San Gimig-
nano 188
Trattoria Contadino 102
Trattoria da Billy, Manarola 217
Trattoria da Giorgio 102
Trattoria Dardano, Cortona 192
Trattoria dei Matti 105
Trattoria dell'Orto 109
Trattoria Garga 103
Trattoria Gianni Franzi, Ver-
nazza 215
Trattoria Il Porticciolo, Man-
arola 217
Trattoria Il Saraceno, Arezzo 196

Trattoria La Lanterna, Riomag-
giore 218
Trattoria Le Mossacce 99
Trattoria Mario 103
Trattoria Nerone 104
Trattoria Papei, Siena 179
Trattoria Zàzà 103
traveler's checks 14
Tre Merli 103
Tuscany 173
Twice 164

U

Ufficio delle Strade del Vino,
Montepulciano 186
university dorms 35

V

Valle dei Cedri 108
Vasari Palace Hotel 92
Vernaccia di San Gimignano 188
Via Maggio 133
Viareggio 203
VinOlio 105
visas 11
Vivoli 101
volunteering 68

W

wine 63
wine tasting 175, 184, 185
wiring money 15
women travelers 22, 36, 82
working 73
  long-term work 74
  short-term work 76

Z

Zimmer La Colonna, Lucca 207
Zoe 170

Maps by Let's Go copyright © 2010 by Let's Go, Inc.

Distributed by Publishers Group West.
Printed in Canada by Friesens Corp.

ISBN-13: 978-1-59880-305-1
ISBN-10: 1-59880-305-0
First edition
10 9 8 7 6 5 4 3 2 1

Let's Go Florence is written by Let's Go Publications, 67 Mount Auburn St., Cambridge, MA 02138, USA.

Let's Go® and the LG logo are trademarks of Let's Go, Inc.

MAP INDEX

Central Florence 236

East Oltrarno 232

Florence 230

Lucca 205

Pisa 199

San Marco 233

Santa Croce 234

Santa Maria Novella 235

Siena 177

Tuscany 174

West Oltrarno 238

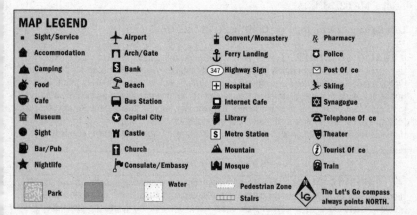

MAP LEGEND

▪ Sight/Service	✈ Airport	⚓ Convent/Monastery	℞ Pharmacy
🏠 Accommodation	⛩ Arch/Gate	⚓ Ferry Landing	✚ Police
⛺ Camping	💲 Bank	(347) Highway Sign	✉ Post Office
🍎 Food	⛱ Beach	✚ Hospital	⛷ Skiing
☕ Cafe	🚌 Bus Station	💻 Internet Cafe	✡ Synagogue
🏛 Museum	✚ Capital City	📚 Library	☎ Telephone Office
● Sight	🏰 Castle	⬛ S Metro Station	🎭 Theater
🍺 Bar/Pub	⛪ Church	🏔 Mountain	(i) Tourist Office
★ Nightlife	🏴 Consulate/Embassy	🕌 Mosque	🚂 Train

		Water	▓▓▓ Pedestrian Zone	N
Park			▦▦▦ Stairs	The Let's Go compass always points NORTH.